The Shore of Expectations:
A Cultural Study of the *Shistdesiatnyky*

The Shore of Expectations:
A Cultural Study of the *Shistdesiatnyky*

Simone Attilio Bellezza

Canadian Institute of Ukrainian Studies Press
Edmonton   •   2019   •   Toronto

Canadian Institute of Ukrainian Studies Press
University of Alberta   University of Toronto
Edmonton, Alberta   Toronto, Ontario
Canada T6G 2H8   Canada M5T 1W5

Copyright © 2019 Canadian Institute of Ukrainian Studies
ISBN 978-1-894865-50-0 (paper)

Library and Archives Canada Cataloguing in Publication

Bellezza, Simone Attilio, author
 The shore of expectations: a cultural study of the *Shistdesiatnyky* / Simone Attilio Bellezza.

Includes bibliographical references and index.
ISBN 978-1-894865-50-0 (softcover)

1. Literary movements--Ukraine--History--20th century. 2. Social movements--Ukraine--History--20th century. 3. Politics and literature--History--20th century. 4. Political persecution--Ukraine--History--20th century. 5. Dissidents--Ukraine--History--20th century. 6. Ukraine--History--1944-1991. I. Canadian Institute of Ukrainian Studies. Press, issuing body II. Title.

DK508.84.B45 2017   947.708'5   C2017-905056-7

The publication of this book has been funded by a generous grant from the Canadian Foundation for Ukrainian Studies. Grants for this publication have also been provided by the Julian and Savella Stechishin Endowment Fund and the Nestor Peczeniuk Memorial Endowment Fund at the Canadian Institute of Ukrainian Studies (University of Alberta).
Cover design by Vitalii Grybov
All rights reserved.

No part of this publication may be reproduced, stored in a retrieval system, or transmitted in any form or by any means, electronic, mechanical, photocopying, recording, or otherwise, without the prior permission of the copyright owner.

Printed in Canada

Як не крути,
на одне виходить,
слід би катюгам давно зазубрить:
можна пострелити мозок,
що думку народить,
думку ж не вбить!

However you twist and turn,
it turns out the same,
torturers should have learned this long ago:
you can blow out a brain
that gives birth to an idea,
but the idea itself can't be killed!

Vasyl' Symonenko

Table of Contents

Acknowledgements /   ix

Introduction
  A Nation of Heroes and Villains /   xi
  The Relaunch of the Soviet Project /   xv
  About Labels and Sources /   xix

Chapter One. The Origins of the *Shistdesiatnyky* (1953–61)
  De-Stalinization and the Dawn of the Thaw /   1
  Khrushchev's View on the New Cultural Course /   15
  The Rise of the Language Question and Educational Reform /   17
  The Debate within Ukraine's Union of Writers /   20
  A New Generation /   28
  Les Taniuk and the Club of Creative Youth /   61
  Andrii Skaba and the Ukrainian Biographic Dictionary /   70
  Levko Lukianenko and the Ukrainian Workers' and Peasants' Union /   72

Chapter Two. The *Shistdesiatnyky* Address the Nation (1961–68)
  Ukraine's Union of Writers against Russification /   92
  The National Question in the Club of Creative Youth /   101
  The Prolisok Youth Club /   104
  The End of the Thaw, and the Appointment of Petro Shelest /   110
  The First Clash: From Alla Horska's Shevchenko Window to the Arrests /   112
  Ukrainian Cinema and the Case of *Shadows of Forgotten Ancestors* /   125
  Ivan Dziuba's *Internationalism or Russification?* /   130
  Covering the Trials: The Work of Viacheslav Chornovil /   141
  In and Out of the Mordovian Camp /   156
  The Braichevsky Case and the Renaissance of Ukrainian Historiography /   170
  A New Sense of Community: The *Shistdesiatnyky* and the Construction of a Public Political Space /   178
  The Case of Oles Honchar's *Sobor* /   191
  The World View of the *Shistdesiatnyky* /   206
  The Scandal Peters Out /   211

Chapter Three. Repressions and Dissent (1968–73)
   The Spring Torch: Smoloskyp and the Prague Connection /   216
   The "Letter from Creative Youth" and the Suppression of Dissent in Dnipropetrovsk /   222
   Attacks in the Stalinist Mould /   227
   Valentyn Moroz and Ivan Dziuba: Rivalry and Solidarity among the *Shistdesiatnyky* /   237
   The Murder of Alla Horska /   251
   The Founding of *Ukraïns'kyi visnyk* /   255
   The Moscow *Shestidesiatniki* and Leonid Pliushch /   260
   Silencing Broader Cultural Initiatives /   275
   The 1972 Pogrom /   281
   The Repression of Minds /   294
   Misplaced Hopes /   300

Epilogue
   What Remained of the Friendships /   312
   What Remained of the Politics /   315
   In Sum: Who the *Shistdesiatnyky* Were /   319

Bibliography /   327
Index /   364

Acknowledgements

First of all, I would like to thank the members of the Scientific Council of the School for Advanced Historical Studies of the University of the Republic of San Marino. Without the trust they placed in me, this research would have never seen the light of day. I am also grateful to the Eugene and Daymel Shklar Fellowship program of the Harvard Ukrainian Research Institute. As a Shklar Fellow I was able to access sources and meet people who turned out to be essential to my work.

Andrea Graziosi was the first to encourage me to study this topic, and I am grateful for his constant support. I also want to thank Oxana Pachlovska, who put me in touch with *shistdesiatnyky* and provided me with many pieces of advice.

My interviewees Lina Kostenko, Les Taniuk, Ivan Dziuba, Mykola Plakhotniuk, and Vasyl Ovsiienko gave me much of their precious time, and I am grateful to them for their help, sincerity, and exemplary honesty. Roman Szporluk spoke with me many times, gave me some files from his personal archive, and acted as a passionate guide during my months at Harvard University. Oleksandr Androshchuk dedicated much time helping me to access the SBU archive, and I am grateful for his patience. Olena Zaplotynska and Oles Obertas discussed my work with me and assisted my research in the Ukrainian archives. Oksana Blashkiv found me a place to live in Kyiv and helped me many times in my search for Ukrainian books. I thank her for her friendship, which endures despite the distance. I am grateful to Tetiana Pastushenko and Serhii Plokhii, who helped me in many ways. Iryna Kashei and Oleh Kotsiuba, both patient and enthusiastic teachers, helped me in my reading and translation of Ukrainian poetry.

I want to thank the journal *Snodi: Pubblici e privati nella storia contemporanea*. Their calls for papers served as a great inspiration and gave rise to the first results of my research.

CIUS Press staff helped to convert my manuscript into a readable book. In particular I wish to thank Marko R. Stech, Ksenia Maryniak, Roman Senkus, and Hannah Wood.

I am thankful to all my schoolmates in San Marino—Maria Elisa Soldani, Chiara Daloja, Sara Barbieri, Nathaël Recoursé, Davide Guerra, and Lorena Barale, who were forced to put up with my bad temper.

Vitalii Grybov corrected my pronunciation when I first read the poems of the *shistdesiatnyky*. He also turned Ukraine into a second home for me, and I hope he knows how thankful I am.

My parents have been an irreplaceable source of support. Words do not suffice in conveying my gratitude and appreciation. I dedicate this book to my father, who taught me the value of honesty.

Introduction

> Ради чого, ви думаєте, я берусь за перо?
> Щоб поганити зло? Щоб уславить добро?
> Нерозлучних братів я візьмусь розлучити?
> І життя білим шовком лише перешити?
> НІ!*

A Nation of Heroes and Villains

The generation of the 1960s—the so-called *shistdesiatnyky* ("Sixtiers," Russian name: *shestidesiatniki*)—played a decisive role twice in the recent history of Ukraine. They first exerted their influence when they challenged the Soviet establishment and exploited the interlude of democratization offered by the so-called Khrushchev Thaw (Russian: *ottepel*, Ukrainian: *vidlyha*). Years later, with the dissolution of the Soviet Union in 1991 and Ukraine's subsequent independence from Moscow, the erstwhile renegade *shistdesiatnyky* were summoned to be nation builders. Despite their seemingly evident contributions, in retrospect their impact is highly disputed in contemporary Ukraine. This underappreciation is apparent in the literary scene, with the post-Soviet generation of intellectuals and writers reading and admiring the writings of the *shistdesiatnyky* but declining to grant them a prominent status in the new national canon that was formed after decades of Soviet marginalization of Ukrainian literature. Rather, the literary debate has focused on the struggle between westernizers and nativists, and in both cases their feelings of national belonging differ radically from those typical of the cultural renaissance of the 1960s.[1]

---

* "Why, do you think, I pick up my pen? / To speak ill of evil and well of good? / Would I separate those inseparable brothers? / Or embroider life with a white silk thread? / NO!" in Ivan Drach, *Balady budniv* (Kyiv, 1967), 53. English translation in idem, *Orchard Lamps*, ed., with an intro by Stanley Kunitz, trans. by Daniel Halpern et al. (New York, 1978), 46.

1 See Oksana Zabuzhko, "Reinventing the Poet in Modern Ukrainian Culture," *Slavic and East European Journal* 39, no. 2 (1995): 270–75; Marko Pavlyshyn, "Literary Canons and National identities in Contemporary Ukraine," *Canadian-American Slavic Studies* 40, no. 1 (2006): 519; and Ola Hnatiuk, "Nativists vs Westernizers: Problems of Cultural identity in Ukrainian Literature in the 1990s," *Slavic and East European Journal* 50, no. 3 (2006): 434–51.

Moreover, Ukrainian historians have severely judged the actions of some representatives of the *shistdesiatnyky* during the 1990s. In his book on independent Ukraine, Heorhii Kasianov—one of the historians who was more sympathetic toward the *shistdesiatnyky*—was highly critical of their weak influence on the course of Ukrainian history.

> Some of the national democrats, especially former dissidents, were so accustomed to opposing Communist rule that the unexpected advent of political freedom left them quite unprepared, both psychologically and organizationally, for constructive action....
>
> Some of the best-known dissidents—Viacheslav Chornovil, Levko Lukianenko, and Mykhailo Horyn—were scattered among the right and centre-right parties and often competed. After their rivalry became public, it did not enhance the social or moral authority of any of the national democrats. A few others made highly dubious (but perhaps inevitable) compromises with their erstwhile enemies, who swiftly appropriated their slogans and ideas—ideas for which the authors had had to pay with years of imprisonment or even with their lives.
>
> Such "pacts with the devil" [that is, with the former Communists] relegated the dissidents to secondary political spheres as bit players in the actual redistribution of power and property, which was controlled by the former Party *nomenklatura*. Some leaders of the national democrats who came from the intelligentsia had been deeply involved with the Communist establishment (Ivan Drach, Dmytro Pavlychko, Mykola Zhulynsky, Volodymyr Yavorivsky, and Pavlo Movchan, among others). They were inclined to be content with maintaining or even increasing their privileges, and they were sometimes in a position to do so because the new state needed them to gain the trust of nationally minded constituents. Indeed, such former dissidents actually legitimized the old Communist leaders as national figures, sincerely believing (or making others believe) that they were carrying out their duty in building the nation-state.[2]

While some *shistdesiatnyky*, such as Lina Kostenko and Yevhen Sverstiuk, never actively participated in politics, the study of

---

2 Heorhii Kas'ianov, *Ukraïna 1991–2007: Narysy novitn'oï istoriï* (Kyïv, 2008), 37–38. Andrew Wilson is of the same opinion in his *Ukrainian Nationalism in the 1990s: A Minority Faith* (Cambridge, UK, 1997) and *Virtual Politics: Faking Democracy in the Post-Soviet World* (New Haven, 2005). Unless stated otherwise, all translations from the Ukrainian and all interpolations in square brackets are the author's. [For readability, the main text usually contains only the English translations of titles of Ukrainian-language works, but they are transliterated in the footnotes.—*Ed.*]

shistdesiatnytstvo (the overall movement of the *shistdesiatnyky*) in Ukraine has always been connected with the later actions of its members and the role they played in the formation of the new nation-state. While the subject was taboo during Soviet rule, after 1991 Ukrainian historians understood the new state's need for legitimacy and thus positioned *shistdesiatnytstvo* within the extended struggle for the national liberation of Ukraine, as though it were one of its phases.[3] Even before 1991 foreign historiography (mostly American and Canadian) presented *shistdesiatnytstvo* from a pro-independence perspective as an episode of the Ukrainian national movement, whose roots stemmed from the nineteenth century.[4] Several interpretations of *shistdesiatnytstvo* that came from North America and England were quite insightful—those of Roman Szporluk, John-Paul Himka, and Bohdan Nahaylo, to name a few—but they were limited to a few articles on singular aspects. Moreover, because these authors' writings were difficult for historians in Ukraine to obtain, they are usually absent from their research.

In her survey of Ukrainian historiography on *shistdesiatnytstvo*, Olena Zaplotynska writes:

> Despite their different approaches to this phenomenon, most scholars consider *shistdesiatnytstvo* to be the result of a limited liberalization of the regime after the Twentieth CPSU Congress. They stress its cultural character, born of a time when literature and art became an "alternative to barricades," when the struggle was not for an abstract political idea but for the individual. The new consciousness that arose from this resistance developed into political

---

[3] On the meaning of history for Ukrainian identity, see Andrew Wilson, *The Ukrainians: Unexpected Nation* (New Haven, 2002). On the use of history in the building of the nation-state after 1991, see David R. Marples, *Heroes and Villains: Creating National History in Contemporary Ukraine* (Budapest and New York, 2007). The first two notable studies on the *shistdesiatnyky* were Iurii D. Zaitsev, "Dysydenty: opozytsiinyi rukh 60–80-kh rr.," in *Storinky istoriï Ukraïny: XX stolittia: Posibnyk dlia vchytelia* (Kyiv, 1992), 195–235; and Iurii O. Kornusov, *Inakomyslennia v Ukraïni (60-ti–persha polovyna 80-kh rr. XX st.)* (Kyiv, 1994), which states that the *shistdesiatnyky* "were the avant-garde of the liberation struggle of the Ukrainian people" (p. 81).

[4] See Julian Birch, "The Ukrainian Nationalist Movement in the U.S.S.R. since 1956," *The Ukrainian Review* 17, no. 4 (1970): 2–47; idem, *The Ukrainian Nationalist Movement in the U.S.S.R. since 1956* (London, 1971); Kenneth C. Farmer, *Ukrainian Nationalism in the Post-Stalin Era: Myth, Symbols, and ideology in Soviet Nationality Policy* (Boston and London, 1980); Jaroslaw Bilocerkowycz, *Soviet Ukrainian Dissent: A Study of Political Alienation* (Boulder and London, 1988); and Bohdan Krawchenko, *Social Change and National Consciousness in Twentieth-Century Ukraine* (Basingstoke, UK, and New York, 1985).

dissent only some time afterward. Most scholars consider *shistdesiatnytstvo* to have been an intellectual phenomenon. Documents have shown, however, that the intelligentsia was not the only group forming the [opposition] movement. Certainly the Ukrainian elite of the 1960s was heir to a specific Ukrainian tradition, according to which the intelligentsia inevitably moves toward dissent and becomes the core around which the national opposition is formed.[5]

The inevitability of the *shistdesiatnyky* moving toward dissent against Soviet rule, though universally accepted, seems to be a teleological explanation of the movement's future development that allows for the incorporation of *shistdesiatnytstvo* into the history of Ukrainian national identity. This interpretation suggests that the way in which the *shistdesiatnyky* demonstrated their national belonging is in line with a coherent process concerning the formation of national identity. Zaplotynska inherited this interpretation from her teacher, Heorhii Kasianov, who authored the book considered to be the best account of *shistdesiatnytstvo* to date. In this work, *Those Who Disagreed*, Kasianov takes into consideration the entire universe of nonconformist thought that animated Ukraine from the end of the 1950s and formed an evolutionary discourse propelling the development of Ukrainian nationalism:

> The opposition movement of the 1960s–1980s and its ideological and political evolution were logical continuations of previous stages in the struggle for national liberation. We must remember that since the nineteenth century the Ukrainian national-liberation movement has generally proceeded through the following stages: apolitical acculturation, the formulation of ideological postulates, the creation of political parties and formulation of political claims, and armed struggle for liberation. With the exception of armed struggle, the opposition movement of the 1960s–1980s likewise progressed through these stages.[6]

---

5 Olena Zaplotyns'ka, "Ukraïns'ke shistdesiatnytstvo: Vyznachennia definitsiï ta istoriohrafiia problemy," in *Ukraïns'kyi istorychnyi zbirnyk (2002)*, ed. Valerii Smolii (Kyiv, 2003), 456.

6 Heorhii Kas'ianov, *Nezhodni: Ukraïns'ka intelihentsiia v rusi oporu 1960–80-kh rokiv* (Kyiv, 1995), 189. I have translated the first word in this book's title in the most literal way to emphasize that it is different from the Ukrainian term for dissidents.

Furthermore, Kasianov viewed this similarity with the nineteenth-century Ukrainian national movement through an ideological lens.

> Thus even a superficial analysis of the ideological output of the opposition movement of the 1960s–1980s shows that with respect to strategic tasks, nothing essentially new was developed.... Of course, one can argue that the tactics did change in relation to their closest predecessors, the OUN and the UPA, but aspiration to legality was characteristic of the Ukrainian liberal democrats as far back as the beginning of the twentieth century.[7]

From this point of view, *shistdesiatnytstvo* indeed constituted an evolutionary stage in the history of the national-liberation movement, albeit not a particularly consequential or successful one.

Such an interpretation is perhaps the outcome of an unconscious underestimation of the Soviet content of *shistdesiatnytstvo*. In my opinion, it is impossible to properly understand *shistdesiatnytstvo* without taking into account the fact that it was also a product of Soviet culture, which by then had been influencing and radically transforming Ukrainian culture for over three decades. When understood in this way, it can be argued that not all of the characteristics of *shistdesiatnytstvo* should be considered as formative factors of Ukrainian nationhood. Therefore the first task of this study will be to re-examine the cultural and political content of *shistdesiatnytstvo* in order to achieve a less teleological understanding of the intellectual ferment that animated Ukraine in the 1960s. An alternative view of the subject will be presented, integrating some of its evolutionary blind alleys and complementing the idea that dissent was not the only logical outcome of this movement. Therefore we shall have to consider various broad interpretations of Soviet history, a field of study that in recent decades has seen unprecedented progress.

The Relaunch of the Soviet Project

In recent years, many historians have identified the decades following the Second World War as a key period to understanding developments in Soviet history as well as the dissolution of the USSR in 1991. The defeat of

---

7   Ibidem, 193. The pro-independence OUN (Organization of Ukrainian Nationalists) and UPA (Ukrainian Insurgent Army) were underground political and guerilla forces that fought all foreign (German, Soviet, Polish nationalist, Romanian, and Hungarian) occupying armies and administrations during the Second World War.

Nazi Germany left the nations that comprised the Soviet Union in positions radically different from where they had been at the end of the First World War. From the 1920s to 1991 Lenin's creation was both an empire, which had reached the very core of Germany, and an international political movement that seemed capable of conquering at least half the earth and enlivening the hopes of nearly half of the population on the other side of the Iron Curtain. In the area of Soviet domestic policy, however, after the immense sacrifices of the Second World War the population of the Soviet Union demanded the improvements in daily life that the Marxist-Leninist prophecy had promised. In the late stages of both the Stalin and Khrushchev eras there were various attempts to formulate a response to the eagerness for change that pervaded Soviet society. For this reason historians speak specifically of a "relaunch of the Soviet project"[8] that took place between 1945 and 1964.

According to Elena Zubkova's classic study of late Stalinism and the early Thaw, both Stalin and Khrushchev missed the exceptional opportunities offered by their two respective crucial moments—in 1945–46 and 1956—preferring instead not to attempt any real reform of the Soviet system. While Stalin was bent on reviving his previous terror regime, Khrushchev lacked the political will or ability to adopt reform proposals and turned instead to a mostly populist policy.[9] Confronted with the unwillingness of Soviet leaders to implement serious reforms, the cultural elite undertook to develop proposals for alternative projects, giving birth to one of the most extraordinary cultural debates of contemporary history, which reflected the inner workings of an entire generation.

In his book on the Russian intelligentsia, Vladislav Zubok traces an evocative portrait of the intellectual life of the Thaw generation,[10] which he calls "Zhivago's children."

---

8   This was also the title of a September 2006 conference organized by the British Academy, University College London, the Hill Foundation, St. John's College, Oxford, and the British Association for Slavonic and East European Studies. The proceedings were published as Juliane Fürst, Polly Jones, and Susan Morrissey, eds., *The Relaunch of the Soviet Project, 1945–1964*, a special issue of *The Slavonic and East European Review* 86, no. 2 (2008). On the relaunch of the USSR, see also William Taubman, *Khushchev: The Man and His Era* (New York and London, 2003).
9   Elena Zubkova, *Russia after the War: Hopes, Illusions, and Disappointments, 1945–1957* (London and Armonk, 1998).
10 I share Marc Bloch's understanding of the word "generation" in *The Historian's Craft* (New York, 1963: "Men who are born into the same social environment [at] about the

> Zhivago's spiritual children were born into a society where everyone was supposed to absorb the Soviet way of life as naturally as the Russian Orthodox had their faith and church. They walked under the Kremlin's red stars and learned Soviet songs. Many of them grew up without their fathers, who had perished during the years of war or the Great Terror. In a sense "Comrade Stalin" became their substitute father, and some of them were taught to love Stalin more than their parents. As the beneficiaries of the Soviet enlightenment project, they were the graduates of the best universities, above all in Moscow and Leningrad, and were destined to become the highly educated group that Stalin cynically called the "Soviet intelligentsia." In reality they were intended to be cadres totally loyal to Stalin's agenda and the Party line. Meeting a foreigner was less likely than seeing a total solar eclipse, and foreign travel was unimaginable. Comparison between the Soviet experience and life in other countries was almost impossible.
>
> Yet something remarkable occurred.... The educated cadres trained for Stalinist service turned out to be a vibrant and diverse tribe, with intellectual curiosity, artistic yearnings, and a passion for high culture. They identified not only with the Soviet collectivity, but also with humanist individualism. This was the unintended result of the Stalinist educational system, the ideas of self-cultivation and self-improvement, and the pervasive cult of high culture that it propagated.[11]

Verifying to what extent this description of the intelligentsia during the time of Khrushchev's Thaw corresponds to the reality of the Ukrainian case will be among the tasks of this study. Additionally, I will attempt to assess the extent to which the *shistdesiatnyky* actually took part in creating an alternative "project to relaunch the Soviet Union." The cultural backgrounds and values of the *shistdesiatnyky* will be explored in order to establish whether they represented an alternative to the political course of Khrushchevism and Brezhnevism, and whether their movement fulfilled the political requirements needed to influence the Soviet authorities. Since the history of Soviet Ukraine seems to suggest that the most plausible answer to these questions is "no," I will also investigate the movement's

---

same time necessarily come under analogous influences, particularly in their formative years. Experience proves that, by comparison with either considerably older or considerably younger groups, their behaviour reveals certain distinctive characteristics that are ordinarily very clear. This is true even of their bitterest disagreements. To be excited by the same dispute, even on opposing sides, is still to be alike. This common stamp, deriving from common age, is what makes a generation" (p. 185).

11   Vladislav Zubok, *Zhivago's Children: The Last Russian Intelligentsia* (Cambridge, Mass., 2009), 21.

flaws, determine who was at fault, and identify crucial moments in *shistdesiatnytstvo* when certain actions were taken or not. This will be achieved by exploiting a series of other heuristic paradigms.

When asked who the *shistdesiatnyky* were, the poet Lina Kostenko elegantly avoided the uncomfortable question by stating "We were a group of friends."[12] In doing so she innocently corroborated recent research on the Thaw that describes the social network of these young intellectuals through the concept of a *kompaniia*. First proposed as a category by Liudmila Alexeyeva,[13] this concept has since been redefined by Juliane Fürst. A *kompaniia* (literally a group of friends) was an "experimental space" that reorganized the relationship between the public and private spheres. These people all engaged in intellectual activity and rejected the notion of privacy in an attempt to create a "forum for private citizens to engage in public life" as an alternative to the all-embracing Soviet state.[14] What these intellectuals were trying to establish was a new *obshchestvennost*. Literally interpreted as 'public opinion' or 'civil society', the Russian term *obshchestvennost* (Ukrainian: *hromadskist*) is a difficult word to translate, because it refers to both a collective identity and a set of values. As Karl Loewenstein put it, the Thaw's intellectuals engaged in cultural debate within the post-Stalinist Soviet Union "did not see themselves as lone freedom fighters but as members of a community trying to re-establish its internal cohesion."[15] Through their artistic activity the *shistdesiatnyky* tried to contribute to the cause of "promoting a new consensus for the direction of the Soviet Union."[16]

Taking Zubok's writing about their origins into account, it would be inappropriate to view the *shistdesiatnyky* as dissidents while they seemingly evinced strong feelings of Soviet patriotism. Benjamin Tromly has claimed that in struggling against Russification, the Ukrainian intellectuals were convinced of the need to restore the Leninist principles of Soviet nationalities policy that Stalin's regime had suspended: "Indeed,

---

12 Interview with Lina Kostenko, 12 June 2009.
13 Liudmila Alexeyeva and Paul Goldberg, *The Thaw Generation: Coming of Age in the Post-Stalin Era* (Boston, 1990).
14 Juliane Fürst, "Friends in Private, Friends in Public: The Phenomenon of the 'Kompaniia' among Soviet Youth in the 1950s and 1960s," in *Borders of Socialism: Private Spheres of Soviet Russia*, ed. Lewis H. Siegelbaum (New York, 2006), 229–49.
15 Karl Loewenstein, "'Obshchestvennost' as Key to Understanding Soviet Writers of the 1950s: *Moskovskii literator*, October 1956–March 1957," *Journal of Contemporary History* 44, no. 3 (2009): 473–92.
16 Ibidem.

the focal point for national aspirations was the promotion of Ukrainian language and culture, and both goals seemed consistent with the creation of a more democratic and supposedly Leninist socialism."[17] Thus a person's support for the rebirth of Ukrainian culture did not necessarily entail identifying him or her as anti-Soviet or anti-Russian.

Therefore this book will analyze the history of *shistdesiatnytstvo* by paying particular attention to the dynamics that transformed a small, cultural "circle of friends" into a political movement. The ways in which the *shistdesiatnyky* addressed their nation and the responses they received will prove particularly important to this investigation. The concepts of *kompaniia* and *hromadskist* and the meaning that the *shistdesiatnyky* attributed to their national identity will form the core of my analysis. The first chapter will illustrate the birth of *shistdesiatnytstvo* as both a cultural phenomenon and a *kompaniia*. The final stage of the formation of the *kompaniia* will be examined in relation to the founding of the Club of Creative Youth in Kyiv. The second chapter, which covers the years 1961–68, will recount the process by which the *shistdesiatnyky* were transformed from a group of private citizens into a movement that directly addressed Ukrainian public opinion and interfered with the activity of the Soviet government. The actions of the *shistdesiatnyky* increased in intensity even after the first repression of 1965–66, when the Soviet authorities condemned *shistdesiatnytstvo* as an anti-Soviet movement. The writings and public initiatives of the *shistdesiatnyky* represented attempts at constituting an alternative *hromadskist* and mobilizing popular support. The third chapter will analyze the final stage of *shistdesiatnytstvo*, examining the reasons that compelled the Soviet authorities to eliminate it. This chapter will also delineate the divisions among the *shistdesiatnyky*, illustrating the fragmentation and lack of leadership that prevented the effective transformation of *shistdesiatnytstvo* into a political movement. Finally, in the conclusion, I will provide a general evaluation of the *shistdesiatnytstvo* era in the context of Soviet and Ukrainian history.

About Labels and Sources

Ivan Dziuba, the standard-bearer of *shistdesiatnytstvo*, has stated more than once that he does not like being labeled a *shistdesiatnyk*, because his

---

[17] Benjamin Tromly, "Soviet Patriotism and Its Discontents among Higher Education students in Khrushchev-era Russia and Ukraine," *Nationalities Papers* 37, no. 3 (2009): 313. Tromly confirms these early conclusions in his *Making the Soviet Intelligentsia: Universities and Intellectual Life under Stalin and Krushchev* (Cambridge, UK, 2015).

political activity was not confined to the 1960s. In these pages you will not find a list of *shistdesiatnyky*, nor will I recount the life and activity of every member of the movement. The task of the present study is to illustrate the defining characteristics of a cultural and civil movement rather than the individuals comprising it, many of whom belonged to *shistdesiatnytstvo* only for a short period or did not share all of its initiatives and ideas. This study will include an analysis of initiatives, texts, and other events that can contribute to an understanding of the development of *shistdesiatnytstvo*. While I made an effort to include all of the central figures, the stories of many *shistdesiatnyky* of medium and minor importance could not be included in this work.[18] For the same reason I decided to include some personalities who technically were not *shistdesiatnyky*, the most evident example being Levko Lukianenko. I hope that the inclusion of his story will assist in the clarification of many aspects of *shistdesiatnytstvo* that would otherwise remain somewhat murky.

This study is widely based on the documents that circulated in Soviet Ukraine in the form of underground literature called samizdat (Ukrainian: *samvydav*; see n. 19 below). Their once illegal nature makes the preservation of these materials unusually difficult.[19] In the case of Ukrainian *samvydav* literature, the Ukrainian diaspora helped to increase their availability. The Ukrainian communities in Poland, Czechoslovakia, Germany, Britain, France, Canada, the United States, Australia, and other countries preserved a strong sense of belonging to the Ukrainian nation, revived after both world wars by the arrival of many of those who had fought against Bolshevism. A contingent within these communities abroad was absolutely convinced of the extraneousness of Communism to Ukraine and was therefore keen to publish any document evincing opposition to Moscow. Owing to the efforts of these communities, important Ukrainian *samvydav* documents were collected and published abroad, making them more accessible to the modern researcher. However, due to the difficulties of travel and the lack of control on the part of the authors, these documents were often published in many different versions: in the original Ukrainian as well as in translation, in their entirety or in abridged versions, and by different editors. Liber and

---

18   More comprehensive accounts can be found in Roman Korohods'kyi, *Brama svitla: Shistdesiatnyky* (Lviv, 2009); and Iryna Zhylenko, *Homo feriens: Spohady* (Kyiv, 2011).

19   Ann Komaromi, "The Material Existence of Soviet Samizdat," *Slavic Review* 63, no. 3 (2004): 597–618. A related Ukrainian term is "*tamvydav*," i.e., published abroad, in which the prefix *sam-* ('self') in *samvydav* is replaced by *tam-* ('over there')—*Ed.*

Mostovych's bibliography of Ukrainian dissent, which traces the different versions of each piece of writing, was indispensable in introducing order to an otherwise puzzling mosaic of texts.[20]

The necessity of relying on underground documents is also a result of the scarcity of official documentation. The documents of the Club of Creative Youth were confiscated and destroyed when the organization was banned, after which the questionable legal status of the overall movement discouraged its adherents from leaving written evidence of their activity. Therefore this study has greatly depended upon the many memoirs, interviews, and diaries that have been published in Ukraine since independence. Though not complete, Babych and Patoka's bibliography of repression in Ukraine was useful concerning Ukrainian publications after 1991.[21]

Because *shistdesiatnyky* were also published in the state-sanctioned press, I have made use of several Soviet Ukrainian newspapers and journals. Some of them, such as the literary journals *Vitchyzna* (Kyiv) and *Zhovten* (Lviv), even had members of the *shistdesiatnyky* on their editorial boards. Others, such as *Literaturna Ukraina* (formerly, until 1962, *Literaturna hazeta*), the official organ of the Union of Writers of Ukraine (Ukrainian acronym: SPU), published works by *shistdesiatnyky* as well as those opposed to them. The literary journal *Dnipro* (Kyiv) published poetry and essays, and many other periodicals contributed to the cultural debate in Ukraine. Their role will be discussed in this analysis.

The Ukrainian émigré journal *Suchasnist'*, founded in Munich in 1961, closely followed developments in the "captive nation" owing to the collaboration of skilful authors such as Ivan Koshelivets and Bohdan Kravtsiv. In particular, among the contributors was the historian Roman Szporluk, who wrote under the pen name Pavlo Chernov.[22]

Preserved in Ukraine's archives are other documents that were useful in reconstructing events. They include the minutes and reports of the Communist Party of Ukraine's Department of Science and Culture, which kept a vigilant eye on the *shistdesiatnyky*, in the Central State Archive of Public Organizations of Ukraine; and the minutes of meetings of Ukraine's

---

20 George Liber and Anna Mostovych, *Nonconformity and Dissent in the Ukrainian SSR, 1955–1975: An Annotated Bibliography* (Cambridge, Mass., 1978).

21 Ievdokiia K. Babych and Valentyna V. Patoka, *Represiï v Ukraïni (1917–1990 rr.): Naukovo-dopomizhnyi bibliohrafichnyi pokazhchyk* (Kyiv, 2007).

22 His selected articles were reprinted some fifty years later in Ukraine. See Roman Shporliuk [Szporluk], *U poshukakh maibutn'oho chasu* (Kyiv, 2010).

Union of Writers (SPU) and the personal archives of several SPU members preserved at the Central State Archive-Museum of Literature and Art of Ukraine.

Furthermore, I had the opportunity to study the personal files of some *shistdesiatnyky* at the archives of the KGB in the Ukrainian SSR, today the Sectoral State Archive of the Security Service of Ukraine in Kyiv. Unfortunately, working in this archive was problematic. There were no lists of records to consult, and hence I had to negotiate which files I would be able to access during my next visit. I was told that I could not see the personal files of living people—yet I was provided with Ivan Dziuba's file. But I could not read the files of Leonid Pliushch or Viacheslav Chornovil and was informed that the KGB did not keep any files regarding people who had not been tried—although, for example, it is unlikely that Lina Kostenko was never under surveillance. Despite this I made efforts to extract information as best I could from what I was given, namely, minutes of interrogations of *shistdesiatnyky* and some witnesses, a few related documents such as essays or transcribed speeches, and reports written by Party officials.

When reading Soviet documents, one should take into account that they were always written with two particular readers in mind—the censor and the KGB agent. In contrast, the writings by *shistdesiatnyky*, especially their *samvydav* pieces, contained a high degree of sincerity, even in the case of letters addressed directly to the Soviet authorities. This forthright stance was partially maintained even during interrogations by the KGB, and the minutes thus revealed themselves to be more useful than I expected. It struck me that a high percentage were written by the accused themselves, likely due to their strategy of abiding by the law, but also likely the outcome of their desire not to be misinterpreted. This may seem somewhat abstract or confusing, but I will provide a practical example in the third chapter.

In May and June 2009 I conducted five interviews: four with prominent representatives of *shistdesiatnytstvo*—Les Taniuk, Lina Kostenko, Ivan Dziuba, and Mykola Plakhotniuk—and one with an activist of the dissident movement of the 1970s, Vasyl Ovsiienko. They were willing to answer all of my questions and provided additional materials I would have been unable to find elsewhere. In two cases, Kostenko's and Plakhotniuk's, my interview uncovered hitherto unavailable information, as neither of them had written memoirs or diaries. Oral sources are very difficult to handle because they contain factual mistakes and anachronisms, and the integrity of an interview often depends on the ability of the interviewer to gain the trust of his subject. I have no doubt, however, that all interviews upon which my research is based were characterized by the same intellectual honesty that had always guided the lives of the *shistdesiatnyky*.

Though far from comprehensive, this study is an attempt at a *prosopography* of the *shistdesiatnyky* and therefore presents various accounts of their lives. I beg the reader's indulgence if not all of the vital details are presented at the first mention of a *shistdesiatnyk*. Such an approach would have transformed the first chapter into a tedious list of short biographies. Instead, I have preferred to present each biography when I think it would best help to illustrate a given figure from the movement. In addition, since Ukrainian culture is not as well known as other national cultures, I have included some brief biographical details about other people who may be unknown to the non-specialist public. I hope I have not over- or underestimated the competence of my readers.

Chapter One

The Origins of the *Shistdesiatnyky* (1953–61)

> Знову чую російську мову,
> мову рідкісної краси.*

De-Stalinization and the Dawn of the Thaw

The death of Stalin, on 5 March 1953, brought about immediate consequences for Ukraine. Russification under the Zhdanov Doctrine and attacks on Jews in the Ukrainian SSR came to an abrupt end. As Borys Lewytzkyj pointed out, several days after the dictator's demise the CPU's first secretary, Leonid Melnikov, was removed from office on the grounds of "deviation from Leninist nationality policy."

> The dismissal was a psychological move ... The change in leadership consolidated the [CPU] and boosted the self-confidence of the Ukrainian leaders, whose sphere of competence was steadily augmented.... There was also a strengthening of Ukrainian representation in the Party apparatus.[1]

This was an outcome of the condemnation of Russification pronounced by Lavrentii Beria, who, in the few months he remained at the head of the USSR, took some steps to foster minority nations' rights, especially in western Ukraine.[2]

Despite these changes, what Stalin's death meant for Ukraine remained unclear. The tercentenary of the Pereiaslav Treaty[3] offered an

---

* "Once again I hear the Russian language / a language of rare beauty," the first two lines of Lina Kostenko's poem 'V poïzdi' (On the Train), in *Slovo molodykh: Al'manakh* (Kyiv, 1955), 15. I thank Roman Szporluk for drawing my attention to these verses.

1 Borys Lewytzkyj, *Politics and Society in Soviet Ukraine, 1953–1980* (Edmonton, 1984), 4. "*Zhdanovshchina*" was a cultural doctrine developed by the secretary of the All-Union Communist Party's Central Committee, Andrei Zhdanov. It resulted in the persecution of intellectuals who did not comply with the regime's wishes.

2 Andrea Graziosi, *L'Urss dal trionfo al degrado: Storia dell'Unione Sovietica 1945–1991* (Bologna, 2008), 149; and Amy Knight, *Beria: Stalin's First Lieutenant* (Princeton, 1993), 186–91.

3 In 1654 Hetman Bohdan Khmelnytsky concluded a fateful alliance in Pereiaslav between the Hetmanate and Tsar Aleksei Mikhailovich according to which Cossack Ukraine accepted the Muscovy's protection. Muscovy, and later the Russian Empire, did not honour their guarantee of autonomy for the Hetmanate.

occasion to present a Stalinist version of history, and the resulting celebrations reaffirmed the inevitable union with Russia as the only way Ukrainians could aspire to prosperity.[4] The cornerstone of this interpretation was the *Theses on the 300th Anniversary of the Unification of Ukraine with Russia (1654–1954)*, produced in 1953 by a group of Party historians led by Andrii Lykholat, officially promulgated by the Central Committee of the Communist Party of the Soviet Union (hereafter CC CPSU), and read at public meetings from 12 January 1954.[5] Despite the official doctrine, in the *Theses* class struggle, born from social oppression, "took place and was progressive not because it accelerated its weakening and final abolition, but because it encouraged unification and served as an 'inflammatory example' of the 'mighty impulse' of the Russian social- and national-liberation movement."[6]

Regardless of the Zhdanov Doctrine's after-effects in historical research, some signs of the new political season were perceptible before the Twentieth CPSU Congress in February 1956. Language changes became evident in 1954 and 1955 as new Soviet Ukrainian journals and scientific periodicals, including *Fiziolohichnyi zhurnal, Mystetstvo, Prapor, Prykladna mekhanika,* and *Ukraïns'kyi fizychnyi zhurnal*, published their inaugural issues. In July 1955 the famous Ukrainian film director Oleksandr Dovzhenko published an article, titled "The Art of Painting, and the Present," in the Moscow literary newspaper *Literaturnaia gazeta*. In this commentary about an art exhibition, Dovzhenko attacked mannerism and expressed his wish for the birth of a new style of painting that could compare with the figurative arts at that time, such as photography, cinema, and television.[7] He hoped that new artists with an individual style might reinvigorate Soviet painting.

The Twentieth CPSU Congress and the final report on Stalin's crimes radically changed Soviet politics. Stalin's successor as the CPSU's first secretary, Nikita Khrushchev, employed only a few words to condemn Stalin's nationality policy, denouncing the forced deportations of entire

---

4 Serhy Yekelchyk, *Stalin's Empire of Memory: Russian-Ukrainian Relations in the Soviet Historical Imagination* (Toronto, 2004), 154–61.

5 In Russian: *Tezisy o 300-letii vossoedineniia Ukrainy s Rossiei (1654–1954 gg.)* (Moscow, 1954); in Ukrainian: *Tezy pro 300-richchia vozz'iednannia Ukraïny z Rosiieiu (1654–1954 rr.)* (Kyiv, 1954).

6 Vitalii Iaremchuk, *Mynule Ukraïny v istorychnii nautsi URSR pisliastalins'koï doby* (Ostroh, 2009), 46–47.

7 Aleksandr Dovzhenko, "Iskusstvo zhivopisi i sovremennost'," *Literaturnaia gazeta*, 21 July 1954.

peoples after the Second World War and stating that the "Ukrainians avoided meeting this fate only because there were too many of them and there was no place to which to deport them. Otherwise [he] would have deported them as well."[8] Though Khrushchev did not mention the repression of the Ukrainian intelligentsia or the famine of 1932–33, by intellectuals in Soviet Ukraine perceived the report as a denunciation of previous policies toward the Ukrainians, and it served as the final catalyst that prompted an unexpected outburst of discontent.

The report arrived in Ukraine on 5 March 1956 and was read at public meetings starting the following day. In a report to the new CC CPSU secretary, Oleksii Kyrychenko, Party members were described as receiving the denunciation of Stalin's personality cult quite positively, expressing sincere regret for the Party's mistakes and accepting the need to repair damages.[9] However, when historians at Kyiv State University and the Institute of History at the Academy of Sciences of the Ukrainian SSR (hereafter AN URSR) read the report during their deliberations on 6 and 7 March, they reacted by attacking the Party. Initial questions about how to teach Marxism-Leninism now and what to do with the *Short Course*[10] were rapidly eclipsed by concerns regarding the lack of intervention by other leaders and the misguided veneration of Stalin that had only recently subsided. Some questions revealed uncertainty about explaining this political shift to Soviet citizens: "The people love Stalin, so how are we to re-educate them now?"[11] At a meeting on 9 March with employees of Kyiv State University, the questions directed at Party representatives became even more politically contentious. Professors demanded clarification of the nationality issue and inquired whether the Tatars would be returning to Crimea. Recriminations against the Party followed ("What if Stalin had not died?") and several stories about loyal

---

8   One of the first translations into English was *The Dethronement of Stalin: Full Text of the Khrushchev Speech*, published as a brochure by the *Manchester Guardian* in 1956. The quote above appears there on p. 17.
9   Report about Party members' reactions to the reading of Khrushchev's 1956 report, 10 March 1956, in Tsentral'nyi derzhavnyi arkhiv hromads'kykh ob'iednan' Ukraïny (hereafter TsDAHOU), f. 1, op. 24, spr. 4255, ark. 3–9.
10 *Istoriia Vsesoiuznoi kommunisticheskoi partii (bol'shevikov): Kratkii kurs* (Moscow, 1938), commissioned by Stalin in 1935. Published in English as *History of the Communist Party of the Soviet Union (Bolsheviks): Short Course* (Moscow, 1939).
11 Party report about meetings with historians, in TsDAHOU, f. 1, op. 24, spr. 4255, ark. 10–13.

Communists being executed under Stalinism provoked doubts about the Party's moral standing.[12]

By 19 March the Soviet authorities seemed to have lost their grasp of the situation. At a meeting with media and state-communication workers in Lviv, the local CPU secretary was unprepared to face their questions. When asked why other Politburo members in the Kremlin had not arrested Stalin, he answered that they feared the outbreak of a civil war. This stirred up more questions about the legitimacy of the Soviet state.[13] On the same day, issues of Ukrainian culture were discussed at a meeting of the Party cell at the Institute of Literature of the AN URSR. Nina Krutikova, the institute's deputy director, painted a troubling portrait of intellectual life.

> With more or less emotional colour, [the members of the institute] have spoken about the fact that until recently every scientific discipline has been repressed; that nihilism toward Ukrainian national culture and fears of new thought have risen among the people; that managing bodies have hindered the creation of fully worthy works of literary criticism and halted the publication of Ukrainian literary classics; that the best writers and critics of Ukraine have been exterminated; and that, as a consequence of the intervention of these managing bodies, the history of Ukrainian literature before the Revolution [of 1917] is one-sided and poor.[14]

A young scholar, Leonid Kovalenko, claimed that "everyone here is concerned only with his own career" and surmised that progress on the compilation of a history of Ukrainian literature and related scholarly research had been frozen due to fear of the KGB. Many agreed with him, citing the 1944 case of official condemnation of Volodymyr Sosiura's patriotic poem "Love Ukraine." The poet Petro Zasenko is quoted as saying "Leninist nationality policy is not being correctly carried out, Ukrainian national culture is not being valued, and Russification is occurring. There are only nine Ukrainian-language secondary schools in Kyiv; there is nowhere to educate our children.... We would do better without the [interference of Party] commissions." The meeting ended with a debate on publishing works by the executed Ukrainian playwright

---

12 Party report on a meeting at Kyiv University, in ibidem, ark. 14–18.
13 Report on the activity of the CPU secretary in Lviv, in ibidem, ark. 46–48.
14 Minutes of the meeting at the Institute of Literature, in TsDAHOU, f. 1, op. 24, spr. 4264, ark. 1.

Mykola Kulish, and Krutikova's report concludes that the trajectory of the meeting resulted from Party officials' failure to prepare adequately for the gathering.[15]

Before long, as Party officials continued making public blunders, the Party's lack of authority became widely recognized by intellectuals. At a meeting with social-studies teachers in Stanislav (today Ivano-Frankivsk) Oblast, CPU representatives were unable to explain how Marxism-Leninism and the history of the Second World War were to be taught. Attendees shouted that strong leadership was needed, and some declared that Stalinism was "the most horrible period in the history of our fatherland."[16] Officials of the Ministry of Culture of the USSR participated in some of the meetings, but the ministry failed to improve the methodology of ideological management. As a report to First Secretary Kyrychenko states, in the SPU, "under false pretenses of condemning the [Stalinist] personality cult, some Communists attempted in their speeches to question Party policy of past years and made demagogic and even anti-Party declarations."[17] A common theme in these speeches was the cultural repression perpetrated by Stalinism. The playwright Oleksandr Korniichuk claimed that many writers in the past had been unfairly condemned for Ukrainian nationalism, and he requested that the Party and Ukraine's Union of Writers (SPU) apologize to Sosiura for denouncing his poem "Love Ukraine" as a "bourgeois nationalist" anthem in 1951.[18] Despite the conciliatory discourses of writers Oles Honchar, Yurii Zbanatsky, and Liubomyr Dmyterko, the majority of writers lamented the mistakes of the past and demanded the rehabilitation of the banned poets Vasyl Chumak, Oleksander Oles, Myroslav Irchan, and Vasyl Blakytny. Poet Leonid Vysheslavsky argued that the time had come to stop thanking the "older brother" (Russia) and to acknowledge that Ukrainians were not inferior to Russians. The most vehement critic was Andrii Malyshko, who "recalled the genocide of the Ukrainian people. He described in dreadful terms the "terrible" past of the Ukrainian people, [saying] "there was no bread or salt; they sent people to prison and tortured them." He even accused Stalin's right-hand man, Lazar

---

15 In ibidem, ark. 2–4. On Kulish, see below.
16 Report to the CC CPU's Department of Agitation and Propaganda, in TsDAHOU, f. 1, op. 24, spr. 4256, ark. 21–25.
17 Report to Kyrychenko, 10 April 1956, in ibidem, ark. 10.
18 About Sosiura's case, see Volodymyr K. Baran and Viktor M. Danylenko, *Ukraïna v umovakh systemnoï kryzy (1946–1980-i rr.)* (Kyiv, 1999), 56–58.

Kaganovich, of being responsible for the death of thousands of innocent people.[19]

On 26 April the Third Congress of Ukrainian Composers played out in a similar vein. In tune with the meeting's motto—"Musical culture is inextricably intertwined with native language"—the outcome of the congress was a condemnation of teaching being conducted in Russian without any linkage to popular Ukrainian culture.[20] Similar opinions were expressed during a meeting of senior theatre directors, along with many reproaches aimed at Soviet cultural institutions.[21] By April 1956 reactions had escalated to the point of verging on revolt. From 3 to 8 April the National Congress of Ukrainian Artists took place at the Kyiv State Institute of Art. There student meetings occurred simultaneously and issued "petitions to the Artists' Congress ... These appeals have a demagogic character, with the intent of disturbing the present order in the institute." Five students—three Party and two Komsomol members—spearheaded this movement. One of them, a Mr. Nikitin, read a statement at a session of the congress, while other students occupied the premises. The authorities brought in the police to restore order.[22]

Khrushchev's report provoked strong feelings of discontent as knowledge workers began voicing doubts about the legitimacy of Soviet authority under Stalin. Although many intellectuals increasingly appeared to be of one mind, they proved unable to organize themselves. On the other hand, after having faltered in the aftermath of Khrushchev's report, the Soviet government decided to reassert its authority by reacting firmly against those who had dared to attack the regime. The designated victim of their crackdown was Andrii Malyshko, whose references to the Ukrainian famine of 1932–33 went beyond the scope of Khrushchev's criticisms of Stalin. In September 1956 Malyshko made "anti-Soviet"

---

19 Report to Kyrychenko, 10 April 1956, in TsDAHOU, f. 1, op. 24, spr. 4256, ark. 11–12. Zbanatsky (1914–94) was a writer of popular novels, several of which were made into films; and Dmyterko (1911–85) was a writer and screenwriter. Honchar will be introduced below. Oleksander Oles (pen name of Oleksander Kandyba) was one of the most popular Ukrainian poets of the early twentieth century. Chumak, Irchan, and Blakytny were modernist poets and proletarian political activists in the 1910s and 1920s. Malyshko (1912–70) was a poet whose strongest works were written in the 1940s.

20 Oleh H. Bazhan, "Narostannia oporu polarytsi rusyfikatsiï v Ukraïns'kii RSR u druhii polovyni 1950-kh–1960-kh rr.," Ukraïns'kyi istorychnyi zhurnal, 2008, no. 5: 148–49.

21 Report to Kyrychenko, 26 March 1956, in TsDAHOU, f. 1, op. 24, spr. 4255, ark. 62–63.

22 Report to Kyrychenko about the Congress of Artists, in TsDAHOU, f. 1, op. 24, spr. 4256, ark. 13–14.

statements in Drohobych during the celebration there of the 150th anniversary of Ivan Franko's birth,[23] but, as reported in a letter denouncing Malyshko to the Party (signed by a V. Geevsky), he asked the audience not to report him once he realized he was in danger.[24] According to a report from the Party's oblast executive committee in Drohobych, Malyshko not only failed to mention the Party's leading role in Soviet society, but went so far as to state that "Karl Marx invented the slogan that the proletariat has nothing to lose except its chains; this is not true, for the proletariat has always been a landowner."[25]

These remarks spurred the SPU to meet and issue a condemnation of Malyshko. Several writers accused him of being a nationalist and refusing to talk to Russian-speakers. However, not all of the speeches were diatribes against Malyshko. Some, such as Oles Honchar (1918–95), saw in these condemnations as an opportunity to mediate between the Soviet authorities and discontented writers. After unequivocally condemning Malyshko's behaviour, Honchar added:

> At the same time I want to say that the declarations of Malyshko, [Mykyta] Shumylo, and [Vasyl] Shvets are a fulsome reaction to our shortcomings, especially in conducting Lenin's nationality policies in Ukraine. During the [period of Stalin's] personality cult, Ukrainian culture suffered greatly; an important contingent of representatives of Ukrainian culture was killed. But now [re]publishing the works of these deceased writers is enriching our Ukrainian literature. In general the decisions of the Party's Central Committee concerning the [Stalin] cult of personality, and the Twentieth CPSU Congress, have opened wide opportunities for creative work. We continue living and working under the light of Lenin's party, under this illustrious example.

Honchar lamented the diminishing number of books published in Ukrainian and the inability to send telegrams in Ukrainian. "Some in the West say that in [Ukraine's] Union of Writers there are people who do not understand [Soviet] nationality policy. In my opinion, those who say that Union members do not understand nationality policy do not properly

---

23 Report to Kyrychenko, 13 October 1956, about Malyshko's speech of 4 September, in TsDAHOU, f. 1, op. 24, spr. 4262, ark. 103–104.
24 Geevsky's letter, 6 September 1956, in TsDAHOU, f. 1, op. 24, spr. 4262, ark. 101–102.
25 Letter, 13 October 1956, in TsDAHOU, f. 1, op. 24, spr. 4262, ark. 65–66.

understand nationality policy themselves."[26] A letter dated 18 January 1957 finally reported to CPSU Secretary Kyrychenko that Malyshko had been severely reprimanded by both the Party and the SPU.[27] Malyshko's case served as an example of the limits to which Soviet leadership would tolerate intellectual discontent.[28]

Another significant occurrence was the condemnation of Vladimir Dudintsev's *Not by Bread Alone*, a novel serialized in 1956 by the Moscow journal *Novyi mir*, which denounced the dishonesty, greed, and hunger for power of the Soviet *nomenklatura*.[29] On 11 December 1956 a meeting of the Party organization within the SPU launched a campaign against *Not by Bread Alone*. The most vehement assailants were the SPU's secretary Yurii Zbanatsky (1914–94) and the Polish-Ukrainian writer Wanda Wasilewska (1905–64), who declared, "We can't take for truth what is clearly an evident lie and slander of our country."[30] The meeting served as a warning that the Soviet leadership would not allow much criticism from writers— the "soldiers of the Party," as defined by Communist orthodoxy. This warning seemed to be effective, for the intellectual establishment showed itself to be unwilling to clash with the regime at this stage.

The most revolutionary voice in 1956 was that of Oleksandr Dovzhenko,[31] who died later that year, on 25 November. In *The Enchanted Desna*, his autobiographical work serialized in the journal *Dnipro*, he explored the deeper cultural roots of Ukrainian identity, reaching even into primordial history.[32] In it the protagonist—a young man modelled on Dovzhenko himself—accompanies his father on a mission to help people

---

26 Collection of statements about Malyshko, in TsDAHOU, f. 1, op. 24, spr. 4262, ark. 72–74.
27 See TsDAHOU, f. 1, op. 24, spr. 4262, ark. 96.
28 For an account of reactions to the Khrushchev's secret speech and how the Party dealt with them, see Robert Hornsby, *Protest, Reform and Repression in Khrushchev's Soviet Union* (Cambridge, UK, 2013), 31–47.
29 In *The Readers of* Novyi mir: *Coming to Terms with the Stalinist Past* (Cambridge, Mass., 2013), 88–109, Denis Kozlov analyzes how *Novyi mir*'s readers reacted to the novel and the debate.
30 Memo on the meeting to the CPU, 14 December 1956, in TsDAHOU, f. 1, op. 24, spr. 4264, ark. 19–26.
31 George S.N. Luckyj, *Ukrainian Literature in the Twentieth Century: A Reader's Guide* (Toronto, 1992), 67.
32 Oleksandr Dovzhenko, *The Enchanted Desna*, trans. Anatole Bilenko (Kyiv, 1982), 249–52, http://sites.utoronto.ca/elul/English/Dovzhenko/Enchanted-Desna.pdf. On Dovzhenko see George O. Liber, *Alexander Dovzhenko: A Life in Soviet Film* (London, 2002); and Vasyl Marochko, *Zacharovanyi Desnoiu: Istorychnyi portret Oleksandra Dovzhenka* (Kyiv, 2006).

in mortal danger from a flood along the Desna and is awakened by refugees crossing the river. He begins the following exchange with his father.

> "Who are those people over there?"
> "They're from far away, from Orel Province. They're Russians, coming from Russia."
> "So who are we? Aren't we Russians?"
> "No, we're not Russians."
> "Who are we, then?"
> "Oh, who knows," Father drawled, with a tinge of sadness in his voice. "We're common folk, sonny ... Ukrainians, the ones who grow bread. [Peasants], so to speak ... Yep, nothing more than [peasants]. Once we were Cossacks, they say, but now it's nothing more than a name."[33]

Dovzhenko's declaration of national belonging hints at the memory of the Cossack past and emerges directly from Ukrainian folk culture. After years of Stalinist homogenization, this was the first, albeit nebulous and vaguely defined, claim to a distinct national identity.

Although the Party regained its control of the intellectuals, it failed to silence the discontent among other educated people. On 2 January Zbanatsky sent to the Party an anonymous letter he had received from a "representative of a sizable stratum of the Soviet middle intelligentsia — brought up in our so-called Soviet reality, i.e., members of a generation entirely grown up under Soviet rule, in the '30s and '40s." The letter's author wrote that he was filled with "resentment and indignation" after he read the short report about the writers' meeting where Dudintsev and his novel were denounced.

> How can you not feel ashamed, you who dare call yourself writers, to play this miserable role of henchman, who's happy to do whatever he's told, as long he gets paid?... You know as well as I do that Dudintsev is right, a million times right: that the Drozdovs, Shutikovs, Nevraevs, [and] Avdiievs are not single men — they are an entire stratum that is a product of those horrible times that have fortunately and irretrievably disappeared into the past. But these

---

[33] Dovzhenko, *The Enchanted Desna*, 27. The term '*muzhik*' in the published translation is replaced here to avoid possible confusion, as some current dictionary definitions specify Russian nationality, which does not apply in this case.

> people are *even now* still in power. And *you know that*. That's exactly why you're ruining Dudintsev, because it's what *they* want. Don't you have any remorse, conscience, or even feeling of personal dignity? After all, you yourselves don't believe in what you say.[34]

The author added that under Stalinism everyone believed in the justness of the Soviet Union and possessed unshakeable faith in the Soviet leadership until Khrushchev's speech opened their eyes.

> And when, finally, this edifice of lies—seemingly erected so quickly—was blown down by the unmasking of Stalin, we suffered and were ashamed of ourselves. We saw truths that our leaders still wish to hide from us. However, we have now learned to tell the truth apart from the lie…. But <u>there cannot be</u> any return to the past. <u>You must know that</u>…. And your names will carry the stigma of shame, the names of dishonest henchmen and miserable, mean lackeys. I will end here. I just wish to add that many people think as I do—and you cannot forbid us to <u>think</u>.

This letter demonstrates that the intellectuals were not wholly appeased by the incomplete Soviet questioning of the Stalinist past. Younger students, in particular, proved to be thorns in the Party's side. For example, while an early report on the university in Stalino (renamed Donetsk in 1961) described unsatisfactory living conditions for students and faculty, the students there did not speak out against the Party.[35] Instead, the decisive factor that inflamed their hearts was the international situation.

In the beginning the Party did not see the events unfolding in 1956 in Poland and Hungary as posing any trouble in Ukraine. As the CPU functionary Stepan Chervonenko wrote in his report to the CC CPSU, in Ukraine the workers were usually "capable of properly evaluating" the political situation in Poland and Hungary—i.e., ascribing the uprising to the forces of counter-revolutionary propaganda. In fact, the opposite was true: university students in Kyiv were largely supportive of the Hungarian and Polish rebels, who, in their opinion, were struggling against the Stalin personality cult and Russification in their own countries

---

[34] This and the next quote are from the original anonymous letter, in TsDAHOU, f. 1, op. 24, spr. 4537, ark. 2–3. Drozdov and the others are all characters in Dudintsev's novel.

[35] A 1956 report to the CC CPU, in TsDAHOU, f. 1, op. 24, spr. 4264, ark. 28–36.

(Konstantin Rokossovsky, they said, was an émigré Russian).[36] Here Ukrainian writers seemed to be in agreement with the political leadership: the poet Maksym Rylsky openly supported Soviet intervention in Hungary, believing that an ideological question was hiding behind the more formal artistic debate.[37]

While many Ukrainian students spent the summers working in the collective farms, they had no access to international news and were therefore initially ignorant of the Soviet repressions in Poland and Hungary.[38] However, by autumn a report on problems at the Kyiv Polytechnical Institute stated that most of the students there, influenced by their Hungarian counterparts, supported Imre Nagy's reforms. Their opinions were validated by the fact that the Party did nothing to improve their living conditions and stipends.[39] This report underlined the role played by Polish students, whose attitude toward the average Soviet student was one of superiority, stemming from their self-perception of being more free and intellectually sophisticated.[40] Party officials noted that Ukrainian faculty were usually unwilling or unable to give students a "correct" interpretation of the Polish and Hungarian situations. Students in the Faculty of History at Kyiv State University showed a great interest toward Hungary, but when they asked their teacher for more information, he provided only a hazy economic explanation. So the students decided to study the question on their own and drew the "wrong" (pro-Hungarian) conclusions instead of falling in line with the Party's position.[41]

The protest ignited by students in Kyiv did not remain confined to the capital. Reflecting on the Polish turmoil, Ukrainian intellectuals began drawing parallels between Ukraine and its neighbours, questioning

---

36 See TsDAHOU, f. 1, op. 24, spr. 4265, ark. 10. Rokossovsky (Polish: Konstanty Rokossowski) was a Soviet career officer of Polish descent and an important commander during the Second World War. From 1949 to 1956 he was Poland's marshal and minister of defence. He authorized the Polish army to put down the June 1956 workers' protests in Poznań, during which seventy-four workers were killed and several hundred were wounded.

37 See TsDAHOU, f. 1, op. 24, spr. 4265, ark. 17–18.

38 Report on the students of the Kyiv State Art Institute, in TsDAHOU, f. 1, op. 24, spr. 4265, ark. 38.

39 See TsDAHOU, f. 1, op. 24, spr. 4265, ark. 30.

40 See ibidem, ark. 31.

41 See the report on the students of history at Kyiv State University, in TsDAHOU, f. 1, op. 24, spr. 4265, ark. 38.

whether the use of Ukrainian was so infrequent because they, too, were victims of imposed Sovietization.[42] In Kharkiv, students at the Institute of Radiophysics protested about their low stipends and crumbling dormitories, leading them to question the Party's policy toward universities as a whole and to lament the lack of freedom of expression and research.[43]

According to Leonid Korenevych, a student in the Faculty of Journalism, Ukrainian students sensed Russians' general disdain toward Ukrainian culture and "felt themselves estranged from their own country." This prompted them to organize a society "to arrange concerts of Ukrainian musical and drama productions, to systematically introduce students to the achievements of Ukraine in the fields of culture and economics, and to recruit new students of Ukrainian literature."[44] Korenevych confided that he had met with an important Ukrainian writer who supported this initiative, but even in later interviews with the CC CPU functionary Fedir Ovcharenko he refused to identify this writer.[45] In the autumn of 1956 a group of Kyiv State University students wrote a letter to Khrushchev announcing their intention to establish a "Union of Youth for Disobedience to Soviet Rule." They stated that they believed the USSR was ruled by lies and wished to make at least a symbolic protest, even if the KGB would inevitably arrest them.[46] They were correct in predicting the reaction of the Soviet authorities, who thenceforth responded strongly to all insubordination.

A report signed by CPSU Secretary Kyrychenko and dated 17 January 1957 describes turmoil at Kyiv State University. As an example, a Komsomol secretary, Zuiev, wanted to organize a conference on social reforms in Yugoslavia and Poland, with anonymous questions permitted from the audience, and two students in the Faculty of Journalism—Marian and Hubanov—distributed a document titled "Minimum Proposals" among their fellow students demanding unrestricted circulation of the foreign press and non-Marxist books. Hubanov stated that he did not

---

42 See the undated report on the intelligentsia, in TsDAHOU, f. 1, op. 24, spr. 4265, ark. 159.
43 See the letter from the Kharkiv Department of Culture and Sciences to the CC CPU, in TsDAHOU, f. 1, op. 24, spr. 4302, ark. 181–82.
44 Dudin's letter, in TsDAHOU, f. 1, op. 24, spr. 4302, ark. 118–20.
45 See Fedir Ovcharenko's letter to the CC CPSU, in TsDAHOU, f. 1, op. 24, spr. 4302, ark. 122–24.
46 See the photographs of the letter, in TsDAHOU, f. 1, op. 24, spr. 4302, ark. 108–10.

believe it was possible to build socialism in a single country. Secretary Kyrychenko reported that these were only examples and that such incidents were a common occurrence in all universities.[47] Zuiev, Marian, and Hubanov were expelled from the university and the Komsomol.[48]

The situation in Lviv and the presence of demagogues within the city worried Kyrychenko. A Mr. Voloshchak had given a speech about the nationality question and defended "Hitler and fascism," while nationalism was spreading in the Faculty of Philology and eventually extended throughout Lviv State University.[49] At Chernivtsi State University, the political views of a Polish student, Werbowa, caused a sensation during an assembly, where she made dangerous declarations about the Polish and Hungarian insurrections. Werbowa was subsequently deported, and the professor who invited her to the meeting was fired.[50] On issues where the political situation in Poland and Hungary was concerned, Ukrainian university students appeared to be the most sensitive demographic group to these realities, and the most vocal against perceived injustices.[51]

The students' frustrations with their living conditions and political climate are further illustrated by two occurrences in 1957. The first was the death of Borys Shypenko, a student in the Faculty of History at Kyiv State University, who killed himself on 27 May 1957. Although the documents concerning his death do not relate the entire story, it is understood that Shypenko had been accused of being an enemy of the October Revolution because of his criticisms of the Soviet system. However, a letter he mailed to his father and the Party before his suicide makes clear that Shypenko did not view himself in this light. He described himself as a victim of the system, noting that even though he believed in Lenin's ideas, Soviet society considered him a counter-revolutionary.

---

47 See Kyrychenko's letter, in TsDAHOU, f. 1, op. 24, spr. 4493, ark. 94–95.
48 See Synytsia's letter, 10 January 1957, in TsDAHOU, f. 1, op. 24, spr. 4493, ark. 99.
49 See Kyrychenko's letter, 14 January 1957, in TsDAHOU, f. 1, op. 24, spr. 4493, ark. 120–28. The particular connotations of protests in Lviv had their roots in students' traditional involvement in the nationalist movement. See Roman Ia. Heneha, "Uchast' Lvivs'koho studentstva v rusi oporu v druhii polovyni 1940-kh–na pochatku 1950-kh rr.," *Ukraïns'kyi istorychnyi zhurnal*, 2007, no. 3: 97–112.
50 See the report, 16 January 1957, in TsDAHOU, f. 1, op. 24, spr. 4493, ark. 133–35.
51 See Zbigniew Wojnowski, "De-Stalinization and Soviet Patriotism: Ukrainian Reactions to East European Unrest in 1956," *Krytyka* 13, no. 4 (2012): 799–829.

> This bureaucratic system mutilates and deforms people. And the tragedy is that this is our Soviet system. It is Soviet but not Leninist, for it is not what Lenin fought for.... We had wonderful ideas, the ideas of Lenin, the idea of Communism. These ideas are very dear and close to me, and I consider them worth dying for. But as it happens, under the powerful facade of these ideas there is much wickedness and filth, much misanthropy and cruelty—all concealed by bright promises. And that truly is a tragedy.[52]

The second case is that of *Kuvalda* (Sledgehammer), a short-lived wall newspaper at the Kyiv Polytechnical Institute (KPI). The editor, second-year student V. Mykhailenko in the Faculty of Mechanical Engineering, published it without the required political oversight. It stated:

> [We] suggest that in Hungary the workers were forced to fight for freedom themselves because of the unsatisfactory governance of the country. In our country ... the resolutions of the Twentieth CPSU Congress are often not being implemented. The authors of this periodical are concerned that the persistence of problems might lead to events similar to those that transpired in Hungary. Here at the Kyiv Polytechnical Institute, the management evidently does not want to adopt new post-congress policies; this could prompt the masses to follow Hungary's suit.... Now, after the Twentieth Congress, we recognize the deeply immoral actions of leading organizations such as the Komsomol and the CPSU, and we will not surrender to brutal and blatantly corrupt pressure from Party members.[53]

Following the publication of *Kuvalda*, Mykhailenko and two other students were expelled from the Komsomol and the KPI. Both the Shypenko and *Kuvalda* incidents demonstrate how the students' protests and demands for better living conditions and freedom of expression became intertwined with sharp criticism of the Soviet past. The Party reacted with the repressions, but it also inadvertently gave youth hope for a change. The most virulent protests seemed to end in 1957 after the Sixth International Youth Festival held in Moscow, but which also included several events in Ukraine. In particular, the World Congress of Democratic

---

52   See Shypenko's letter, in TsDAHOU, f. 1, op. 24, spr. 4587, ark. 48–57. The quotes are on ark. 53 and 56.
53   See the memo to the CPU Secretary, in TsDAHOU, f. 1, op. 24, spr. 4537, ark. 14–23.

Youth took place in Kyiv on 16–23 August 1957 under the aegis of the United Nations. There more than three hundred and twenty delegates from eighty countries assembled to discuss the future. The congress went smoothly, without any protests from Kyiv's students. The main subjects of discussion were fear of nuclear war and the end of colonialism brought about by the liberation of millions of people in Asia and Africa. The Soviet delegates expressed reformist views, while the Chinese delegates assumed the role of the Stalinist "old guard."[54]

Khrushchev's View on the New Cultural Course

The Soviet leadership made several concessions facilitating the development of Ukrainian culture. Between 1957 and 1958 new academic periodicals were created (e.g., *Ukraïns'kyi istorychnyi zhurnal*, *Radians'ke pravo*, and *Ekonomika Radians'koï Ukraïny*) and the Union of Journalists and the Union of Cinema Workers were founded, respectively, in 1957 and 1958. A broad process of rehabilitation began in Ukraine, where, owing to Maksym Rylsky's efforts, dozens of writers and artists who had been repressed during the 1930s and 1940s were readmitted to cultural life and their works were republished.[55] This rehabilitation of former victims of the Stalinist Terror restored to Ukraine's cultural milieu "the artistic inheritance of those who are known in history as the 'Executed Renaissance,' and also a number of figures of [Ukraine's] cultural past."[56] Prominent pre-revolutionary Ukrainian cultural figures, such as Mykola Kostomarov, Mykhailo Drahomanov, Serhii Podolynsky, Panteleimon Kulish, and Borys Hrinchenko, were included in this process. This fostered the recognition of the Ukrainian literary classics as "revolutionary democrats," and the works of Taras Shevchenko, Ivan Franko, Lesia Ukrainka, Pavlo Hrabovsky, and Mykhailo Kotsiubynsky were reintegrated into the Ukrainian literary canon.[57] The literary critic Oleksandr Biletsky assisted greatly with these rehabilitative endeavours through his writings and editing activity. His sense that Ukraine had a

---

54 See the report about the congress in TsDAHOU, f. 1, op. 24, spr. 4493, ark. 177–83.
55 Baran and Danylenko, *Ukraïna v umovakh systemnoï kryzy*, 120–21.
56 Lesia Shevchenko, "Kul'turno-ideolohichni protsesy v Ukraïni pislia XX z'izdu KPRS," in *Pochatok destalinizatsiï v Ukraïni (do 40-richchia zakrytoï dopovidi M. Khrushchova na XX z'ïzdi KPRS)*, ed. Stanislav V. Kul'chyts'kyi (Kyiv, 1997), 98.
57 Vasyl Markus', "Ukraïns'ka kul'tura v prokrustovomu lozhi," *Suchasnist'*, 1961, no. 2: 13. Kostomarov, Drahomanov, Podolynsky, Kulish, Shevchenko, Lesia Ukrainka, Hrabovsky, Franko, and Kotsiubynsky were major Ukrainian literary or intellectual figures in the nineteenth century.

specific national-cultural identity has been reflected in the writings of other writers, such as Roman Szporluk:

> Ukraine's situation, especially at the beginning of the age of its existence, was such that it could be completely absorbed by a mightier neighbour, or in the best case reduced to the status of Provence, Catalonia, or Flanders. But that did not happen. Poland did not swallow up the Ukrainian people. The Ukrainian people did not dissolve themselves into tsarist Russia or into the Austro-Hungarian monarchy. Even islands of "Ukrainianness," such as "Subcarpathian Rus'" [Transcarpathia], survived until the moment of the unification with the entire Ukrainian people.[58]

This atmosphere of cultural development was also fostered by Nikita Khrushchev, who spoke about the new goals of Soviet culture at a convention of the USSR writers', artists', sculptors', and composers' unions on 13 May 1957. Tracing the line of political orthodoxy in artistic activities, he said that despite the condemnation of his personality cult, the overall evaluation of Stalin as a Soviet leader by the Ukrainian people was nevertheless positive.

> When the Party developed the critique of the Stalin personality cult and condemned his mistakes, some writers began considering their past artistic output as misinformed or misguided. Certain members of the literary community even expressed the opinion that all of their books should be rewritten. One has to acknowledge that among the intelligentsia there were also those who did not actively take part in the fight for our cause, who began to blame and defame those labourers in literature who had celebrated the successes attained by our people under the guidance of the Party.[59]

Khrushchev claimed that these writers formulated the label *"lakirovka"* to attack honest Soviet writers, undermine the Party's leadership, and sow doubts about the contribution of artistic works to building Communism. He attacked Vladimir Dudintsev rather mildly and stated that Maksym Rylsky was an example of a wrongly persecuted

---

58 Pavlo Chernov [Roman Szporluk], "Zamitky pro polityku peretryvannia i vik chesnosty," *Suchasnist'*, 1961, no. 11: 39.
59 Mykyta Khrushchov [Nikita Khrushchev], "Za tisnyi zv'iazok literatury i mystetstva z zhyttiam narodu," *Zhovten'* 7, no. 9 (1957): xi.

intellectual, whom he had tenaciously defended from Lazar Kaganovich and Stalin's accusations of being a "bourgeois nationalist."

> The Party has resolutely condemned and consequently corrected the mistakes made during the period of the [Stalin] personality cult in all areas of society, including ideological work. But at the same time it resolutely stands against those who are trying to exploit these past mistakes in their attacks on the guidance of literature and art by the Party and [Soviet] state.[60]

Thus Secretary Khrushchev outlined the permissible limits of artistic expression using opposing examples of a bad writer and a good poet who were affected by the rehabilitation of repressed artists under the eye of the Party. He then reasserted the writer's central role in the promotion of Communism, and the need for the Party to exert strict control over cultural output. Khrushchev's speech was published in many newspapers and was regarded as a guideline of sorts for cultural workers.[61] In it he asked the unions to collaborate among themselves and with the Party. The speech was generally somewhat vague, however, and it failed to address many sensitive matters. Problems arose when the Party needed to address practical issues, which in Ukraine's case predominantly concerned the language question.

The Rise of the Language Question and Education Reform

After the denunciation of the Stalin personality cult, the issue of Russification began to trouble an increasing number of people in Ukraine. According to Volodymyr Baran, during the autumn of 1956 the CPU and other state institutions received many letters lamenting the exclusion of the Ukrainian language from public life and requesting its broader use, especially in schools and sports associations.[62] The intellectual turmoil in other socialist countries worsened the situation. Secretary of the CPSU Kyrychenko wrote to the CC CPSU that Ukrainian intellectuals, influenced by their foreign colleagues, were lamenting the Russification of public life. These colleagues were often surprised by the scarce use of

---

60 Ibidem, xvi.
61 It was defined thus in both *Zhovten'* and *Kommunist*, 1957, no. 12: 2.
62 Volodymyr K. Baran, *Ukraïna 1950–1960-kh rr.: Evoliutsiia totalitarnoï systemy* (Lviv, 1996), 223, and Hryhorii Vashchenko, "Soviet Educational Policy," *The Ukrainian Review* 3, No. 4 (1956): 55–60.

Ukrainian in everyday life, which they claimed they would not tolerate in their own country.[63]

In 1957 and early 1958, professional translators from Russian into Ukrainian sparked a debate in the major literary journals about pressure from Party officials to assist in imposed Russification of the Ukrainian language. Such Russification entailed ignoring idiomatic Ukrainian expressions in favour of literal translation from the Russian. In May 1958 Anton Khyzhniak's essay "Let us love and respect our native tongue!" in *Literaturna hazeta* effectively brought an end to the dispute.[64]

In November 1957 Taras Franko, a son of the famous writer Ivan Franko, sent a letter to the Moscow newspaper *Pravda* in which he condemned discrimination against the Ukrainian language. He stated that Ukraine's current linguistic situation was the result of Stalin's neglect of Leninist nationality policy, and he identified the decreasing number of Ukrainian schools as "concrete proof of [Russian] imperialist chauvinism." In Soviet Ukraine the study of Ukrainian was not compulsory, and Russian-speaking students were favoured in university-entrance examinations. Franko recounted that after Ukrainian-Canadian visitors to Kyiv interacted with public officials who pretended not to understand Ukrainian, they were left with the impression that Ukrainian was more widely spoken in Toronto.[65]

Two particular cases of discrimination contributed to the worsening of this situation in the scientific and scholarly spheres and in everyday life. First, the field of Ukrainian linguistics was regarded as a minor discipline. Its disparagement was evident in the absence of a scholarly journal dedicated to the subject, thus forcing Ukrainian linguists to publish their writings haphazardly in non-linguistic periodicals and preventing the formation of a dedicated platform for academic debate.[66] Second, the number and circulation of newspapers in Ukrainian were conspicuously low during the years 1954–60, especially in urban areas. The scarcity of Ukrainian periodicals contributed to the unhindered of Russification of

---

63 Bazhan, "Narostannia oporu polityrsi rusyfikatsiï," 151.
64 The debate is described in Vasyl Chaplenko, "The Struggle against the Russification of the Ukrainian Language," *The Ukrainian Review* 14, no. 2 (1967): 2–3.
65 Franko's letter is preserved in TsDAHOU, f. 1, op. 24, spr. 4587, ark. 87–94.
66 See Oleksa Horbach, "Pisliavoienni movoznavchi publikatsiï v URSR," *Suchasnist'*, 1961, no. 12: 101–13.

Ukraine's urban-dwellers and widened the gap between the predominantly Russophone cities and the countryside.[67]

Khrushchev's school reform prompted great dissatisfaction. Parents were thereby allowed to choose the language in which their children are taught. The correct choice was obvious: the benefits of an education in Russian often outweighed those offered by instruction in Ukrainian; a good command of Russian was required to receive a good university education and a decent job; all Union-level and economic institutions worked in Russian; and it was the language of the Soviet Army. Furthermore, the teaching of Russian as an optional language was conducted only at the elementary level. As a result, parents living in the non-Russian republics tended to choose education in Russian to guarantee their children a better future. Consequently the seemingly democratic reform effectively resulted in increased Russification.

The language of instruction issue sparked a fierce dispute in the Ukrainian press. The SPU expressed its members' disapproval of the new policy in its organ *Literaturna hazeta*, stating that "one should not leave it solely to parents to decide which language is compulsory for their child to learn."[68] The poets Maksym Rylsky and Mykola Bazhan sent a letter to *Pravda* (published on 22 December 1958) in which they diplomatically proposed that "the only acceptable solution to the problem of language study in secondary schools is the enforcement of compulsory and equal study of both Ukrainian and Russian in all schools of the Ukrainian SSR."[69]

In April 1959 the writers Andrii Malyshko and Oles Honchar, both of whom were then members of the Supreme Soviet of the Ukrainian SSR, sent a letter to all of the highest Soviet officials requesting revision of the language law in accordance with Rylsky and Bazhan's proposal.[70] Nevertheless the Council of Ministers of the Ukrainian SSR adopted the all-Union law without any modifications on 24 April 1959.

Two months later Rylsky lamented the increased use of the nominal ending "-u" (as in Russian) in the dative case instead of the Ukrainian

---

67 See Pavlo Chernov, "Mis'ki hazety v URSR," *Suchasnist'*, 1961, no. 5: 11–21.
68 Quoted in Volodymyr Derzhavyn, "School and Russification," *The Ukrainian Review* 4, no. 3 (1959): 16.
69 Quoted in Baran and Danylenko, *Ukraïna v umovakh systemnoï kryzy*, 118. Bazhan (1904–83) was the SPU' secretary from 1953 to 1959.
70 The letter is preserved in the Tsentral'nyi derzhavnyi arkhiv-muzei literatury ta mystetstva Ukraïny (Central State Archive and Museum of Literature and Art of Ukraine, hereafter TsDAMLMU), f. 22, op. 5, spr. 95, ark. 1–2.

ending "-ovi."[71] In spite of this and other specific aspects of the Russification policy during Khrushchev's rule, the new leadership of the SPU revitalized cultural life within the organization. The émigré scholar and political journalist Vasyl Markus, who had a largely negative opinion of the Khrushchev Thaw, described those years as follows.

> Every week or month a new development occurred, slightly distinct from the hundred that had arisen before it: a new periodical was released after a twenty-year drought; Dovzhenko's letters, republished at last, brought in a wind of new romanticism; [the playwright] Mykola Kulish and [theatre director] Les Kurbas were rehabilitated; a collection of poems by ... [the émigré poet] O. [Oleksander] Oles was published; and there were some who spoke passionately about purging Russian words from the Ukrainian language. During this period new and exciting ingredients were being added to Ukrainian cultural life. Though at first glance seemingly minor, these aforementioned occurrences gave birth to discussions, created ferment, generated hopes. In the Union of Writers, at Kyiv's Shevchenko [State] University and Lviv's Franko [State] University, in student residences, and even at Komsomol meetings, discussions on these topics were taking place.[72]

The Debate within Ukraine's Union of Writers

It is difficult to find documentation of the largely informal discussions inside the SPU. The minutes of its meetings, where discussions regarding the cultural revival were often on the agenda, have proven to be a most useful source. When Oles Honchar replaced Mykola Bazhan as secretary of the SPU in 1959, the organization was undergoing a temporary crisis. After the turmoil in 1956, all major figures (such as Pavlo Tychyna and Maksym Rylsky) had moved away from active participation in the life of

---

71 See Chaplenko, "The Struggle against the Russification of the Ukrainian Language," 2–16.
72 Markus', "Ukraïns'ka kul'tura v prokrustovomu lozhi," 11. Les Kurbas (1887–1937) was an outstanding avant-garde theatre organizer, director, filmmaker, actor, and teacher during the 1920s and early 1930s. He was arrested in December 1933 and imprisoned in labour camps in Soviet Karelia and the prison on Solovets Island. On 3 November 1937 the NKVD shot and buried Kurbas and his fellow political prisoners, Ukrainian writers Hryhorii Epik, Pavlo Fylypovych, Myroslav Irchan, Yakiv Kovalchuk, Antin Krushelnytsky, Mykola Kulish, Andrii Paniv, Valeriian Pidmohylny, Valeriian Polishchuk, Oleksa Slisarenko, Mykhailo Yalovy, Marko Vorony, and Mykola Zerov, in Soviet Karelia's Sandarmokh forest. From August 1937 to December 1938 more than 9,500 political prisoners, including many participants in the Ukrainian "executed renaissance" of the 1920s and 1930s, perished there.

the organization, citing personal reasons or commitments to other political institutions.[73] The new cultural policy introduced by the Twentieth CPSU Congress required strong leadership to ensure the proper development of existing journals (such as *Vitchyzna*) as well as new ones (e.g., *Vsesvit, Prapor*, and *Radians'ke literaturoznavstvo*).[74] According to a Party report,

> In the poems one does not strongly feel a pulse of life, a high civic fervour. A number of poets, especially the young ones, actually took as their symbol a "lyrical nightingale" and are praising only "booklets and love letters," refraining from addressing the high and strong feelings of Soviet man and the theme of his mighty work....

The work of these "pessimistic and desperate" poets

> ...advances some assertions that in fact resemble inimical bourgeois-nationalist propaganda. The key point of all of these conversations and speeches is that since the [Second World W]ar a conscious policy of Russification has been carried out in Ukraine and that Ukrainian national culture has fallen into decay.[75]

It is worth noting that the conflict was not actually between two generations of intellectuals, though it was common to represent it as such.

The report singled out two younger literati as negative examples. The first was Ivan Dziuba, a literary critic from Stalino (now Donetsk) who worked at the journal *Vitchyzna* and had recently published a "pernicious" essay in *Literaturna hazeta*, titled "An Ordinary Person or a Philistine?"[76] The second was Lina Kostenko, whose poems were criticized for their underlying messages.

> Among [her] recent poetry collections, "Sails" ... by the young poet Lina Kostenko make[s] the most worrying impression. Some of the verses in the collection represent a social defence of Tsvetaevism and Gumilevism. The poem "Fern" is a vivid example. Even if one takes it as a description of nature, one cannot help but object to this poem,

---

73 See the report of the Department of Science and Culture, 21 November 1958, in TsDAHOU, f. 1, op. 24, spr. 4703, ark. 77–78 and 95–100.
74 See the report, 18 November 1958, in TsDAHOU, f. 1, op. 31, spr. 992, ark. 62–64. Tychyna and Rylsky were two of the most esteemed Ukrainian poets of the first half of the twentieth century.
75 Report, 21 November 1958, in TsDAHOU, f. 1, op. 24, spr. 4703, ark. 86 and 94.
76 Ibidem, ark. 84.

imbued as it is with despair, hopelessness, and fatalism. If one takes the poem to be an allegory, then it is from the first to the last verse anti-social and apologetic.⁷⁷

The most castigated of Ukraine's literary journals was *Vitchyzna*, which in 1958 published several problematic works. The first of these was the poem "Fairy Tale" by Leonid Pervomaisky, who wrote it as a meditation on the art of poetry. This poem was deemed politically "incorrect" because it presented the past as a golden age in comparison with the present and revealed "the "poet's egotistic nature."⁷⁸ Some of the short stories (such as Liubomyr Dmyterko's, *Vitchyzna*'s editor) and essays published in *Vitchyzna* were also considered unsuitable. An essay by the linguist Antonina Matviienko, titled "In Favour of a High Culture of the Native Language," was condemned because it accused attacked leading Party members in Ukraine of being "bourgeois" and "narrow-minded" promoters of Russian chauvinism.⁷⁹ Other essays also had "dangerous" content: "From the Life of Ukrainians in Poland," by the Kyiv history professor and former Soviet diplomat Vasyl Tarasenko (1907–2001) referred to the forced deportations at the end of the Second World War; and "The Economic Problems of Collective Farms in the Ukrainian Republic's Carpathian Agricultural Region" by the Lviv economist Liubomyr Olesnevych (1921–83) pointed out the serious inefficiencies in Soviet agriculture.⁸⁰

According to official reports, the "worsening" of literary works in Ukraine and the increasing distance between the writers and the people could be attributed to the admittance of the younger generation into the SPU. These young intellectuals, who had typically moved from rural areas to Kyiv to study at the university there, were customarily welcomed into the SPU upon graduation.⁸¹ The reports outlined the repercussions of this immediate inclusion.

---

77 Ibidem, ark. 87–88; Tsvetaevism and Gumilevism refer to the poetic styles of Marina Tsvetaeva and Nikolai Gumilev.
78 These critical remarks were also in an earlier report. See TsDAHOU, f. 1, op. 31, spr. 992, ark. 72.
79 Ibidem, ark. 79.
80 See the report from censors in the Soviet Army, in TsDAHOU, f. 1. op. 24, spr. 5024, ark. 15–21. As the head of Soviet Ukraine's delegation at the United Nations, Tarasenko was famous for the role he played in May 1948 in the UN General Assembly's vote in favour of the creation of the state of Israel.
81 Report, 21 November 1958, in TsDAHOU, f. 1, op. 24, spr. 4703, ark. 93.

> Their early professionalization [as writers] tears them away from the creators of the material richness of Soviet society. As soon as their first book is published, these young intellectuals stop any physical labour and, exploiting the rights of union members, dedicate themselves to creative work, [thus] obtaining easy profit from their literary occupation. They visit one publishing house then another, one editorial board then another, and end their day at a restaurant. However, the union's leaders have never discussed the problem of these young intellectuals' lifestyle or their literary and artistic activity.[82]

According to one report, responsibility for this situation lay with the SPU's past leadership, which had accepted young writers who lacked a political education and defined themselves as "self-taught." Because of the accelerated career trajectories of these young intellectuals, the editorial boards of the publishing houses and periodicals they worked for lacked "a genuine atmosphere of highly principled diligence, of Party criticism and self-awareness. As a consequence, today the pages [of these publications] are devoted [disproportionately] to the early writings by undistinguished authors."[83]

Despite the frictions within the SPU, its secretary, Yurii Zbanatsky, was able to reconcile the writers with their readers and soothe the tensions that arose as a result of one report on the Stalin personality cult.[84] Oles Honchar's appointment chairman of the SPU in 1959 marked the first step of including younger generations of writers in the new cultural *nomenklatura*. Honchar promoted the integration of these new forces into the SPU in order to prevent opposition and to channel their desire for change within Soviet institutions.[85] At the same time, he still showed himself to be a dependable Soviet citizen: his trilogy *Praporonostsi* (The Standardbearers), which he wrote between 1946 and 1948, was one of the most popular literary works about the "Great Patriotic War" and brought Honchar great renown. Honchar showed his enduring loyalty to Soviet

---

82 Report, 18 November 1958, in TsDAHOU, f. 1, op. 31, spr. 992, ark. 83.
83 Ibidem, ark. 84.
84 See the report, 21 November 1958, in TsDAHOU, f. 1, op. 24, spr. 4703, ark. 95.
85 Honchar's attention to the new generations of writers dates back to at least 1956: see his "Slovo do molodykh," *Dnipro* 30, no. 2 (1956): 120–22. According to Olia Hnatiuk, Rylsky initiated this strategy: see "Shistdesiatnyky: Doli ta roli," in her *Mizh literaturoiu i politykoiu: Eseï ta intermediï* (Kyiv, 2012), 17–27.

orthodoxy in his speech at the celebrations of the centenary of Ivan Franko's birth. His words seemed to render perfectly the moderate meaning of Khrushchev's criticisms.

> Today—especially after the inspiring decisions of the Twentieth Congress of the Communist Party—unprecedentedly extensive and bright prospects have come to light for our literature, [and] for every single writer. We now tread the Leninist path in literature, and there are plenteous possibilities [of development] for every artistic individual. Each [literary] artist can uncover his creative talents and provide an even wider scope for his thoughts, his emotional experiences, in a fresh and brave way.[86]

To understand how Honchar could reconcile Soviet political conformism, the demands of the younger generation, and the shifting attitudes within the SPU, it is helpful to compare the SPU's activities before and after his appointment as head of that organization. The SPU's Presidium convened on 6 February 1958 and was followed by a meeting of the board of governors on 28 February. Both sessions began with harsh criticism of Vladimir Dudintsev. In his report about Ukrainian poetry at the 6 February meeting, Anatolii Moroz, editor in chief of the Radianskyi Pysmennyk publishing house, highlighted Dudintsev's shortcomings by comparing him with the "more virtuous" Mykola Bazhan. Yurii Smolych condemned not only Dudintsev's novel but also "Dudintsevism" as a whole.

> At this time our Ukrainian organization of writers is one of the first among many such organizations within the Soviet Union to unanimously condemn notorious "Dudintsevism," a movement that has attempted to distort and defame our brilliant Soviet socialist life. We reject the clannish motives that have distanced literature from Soviet life, operating under [Dudintsevism's] slogan "Not by bread alone."[87]

---

86 Minutes of the plenum on the centenary of Ivan Franko's birth, TsDAMLMU, f. 590, op. 1, spr. 253, ark. 5.

87 Minutes of the plenum of the board of governors, in TsDAMLMU, f. 590, op. 1, spr. 307, ark. 23. Smolych (1900–76) was a writer and literary critic and a former member of Vaplite (see n. 183).

The discussion about poetry in Ukraine—a discussion that had reached a decisive stage in its development—continued during the 6 February meeting. Many in attendance acknowledged the positive efforts of the younger literary critics, such as Ivan Svitlychny and Ivan Dziuba, but attacked *Vitchyzna* and suggested the entire editorial board should thoroughly discuss an article before accepting it for publication.[88] The last to speak was Bazhan, who discussed the meaning of rehabilitation and freedom in the literary press.

> I believe that the process of correcting those inequities that had been perpetrated against many figures in Ukrainian literature is good and beneficial, and we are extremely grateful for the Party's efforts in this respect. But in this process of rehabilitating literary figures and our culture, we must not lose awareness of our Party affiliation. In this regard there have been troublesome instances on the pages of *Vitchyzna* and even in *Literaturna hazeta*. I applaud the rehabilitation of Les Kurbas, an extremely interesting and talented individual who is worthy of our respect, but warn against the rehabilitation of Kurbas's formalist followers, which would result in the upset of our Party order in literature, art, and theatre. [Oleksii] Poltoratsky's article concerning the rehabilitation efforts is politically incorrect and distracts from our perception of this wonderful process, which stems from a profound understanding of the development of Soviet Ukrainian literature. We writers must offer correct ideas and interpretations of these revisionist tendencies in our articles.[89]

The SPU Presidium's meeting ended with the adoption of a resolution condemning Boris Pasternak, who had been expelled from the Union of Writers of the USSR. This document of condemnation was drawn up during a meeting chaired by Honchar, who spoke especially harshly against the author of *Doctor Zhivago*, claiming that Pasternak "had sold out to foreigners."[90] Although sympathetic to some of the new generation's ideas, Honchar demonstrated that he was well aware of the line that the Soviet intelligentsia could not cross.

---

88 See Yevhen Adelheim's and Prokip Mysnyk's reports, inTsDAMLMU, f. 590, op. 1, spr. 308, ark. 92–128. Poltoratsky (1905–77) was a writer, literary critic, and the first editor in chief (1958–70) of *Vsesvit*, the Kyiv journal of foreign literature in Ukrainian translation, when it was revived after a twenty-four-year ban.
89 Ibidem, ark. 132.
90 See the minutes of the preparatory meeting of the SPU's the Presidium, in TsDAMLMU, f. 590. op. 1, spr. 308, ark. 203ff.

The atmosphere of the meeting on 28 February was similar to that on 6 February, but several more practical problems arose. The writer (and wartime Soviet partisan) Yakiv Bash lamented the insufficient print-runs of Ukrainian books (for example, only 30,000 copies of Honchar's famous trilogy *Praporonostsi* (The Standard-Bearers) were printed. Yurii Dold-Mykhailyk noted that a new kind of advertising was needed to promote reading, arguing that promotional posters ought to include the names of authors in addition to the existing slogan "Read Books." The Presidium applauded the revival of *Vsesvit*, but Poltoratsky (1905–1977), the journal's new editor, though pleased, stressed the difficulty of finding qualified staff, for few young Soviet persons knew any foreign language well enough to be professional translators. Upon hearing this, the writers in attendance expressed their concern, since knowledge of foreign cultures was considered crucial to the fruitful development of Ukrainian literature.[91]

Thus the meetings on 6 and 28 February showed some signs of cultural revival, but the tone and content of the views expressed there were reminiscent of the Stalinist era.

On 10 March 1959 the Fourth Congress of Writers of Ukraine—the first one chaired by Honchar—gave rise to a completely different debate. There Mykola Bazhan began his remarks by stating that the Twenty-First Congress of the CPSU had affirmed the guidelines set out in Khrushchev's speech at the Twentieth Congress. This announcement received sonorous applause. Bazhan cautioned those who wished to exploit the denunciation of the Stalin personality cult and gloss over the conquests of Soviet socialism. He then remarked on the lack of promising prose in the aftermath of the cult, indicating that the cultural legacy of Stalinism could be held responsible for this: "Under the cover of the mighty cult of a great personality, many have created little cults of insignificant personalities."[92] Bazhan refuted the SPU's past criticisms of new poetry, defended Leonid Pervomaisky, and praised the "talented young poetess" Lina Kostenko: "Her books are surely among the most interesting creations of the young poets.... She only needs the following advice. The notes of disharmony and exaltation [in her poems] are not proper for the polyphonic music of our lyric poetry that is emerging now and beginning to gain strength."[93]

---

91 See the minutes of the Plenum, in TsDAMLMU, f. 590, op. 1, spr. 307, ark. 82–102. Dold-Mykhailyk (1903–66) was a writer and screenwriter.
92 Text of Bazhan's speech, in TsDAMLMU, f. 590, op. 1, spr. 347, ark. 13.
93 Ibidem, ark. 31.

Bazhan also welcomed the revival of *Vsesvit* and lauded Honchar's and Mykhailo Stelmakh's novels.[94] He reminded the audience of the greatness of Dovzhenko's cinematic masterpiece, *Zemlia* (Earth), and he stated that Ukrainian authors should be inspired by Dovzhenko's poetic novel *Enchanted Desna*. Bazhan rejected the notion that there was any discord between the Ukrainian and Russian languages, both of which he loved, and condemned Dudintsev's novel as "slanderous." He was alone in this opinion, however, as everyone who spoke after him declared that they loved Dudintsev's book. Frequently voiced was the word "honest," denoting a clear change from the past conception of literature and contradicting even Khrushchev.[95]

The remainder of the congress was dedicated to the Ukrainian national question and the need for a new honesty in literature. The writer Semen Zhurakhovych (1907–97) stated that despite the promotion of "internationalist values," the real problem in Ukraine was Russian chauvinism. The film scholar and philosopher Viacheslav Kudin (1925–2018) noted that "Art cannot be of high quality by contemporary standards if it does not provide people with answers to real problems of everyday life, if it does not solve at least a small number of the most troubling questions for people."[96] He added that the problem of decreased numbers of readers was not due to the introduction of television, as some claimed, but rather to the proliferation of low-quality literature. Television, Kudin argued, should be considered an opportunity.

This opinion was supported by Borys Antonenko-Davydovych, who also brought up the question of writer's royalties.[97] During the Stalin period publishing houses had introduced a payment method that was not dependent on the number of copies sold. The press-run of each book was not linked to its actual success, causing discontent among the more accomplished authors. Antonenko-Davydovych's suggested change caused a commotion: "It must be said that establishing a basis for the

---

94 Stelmakh (1912–83) was one of the most popular Soviet Ukrainian novelists of the 1950s and 1960s.
95 For example, Semen Zhurakhovych stated: "I've finished reading Dudintsev's *Not By Bread Alone*—it's an honest book" (TsDAMLMU, f. 590, op. 1, spr. 345, ark. 21).
96 Ibidem, ark. 27.
97 Antonenko-Davydovych (1899–1984) had become a popular writer by the mid-1920s. He was arrested in 1935 and survived ten years of imprisonment and hard labour in Siberia. He was not allowed to return to Ukraine until 1957, after which he resumed his literary career. His presence at SPU meetings after the Twentieth CPSU Congress was highly significant.

payment of writer's fees is very difficult. But there has to be a single principle: if a book is successful and sells quickly, it must be reprinted. If a book remains on the bookshelf for one, two, [or] three years, one should not hurry to reprint it."[98] He also addressed the issue of authenticity in Ukrainian literature, encouraging writers to follow the example of the young poet Vasyl Symonenko.

> We have to show people as they are. Teach them how to live, to love, and to suffer in a human way. That is something no one except us writers will ever do. So let us pledge that we will commit to this cause, lest they say in the future, as Vasyl Symonenko said, "There were no such writers on the earth ..."[99]

The remaining speakers complained about the difficulties of Ukrainian cultural life, including paper shortages that sometimes affected the publication of *Literaturna hazeta*, and advocated the printing of works by Volodymyr Vynnychenko and the diaries of Dovzhenko, who were considered the only intellectuals who had represented Ukrainian culture during Stalinism.[100] Serhii Plachynda stressed that educational reforms had harmful consequences and reported that he "heard a conversation among parents of schoolchildren in which they said that they had fought to make their children study only in Russian. These people cannot even speak Russian themselves, they are not very culturally aware…and it's obvious that they do not have any sense of national pride."[101]

In the final resolution adopted at their congress, Ukraine's writers reaffirmed their condemnation of "bourgeois nationalism" but also took pains to extol the Soviet Union's "multinational culture."[102] The congress recognized the successes of those who were trying to gain more freedom for the expression of national culture. Dovzhenko's growing reputation and the re-evaluation of emerging young poets were indicative of a

---

98 Ibidem, ark. 38.
99 Ibidem, ark. 42.
100 See Ibidem, ark. 43–97; Volodymyr Vynnychenko (1880–1951) was one of the best Ukrainian writers of the first half of the twentieth century. He was also a prominent left-wing political figure and served as the first head of the Ukrainian government of the Ukrainian National Republic and its Directory in 1917–18. From 1919 he lived in Vienna, Prague, and Berlin, and from 1934 in France.
101 Ibidem, ark. 102.
102 The resolution is in TsDAMLMU, f. 590, op. 1, spr. 346, ark. 34–36.

renewed willingness to embrace Ukrainian culture within the Soviet context.

A New Generation

The Communist Party was concerned about the emergence of a new generation of writers whose work was powerful enough to transform and challenge Soviet writer's role as an intellectual proponent of Party ideology. For these intellectuals, the impact of the Khrushchev Thaw was enhanced by the influence of books published in the West that began circulating in the USSR in the late 1950s through the samizdat network.[103] A vivid example is *The Executed Renaissance*, a famous anthology of Soviet Ukrainian literature of the 1920s and early 1930s compiled and edited by the émigré scholar Yurii Lavrinenko.[104] Sverstiuk recalled:

> The book *Executed Renaissance* was a rare and brilliant star in the darkness of the 1950s. If it could have materialized simultaneously on the desks of students, teachers, and scholars, then our cultural environment would have been radically different.... Several important revelations would have been made: that Pavlo Tychyna— "the bard of the Revolution" [and a]member of all of the Presidiums—indeed also belonged to the "Executed Renaissance" as a participant in the former struggle for national liberation ... that even Maksym Rylsky and Volodymyr Sosiura were not as Soviet as they were described in the state literature, and that works by both of them had been banned by the censors.... The *shistdesiatnyky* passed around the book as rapidly as possible, a practical consideration so that no one kept it for too long. For many it was a true joy to hold it in their hands. A worn-out copy is preserved in Alla Horska's archive.[105]

The *Executed Renaissance* substantiated the idea that the Ukrainian cultural renaissance had been abruptly suppressed in the 1930s, when

---

103 For an introduction to the phenomenon of samizdat (and *samvydav*), see F. J. M. Feldbrugge, *Samizdat and Political Dissent in the Soviet Union* (Leyden, 1975); Jurij V. Mal'cev, *L'altra letteratura (1957–1975): La letteratura del samizdat da Pasternak a Solzenicyn* (Milan, 1976); and Dimitri Pospielovsky, "From Gosizdat to Samizdat and Tamizdat," *Canadian Slavonic Papers* 20, no. 1 (1978): 44–62.
104 Iurii Lavrinenko, comp. and ed., *Rozstriliane vidrodzhennia: Antolohiia 1917–1933: Poeziia, proza, drama, eseï* (Paris, 1959).
105 Ievhen Sverstiuk, "Pro 'Rozstriliane vidrodzhennia,'" in the new edition of Lavrinenko's *Rozstriliane vidrodzhennia* (Kyiv, 2002), 968 and 970.

Stalinism set limits on cultural activity. With the official denunciation of Mykola Khvylovy and Mykola Skrypnyk[106] it became clear that Stalinism would sanction the death or imprisonment of any artist who refused to follow the Party line.

> The Soviet system shared with other modern political systems an emphasis on its citizens' sense of self, [but] it was distinguished by the type of self it sought to cultivate. This self was not to be individualistic; instead, according to Soviet ideology, individuals could find fulfillment only by joining the collective. In contrast to Western societies, where the liberal self was constituted by ownership of private propriety and a system of legal protections and individual rights, the Soviet system promoted an illiberal subjectivity, in which private life was diminished and individuals reached their full human potential through participation in social life.[107]

During the Thaw, Soviet intellectuals reconsidered Soviet morality, attacking the class approach and re-evaluating universal values. A new set of ethical principles emerged from this turmoil.

> Two basic themes can be identified in this regard. The first was related to the defense of universal civic values, such as openness, political freedom, and equality. The second stressed more humanistic universal values such as love, friendship, honesty, and devotion to parents and family.[108]

This code of behaviour entailed a different concept of self, which was particularly evident among the poets who attempted to define it.

> Without exaggeration one can say that the individual "I" that was openly and loudly affirmed by the young Ukrainian poets of the 1960s was not only an original *anthropological-personal marker* of a literary generation but also significantly determined their artistic-

---

106 On Skrypnyk, Khvylovy, and Ukrainian national communism in general, see James E. Mace, *Communism and the Dilemmas of National Liberation: National Communism in Soviet Ukraine, 1918–1933* (Cambridge, Mass., 1983).
107 David L. Hoffmann, *Stalinist Values: The Cultural Norms of Soviet Modernity, 1917–1941* (Ithaca and London, 2003), 46.
108 Vladimir Shlapentokh, *Soviet Intellectuals and Political Power: The Post-Stalin Era* (London and New York, 1990), 163.

stylistic approach. In those years the ideologists of art interpreted such accentuation of the personal, featuring an emphasis on one's "self," as a serious challenge to social norms with their dogma of massification, standardization, and a depersonalized collective "us" imposed and ever-supported by the authorities.[109]

This new concept of the self was a take-off point for the emerging process of redefining the relationship between the individual and the collective subjects of society and the nation (their own, Ukraine, but also others, particularly Russia). The birth and first steps of this nascent cultural revolution can be traced in the writings of the three standard-bearers of literary *shistdesiatnytstvo*—Lina Kostenko, Vasyl Symonenko, and Ivan Dziuba.[110]

Lina Kostenko was born on 19 March 1930 in Rzhyshchiv, a town on the right bank of the Dnipro River seventy-six kilometres south of Kyiv. For the first six years of her life she lived in the countryside, largely under the care of her grandmother. According to Kostenko, her childhood was the happiest period of her life, and she has often reminisced about it in her writing.

> I grew up in orchards,
> where warm pears ripened
> where a leaf was covered with dust,
> and juicy stalks were fragrant.
>
> I grew up in fields,
> where the sunrise was like a flare,
> where disturbed tillage
> softly steamed at noon.
>
> I grew up in forests,
> where pines like slender waists grew pink,
> where dew fell heavily

---

109 Liudmyla Tarnashyns'ka, *Ukraïns'ke shistdesiatnytstvo: Profili na tli pokolinnia (Istoryko-literaturnyi ta poetykal'nyi aspekty)* (Kyiv 2010), 8.
110 Besides Tarnashynska's study, interesting analyses of the poetry of the *shistdesiatnyky* (with attention also to other authors of this generation, such as Mykola Vinhranovsky, Ivan Drach, and Vitalii Korotych) can be found in Bohdan Kravtsiv, "Velyka vedmedytsia," *Suchasnist'*, 1962, no. 2: 24–49; Anna-Halia Horbatch, "The Young Generation of Ukrainian Poets," *The Ukrainian Review* 12, no. 4 (1965): 23–34; and Ostap Tarnawsky, "Dissident Poets in Ukraine," *Journal of Ukrainian Studies* 6, no. 2 (1981): 17–27.

on light blue sylvan glades.

I grew up on the Dnipro,
where blue slopes tower above,
where fishermen –a not very talkative people—
set out their nets for the night.

And the hues of those distant years—
wherever I may go,
whatever I may write, lie like a reflection
on white paper. [111]

These verses, written in 1956, are the polar opposite of what the Soviet leadership expected from its "ideological fighters." All attention is focused on the personal experience of the author, whose individuality is reaffirmed through the use of anaphoras. These verses contain no didactic purpose. Rather, they are Kostenko's attempt at recreating and describing the bucolic universe of her childhood and expressing her emotional attachment to her native land—an attachment reminiscent of Dovzhenko's writings.

Kostenko claims to have always enjoyed freedom, even as a child. When she was five years old, she would swim in the Dnipro, and when her grandmother would tell her to come out and dry off, she would answer, "Leave me be, I want to be here!"[112] When she was six, her family moved to Kyiv's Rusanivka district, known as the "Kyivan Venice"— another *locus amoenus* idealized in her poems. The harmony of Kostenko's family life was disrupted by the arrest of her father, a school principal in Kyiv, and his ten-year imprisonment. Kostenko, who acknowledges a

---

[111] Lina Kostenko, *Selected Poems: Wanderings of the Heart*, trans., with an afterword, by Michael Naydan (New York and London 1990), 4, a translation of "Ia vyrostala u sadakh," *Dnipro* 30, no. 10 (1956): 36. A considerable problem in analyzing Kostenko's poetry is the fact that it is difficult to determine the exact date when she composed certain verses. The Soviet authorities quickly forbade the publication of much of her early work, and it was disseminated instead through *samvydav*. The poetry Kostenko wrote in the 1960s, such as her historical novel in verse *Berestechko*, which she completed in 1966, were often not officially published until the 1980s. There is no critical edition of her poetry, and she herself told me that determining the date when she composed every poem is beyond her ability. Liudmyla Tarnashynska has compiled an incomplete bibliography of Kostenko's official publications and also uses Kostenko's later poetry in her study of the *shistdesiatnytstvo* phenomenon. To avoid anachronism, in this study I refer only to poems that she undoubtedly wrote in the 1950s and 1960s.

[112] My interview with Lina Kostenko, 12 June 2009.

significant intellectual debt to her parents, remembers that when the NKVD agents came to their home to arrest her father in 1936, they asked him to show them his weapons. He pointed at his daughter and declared, "That is my weapon!"[113] After the Second World War—a war that Kostenko remembers as a period of destruction and violence perpetrated by German soldiers—Kostenko finished high school and attended the Kyiv Pedagogical Institute. She did not graduate with the top marks required to enter Kyiv State University, but in 1952 she was admitted to the Gorky Institute of Literature in Moscow.

Although the Kostenkos spoke only Ukrainian at home, Lina had learned to speak and read Russian during her years in Russified Kyiv. During our interview she noted that she did not consider it a foreign language. Moreover, Russian culture, especially Russian literature, was an organic component of Kostenko's education—she loved the poetry of Marina Tsvetaeva, Aleksandr Blok, and Boris Pasternak. She used to read the many Russian books in her father's library, and she defined her use of Russian as "natural."[114] Moving to Moscow appeared to have been a seamless transition. Kostenko's poem "On the Train," for instance, begins with the verses used as this chapter's epigraph. Another, untitled, poem reads:

> When I walked out of the railway station
> I forgot all lofty words
> and wholeheartedly exclaimed:
> "Greetings, Moscow, mother of mine!"
>
> I'd traveled a long time from home
> and my head is buzzing from the journey,
> but do I care that I'm tired
> when I'm in Moscow itself?
>
> It's no matter that the evening is getting cold
> and the autumn rain is pouring—
> I'll promptly seek out Red Square
> amid Moscow's other plazas.
>
> So I went where my eyes led me—
> onto boulevards, thoroughfares, and bridges—

---

113 Ibidem.
114 "Pryrodno" in the original. Ibidem.

and searched for it until night fell
in that great city, Moscow.

I asked no one the way
and no one drew me a map:
that road in Moscow is the kind
that everyone discovers alone.[115]

Kostenko's enthusiasm was bolstered by the atmosphere at the Gorky Institute, where her fellow students represented more than forty different nationalities and the use of Russian as a common language did not seem to be a chauvinistic imposition. When she read her own Ukrainian poems in the literature seminar, the professor acknowledged her as a genuine poet, even with his limited knowledge of Ukrainian. Kostenko remembers that there were some Russian nationalists at the institute, but they were more concerned about other nationalities than the Ukrainians. When the Doctors' Plot conspiracy was set in motion in 1953, people at the institute were afraid that the purge might include its own Jewish students.

Kostenko made many friends among the Polish students at the Gorky Institute. Among them was her first husband, the novelist Jerzy Pachlowski, who had fought as a Polish partisan against the Nazis during the Second World War and maintained a high level of national pride. Observing the Poles' evident sense of patriotism and loyalty to their nation, Kostenko began wondering about her own national identity, and further events spurred her to reflect on Ukraine's history. In 1953 she noticed that while most people were gripped by hysteria when Stalin died, her only friend who did not mourn the dictator's demise was her Estonian roommate. Kostenko came to comprehend her roommate's lack of grief only later, back in in Kyiv when, during a car ride, a Latvian couple told her about the Soviet deportations there after the war. It was then that Kostenko first connected these repressions with the Terror of the 1930s and her father's incarceration. Her shock was so great that she considered leaving the car and returning home on foot so that she might be able to reflect better upon the realities of Ukrainian history. This experience sheds light on the meaning of her poem "Lydia Koidula in a Foreign Land."

There once stood a woman alone
on the shore of a sea....

---

115 In *Slovo molodykh: Al'manakh*, 16.

> And the woman cried
> "Eesti!
> My beautiful land!
> I have never seen deceit,
> For you are forever faithful."[116]

In Kyiv Kostenko noticed that people were surprised when she spoke in Ukrainian. When she was pregnant with her first daughter, another pregnant woman she encountered at the hospital asked her: "Why do you, a member of the intelligentsia, speak this language of the Red Indian tribes?"[117] Kostenko maintains that this incident convinced her of the need to defend Ukrainian culture in her homeland.

Kostenko graduated from the Gorky Institute in 1956, presenting as her dissertation a collection of poems that would be published a year later as *Rays of the Earth*. One of the members of the graduation review committee, the writer Vsevolod Ivanov, gave these poems quite a positive evaluation.

> This is a very talented poet with a great future. Lina Kostenko's verses impress with their sincerity, warmth, and rare honesty, which uncovers the soul of humanity without falling victim to any small-minded concerns, tension, or cynicism.[118]

After Kostenko moved back to Kyiv, she gained popularity with her poetry published in literary journals and two further collections, *Sails* (1958) and *Wandering of the Heart* (1961). In her poems the significance of the self apparently contradicted the economic determinism of Marxist theory, as communicated in the final lines of "Destiny."

> I alone chose my destiny,
> and whatever happens to me
> I won't have any claims
> on the Destiny I've chosen.[119]

---

116 Lina Kostenko, *Selected Poems*, 42. The poem was first published in Ukrainian in *Dnipro* 31, no. 6 (1957): 39–40. Lydia Koidula is the pen name of Lydia Emilie Florentine Jannsen (1843–86), an Estonian poet who lived in Kronstadt and was famous for the nostalgic sentiments in her poetry.
117 My interview with Kostenko.
118 Quoted in Mariana Savka, "'Ia vybrala doliu sobi sama': Zhyttievymy shliakhamy Liny Kostenko," *Use dlia shkoly*, 2001, vyp. 6: 7.
119 In Lina Kostenko, *Vybrane* (Kyiv, 1989), 35.

During our interview Kostenko noted that, unlike Pavlo Tychyna, she could not write an ode to the Communist Party, because she felt that it did not fit her personality. Instead she pursued an expressive style that differed from socialist realism.

> One can live in this world without blinders,
> One can look many ways upon the world:
>
> with eyes wide open,
> from under a brow,
> through one's fingers,
> through open windows,
> or
> through a crack in the door.
>
> From this the world will not change one iota.
> It all depends upon the person's eye[s] —
> In the wide open ones, the whole world will be reflected.
> The narrow ones will only mirror pettiness. [120]

The time during which Kostenko was living did not seem to her a golden age for poetry or for society as a whole. For this reason she turned to Taras Shevchenko for guidance in "To the Kobzar."[121]

> Beloved kobzar!
> Again I come to you,
> For you are conscience and law to me.
>
> Forgive me the intrusion of this interview
> Disturbing your sleep in eternity.
>
> Perhaps it is not a trivial matter.
> See for yourself how complex are the times:

---

120 idem, "Na sviti mozhna zhyt' bez etaloniv," *Dnipro* 32, no. 2 (1958): 62. English trans.: "If You Cannot Paint the Wind," *The Ukrainian Review* 21, no. 3 (1975): 84.

121 idem, "To the Kobzar," *Zhovten'* 11, no. 3 (1961): 3–5. A *kobzar* was an itinerant, often blind or disabled, bard who sang epic folk poems while playing a *kobza*, a lute-like Ukrainian folk instrument. *Kobzar* is also the title of Taras Shevchenko's first published collection of poetry and thus closely associated with Ukraine's national poet and metaphoric *kobzar* par excellence.

> Great upheavals,
> Old traditions shattered,
> Concepts of beauty redefined.
> Eternal flux —
> Both cosmic and earthly.
> Only the graves are silent and still.
>
> Oh, how many souls in the last century
> Were maimed, made destitute and ill![122]

As the poem continues, Kostenko describes a cultural universe where poets "look for the newest forms / for meaning / that is lacking in their soul." Shevchenko, the symbol of genuine Ukrainian culture and poetic revolution, answers the question.

> But how could you write poems?
> I didn't write. I wept and laughed.
> I blessed and sang and cursed.
> Frankly I worried little
> about how I appeared to bystanders
> ...
> For remember that on this planet,
> from the time our Lord God created it,
> there hasn't been an epoch for poets,
> but there have been poets for epochs.

Conscious of the perceived duty of the poet, Shevchenko nevertheless advises Kostenko not to feel shackled to the truth. Kostenko accepts this advice.

> And it's true that winged creatures
> do not need the ground.
> ...
> For birds this is most likely the truth ...
> But how about humans? And what about humans?
> They live on earth.
> They do not fly themselves.

---

[122] This portion of the poem was translated by Tatiana Shevchuk and published as "To the Kobzar," in *Nashe zhyttia/Our Life* (the magazine of the Ukrainian National Women's League of America) 27, no. 3 (1970): 26.

> But they have wings. They have wings!
>
> They, those wings,
> are not made of down or feathers,
> but of truth, sincerity, and trust.
>
> For some they are made of fidelity in love.
> For others, of constant striving.
> ...
> For some, from a song or hope,
> or from poetry or a dream.
>
> A person supposedly doesn't fly ...
> But he has wings. But he has wings![123]

This poem, "Wings," reveals a spectrum of values important for the poets of the *shistdesiatnyky* generation—honesty, trust, love, passion, hope, dreams, and, of course, art. These values are what allow a human being to rise above his/her material existence and follow that winged value, truth. In her poetry Kostenko did not confine herself to solely expressing her imagination and thoughts. She also encouraged other poets to improve their work by practising introspection.

> There are ever more poets on earth—
> more accurately
> those who know how to rhyme.
> In the jungles of words they set their nets,
> but it's too early to catch any quarry.
> Hares, parrots, sparrows' nests ...
> A great chirping, squeaking, and tweeting,
> such that a person sometimes wants
> to search for poetry in the stillness.
> Let the many-coloured small fry bustle and change their skins according to the weather ...
> O Poet,
> learn to search and wait!
> The best verse is still at large.[124]

---

123 Idem, "Kryla," *Vitchyzna* 29, no. 2 (1961): 5. The Ukrainian word *"pravda"* has two meanings: truth and justice." So does *"volia"*: liberty/freedom and will.
124 Idem, "Vse bil'she na zemli poetiv," *Vitchyzna* 30, no. 7 (1962): 123.

The *shistdesiatnyky* poets encouraged introspection and rejected those who wrote panegyrics to the Party and the Soviet Union, even if they claimed to be following the whispers of their soul. If we consider Soviet society as a "civilization of whispers," then the *shistdesiatnyky* tried to transform those whispered conversations into poetry. The first enemy of the truthful poets was not external censorship, but self-censorship.

> Look for the censor inside you.
> He lives there, slumbering, unshaven.
> He sits there like an imp in a stove
> and silently removes your conscience.
> From inside, a little at a time, not at once.
> He'll take down everything, wherever there's a little icon.
> And will imperceptibly take you out of yourself.
> All that will remain will be a husk.[125]

Real poets wage battles against themselves, according to their sense of duty toward society. The revolutionary sense of Kostenko's work is explicitly stated in one of her most famous poems, "The Alternative to Barricades".

> During historical rifts,
> in the smoke of someone's ravings,
> people are
> always
> on the barricades,
> whether they know it or not.
>
> Barricades of bricks against homelessness.
> Barricades of poetry against thoughtlessness.
> Barricades of conscience against Berias.
> …
> The distribution of courage is not allowed.
> …
> So please step aside
> if you are afraid to be bowled down like skittles.
> Death is not yet a defeat.
> In victorious battles
> There are also those who die.

---

125 Idem, *Vybrane*, 12.

> Descend from the barricades you who are heroes until it gets tough.
> And cease your philistine claptrap.
> The right to be on the barricades only have
> rebels,
> their enemies,
> and medics.[126]

Kostenko describes her work as a rebellion against thoughtlessness through which she distances herself from Soviet *mishchany*—meaning both burghers/petits bourgeois and philistines—the true children of Stalinism.[127] Although Kostenko does not identify a specific enemy in her work, and although the Soviet authorities had not yet begun repressing the *shistdesiatnyky*, the sense of an impending battle against censorship was already spreading among the intelligentsia. In 1963 publication of Kostenko's fourth book, *Zorianyi intehral* (The Stellar Integral), was forbidden, and publishers rejected many of her other works. Kostenko's frustration with the increasing hindrances to freedom of expression even surfaced in her poems, where she hinted at the *samvydav* option. In "Letter" Kostenko depicts herself in the act of writing unsanctioned poems.

> I've lain the paper on my knee, I'm writing
> distraught verses. As if I'm writing prose—
> various layers without line breaks
> so that at first glance it seems I'm writing regular letters.
> Actually, that's not far from the truth.
> It has a different form—but the very same content.
> Verses addressed to people are the most sincere letter in the world.[128]

Underlying Kostenko's poems are the desire and tentative bid for freedom in Soviet society during the Thaw. Though she does not name the adversary, attacks against the cultural establishment are evident in both the content and structure of her work. Kostenko's use of Ukrainian, her references to Shevchenko, and her emphasis on oneself and one's own

---

126 This poem was first published in *Dnipro* 38, no. 12 (1964): 60–61. Here I present the better-known version that circulated in *samvydav*. See idem, *Vybrane*, 145.

127 The classic definition of the Russian word *meshchanstvo* (*mishchanstvo* in Ukrainian) is in Vera S. Dunham, *In Stalin's Time: Middleclass Values in Soviet Fiction* (Cambridge, Mass., 1976): 19–20.

128 "Lyst," in Kostenko, *Vybrane*, 135. The poem was also published earlier in *Sails*.

values make her a perfect representative of the cultural turmoil of the 1960s. In this respect she actually belongs to the broader literary movement within the Soviet (and therefore also Russian) culture of that time. In Kostenko's work we find no suggestion of hatred toward Russians. The affirmation of her own nationality through the use of Ukrainian did not conflict with the appreciation she had for other nationalities. While Kostenko never directly questioned Marxism-Leninism, her love of truth and freedom of expression were enough to induce the Soviet authorities to silence her. Although she never actively took part in *samvydav*, her works were disseminated by others. The quality and emotional appeal of her poetry made her one of the most famous poets of the entire movement.

All of the themes in Kostenko's verses are present in the works of another poet, Vasyl Symonenko, whose short yet impactful poems, paired with his tragic life story, made him an icon of the *shistdesiatnyky* generation. Recounting Symonenko's life is a difficult task, as he died in 1963 and left very few documents concerning his life and intellectual development. The unusual communicative strength of his poetry and writings, however, helps to fill this gap.

Symonenko was born on 8 January 1935 in Biivtsi, a small village in Lubny Raion, Poltava Oblast. As he wrote in his requisite autobiographies for the Soviet authorities, "my father … abandoned [our] family when I was less than a year old. Our paths have never crossed since then."[129] As a result Vasyl was very attached to his mother, who worked on a collective farm. During his childhood he changed schools often but his grades were consistently very high, and he finished high school with high honours (a gold medal). Symonenko enrolled at Kyiv State University, where he studied journalism from 1952 to 1957. After graduating he was hired as an editor at the literary departments of two oblast newspapers, *Cherkas'ka pravda* and *Molod' Cherkashchyny*, in Cherkasy, where he moved with his mother. In 1950 Symonenko had joined the Komsomol, and he remained a member until 1959, at which point he became a candidate member of the Communist Party. His ties to these organizations were troublesome. Symonenko's friend Yurii Yacheikin recounts that in 1953 he was accused at a Komsomol meeting of reading the works of the "racist" Mark Twain. There Symonenko spoke out in his defence and was banned from his student residence as a result. he then lived with the Yacheikin family in

---

129 Document no. 4 in Vasyl Symonenko, *Spadshchyna*, vol. 2, *Proza*, bk. 2 (Kyiv, 2008), 482.

Kyiv for a year and a half. During this time he and Yacheikin collaborated on producing an underground periodical called "UTYuH," which they typed out on a Remington portable typewriter.[130] Years later Symonenko self-published his first collection of poems on the same typewriter. The few notes he left about his university life suggest that he found it difficult to make real friends, and that generally he did not enjoy the classes or life at the student house. On the other hand, many of his housemates were studying literature, so he and they had a common interest in writing and reading poetry.[131]

Some of Symonenko's compositions, written largely for publication in Communist Party almanacs, address topics to do with the Komsomol and the Party, as well as Ukrainian-Russian relations. Like Lina Kostenko, Symonenko seemed to love Russia and appreciate its actions in "saving Ukraine from the Nazis and Ukrainian nationalists" during the Second World War. In his poem "Ukraine Has Not Yet Died," whose title is borrowed from the first line of the Ukrainian national anthem (banned in the USSR), Symonenko directly addresses those Ukrainians who allegedly collaborated with the Germans.

> Then the people called you dogs
> Because you licked the Germans' boots,
> Cried "Heil" with hoarse bass voices,
> And roared "Ukraine has not yet died."
> ...
> Then if to aid Ukraine
> "Muscovites" hadn't arrived again from the east.
> ...
> You'll roam about in foreign lands
> Until the devil has taken you all,
> Because you know: Ukraine has not yet died,
> And it won't![132]

---

130 The incident is referred to in Vasyl Iaremenko's foreword to Symonenko, *Spadshchyna*, vol. 1, *Poeziia*, bk. 1, 28–29. The name "UTYuH" is the acronym of a presumably parodic Universal Society of Young Humourists. It mirrors the Russian word *utiug* (clothes iron).

131 Vasyl Symonenko, "Storinky shchodennyka: Zi students'kykh zapysiv," in his, *Spadshchyna*, vol. 2, *Proza*, bk. 2: 230–35; on Symonenko's poetry, see Igor Shankovsky, "Vasyl Symonenko and His Background," *The Ukrainian Review* 14, no. 1 (1967): 20–30; no. 2: 33–43, and no. 4: 44–55.

132 Symonenko, *Spadshchyna*, vol. 1, *Poeziia*, bk. 1, 447.

This interpretation of what happened during the Second World War is very much in tune with the official Soviet line of history, in which the Ukrainian nationalists were portrayed as enemies of the Ukrainian people while Soviet soldiers—usually considered foreign, totalitarian invaders in the nationalist version of history—were presented as liberators. This poem distances Symonenko from one Ukrainian nationalist perspective that has considered collaboration with the Nazis as a lesser evil compared to the threat of Soviet/Russian reconquest.

Symonenko was loyal to the Red Army not only because they fought the Nazis, but also because he apparently felt a sincere affinity for the Soviet system, a sentiment he expressed in his poem "My Heart is in the Komsomol."

> There are those who know how to live quietly.
> They bend under the wind like grass.
> At twenty their souls turn grey,
> Only their heads do not.
> But I say: are locks of hair the issue
> If rust has devoured the soul?
> Eternal respect, eternal honour and glory
> To those whose soul does not turn grey!
> ...
> O Komsomol, I am proud of you,
> I am happy that I'm in your ranks,
> ...
> We have stood shoulder to shoulder forever.
> For there is no reward in the world,
> No better road to be found,
> Than serving the Party and the people,
> Than heading toward the future with the Party![133]

Symonenko's enthusiasm for the Komsomol indicates that he was not anti-Soviet. But his writings about the Soviet Union did not always deliver a forthright message. The aim of these quotes is to show that *shistdesiatnytstvo* was not born from the same milieu as other currents of the Ukrainian national movement, although the histories of these currents are often fused in the popular imagination into one broad national-liberation movement.

---

133 Ibidem, 450.

The themes of subjectivity and need for self-expression are also present in the verses Symonenko wrote for Soviet almanacs. However, he imbued them with a new concept—namely, of individuality.

> We are all different in character,
> And our tastes are dissimilar,
> But a unique Fatherland raised us
> In greatly troubled times.[134]

Symonenko highlights the importance of individuality, but he takes a different approach in noting that the common denominator within the collective is not class or the Party but rather the fatherland. In 1960, when this poem was published, the call to the fatherland was surely interpreted as alluding to the "great Soviet Fatherland." But the intended meaning of the word changes considerably if we consider Symonenko's subsequent poems, such as those in his first officially published collection, *Silence and Thunder* (1962). Symonenko's poetry focused on innovative approaches to a unique individual personality, as demonstrated in his poem "You Are a Person."

> You know that you're a person;
> You know this; or do you not?
> Your smile is unique,
> Your pain is unique,
> Your eyes only you have got.
>
> Tomorrow you'll be here no longer;
> No more on this earth will you be.
> Others will walk
> And will love and will talk,
> Others much better, much eviler than we.
>
> Today all is here just waiting:
> The meadows and lakes and the unbounded steppe.
> And to live you must rush,
> To love you must rush.
> Hurry up, wake up, don't sleep.
>
> For on earth you are still a person.

---

134 Ibidem, 421.

> And whether you like it or not,
> Your smile is unique,
> Your pain is unique,
> Your eyes only you have got.[135]

Nonetheless, his poetics of the self did not ignore the presence of a broader collective dimension, as in the poem "I."

> He looked at me as if I had no worth.
> I saw his eyes were empty when he finally withdrew.
> "Why do you see yourself the centre of the earth?
> There are many millions just like you."
>
> He was gruff and angry—that I could see.
> His wrathful face would twist and swell;
> And if he could, he'd have crucified me,
> Because I respected myself.
>
> But my pride didn't want to kneel,
> Every minute stretched long before it was done;
> There are millions like me, but I feel
> That I will always be ONE.
>
> For everyone has his own style,
> Not everyone can be coerced.
> WE isn't many standard I's,
> It's many different worlds.
>
> WE is the bosom of nations, of billions,
> WE is the clan that all persons comprise.
> And only he will get respect from millions
> Who can respect a million I's.[136]

These verses are an anthem to freedom of expression, which the *shistdesiatnyky* upheld. They rejected the homogenization of Stalin's socialist realism and sought personal realization through art. Symonenko wrote about this in his diary, commenting on cultural life in the first six months of 1963.

---

135 Vasyl Symonenko, *Hranitni obelisky / Granite Obelisks*, trans., with an intro., by Andriy M. Freishyn-Chirovsky (Jersey City, 1975), 54–55.
136 Ibidem, 80–81.

> Almost suffocated in the gun-smoke of ideological warfare. Realism has achieved victory, true, not by its creations, but through administrative wheeling and dealing....
>
> Formalistic inaneness [sic] has remained, as in the past, the real threat to literature. For what is it but formalism, when hundreds of hacks suck away at such so-called eternal, but in reality secondary, ideals—love work, honour your father and mother, and don't give your neighbor the evil eye? Formalism begins when thought ends. If a poet doesn't bring new thoughts and emotions—he's a formalist. No matter how he advertises his supposed membership to the realistic school.[137]

For Symonenko the true realist was Taras Shevchenko, not the hundreds of Soviet poets and literary critics who condemned Symonenko's work. His hatred for the supposed moralism of Soviet poetry emerges in "Moralists."

> Moralists have long taught us,
> ...
> That a person supposedly needs wings,
> That he can't do without wings.
>
> I strenuously spit on these words,
> They endlessly outrage me—
> Hens and geese always have wings,
> So do sparrows and tits!
>
> I am ready to shout with all my strength,
> Straining my voice:
> A person doesn't need wings,
> He needs a heart and an intellect![138]

Symonenko despised the empty formulas of socialist realism, which for him were equivalent to hypocritical moralism. He was interested in the truth, as he declares in "To the Noisy Mentor."

> You don't need! Don't need! Don't need
> To read me a primer!

---

137 Ibidem, 133.
138 Vasyl Symonenko, *Spadshchyna*, vol. 1, *Poeziia*, bk. 1, 184.

> Leave me the truth
> About your time and you,
> Without trifling details, without a "hurrah."
> So, why, my friend, do you feel
> It's not a sin to rebuke
> Me for being born
> Later than you?
> It would be better to teach me to plow a field,
> To remove the knife from the heart of the truth.[139]

The truth was paramount to Symonenko, as was the ability to exercise his own intellect. However, the right to doubt was forbidden within the Communist Party, especially if one belonged to the special category of artists Symonenko describes in "Doubts."

> Today we have, so it seems,
> Nothing at all to doubt!
> Live, create, and experience
> The praise of our leaders and the Party ...[140]

The disenchantment expressed in these 1963 verses stands in stark contrast to Symonenko's pro-Komsomol poetry of 1960, revealing the evolution of his thoughts and feelings. Within three years the once enthusiastic Komsomol member had become transformed into a disappointed critic. Symonenko never quit the Party and never criticized Marxism itself. His qualms about Marxism, as he noted in his diary, lay in its perception as a quasi-religion, which he equated with a means of enslaving people's minds.

> I speak out against new religion, against hypocrites, who try in vain to transform Marxism into a religion, into a Procrustean bed for science, art, and love....
> If Marxism does not withstand the wild onslaught of dogmatism, it is destined to become a religion. No teaching has the right to monopolize the spiritual life of mankind.[141]

---

[139] Ibidem, 346.
[140] Ibidem, 450.
[141] Symonenko, *Hranitni obelisky*, 129.

The essence of Symonenko's criticism of Soviet cultural policies was that they threatened intellectual independence. Symonenko spoke not only of science and art in his poetry but also of love. In doing so he attempted to carve out an artistic space in which his generation might express their personal experience of universal human emotions. The following lines, which reveal an adherence of sorts to the principles of Marxism, are highly significant when placed side by side with Symonenko's condemnation of Stalin.

> It's true, Stalin did not descend upon the pedestal; neither did the people put him there. He *climbed up* himself—through treachery, turpitude, he climbed up bloodily and insolently just as all tyrants do.[142]

Symonenko also continued working at Soviet periodicals, even as his health worsened. Confined to the provincial town of Cherkasy, he was unable to find proper medical care there for his tumour. His feeling of helplessness translated into severe self-judgement in his poetry, as seen in "The Call of the Twentieth Century."

> The great mother lamented,
> Implored, shouted at me,
> To become a brutal torturer
> Of stupidity, baseness, and mendacity.
> ...
> I'm bawling and shouting, striking my chest,
> I'm plucking the hair from my graying head:
> What can I [do] when people are slumbering?
> What can I [do] when you've fallen asleep?

This despair for having neglected his duty impelled Symonenko to start a diary, which became a respite from the loneliness of Cherkasy.

> I am not starting this diary for want of playing at greatness. I need a friend with whom I can share my doubts. I know of no companion more faithful, more sincere than paper.
> The earth is carrying me around the sun for the twenty-eighth year now. I haven't done much of anything that's good or beautiful during all this time. Instead, I've learned to be silent and cautious,

---

142 Ibidem, 127.

> when I should scream. And—most horrible of all—I've learned to be insincere.
>
> Lying is perhaps my profession. I was born with a talent for lying.[143]

Symonenko viewed the revitalization of national culture to be the solution to the stalemate he was caught in. In his poem "My Language," whose polysemous title refers to both the language of truth and the Ukrainian language, Symonenko uses the image of wings as a metaphor for people's enlightenment.

> You give the poet stalwart wings
> That lift the truth into the heavens,
> For the scholar you gently revealed
> The depth of human wisdom.
> And by nature you'll grow and not fade,
> You'll flourish in poems and verses,
> Because in you resides a great people's
> Tender and wistful soul.[144]

For Symonenko the Ukrainian language was the means by which people might achieve greatness and uncover truth amidst the lies perpetuated under the condition of national enslavement. National pride resounds in Symonenko's best-known poems, but it is yoked to the struggle for truth and a persistent feeling of inadequacy.

> Ukraine! I can't stand you,
> I hate you with all my senses
> When you're primitive and like a plank,
> When you don't have a single thought in your head.
> I love a different you—when you rebel,
> When the Dnipro seethes with anger below the cliffs,
> When you think, when you see and hear
> And carry a heavy pail from the well.

---

143 Ibidem, 123. It is worth noting that Symonenko was perhaps hinting at his work as a journalist rather than his work as a poet, despite having been forced to modify his poetry for it to be published. All of his writings published in various Soviet newspapers and other periodicals are now collected in the two parts of the second volume of his collected works. Overt betrayal of his ideals is not immediately evident in his journalistic pieces.

144 Symonenko, *Spadshchyna*, vol. 1, *Poeziia*, bk. 1, 400.

> Ukraine, be silent! Ukraine, be quiet!
> You're not rich enough to waste words.
> May mendacity not bend your words,
> May your intellect not believe in poor wonders.
> ...
> Don't sit in diapers over foreign ages,
> But go proudly through death into immortality![145]

The struggle for Ukrainian independence is a recurrent theme in Symonenko's poetry, and it is one of the reasons why he achieved such renown and success. He speaks of being the victim of an evil regime, sparing no strength of expression to communicate the gravity of Ukraine's situation and the need for her people to rise up.

> Where are you now, oh torturers of nations?
> Where is your Majesty; your power — where's
> it gone?
> You will no longer have the quiet, sacred places
> To lay unholy waste upon.
>
> My nation grows, expands, is acting,
> Without your whips, without your scorn.
> It will outlive all those whose fortitude was lacking,
> All those whom evil hordes have borne.
>
> My nation is! My nation lives eternally!
> And no one will destroy my nation's life!
> It constantly grows young internally,
> Its soul with tenderness and fury rife.
>
> You! Bastard sons of torturers satanic!
> Forget this not, you harvest of the mud:
> My nation is, its vibrancy is titanic,
> My nation's veins still throb with Cossack blood![146]

These verses are a denunciation of colonialism, subtly blaming both imperial Russian and Soviet exploitation. Uninterested in international politics and internationalism, Symonenko claimed a place for his nation

---

145 Ibidem, 242–43.
146 Symonenko, *Hranitni obelisky*, 31.

as a self-sufficient entity. In his poem "Filial," Ukraine is described in the most classical of its guises—as a mother.

> I peer intently in your eyes,
> As blue and frightening as the fire's core;
> And from within a scarlet lightning flies—
> The light of riots, revolts, and war.
>
> Ukraine! You are truly a marvel;
> And may the timeless ages flow,
> My proud and gracious, handsome mother,
> For me your wondrousness but grows.
>
> For you I sow pearls on my spirit,
> For your sake is all that I think and I do—
> May Russians and Americans be silent
> When I elect to speak with you.
> ...
> And high above the world a battle's fought today
> In the cause of your rights and your life.
>
> May the beet-coloured clouds burn forever,
> And may the insults fly or not—
> I'm determined to sprinkle your sanctified banner
> At least with a drop of my blood. [147]

The love of truth and hatred of lies, national consciousness, a strong sense of the poet's duties toward his people, and willingness to fight for his culture are the defining traits of Vasyl Symonenko and his poetry. However, feelings of inadequacy and self-criticism permeate his personality. About three months before dying of cancer, Symonenko commented on the censorship of his writing. Loneliness, defeat, and a sad irony fill the lines he wrote on 5 September 1963.

> My friends have fallen silent, not a word can be heard of them. The organs of the press have grown more obtusely impudent. *Literaturna Ukraïna* castrates my essay; *Ukraïna* mistreats my poems. Every lackey does as he pleases. How can you shine with gratitude, how can you not pray every day and night for those who granted us such freedom? To this it may be added that in April my poems were

---

147 Ibidem, 38–41.

removed from *Zmina*, slaughtered in *Zhovten'*, and later rejection came from *Dnipro* and *Vitchyzna*.
Oh what a joy! And we all are oppressed;
That's what it takes for this place to progress.[148]

When he died on 14 December 1963, Symonenko's friends rallied to pick up his torch and share his legacy. Among them was the literary critic Ivan Dziuba, to whom Symonenko had dedicated this poem:

It's not worth only flitting about like a hummingbird,
Young people have an honorary role:
Here the meaning is not only in the free verse,
For them Poetry is the password!

Ivan Dziuba (aka Dzyuba) was born on 26 July 1931 in the village of Mykolaivka, now in Volnovakha Raion, Donetsk Oblast. His father was a labourer, and his mother, a nurse. Shortly after his birth, Dziuba's parents went to work in a nearby city, so for the first three years of his life—which coincided with the 1932–33 famine—he lived in the village with his grandparents. Though Dziuba's memory of the famine is limited, his mother recounted stories of the dying people who were brought to the hospital to be treated for starvation.[149] After his parents brought young Ivan to live with them in the city, his mother would take him with her to the hospital where she worked, and there a doctor taught him to read. Dziuba read the newspaper for his father every day and managed to complete his first two years of schooling before the Second World War broke out.[150] While speaking Ukrainian at home with his parents and relatives, he learned Russian by osmosis in the prevailing Russian-speaking environment of the city.

In everyday life we spoke in Ukrainian, on official occasions in Russian; schools, social life, newspapers, and the radio were in Russian. This dichotomy seemed to be natural; at least I did not see anything wrong with it.[151]

---

148 Ibidem, 137.
149 My interview with Ivan Dziuba, 13 June 2009.
150 "Tsia knyzhka zminyla use moie zhyttia: Rozmova z Ivanom Dziuboiu," in Bogumila Berdykhovs'ka and Olia Hnatiuk, *Bunt pokolinnia: Rozmovy z ukraïns'kymy intelektualamy* (Kyiv, 2004), 91–92.
151 Ibidem, 93.

Besides this linguistic duality, Dziuba noticed other social dichotomies and that there was often a difference between people's speech and their actions and between their public and private lives. But no one seemed to find fault with such disparities. The wartime German occupation was a difficult time for the Dziuba family. It was then that the local schools began operating in Ukrainian, but many of the teachers were persecuted after the Soviet reconquest. Dziuba did very well in the Soviet school system and went on to join the Komsomol. His words about communism are particularly interesting.

> I did not only believe. I was romantically in love with this idea. It seemed to me that this was just.... I imagined that communism was the idea of justice. And in a young person the idea of justice evokes an emotional enthusiasm. I was, let's say, a typical specimen of a communist romantic. As a lecturer at the raion committee I travelled about the neighbourhood on my bicycle to lecture about international politics.[152]

This infatuation with communism, however, did not prevent Dziuba from criticizing various facets of Soviet society. He recalls wondering why Party leaders had declared Stalin to be the author of all Soviet conquests when, according to Marxism, it was the people who were the real actors of history. Nevertheless, for Dziuba Marxism and faith in communism seemed to hold a Gramscian cultural supremacy, which made it difficult for him to conceive of holding a position outside the framework of Marxist ideology.

> We could not even consider the idea that someone among us could betray and denounce us to [the political police]. We were naive and trusting, as only young people can be. In addition, we were highly principled members of the Komsomol.[153]

Despite problems with his health, Dziuba was an excellent student. He was a devoted admirer of the famous Soviet Russian poet Vladimir Mayakovsky, whose book of poems he had taken pains to rescue from destruction during the Nazi occupation, and he decided to study Russian

---

152 Ibidem, 99.
153 Ibidem, 100–101.

philology at the university in Stalino (now Donetsk). Dziuba enrolled there and in the Komsomol as a Russian.[154] He admits that his Ukrainian identity was a much later acquisition.

> I spoke Russian not as a matter of principle but because the situation demanded it. Russian was the "norm," but I happily switched to Ukrainian when somebody addressed me in Ukrainian. I wrote my sporadic "diarist" writings in both languages, depending on the material. Therefore I was, as a matter of fact, not "Russian-speaking" but "bilingual."[155]

While I was interviewing him, Dziuba offered a subtly different testimony: he said that he decided to study Russian literature because he "had the impression that Russian was somewhat superior, more important."[156] He claimed that his "self-Ukrainianization" began while he was working at the local newspaper *Radians'ka Donechchyna* and his boss, the writer Andrii Klochchia (1905–72), questioned his passion for Mayakovsky. Klochchia gave Dziuba works by the banned writers Volodymyr Vynnychenko and Mykola Khvylovy to read, and he introduced him to the young poet Vasyl Stus. Dziuba was also strongly influenced by Pavlo Baidebura (1901–85), the longtime secretary of the oblast's branch of Ukraine's Union of Writers, which Dziuba had joined.

> All of these acquaintances in the literary and journalists' circles of the "miners' capital" opened my eyes to the fact that a Ukrainian intelligentsia existed, not just a Russian one, and that the Ukrainian language could be spoken not only in the lower strata of society, as I did in Olenivski Kariery.[157]

In Stalino Dziuba became the secretary of the university's Komsomol branch, but his enthusiasm toward this organization was nearing an abrupt end. After the Nineteenth Congress of the CPSU in 1952, which had urged Party members to engage in self-criticism, at an oblast meeting Dziuba directly attacked the local Party secretary and the university rector for several cases of favouritism. "I saw a discrepancy between ideology

---

154 Ivan Dziuba, *Spohady i rozdumy na finishnii priamii* (Kyiv, 2008), 118.
155 Ibidem, 123.
156 My interview with Dziuba.
157 Ibidem, 125. Olenivski Kariery (renamed Dokuchaievsk in 1954) is the town in Donetsk oblast where he lived with his parents.

and reality, which tormented me, so I spoke out against it."[158] Dziuba won over the audience, but the local Party bosses abruptly the meeting and telephoned Moscow for instructions on how to proceed against him. This incident could have ended tragically, for a KGB agent announced that Dziuba would be arrested during the imminent purge of Jews in the USSR in 1952 and 1953. Stalin died in 1953, however, and all that happened was Dziuba's dismissal as secretary of the local Komsomol branch. "With that my activism within the Komsomol broke off, and there came a period of deep disillusionment, of depression, and a crisis in my own world view."[159]

Dziuba was saddened by Stalin's death. But he felt the effects of the Khrushchev Thaw as soon as *Pravda* published several lines from President Dwight D. Eisenhower's speech on the occasion of Stalin's demise. The fact that the speech was published in *Pravda* convinced Dziuba that subtle political changes had begun in the USSR.

In 1953 Dziuba was accepted into the graduate program at the Institute of Literature of the AN URSR in Kyiv, intending to write a dissertation on Mayakovsky's satire. As soon as he moved there, he felt the different atmosphere of that city. Stalino was considered a stronghold of Russianness, but it had a more liberal environment in which criticism of the Party leadership was tolerated. In Kyiv, on the other hand, everyone took great care not to arouse suspicion.[160] During the three years of his graduate studies, Dziuba became interested in Ukrainian literature, largely because it was now possible to obtain and read works that had been unavailable before the Thaw. His new acquaintance, the writer Borys Antonenko-Davydovych, introduced him to the works of the nineteenth-century Ukrainian literati Mykhailo Drahomanov and Borys Hrinchenko, among others. Furthermore, Dziuba was able to access Polish literature and translations for the first time.

> It must also be said that the Polish press in the latter 1950s had a phenomenal significance for us [Ukrainians]. That was our only window to the Western world, and what a window it was. I

---

158 *Naspravdi bulo tak: Interv'iu Iuriia Zaitseva z Ivanom Dziuboiu* (Lviv, 2001), 47–48.
159 Dziuba, *Spohady i rozdumy na finishnii priamii*, 139. For a broader discussion of the meaning of Komsomol membership for youth after the Second World War, see Juliane Fürst, *Stalin's Last Generation: Soviet Post-War Youth and the Emergence of Mature Socialism* (Oxford, 2010).
160 Ibidem, 144.

> subscribed to [the Polish periodicals] *Polityka, Kultura, Życie Literackie*, [and] *Twórczość*, and to [the Czech periodical] *Literární noviny*. Many others did the same. At that time the most popular section in the bookstore on Kreshchatyk [Boulevard], Kyiv's main street, was the Polish one. This shop sold books from the Eastern bloc countries. The Polish section was frequented by the intelligentsia and youth....
>
> The Ukrainian[-language] journal *Duklia*, which was published in Czechoslovakia, was very important to us.... [in it] we could read authors whose works were banned in Ukraine.[161]

Dziuba needed to work to survive, and he wanted to be employed in the field of Ukrainian literature. When he was offered an editing job in 1956 by the Dnipro Publishing House, he decided to put aside writing his dissertation. In the following year was hired as the editor in charge of literary criticism by the monthly literary journal *Vitchyzna*. The half-decade (1957–62) that Dziuba was in that position was significant for his intellectual development, for it was then that he became acquainted with many writers and critics, including Yevhen Sverstiuk, Ivan Drach, Leonid Kovalenko, and Ivan Svitlychny. Although *Vitchyzna* was run by Oleksii Poltoratsky and then Vasyl Kozachenko—critics with rather old-fashioned tastes—Dziuba was able to secure the publication of some innovative articles. His closest ally at the journal was its deputy managing editor, Volodymyr Pianov (1921–2006), a stalwart defender of Ukrainian culture.

> As for Volodymyr Yakovych Pianov, I am thankful to him not only for welcoming me to *Vitchyzna*. He also had a great influence on my Ukrainianization. Moreover, I know that he had a great influence not only on me (although later we, the youth, went farther, and some lost a good sense of judgement). Characteristically, no one in the Institute of Literature, not even the staunch Ukrainian Serhii Plachynda, tried to Ukrainianize me, but Pianov always stoked the embers of my national self-consciousness. Every now and then Volodymyr Yakovych [Pianov] took me under his wing, acquainted me with [the famous poet] Pavlo Hryhorovych Tychyna, and insisted that he [Tychyna], as a deputy of the Supreme Soviet of the Ukrainian SSR, deal with my registration [to reside] in Kyiv—what a long and troublesome procedure it was to obtain permission to live

---

161 "Tsia knyzhka zminyla use moie zhyttia," 107–108.

in the capital! When I contracted tuberculosis again, he searched for renowned doctors and brought me some warm boots to prevent my feet from freezing.[162]

Working at *Vitchyzna* helped Dziuba to evolve intellectually and galvanized his participation in Ukrainian literary life:

> Thus as of 1956 a revision of my world view took place with gradually increasing speed, first on a social and democratic level, and then also on a national level. From that point we could claim that [my] conscious Ukrainian activity had begun. In the beginning it was an exclusively literary phenomenon, but the momentum of the [*shistdesiatnyky*] movement pushed us into political opposition, with little regard for the fact that this momentum was blind.[163]

Dziuba and his colleagues welcomed Khrushchev's denunciation of the Stalin personality cult. He and many of his Ukrainian intellectual peers were critical of the Soviet Union and convinced of the need for change. Excited but unsurprised about Khrushchev's speech, they were ready to engage with Khrushchev's Thaw.

Dziuba's initial forays into Ukrainian literary criticism were condensed into his first book, *An Ordinary Person or a Philistine?* (1959). It was much less revolutionary than the poetry of Kostenko and Symonenko described above. In it Dziuba quotes Lenin and Maxim Gorky, presents Khrushchev as an innovator who broke new ground at the Twentieth CPSU Congress, and the subjects he addresses and the points he makes are both orthodox Soviet and orthodox Marxist. Nonetheless Dziuba's book added something novel and significant to the development of *shistdesiatnytstvo*. Each of its four chapters is dedicated to a different subject. The first chapter addresses the problem of *mishchanstvo* (babbittry or philistinism) in Ukrainian literature, and Dziuba devotes many pages to condemning it as a way of life characterized by *kulturnist'* (culturedness), a mixture of social refinement and prudishness. Though some of his observations are typical of Soviet society in this period, Dziuba's originality resides in his analysis of how the stories by most of

---

162 Dziuba, *Spohady i rozdumy na finishnii priamii*, 483–84. Soviet authorities deemed the prose collection *The Burning Bush* (1968) by the writer Serhii Plachynda (1928–2013), Dziuba's fellow doctoral candidate at the Institute of Literature, a "nationalist deviation" and ordered it removed from Soviet libraries.
163 "Tsia knyzhka zminyla use moie zhyttia," 54–55.

the authors he discusses reaffirmed the success of Soviet philistinism and conformity even though these writers struggled against them.

The multifaceted ideology of babbittry was grounded in the ideas of egotistic individualism, parasitism, and aspiration to "live richly" off society and the people. Associated with the acculturation, refinement, and "daintiness" that defined a *mishchanyn* (burgher or philistine) was his ideal of life—which, according to Gorky, could be summarized in the maxim "to work very little, to think very little, [but] to eat a lot."[164] Soviet novels tended to portray certain types positively: a young girl who joins the Komsomol with the intention of gaining easy admission to university; or a spoiled boy who, rather unbelievably, becomes the best worker in his factory after a week of employment. In these novels the Communist Party plays the role of a *deus ex machina* that resolves troublesome situations, and the authors fail to acknowledge the important role of the collective in directing these fictional characters toward socialism. Dziuba identifies Oleksandr Dovzhenko as an author who properly situated and contextualized his characters' psychological changes.

> For Oleksandr Dovzhenko, a person does not exist isolated from the surrounding world. The person and the people, the person and his life, the person and his epoch—these are the themes and the relations with which the author's intellect struggles. In a single character he [Dovzhenko] wants to see an entire people and an epoch; in the existence of the collective he wants to feel the pulse of the blood and the breath of the entire country and of all time. He wants to see, feel, and show how a people recreates itself by recreating its life.[165]

The key to a successful story lies in the realistic description of the character's transformation from a selfish bourgeois-philistine into an everyday hero, into that elusive "ordinary person" who serves as the hero of Soviet socialist realism. In *An Ordinary Person or a Philistine?* the second chapter is dedicated to literature describing and written for young people. In it the national factor plays a major role. Dziuba laments the scarcity of believable characters and the standardized plots of Ukrainian prose, which resulted in the publication of many similar novels. For him the heart of the problem is the overly rigid standardization of the language in Soviet authors' descriptions and dialogues, thereby making it impossible

---

164 Ivan Dziuba, *Zvychaina liudyna chy mishchanyn: Literaturno-krytychni statti* (Kyiv, 1959), 27.
165 Ibidem, 99.

for them to effectively describe a character and his inner world. The problem with a standard young character is that

> In his words and manners one can always find something false, something alien, [and] unreliable. We would rather see a character who is less talkative and more inwardly strong and pure.
>
> In life, language, the style of phrasing, and the manner of conversing can reveal so much about a person. In literature [this is the case] even more! They reveal his or her spiritual energy, [and they] portray the more characteristic and valuable factors in his or her life. A main character who is loud, vain, and blathering will never gain the reader's sympathy. That is why we strongly want Soviet youth in literary works to speak, at last, a genuine Ukrainian language—precise and expressive, fiery and sparkling, poetic and charming—the language of Ivan Kotliarevsky and Taras Shevchenko, of Lesia Ukrainka and Mykhailo Kotsiubynsky, and of Hryhorii Kvitka-Osnovianenko and Ostap Vyshnia. If a youth in literature spoke this way, he would appear as a hero, whose expressions and witty words could grow wings and reach young people, forcing out the foolish and distasteful, hybrid [Ukrainian-Russian] speaking, motionless characters and idlers, the so-called *stiliagi* [privileged Soviet "mods"]....
>
> The time has come to begin a decisive and widespread struggle for the language culture of our youth. In this struggle, literature, and especially the "young" literature for and about youth, has to play a decisive role.[166]

Without explicitly condemning the Russified standardization of Ukrainian orthography, Dziuba did so by providing examples of genuine Ukrainian expressions. He demonstrated how the psychological development of a character can be traced through his or her linguistic evolution.

The third chapter of *An Ordinary Person or a Philistine?* concerns the relationship between work, particularly manual labour, and the maturation of young people. The most thought-provoking sections are those where this Soviet theme gives way to a discussion of the importance of genuine emotions. Comparing the characters in Ivan Senchenko's[167]

---

166 Ibidem, 150–51.
167 Ivan Senchenko (1901–75) was a popular Soviet Ukrainian writer from the mid-1920s, when Khvylovy invited him to join the Vaplite writers' organization (see n. 183). He survived the Great Terror and had a successful career as a writer, critic, and journal

cycle of 1950s stories about life in Kyiv's Solomianka district with those in Dovzhenko's oeuvre, Dziuba underlines the importance of feelings as they emerge in the personality of the protagonist, Denys. Dziuba implies that through the incorporation of a private, familial dimension, the character is imbued with added depth. Thus he hints at the importance of the community and the nation.

> This husband's (the father's) respect for [his] wife (the mother); [his] respect for and readiness to defer as the stronger one to his weaker lifelong companion; his humane tact and courtesy; and the son's respect for his elders; his deference to his mother and his sensitivity; the general atmosphere of sincerity, mutual respect, and readiness to help one another within the family—all of these factors inspire us to remember Dovzhenko's characters, with their inner culture and the vivid [traditional] national type of their relations.[168]

The book's fourth and final chapter examines contemporaneity in literature, focusing on the ways in which writers have described the reality of collective farmers' lives. Although the chapter's general tone is not confrontational, the literary examples Dziuba includes cast light on the often disagreeable human dimension of Soviet agriculture.

> The writer speaks about the most important and most unpleasant of subjects: people have lost their dignity, and they are afraid of affirming their indisputable rights, even when they are called to do so.[169]

The problem at the collective farms, as Dziuba argues, is that the management does not care about the needs of the people and manages state enterprises solely for their own profit. Even if Dziuba's logic is not provocative, his giving credence to the literature that described collective farms in such stark terms was revolutionary. Nonetheless, these criticisms were not enough to make Dziuba doubt the Marxist credo, which he reaffirmed through his many praises of Lenin and Khrushchev.

With this masterpiece of diplomatic criticism, Dziuba cemented his role as the best spokesperson on behalf of the revival of Ukrainian culture.

---

editor in postwar Kyiv. In 1972 his wife, the historian Olena Kompan (1916–1986), was fired from her research position at the Institute of History of the AN URSR for her ties with Ukrainian dissidents.

168 Ibidem, 204.
169 Ibidem, 258.

He doubtlessly kept his more inflammatory comments to himself. In a note he wrote in 1961, his ideas about Symonenko's poetry testified to the culmination of his Ukrainianization: "Symonenko has shown our society the problems that we had cast off onto others. We have been the premier fighters for the freedom of all peoples... In addition, Vasyl has begun to speak about the liberation of our own people. That, in its own way, is a historic turning point in our literature."[170]

Like many other intellectuals, in the late 1950s Lina Kostenko, Vasyl Symonenko, and Ivan Dziuba were ready to step forward into the public eye. They were all friends and members of the SPU, but they lacked a place or an institution where they could unite, work together, and develop their ideas, which remained merely artistic at the time. Kyiv's intellectuals were provided this "common space" by a special Komsomol club founded by Les Taniuk.

Les Taniuk and the Club of Creative Youth

Les (Leonid) Taniuk (1938–2016)[171] was born in the village of Zhukyn in Dymer raion, Kyiv Oblast, to a mother of German descent and a Ukrainian father. Although he grew up bilingual, he considered German his true mother tongue.[172] But he was very sensitive to the state of the Ukrainian language. As a high-school student in Lutsk, in his diary Taniuk described how Russian speakers reacted with disdain and derision to people who spoke Ukrainian. Consequently he felt so uncomfortable that he spoke Ukrainian "only in the street and at home."[173] He also began keeping his diary in Russian until his father discovered it and lectured him on the matter of language and national pride. This occurred a few months before Taniuk was ordered to read Khrushchev's report on the Stalin personality cult at a local Party meeting. Taniuk was shocked by Khrushchev's condemnation of Stalin's nationality policy, as he was by what he read in Vladimir Dudintsev's controversial novel *Not by Bread Alone*: In response he wrote: "It appears that we are on the eve of a new revolution. People are thinking in a completely different way than

---

170 Ivan Dziuba, *Spohady i rozdumy na finishnii priamii*, 193.
171 Taniuk was born in 1938. After the prohibition of the Club of Creative Youth (*Klub tvorchoï molodi*, or KTM) he moved to Moscow, where he worked as a director in theatre, cinema, and television. In 1986 he returned to Ukraine and began a political career, and in 1990 he was elected to the Verkhovna Rada (Ukrainian parliament).
172 My Interview with Les Taniuk, 28 May 2009.
173 Les' Taniuk, *Slovo, teatr, zhyttia*, vol. 3, *Zhyttia* (Kyiv, 2003), 12.

yesterday ... I can't stop wondering about the newness that I smell, that I divine, that I sense on the wind of the year 1956."[174]

Even before moving to Kyiv in September 1958 to study theatre and film directing (1958–63) at the Karpenko-Kary State Institute of Theatre Arts, the national institute for the performing arts, Taniuk had grown increasingly skeptical of Marxism and Soviet policy. After he began studying Esperanto, Taniuk sarcastically noted that Russian was the USSR's Esperanto. Despite his misgivings about some aspects of the Soviet Union, he did not immediately embrace nationalism as an alternative. Upon reading Dmytro Dontsov's *For Which Revolution*, Taniuk assessed the ideas of that influential proponent of Ukrainian nationalism as follows.

> The question is: can nationalism be a political idea?
> With all due respect toward the word 'nation'—absolutely not.
> The idea of a nation and nationalism are not the same thing. The difference consists above all in the attitude toward other peoples. They are well disposed toward me, as I am well disposed toward them, following the logic of returning kindness. As a rule, they pay you back with the same coin.
> His [Dontsov's] hatred of democracy gives the old man away from the beginning. The Zaporozhian Sich itself, which he honours so much, was indeed a democracy, but in this case he does not wish to take it into consideration.[175]

In February 1958 Taniuk devoted many pages of his diary to reviewing *V. I. Lenin on Ukraine*, a book recently published by the Institute of Party History of the Central Committee of the Communist Party of Ukraine (hereafter the CC CPU). Although Taniuk did not keep his criticism of Lenin in check, he appreciated that Lenin had been able to modify Marxist theories on the national question, adapting them to the multinational reality of the Soviet Union.

> At the end of his life Lenin reached an understanding of the complexity of the national question ....
> Stalin did not understand it and merely resumed where Lenin had left off. Stalin thought that the national contradictions themselves were the glue with which he could hold the brotherhood together,

---

174 Ibidem, 58.
175 Ibidem, 224.

and he began placing them into groups, to mix them, divide them, and then again so on and so forth ..."[176]

As a supporter of Lenin's idea that Ukraine needed a Ukrainian-language educational system, Taniuk acknowledged the deteriorating condition of the Ukrainian language and was gripped by a sense of duty to improve its status. He kept notebooks in which he wrote down the new Ukrainian words he came across as if he were studying a foreign language, solemnly stating that "today we need to work on the creation of an *aristocratic* Ukrainian language—on the development of the 'language' of Shelmenko and even the 'language' of a normal collective farm in Poltava Oblast."[177] Taniuk's concern was spurred by the state of Ukrainian language use in the artistic community. He regretted that in Ukrainian comic theatre the audience was goaded into laughing at the language used on stage—usually the mixed, Russian-Ukrainian patois called *surzhyk*. Taniuk hoped that one day Ukrainian spectators could laugh as an Englishman does at a play by George Bernard Shaw or an Italian does at a play by Eduardo de Filippo, whose humour in the plays' content rather than in their characters' manner of speaking.[178]

According to Taniuk, during his time at the Karpenko-Kary Institute the majority of its teachers were "anti-Ukrainian" and held conservative views on art. A notable exception was Marian Krushelnytsky (1897–1963), the head of the directing department, who helped Taniuk to find a mode of expressing himself as an actor. Krushelnytsky introduced Taniuk to several members of Kyiv's intelligentsia, but these encounters only cemented Taniuk's impression that speaking Ukrainian was unwelcome in intellectual circles, where it was used only if it was "unavoidable."[179]

Taniuk's busy social and academic calendar during his first year in Kyiv prevented him from contributing directly as an artist to the *shistdesiatnyky* movement, its themes emerged in his diaries, where they contrasted with the typical values of Stalinism. In the spring of 1959 Taniuk commented on a speech Maksym Rylsky delivered to the Third

---

176 Ibidem, 378.
177 Ibidem, 417. Shelmenko, the hero of a popular eponymous play by Hryhorii Kvitka-Osnovianenko, speaks in the substandard language of the author's nineteenth-century comical characters.
178 Ibidem, 420–21. *Surzhyk*, though widely used by many, usually less educated, people in Ukraine, is considered déclassé.
179 See ibidem, 453 and 697–98.

Congress of Soviet Writers: "The title of the speech was 'About the Person, for the Person.' In it the socialist was not separate from the capitalist person, nor the Party member from the trade unionist—there is just *one person*."[180] Taniuk's desire to find a new side to the individual was one reason why he defended Dudintsev's novel: "It is really an epochal novel, [about which] I have not changed my mind. Maybe for the first time, *despite* the ideology of the *herd*(!), this is a novel about the bread of the soul, about a personal 'I.'"[181]

Taniuk thought that the main shortcoming of the past and present generations of Ukrainian intellectuals was their lack of a strong concept of individuality. Only his favourite authors of the Ukrainian cultural renaissance of the 1920s seemed to have addressed this problem.

> In the ideas [of those intellectuals] a major factor was absent: "I" in the first person and capitalized.[182] The members of Vaplite perhaps got closer to it than anyone ... It resonated louder in the most ephemeral of forms—in poetry. Here the "I" was elemental, instinctive. Not supported by theory or by strategy, it became silent in the 1930s, when the days of the masses came."[183]

Taniuk was a passionate reader of theatre reviews published during the 1920s and 1930s, and he particularly admired the works of Mykola Kulish and Les Kurbas, two major Ukrainian theatre figures who suffered repression and eventually death in the Soviet Gulag.[184] Taniuk considered himself and his peers to be responsible for the current crisis of Ukrainian culture, and he wanted to restore the tradition of Ukrainian theatre that had been destroyed in the Stalin era. In August 1959 he wrote in his diary:

---

180   Les' Taniuk, *Tvory v 60-y tomakh*, vol. 4, *Shchodennyky 1959–1960 rr.* (Kyiv, 2004), 44.
181   Taniuk, *Slovo, teatr, zhyttia*, 319.Regarding the criticism of Dudintsev by the prominent Ukrainian poet and official Mykola Bazhan, Taniuk wrote: "I cannot believe that an encyclopedic person such as Bazhan does not realize the meaning of Dudintsev's novel. They have already experienced it all more than once—[so] why oppose him? Why are they recreating the same mistake again and again?" (Taniuk, *Tvory*, 4: 73).
182   In Ukrainian the word "*ia*" (I) is not capitalized.
183   Ibidem, 238. *Vaplite* — the acronym of *Vilna akademiia proletarskoi literatury* (Free Academy of Proletarian Literature)—was a short-lived (November 1925–January 1927) elite Soviet Ukrainian writers' group. Bazhan was a member. Most of the members perished during the Great Terror.
184   See note 72 above.

> Perhaps we are indeed guilty, my generation ... the boys and girls in my course.... Why is the theatre only Krushelnytsky's problem? Why is language troubling only Rylsky? Where are the people who should sound the bell already?
>
> Perhaps the people who could be heroes are not interested in this problem. This leaves me in a sour mood. Even if I swim in the Styr or hide myself in a book, I can't help but feel that everything is going wrong. There has to be a way out of this dead end, and it is *our* problem, *my* problem.[185]

This concern prompted Taniuk to contact several classmates and propose that they establish an experimental Ukrainian theatre group. He also invited students from other programs at the Karpenko-Kary Institute to join this initiative. After a lengthy preparation period, the official inauguration of the group took place on 8 March 1960. Besides theatre students, it included singers and musicians, a figurative artist, and one writer. They were all enthusiastic and convinced of the cultural significance of their group, soon named the Club of Creative Youth (Ukrainian acronym: KTM), also known as Suchasnyk (the Contemporary).

> You can feel that people really need this, that the time has come, and that the fruit is ripe for picking. I spoke about the axiom of a new cycle and tried to give an assessment of the overall Ukrainian situation ... Nearly seventy people gathered to listen; the hall was almost full. To facilitate administration and placate the institute's rector, we explained that it was an initiative group of the Komsomol. He walked away laughing.[186]

The decision to establish the KTM under the aegis of the Komsomol was made in order to receive official status and allow the club to evade more severe forms of censorship. Ivan Dziuba, who later joined the KTM, remembered that joining the Komsomol "in those days ... could be, and often was, a form of exposure to juvenile maximalism and indeed resistance to bureaucracy.... Not surprisingly, the Party kept the Komsomol under constant surveillance."[187] This was also the opinion of Les Taniuk, who in the 1990s thus described the KTM:

---

185 Ibidem, 115.
186 Ibidem, 385.
187 Dziuba, *Spohady i rozdumy na finishnii priamii*, 119.

> The Club of Creative Youth was also born from the need to stop living an incomplete life, as an attempt to unify the youth, particularly the creative youth ... against the stiffness of the old people who were the embodiment of the system. It was an idea of Ukrainian self-expression—we literally desired a new understanding, a new knowledge that we could not share with anyone officially. Censorship, Party committees, clans of untalented popular bootlickers, directives of the [Party] plenums and congresses about the uniqueness of socialist realism, whose tenets must not be violated, and a lot of other useless vapidity—all stood before us like a prison wall, beyond which, we felt, there was another life.[188]

At its meeting on 23 March 1960, the group chose its official name and elected Taniuk president. The KTM's first official initiative was a telegram to France's President Charles de Gaulle on the occasion of Khrushchev's visit to Paris. In it the KTM expressed hope for "the beginning of a new phase in the exchange of cultural values and national talents" between France and Ukraine.[189]

Three days later Taniuk discussed the matter with Krushelnytsky, who welcomed the initiative and the opportunity it afforded for members to do "something real." Krushelnytsky recommended recruiting as many people as possible and opening membership to others outside the art community. He also suggested that the club organize a theatrical performance as part of a competition among new theatre companies. Taniuk decided to contact Viacheslav Chornovil, then a student at Kyiv State University's Faculty of Journalism whom Taniuk had met a few months earlier, to offer him a part in the production. Chornovil, who had come from Cherkasy Oblast to study in Kyiv, enthusiastically accepted Taniuk's invitation. From their first encounter Chornovil had been struck by Taniuk's charisma. Meanwhile Taniuk was surprised that Chornovil approved of the KTM's Komsomol affiliation and believed in the possibility of change from within.

> This phrase of his [Chornovil's] is particularly important: "When I become secretary of the Central Committee of the Komsomol, we will change everything, everything completely." "Who will let you do that?" [I asked] "I'll force it through! Now you have to take

---

188 Les' Taniuk, *Parastas* (Kyiv, 1998), 13.
189 Taniuk, *Tvory*, 4: 438–39.

everything in your hands—otherwise it will come to a stop, and stopping means going backwards. It is evident even to an idiot that the old people have recovered and are gradually tying our hands." He was convinced, even from that dated conversation, that we needed to make our headquarters in the Komsomol, where there are a lot of wonderful boys and girls who sincerely want change and believe in such an opportunity.[190]

Chornovil took part in all of the KTM's rehearsals of Mykola Kulish's play *Sonata pathétique*, in which he had the main role. Unfortunately he never performed that role on the stage, for upon graduating from university in 1960 he was hired as an editor by the Lviv Television Studio and did not return to Kyiv until 1963.

One of the KTM's first successful initiatives was an assembly that took place in the main hall of the Kyiv Institute of Art on 29 May 1960. During its first half Taniuk read and commented on *The Murderers' Rotunda*, a novel by the Ukrainian émigré writer Todos Osmachka, whose work was officially forbidden in Soviet Ukraine. Taniuk was inundated with questions after his reading, and he accepted the audience's suggestion that the subsequent meeting be dedicated to Mykola Kulish. The second half of the session was run by the actor Petro Masokha (1904–91), who shared his memories of Les Kurbas and Oleksander Dovzhenko. The meeting's success was evident not only in terms of quality and number of the participants—nearly seventy people, not all of whom were members of the KTM—but also because it attracted other artists. After the show a group of sculpture students at the Kyiv State Institute of Arts offered to take on the role of set designers and suggested staging a show about a group of mountain climbers.[191]

When news about the KTM spread, another group of artists, mainly painters, approached Taniuk about joining the club. They were led by Alla Horska (1929–70), who became one of the KTM's most active members. Taniuk recalled: "As a matter of fact, the real Club of Creative Youth began with the arrival of [these artists,] nonconformist members who brought with them a spirit of active rebellion and rejection of the old dogmas and forms."[192] Horska's studio apartment became the KTM's second home, and she was often instrumental in transforming ideas into practical

---

190 Ibidem, 395.
191 Ibidem, 601–602.
192 Taniuk, *Parastas*, 61.

projects. Horska shared Taniuk's interest in Kulish and Kurbas and was a good friend of Nelli Korniienko, Taniuk's future wife. In injecting the KTM with a desire for artistic revival, Horska received something significant in return. While not knowing Ukrainian very well, by immersing herself into a milieu where Ukrainian was the only language spoken she began thinking of herself as a Russified Ukrainian. To further her linguistic facility, she asked her KTM colleagues to give her lessons in the Ukrainian language, and she studied it every evening.[193] The KTM's reputation generated several waves of new members, including among Kyiv State University's students of physics and cybernetics. The medical student and later dissident Mykola Plakhotniuk described how a friend convinced him to attend a KTM gathering for the first time.[194]

During the KTM's first two years, the participation of writers and literary critics was sporadic, with two notable exceptions. The first was Ivan Svitlychny (1929–92), by then a well-established critic and member of the SPU. On 23 June 1960 Taniuk ran into Svitlychny at the SPU building, where Taniuk had come to meet Krushelnytsky. The commotion caused by the visit of Palmiro Togliatti, the leader of the Italian Communist Party, to Kyiv gave Taniuk the opportunity to approach Svitlychny to join the KTM, only to discover that Svitlychny had already attended some of its events.[195] Svitlychny, whose apartment was one of the most active Ukrainian literary salons in the capital, welcomed the opportunity to become Taniuk's friend. In November 1960 Taniuk visited Svitlychny to consult with him about the KTM's future activities. Svitlychny "suggested that the club should become 'more literary,'" but he also "complained that writers were too individualistic" and therefore reluctant to join any group.[196]

The second exception was Vasyl Symonenko, whose acquaintance Taniuk made on 12 November 1960, the day when the Kyiv Metro first opened. They were introduced to each other by a mutual friend, the writer and critic Stanislav Telniuk (1935–90). Taniuk wrote down his impressions of the encounter in his diary.

> Telniuk arrived along with a young man, a journalist from Cherkasy named Vasyl Symonenko. During [our] hour of

---

193 My interview with Taniuk, 28 May 2009.
194 Ibidem and my interview with Mykola Plakhotniuk, 3 June 2009.
195 Taniuk, *Tvory*, 4: 620.
196 Ibidem, 729.

> conversation he did not laugh once. But there is something roughly pleasant about him. Maybe it is [his] language—a Cossack pronunciation, perhaps derived from the ascetic people of the Sich. We walked along the Khreshchatyk and even went up the hill [to the ancient citadel area].
>
> He graduated from our university. Stanislav said that Vasyl writes very good poetry. Symonenko and I immediately found a common language, but we talked about everything except poems. Stanislav's words surprised me.[197]

The KTM offered the young intellectuals of the capital a platform to present their works to the public, and soon people such as Lina Kostenko, Ivan Dziuba, and the historian Mykhailo Braichevsky became members. The KTM was also a place where different artists could engage in discussions and present their own ideas, in hopes that input from others would help to develop them further. As Kostenko stated, "Our characteristic trait was that we liked each other a lot, we respected one another, and everyone found each other's work interesting."[198] The KTM's mandate could be reconciled with the Zeitgeist of the 1960s, which the literary critic and KTM member Mykhailyna Kotsiubynska described thus.

> The *shistdesiatnyky* were the spontaneous manifestation of a spiritual ripening, a new mentality, a new system of values, and a new understanding of the national experience within the depths of the totalitarian system. They had been educated in this system, marked indelibly by this environment that had given birth to them, and passed through the different stages of its development, unable to free themselves of all its prejudices. Initially many of them were profoundly imbued with those ideological myths, which they would later discard on their own as illusions and hindrances.[199]

As a sanctioned offshoot of the Komsomol, the Club of Creative Youth can be considered an attempt on the part of the Soviet establishment to co-opt the cultural ferment brewing among young, educated Ukrainians. For the Soviet leadership, endorsing such initiatives was a means of shaping

---

197 Ibidem, 764. The Kreshchatyk is Kyiv's central boulevard. The Sich was the principal fort of the Zaporozhian Cossacks, located on the island of Khortytsia below the now inundated rapids of the Dnipro River near the present-day city of Zaporizhzhia.
198 My interview with Kostenko, 12 June 2009.
199 Mykhailyna Kotsiubyns'ka, "Ivan Svitlychnyi, shistdesiatnyk," foreword to Ivan Svitlychnyi, *U mene ie til'ky slovo* (Kharkiv, 1994), 5.

the generation born in the 1930s and 1940s, whom they did not consider—and who did not consider themselves—as alien to Soviet society. But this was not the only way in which the Communist state was trying to manage the cultural renaissance of the early 1960s.

Andrii Skaba and the Ukrainian Biographic Dictionary

Some Party members were convinced that the Soviet Ukrainian government needed to exert stricter control over artistic activity. One of them was Andrii Skaba (1905–86), the CPU's former propaganda secretary in Kharkiv Oblast who had been appointed Ukraine's minister of higher and secondary special education in 1959. Skaba presided over a meeting of contributors to a proposed Ukrainian biographic dictionary project[200] held on 2 February 1961, and the minutes of this meeting offer an insight into how he understood his ministerial duties. Skaba opened the assembly with an attack on many dictionary entries that failed to conform to Party guidelines. He questioned why Musii Kononenko's 1919 poem "Mazepa" was listed among his works, and he found fault with the sentence "Mazepa faced the world with pure ideas, and he fought for the success of the whole country," sarcastically deeming it "American, Canadian, Western Ukrainian."[201] Skaba accused the project's contributors of using "nationalist" sources written before the October Revolution or by non-CPU members, and he claimed that certain entries failed to describe their subject from a Communist point of view. As examples, Skaba stated that the authors of the entries about Mykhailo Drahomanov and Mykhailo Hrushevsky neglected to highlight the "errors" of these two historians, such as their involvement in nationalist organizations.

One of the contributors, a Mr. Pyvovarov, tried to defend the project by saying that it was meant for educated readers who were able to make their own judgements. He courageously added: "We cannot write that Ukrainian literature developed only in a revolutionary direction and that

---

200 This project was ostensibly an attempt to revive the "Biographic Dictionary of Ukrainian Figures in Science, History, Art, and the Civic Movement" project initiated in 1918 by the Ukrainian Academy of Sciences. The project was shut down by the Soviet regime in 1933, and many of its contributors were repressed. In post-Soviet Ukraine a new national biographic dictionary project has been undertaken by the Institute of Biographic Research at the V. I. Vernadsky National Library of Ukraine in Kyiv.

201 TsDAHOU, f. 1, op. 1, spr. 5373, ark. 1–2; Kononenko (1864–1922) was a prose writer, poet, and Ukrainian co-operative functionary in Lubni and Poltava who was persecuted by both the tsarist (1905) and Bolshevik (1918) regimes. He died prematurely from tuberculosis.

no one distanced themselves from these positions. As members of the editorial board, we did not wish to embellish history or any given writer."[202] To support his argument, Pyvovarov noted that in Russia it was normal to refer to the famous Russian writer and Nobel laureate Ivan Bunin and even publish his works although he had been an anti-Soviet émigré in France from 1920 until his death in 1953.[203]

Skaba derided Pyvovarov, declaring his astonishment and inquiring where Pyvovarov had picked up such ridiculous notions. As a result the remainder of the meeting was noticeably tense. The editorial board's members concluded that the biographic dictionary was intended for scholars and asked Skaba to specify which of Hrushevsky's works could be mentioned. Since the pre-eminent Ukrainian historian was referred to in many Russian books, Skaba agreed with the editorial board that the titles of Hrushevsky's works that were not banned could be listed. Other contributors emphasized the fact that they had not included any authors of the 1920s and 1930s with dangerous political views. Pyvovarov responded that if all those individuals were excluded, what would remain would be a "history of Lilliputians."

Skaba silenced Pyvovarov, stating

> "I am not saying that Kononenko must not be included, I am saying that it must be made clear that he wrote a whole set of loathsome works, which were not in the interests of the Ukrainian people. That is what I am talking about. Of course, not using the words that I have used now, but in academic language—that is the point, Comrade Pyvovarov."[204]

The meeting closed with a decision to publish the dictionary because it was an important work, with the condition that several new authors be included on the editorial board and several entries deleted. However, the dictionary was never published.

Skaba again proved himself a champion of Soviet orthodoxy at a meeting of Party members in the SPU and Ukraine's Union of Artists held on 25 April 1961. After formally complimenting the newest Lenin Prize

---

202 Ibidem, ark. 10.
203 Bunin's writings were forbidden after he left Bolshevik Russia in 1917, but were accepted again after Stalin's death.
204 TsDAHOU, f. 1, op. 1, spr. 5373, ark. 19.

winner, Mykhailo Stelmakh (1912-83), Skaba called the audience's attention to its duties toward the Party.

> The Party's call to strengthen the ties or literature and art with the lives of the people has a great significance. With unusual strength this call sounded after the Twentieth Congress of the Party [CPSU]. It has played a major role in the reunion of all creative forces around the Party—a reunion of attitudes of those who unselfishly serve the Party and the people.[205]

Skaba urged the writers and artists not to sit at home but to see what was going on, be inspired by current affairs, and devote attention to the working class and the "friendship of peoples" of the Soviet Union. In his long and pompous speech, only one line was dedicated to a revision of the past directives of Stalinist culture: "Life often brings in correctives for what yesterday was considered indisputable."[206] Under Mykola Pidhirny (Russian name: Nikolai Podgorny), the CC CPU's first secretary (1957–63), the Party tried to reaffirm the political leadership's control over "artistic workers," whose work was deemed very valuable in the efforts to redesign the Soviet state after the Twentieth CPSU Congress. The Party was prepared to fight all attempts at contesting Moscow's dominance in Ukraine. In the late 1950s and early 1960s the KGB uncovered several nationalist organizations, particularly in western Ukraine, where the resistance of the underground Ukrainian Insurgent Army (UPA) had remained significant.[207]

Interestingly, one Ukrainian underground organization differed from all of the others, in both its principles and the public manifestation of its struggles.

Levko Lukianenko and the Ukrainian Workers' and Peasants' Union

On 20 and 21 January 1961 four Lviv jurists—Levko Lukianenko, Ivan Kandyba, Stepan Virun, and Vasyl Lutskiv—were arrested, accused of having founded an illegal and dangerous anti-Soviet organization, the Ukrainian Workers' and Peasants' Union (Ukrainian acronym: URSS). In what became known as the Jurists' Affair, the prosecution of these URSS

---

205 Minutes of Skaba's speech, in TsDAHOU, f. 1, op. 1, spr. 5372, ark. 5.
206 Ibidem, ark. 6.
207 See Anatolii Rusnachenko, *Rozdumom i sertsem: Ukraïns'ka suspil'no-politychna dumka 1940–1980-kh rokiv* (Kyiv, 1999), 7–28.

members was handled quietly and therefore did not affect other members of the local intelligentsia. Nonetheless this organization's character and the fame it received about five years later make it a vital facet of the *shistdesiatnytstvo* movement.

The leader of the URSS was Levko Lukianenko (1928–2018), later an influential politician in independent Ukraine. In 1994 he published the first of many volumes of memoirs of his life as a dissident in the hope that they would be of use to the country's new leaders.[208] But these writings do not clearly illuminate the trajectory of Lukianenko's political and cultural development. For example, documents from the 1960s do not always square with his later writings and sometimes even contradicted, providing different facts or interpretations. Let us consider these complexities and try to explain them.

The main source about Lukianenko's early life is a memoir he wrote in 1988, during his second period of imprisonment in the Siberian village of Berezovka. It was first published in 2005 in a small collection of documents concerning his life.[209] Lukianenko was born on 28 August 1928 in the village of Khrypivtsi, now in Horodnia Raion, Chernihiv Oblast, the first of three sons and a daughter. His father had only an elementary education, but he enjoyed expanding his knowledge through reading, especially books about Cossack history. Lukianenko's mother, who had attended secondary school, often sang traditional Ukrainian songs to him (including the prohibited Ukrainian national anthem, "Ukraine Has Not Yet Died") and passed her passion on to her son. Lukianenko made it clear in his writings that the family did not think highly of Soviet rule.

> Autumn 1943. Our family was in a trench in the garden, for the front was approaching as the Red Army advanced from the neighbouring village of Pivnivshchyna. My father was standing in the garden watching the grey mass move closer along the road. "The Russian horde is pressing forward again. Again we shall [be forced to] labour and labour, again we shall have to hand everything over—in vain. Again there will be famine and torture. Children, my children, again you are going to starve...." My father's lips began to tremble, he grimaced convulsively and shed bitter tears. "Divine punishment," he added and slowly walked from the garden to [our] cottage, as if

---

208 This goal in the introductions to each volume. The most explicit statement is in Levko Luk'ianenko, *Z chasiv nevoli: Sosnovka-7* (Kyiv, 2005), 8–9.
209 Idem, *Spovid' u kameri smertnyka* (Kyiv, 2005).

to the gallows. The 'new lords' opened the gate to the courtyard of my father, to his home, and to all of Ukraine, and my father did not dare say a word to them. Those few bitter tears dripped deep into my soul.[210]

During the war Lukianenko's father was conscripted into the Red Army and served in it until Germany's defeat. Young Levko was also drafted, in 1944, because he looked older than he was and did not have a birth certificate. During army training he befriended Vasyl Kotsiubera, a young man from Kyiv Oblast, who first told him about the Ukrainian nationalist resistance to Soviet authority. As Lukianenko admitted years later while in a prison camp, his reaction to this news was informed largely by his youth rather than any real political reasoning.

> If [Kotsiubera] had told me something about the struggle of the OUN and the UPA and had proposed that I join the underground [insurgency] with him, I would have gone. Other than a general idea, I did not know anything about the independence movement, but I would have gone with Vasyl out of fellowship with him, out of simple audacity, and perhaps partly out of the love of risk. Sometimes I blame myself for not having asked him, for I was merely a silent and devoted executor of his orders, like a dog. To tell the truth, I understood his requests as favours for a friend, not as orders.[211]

Lukianenko had no other ties with the world of Ukrainian nationalism or the resistance in Western Ukraine. He was sent off to serve with the Soviet troops occupying Austria and remained there from October 1945 to the summer of 1949. In 1948 Lukianenko attended a year-long mechanics course in Mödling, a city near Vienna, but he soon missed his homeland and applied to return to the Soviet Union to attend an auto-mechanics institute in the Azerbaijani city of Julfa. He recalled that "pleasant Austria charmed me with its high degree of civilization" and its high living standard. Soviet conditions were a stark contrast, as Lukianenko realized upon his return to the USSR. His first encounter there was with a group of hungry children: "I was astonished to see that their shoes and clothes

---

210 Ibidem, 8–9.
211 Idem, *Z chasiv nevoli*, bk. 2 (Kyiv, 2007), 111.

were of incredibly bad quality and [yet] cost so much more compared to those in Austria."[212]

According to Lukianenko, in discussions with his father he would single out Russian exploitation as the reason for the poor economic situation in Ukraine. Nevertheless he joined the Komsomol after he was demobilized in 1950 and embarked on a typical Soviet career. He aligned his participation in the Komsomol with his desire to fight poverty in Ukraine.

> In 1950, after spending some time at home, I came to this line of thought: since poverty is rampant both in Ukraine and at home, I have to fight for Ukrainian independence. That is the goal to which I will devote my life. Secondly, I will be able to achieve more if my profession is as powerful as possible ... Within the state, and as long as authority in the USSR is concentrated in the Party, my profession will have to be in a Party post. And as long as the Komsomol remains the only route into the Party for a young man, then I have to join the Komsomol.[213]

In the following years Lukianenko joined the Party, attended an evening school for Red Army officers, and changed his language of education from Ukrainian to Russian. In 1953 he passed the entrance exam for one of the most prestigious law faculties in the USSR, at Moscow State University (MGU). According to his memoirs, his choice to study there was linked to the need to acquire more knowledge about the enemy from within. The atmosphere at that university was heavily politicized in those years.

> The MGU dorm was a "mini Soviet Union," populated by students from many regions and many ethnic backgrounds. For all of them, life in Moscow, with its symphony orchestras and art galleries, the Bolshoi, and the Moscow Art Theatre, offered their first encounter with high culture and fine arts.... The students' daily existence was outwardly politicized. They attended numerous Komsomol meetings, where they were allowed to simulate "political democracy" by nominating their candidates and arguing their agenda (although the party and Komsomol leaders always supervised).... At the same time, the dictates of ideology began to exist separately from real life in their minds. This division allowed

---

212 Idem, *Spovid' u kameri smertnyka*, 10–11.
213 Ibidem, 13.

students to combine common sense and total faith in the Soviet regime and its propaganda.[214]

Lukianenko did not feel at home in this multicultural climate. In 1954 he married Nadia Buhaievska, a Ukrainian student of agriculture at Kyiv State University, whom he had met during the summer in his home village. The next two years seemed to pass without any remarkable occurrences. Khrushchev's secret speech was as much a shock for Lukianenko as it was for others. However, as he was officially a committed Communist, he tried to reconcile this apparent hypocrisy.

> The year 1956 changed the strategic conception of my struggle. First, it became hard for me to keep wearing the mask of an active Soviet Communist. The stronger the idea of Ukrainian independence became in me, the more I felt myself a stranger in civil society (and an underground society did not exist at that time). The hypocrisy of my position emerged through my activity as a Communist, and the moral burden became heavier and heavier for me. The only way out that I could see was to end my civic activity and admit my ideological status as an underground dissident. Thus my moral conflict ended and a relative harmony settled in my soul, for now no one could hold my ideas against me and say, "You were active as a Communist, but then you went against the Party." The hypocrisy was removed. I convinced myself of the necessity of Ukrainian independence, which was the most anti-Party of ideas, but openly I occupied the position of an extreme opponent and allowed myself to criticize Party policy, as far as it was considered acceptable in 1956–57. Therefore my licit position did not contradict my illegal goal but paved the way for it and helped it to avoid the risk of crossing the boundaries of what was permitted, as far as it was possible. (I considered it unnecessary to cross this line, because in Moscow the opposition in its positive component had a goal of allowing more democracy, but what was important for me was the separation of Ukraine from Russia, not the democratization of Russia. And besides, I wanted to finish university, [and] not be expelled before graduation).[215]

It appears that Lukianenko's first concern was to justify his decision to remain a Party member. This second *excusatio non petita*, when he had

---

214 Zubok, *Zhivago's Children*, 35 and 37.
215 Idem, *Spovid' u kameri smertnyka*, 14–15.

already stated that his enrolment was a means of reaching his anti-Soviet goal, cannot be easily dismissed. Lukianenko's desire to highlight 1956 as a turning point in his development may indicate that Khrushchev's secret speech and its consequences influenced the way Lukianenko viewed the Party more than he cared to admit. Otherwise we have to accept his nearly perfect duality as a devout Ukrainian nationalist who pretended to be a Communist so convincingly that he was able to enrol at the MGU.

Another of Lukianenko's reminiscences seems to preclude the latter statement. When telling the story of his encounter with a fellow university student, Lev Krasnopevtsev, in the prison camp, he wrote: "In 1957 I was a Communist and was in [my] fourth year of studies in the law faculty in Moscow." Lukianenko is recounting an incident he experienced in 1957, after the World Youth Festival in Moscow. A group of MGU students, headed by Krasnopevtsev, had become acquainted with several foreigners, with whom they exchanged addresses and reading materials and talked about the Soviet Union. The KGB accused these students of anti-Soviet activity and sentenced Krasnopevtsev to ten years in a prison camp. A meeting of the Party cell at the university was called, and there a KGB agent reprimanded the members for their lack of surveillance over their comrades. Lukianenko attended the meeting, and his reaction reveals his attitude toward the situation.

> I carefully listened to the accusations themselves, as well as the conversations of Krasnopevtsev and his friends with the foreign youth, including their exchanging addresses and agreeing to correspond, and I did not hear anything criminal. It seems they gave the foreigners some newspaper articles. *"Then what was criminal in their actions?"* This question beat against my brain. I put up my hand to ask the Chekist [KGB agent] precisely what crime the students had committed. I stood up a little bit. And looking around me, I saw on the other faces the same indignation that was displayed on the Chekist's face; my hand came back, and I sank down onto my chair. This idea flashed in my head: that they will perceive my doubt about the legality of the arrest as a defence of this group of students and banish me from the university. I very much wanted to finish university, and therefore I thought that I would put off my defence of democracy until I had graduated. And it was good that I refused to come to their aid. In another year I finished university, and three

years later I changed my life to be an advocate for freedom while in captivity in a prison camp.[216]

In his memoir Lukianenko writes that he decided to abandon his active commitment to the Communist Party as a result of this incident. But this does not tally with his self-portrayal as an experienced double agent. Rather, it shows him to have been a typical Soviet student who, became progressively disillusioned during the Khrushchev Thaw because of the contradictions between his ideals and everyday life in the USSR. I am not suggesting that Lukianenko did not have any national pride, but such feelings coexisted in him with an adherence to socialist ideals more than he was willing to remember after 1991.

Lukianenko's stay in Moscow reinforced in him a sense of exasperation as a Ukrainian. There he was frequently called a *"khokhol"* (a Russian derogatory term for a Ukrainian), but he could not respond by calling someone a *"katsap"* (a Ukrainian pejorative for a Russian) if he did not want to be accused of being a bourgeois nationalist. The Thaw's relative liberalization made many formerly forbidden books available in the capital's libraries, such as the writings of Georgii Plekhanov and Mykhailo Hrushevsky, which Lukianenko read avidly. In the Lenin State Library in Moscow, Lukianenko came across some issues of the Ukrainian journal *Haslo* published in Chernihiv in 1902, containing materials on the clandestine Revolutionary Ukrainian Party (RUP). He writes: "After listening for four years to professors criticizing all other parties except the CPSU as being anti-democratic and against the people, the materials from the RUP program astonished me with their democratic and socialist content."[217]

After graduating from the law school in 1958, Lukianenko returned from Moscow to Ukraine to work in Radekhiv Raion in Lviv Oblast, where he had agreed to take a job as a Party propagandist the previous summer. In September he moved there with his wife, and soon thereafter he began travelling around other raions. Because it presumed an active role within the Party bureaucracy, being a propagandist may seem a peculiar job for a self-professed nationalist. However, during his frequent travels as part of his job, Lukianenko had the opportunity to speak with local denizens

---

216 Lukianenko, *Z chasiv nevoli*, bk. 2, 222–23. The events involving the Krasnopevtsev group were considerably more complicated than Lukianenko reveals in his memoirs. See Hornsby, *Protest, Reform and Repression in Khrushchev's Soviet Union*, 102–107.
217 Luk'ianenko, *Spovid' u kameri smertnyka*, 17.

and ask them about their past and present situations. What he was told about the Second World War horrified him. "Their feelings exceeded all of my expectations: everyone, with the exception of a small handful of sycophants in each village, considered the [Ukrainian nationalist] insurgents and members of the underground organizations to be the knights of the national liberation cause, and at every opportunity [they] described to me their achievements, about the suffering in the countryside, and about the brutality and ruthlessness of the *moskali* [Russians]."[218] Moreover, Lukianenko himself witnessed incidents of cruelty that collective-farm directors inflicted upon the rural population already suffering from famine.

Through his job Lukianenko became acquainted with several colleagues who shared his concerns about the plight of Ukrainians. They included Stepan Virun, a fellow propagandist in Lviv Oblast; Vasyl Lutskiv, the manager of a village club; and Oleksandr Libovych, a land surveyor working for the Lviv administration. In 1960 Lukianenko, who had left his Party job to work in the legal sector, met Ivan Kandyba (1930–2002), a lawyer in Lviv; Yosyp Borovnytsky, an investigator working for the Lviv state prosecutor's office; and Ivan Kipysh, a *militsiia* (police) official in Lviv. All of them were born between 1923 and 1935, and four of them (Lukianenko, Virun, Lutskiv, and Borovnytsky) were Party members. Kandyba described this group in a subsequent appeal letter to the Soviet authorities: "We were individuals who saw many different outrages happening around us—mass violations of socialist law and of the political rights of citizens, as well as national oppression, Russian chauvinism on the rampage, mistreatment of the rural population, and many, many other abnormalities."[219] Lukianenko and Virun had the idea of forming an organized group or party with the goal of improving conditions in Soviet Ukraine. Virun described it thus:

> Working in Party and legal agencies, we could not remain indifferent to whatever was hindering [the country's] development, whatever caused people distress. We wrote about these problems in letters to newspapers and periodicals, as well as to the highest Party and Soviet organs. The absence of any response to our protests and the indifference of the aforementioned agencies compelled us [Lukianenko and Virun] to issue a pamphlet that examined the

---

218 Ibidem, 18.
219 Document no. 6 in Michael Browne, ed., *Ferment in the Ukraine* (Woodhaven, 1973), 60–61.

existing conditions in our country from a Marxist-Leninist point of view. It sharply criticized the years of famine and unjustified repressions—the years of the "personality cult," as it has been delicately called [concerning Stalin and Stalinism]. Our assessment of this period [in the pamphlet] did not diverge from the assessment given to it in official Party documents.[220]

The previous two quotes were extracted from letters of appeal written around 1966, when Lukianenko and Virun were in the same Mordovian prison camp and seeking reviews of their cases. They seem to be much more consonant with the spirit of the program of the URSS (and with the "Notes" described below) than with Lukianenko's memoirs.

The group (without Libovych, Kipysh, and Borovnytsky) convened for the first time in the evening of 7 November 1960—the anniversary of the October Revolution—in Kandyba's apartment, where they were joined by Mykola Vashchuk, a student at the Lviv Communist Party School who turned out to be an informant for the KGB. There they discussed the URSS program, which Lukianenko wrote on the basis of his conversations with Virun.

With several verses by Taras Shevchenko as the epigraph, the document (first published thirty-four years later, in 1994) began by stating that after the turning point of 1953, the Soviet Union had revealed itself to be ill-suited for bringing about the "material security and political freedom" of Ukraine. More and more people were convinced of the necessity of fighting for Ukrainian independence, but this struggle needed a precise program and organization, which the URSS aimed to provide. In the preamble, the program stated that "the new stage of the struggle for independence substantially differs from the previous one, which ended nearly ten years earlier."[221] The meaning of the struggle had changed from that of the old independence movement, for the members of the URSS were now

> fighting for an independent Ukraine of the sort that, highly guaranteeing the material and spiritual needs of its citizens on the basis of an independent economy, would develop in the direction of communism, [and] secondly, in which all citizens would truly take advantage of political freedoms and determine the direction of

---

220 Document no. 4, in ibidem, 46.
221 "Rozshyrenyi proekt prohramy Ukraïns'koï robitnycho-selians'koï spilky (URSS)," in Levko Luki'anenko, *Ne dam zahynut' Ukraïni!* (Kyiv, 1994), 10.

Ukraine's economic and political development—this is our party's ultimate goal.[222]

According to this program, the URSS wanted to build an independent Ukrainian state where political freedoms would be respected and all citizens would collaborate to build communism. Since the Soviet constitution granted the right to secede from the USSR, the means of this struggle were defined as follows.

> ...The goal of this first stage of our struggle is securing the political freedoms necessary for organizing the entire Ukrainian people to fight for the creation of their independent national state.
> The methods for attaining this goal are peaceful and constitutional.[223]

The program's first two articles examined Ukrainian history, recounting how foreign overlords had continuously kept Ukraine in servitude, exploited its rich natural resources, and prevented its development. Lukianenko viewed the Soviet Union as a colonial empire in spite of his enthusiasm for the October Revolution, which held "great significance" in the "growth ... of the national-liberation struggle in the East."[224] The fourth article called attention to the presence of various national-liberation movements throughout the world. However, while in some regions the proletariat was still struggling against colonial forces only to surrender power to the bourgeoisie, Lukianenko thought that the working class should go one step further: "resolving the second national task—the overthrow of its own exploiters and the establishment of a socialist order."[225]

> ... The URSS stands on a foundation of international communism and shares the theory of revolutionary Marxism-Leninism.
> In the current period the Ukrainian national-liberation movement cannot be victorious without leadership from a party armed with the knowledge of Marxism-Leninism.
> Marxism-Leninism as the science about the laws of the development of nature and society, about the revolution of the

---

222 Ibidem, 11.
223 Ibidem.
224 Ibidem, 12.
225 Ibidem, 13.

exploited masses and national liberation, [and] about the victory of socialism and the construction of communism, is the URSS's ideational weapon. The study and mastering of this weapon is one of the more important tasks of every member of the URSS, because knowing Marxism-Leninism reveals the bottomless chasm between contemporary Soviet reality and those ideals for which the proletarians of all countries fought together with their leaders, Marx, Engels, and Lenin, [because] knowing Marxism-Leninism helps us to understand what kind of independent Ukraine we need and how more easily to achieve it.[226]

Contrary to Lukianenko's memoirs, the URSS's ideological framework was Marxism-Leninism, which was adopted as the ideal governing an independent Ukraine despite the perceived betrayal of the Soviet Union. Although Marxism-Leninism was the official ideology of the struggle, Ukrainian independence was still considered the only way for Ukrainian people to best manage their own assets and destiny. However, the actual move toward national independence was to be delayed until political freedoms had been achieved for all Soviet peoples. In the opinion of the program's authors, the Soviet Union was failing, in part, because the leadership of the Communist Party (CPSU) was unable to propose a general secretary of proper "political intelligence" after Lenin's death. This resulted in successive races for the Party's leader being won by brute strength. Just as power was concentrated in Stalin's hands within the Party, power was concentrated in the hands of the bureaucracy within society, giving birth to dictatorship. "The limitations to liberty that had already been introduced in 1917 and directed against the 'exploitative' classes were not abolished even after the destruction of the last exploitative class, the kulaks. On the contrary, these limitations have been used against the workers themselves for a long time."

The lengthy eighth article is dedicated to illustrating the conditions of "colonialism" under which Ukraine existed within the Soviet Union, with a focus on economics, politics, and culture. Though reaffirming friendship with the Russian people, the program states that real friendship is only possible when grounded in equality, and it accuses the predominantly Russian leadership of the CPSU of betraying its own ideology.

---

226 Ibidem, 14.

> Marxism-Leninism, which is the official ideology of the CPSU, demands that the national question must be always and everywhere resolved not from the point of view of the interests of a neighbouring or other nation or group of nations, but by the people of the given nation. But the CC CPSU will never offer the question of Ukrainian independence to the Ukrainian people for determination. It is all too aware that the day when the Ukrainian people raises its hand to determine this question would be the day of Ukraine's secession from inclusion in the USSR. As for Marxism-Leninism's just demands, the Russian leadership acknowledges them on paper but acts in practice according to the motives of its [personal] benefit.[227]

The program goes on to assert that national liberation is dependent on the achievement of a worldwide socialist revolution and the internationalist character of the URSS, and it attacks the privileges of the Soviet *nomenklatura*. The fifteenth paragraph reaffirms that ultimate power in industry should be in the hands of the workers, not the bureaucracy: "Communism is the bright future of humankind. But the Party-Soviet bureaucracy transformed this most noble idea into an object of speculation." The Party is further accused of permitting the Soviet leadership to neglect improving workers' everyday lives: "It highly values work but does not value the worker himself at all."[228]

The accusatory tone becomes stronger in the sixteenth paragraph, where Lukianenko examines rural life and blames the CPSU for the Soviet Ukrainian famine of 1933. He claims that just in that year three million inhabitants of Soviet Ukraine were starved to death so that there would be "strengthening of union [inter-republican] ties"

> In the revolution [of 1917] the peasantry fought [for ownership of] the land, but it does not possess it at all. It is not land that serves the peasants, but, on the contrary, the peasants became transformed into an appendage of the land [owned] by the state (Party), and therefore the Party-Soviet leadership is more concerned with the collective farmers' production than with the collective farmers.[229]

---

227 Ibidem, 20.
228 Ibidem, 30.
229 Ibidem, 31.

Lukianenko condemned the organization of labour in the rural economy and accused the Soviet state of lying about the achievements and wealth of agriculture in the USSR.

The program's conclusion re-emphasized that the URSS's goal was to continue the struggle that Marx, Engels, and Lenin had led. It quoted the Soviet Constitution and the Criminal Code of the Ukrainian SSR to indicate that the goal was constitutional and not criminal, and that the means of achieving it would absolutely non-violent.

Lukianenko recalls that the group's members had a brief discussion after first reading the program, and that during it everyone was in agreement about its two main points: (1) the struggle had to be non-violent, and (2) democratization had to be the primary goal because a widespread campaign for an independent Ukraine could be conducted only in conditions of freedom and democracy. Otherwise the feedback was that the program was too blunt, and Lukianenko was asked to write a second draft that emphasized democratization of the country as the main goal.[230]

The references to Marxist-Leninist ideology in the program's first draft are indisputable, and the call for national independence is interwoven with the problem of democratic freedoms and with social issues. Ukraine's poor economic conditions are ascribed to the Soviet leadership's betrayal of Marxist-Leninist principles. The ideological framework of the URSS was much the same as that of the *shistdesiatnyky*. But its members' educations and professions inspired them to seek a more concrete action plan, and this spurred them to found a political organization. In 1966, recounting the discussion that ensued after the reading of the draft program, Lukianenko wrote:

> During the conversation on 6 November 1960, members of the group discussed the question of what theory we intended to use as the basis of our work. This question was raised in order to focus attention on the importance of theory, not because we suspected there to be supporters of some other (theory) [or] philosophy among us. We had all been brought up in the spirit of Marxism-Leninism, and therefore we unanimously agreed in the course of our conversation that we ought to be guided by Marxist-Leninist theory

---

230 "Vstupne zauvazhennia,' in Luk'ianenko, *Ne dam zahynut' Ukraïni!* 35.

when working to eliminate illegal [Soviet] limitations on democratic liberties.[231]

This declaration seems to suggest that for Lukianenko's generation—and perhaps for the entire 1960s generation—Marxism-Leninism was a sort of "transcendental structure" through which people saw social reality. The Lukianenko who emerges from what he wrote in the 1960s is very different from the Lukianenko we see in his works published after 1991. The gulf between the two widens as we take his "Notes" into consideration.

In a Lukianenko wrote in 1966, he describes his political evolution between 1959, when he was absolutely convinced of need for an independent Ukraine, and 1960.

> As a result of examining the Soviet reality, in 1960 I came to revise the earlier conclusion reached by the [URSS] draft program and began to think that it was not independence of the Ukrainian SSR that was essential for improving the lives of the people, but rather the elimination of bureaucracy. And it seemed to me that bureaucracy could only be eliminated by giving greater scope to socialist democracy. I discussed this question with Virun and [Ivan] Kandyba even before our meeting on 6 November 1960, and as a result the URSS draft program was rejected on 6 November 1960. We then turned to the formation of a lawful organization, the purpose of which would be to remove illegal limitations on citizens' rights. In compiling the new draft program, it was proposed that we incorporate only the paragraph dealing with democratization from the rejected draft.[232]

One could argue that because Lukianenko wrote these words in his letter appealing the verdict of a criminal trial, he was unlikely to admit to having committed any crime. However, because this letter's real audience was not the Soviet authorities but the readers of *samvydav*, more sincere and unrestrained writing was needed. Another version of the meeting of 6 November 1960 is provided by the "Notes" that Lukianenko wrote after the meeting in order to prepare a new draft of the URSS's program. The "Notes" were not intended for anyone else besides him. Contrary to what Lukianenko wrote in his memoirs, they confirm the progressive

---

231 Document no. 2 in Browne, ed., *Ferment in the Ukraine*, 40.
232 Ibidem, 37.

"democratization" of his thinking. According to his "Notes," after the reading of the draft program those present quickly dismissed it as too nationalistic. The subsequent discussion of how the program ought to be constructed focused on three crucial issues: identifying the group's ideology, defining the goal of its struggle, and determining how this goal might be achieved.

On the point of ideology, Kandyba dismissed Marxism-Leninism because it "had become loathsome to the people."[233] This claim kindled an impassioned debate. Lukianenko's summary of the meeting suggests that those present agreed that the Soviet people could be divided into two categories. The first category, the majority of whom were workers and peasants, consisted of those who did not have the opportunity to study the texts of Marxism-Leninism. The meeting's participants attendants posited that because all changes in the autocratic Soviet Union were publicly aligned with Marxism-Leninism, the people could and often did attribute harmful policies to Marxist-Leninist ideology. On the other hand, the second category of people were those who had studied Marxism-Leninism and understood that Soviet society did not encapsulate the true nature of this ideology.

> Marxism-Leninism, being a powerful weapon for comprehending social processes, gives [us] the possibility to understand that Soviet society is not that society that all of advanced humankind dreamed about and which the peoples of the former Russian Empire fought for with such heroism and self-sacrifice.[234]

Despite the fact that the Soviet leadership exploited a false Marxism-Leninism as a means of honing the methods and forms of exploiting peoples, the group asserted that its members, "who seek to improve the people's destiny, should continuously study the theory of Marxism-Leninism and convey its true content to the people, expose the hypocrisy and mendacity of the bureaucratic leadership,[and] demonstrate with concrete examples the contradictions between, on the one hand, the CPSU's activity and its slogans, its words, in practice and, on the other, the principal ideas of Marxism-Leninism."[235]

---

233 "Notatky uchasnyka 1-oï narady spilky borot'by za demokratiiu," in Lukianenko, *Ne dam zahynut' Ukraïni!* 36.
234 Ibidem, 37.
235 Ibidem, 39.

An independent Ukraine was part of a broader program whose main objective was the satisfaction of material needs and the exercise of all democratic freedoms and rights, to be achieved by "broadening the sovereignty of the people." Restoring democracy meant improving the government in every sphere of activity:

> ... [D]emocracy is necessary not only for managing the economy and satisfying the people's material needs more rationally than they are now; it is [also] necessary in order to satisfy the people's spiritual needs, many of which can only arise under the conditions of democracy.[236]

Only democracy could ensure a conducive environment for the development of the Ukrainian nation. The struggle for independence became a practical consequence of the achievement of real democracy, a goal that was at the centre of the meeting's discussion.

All of the participants agreed that since the goal of their struggle was implementation of the rights and freedoms guaranteed in the Soviet Constitution, the means of the struggle should be constitutional and peaceful. The group acknowledged the problematic aspects of this method: the struggle for implementing the Constitution had to be conducted underground, for the Soviet authorities would not tolerate any public discourse on this issue. However, to achieve any success the group had to try to broaden and circulate its ideas as far as possible. Several methods of disseminating the group's mandate were suggested for inclusion in the revised draft program. URSS members could inform the people by distributing issues of *Nashe slovo*, a Ukrainian newspaper published in Poland. Reading a Ukrainian newspaper published abroad, where the press was decidedly freer, would open the eyes of many Ukrainians to their enslavement. "It is indispensable to familiarize the people, especially the youth, with literature that is now being printed bit but was forbidden earlier, especially with historical literature." Lastly, the group resolved to encourage the use of Ukrainian and convince the working class of the need for broader democratization of society. This could be achieved by "[d]ispatching delegations, sending petitions (letters signed by a significant number of people), and, most simply, the mass mailing of individual letters."[237] This last point is particularly significant,

---

236 Ibidem, 41.
237 Ibidem, 42–43.

because these methods would become the primary tools that the older *shistdesiatnyky* would use from 1961 on.

As this analysis has shown, the "Notes" contradict the idea of a disenchanted Lukianenko. Instead they illustrate his involvement in a neo-Leninist group and his desire to democratize his country. His worries about the proper development of the Ukrainian nation coexisted with his aspirations to freedom, but they were not the primary focus of the URSS's subsequent actions.

The group's second meeting, scheduled for 22 January 1961, never took place. On 20 January the KGB arrested Ivan Kandyba, and the following days saw the detention of all of the other members. Soviet prosecutors and special agents did not have any qualms about intimidating those arrested during questioning. Vasyl Lutskiv recalls that he was forced to confess his anti-Soviet activity and denounce Lukianenko under the threat of physical harm.[238] The illegal conduct of the questioning was recounted in letters that URSS members wrote in 1966 to the Soviet authorities. Kandyba recalls that

> They planted their agents in each of our cells.... All the agents posed as Ukrainian nationalists who had been arrested in some imaginary case. They continuously tried to provoke [discussions] about various anti-Soviet topics, told us of various fear tactics that KGB agencies were capable of using against prisoners, and said that the only means of avoiding various torture was to admit one's crimes and repent; they also employed other methods of provocation.[239]

Lukianenko's memories of his time in prison are also illuminating and do not spare any bitter irony.

> [The KGB undercover agent] told me all sorts of horror stories about Chekist activities, in his attempt to make me believe that I had left my civil rights at the door and that here—in remand solitary—the Chekists could do with me as they liked. [It was suggested to me that] the best way for me to behave under these circumstances, therefore, was not to insist on the truth but to convince the investigating agents that I repent; in order to substantiate this, I would have to sign any testimony presented to me by the investigator.... He tried to sow in my mind the seeds of hatred for

---

238 Document no. 3 in Browne, ed., *Ferment in the Ukraine*, 43–45.
239 Document no. 6 in ibidem, 64.

the security agencies and Soviet rule in general. Attempts were later made in the investigator's office to spur such hatred on my part. But I did not give in ... Strangely enough, the KGB Administration for Lviv Oblast did everything first to educate me in an anti-Soviet spirit, and then to punish me. Although they failed in respect to the former, the latter was carried out with a vengeance.[240]

The prisoners' trial took place behind closed doors, and there on 20 May 1961 the judges sentenced Lukianenko to death and Kandyba to eleven years, Lutskiv, Virun, and Libovych to ten years, and Borovnytsky and Kipysh to seven years in prison camps. A shocked Lukianenko somehow found the strength to organize an appeal, which took place on 20 July and reduced his sentence to fifteen years of incarceration.

Lukianenko and his fellow prisoners were sent to a prison camp in the Mordovian ASSR. The Soviet public remained completely unaware of their destiny at least until 1965–66, when the first wave of repressions against the *shistdesiatnyky* would provide Lukianenko with an unexpected opportunity to communicate with the outer world.

The perceptions of the significance of Lukianenko's and his friends' political actions differ substantially between the documents written in the 1960s and his post-1991 writings. Unfortunately, the other URSS members did not leave any memoirs to compare with Lukianenko's. The reasons for this difference in perception will be explained below, in our description of the reality of the prison camp and Lukianenko's encounters with the old and new generations of Ukrainian nationalists. At this point, it is possible to agree with Heorhii Kasianov's assessment that the Lukianenko affair

> testifies to the beginning of a new phase of the opposition movement, whose members did not exclude themselves from the Soviet system. For the first time in Soviet-era Ukraine, a determined group of intellectuals tried to unite in order to implement a political alternative within the framework of the existing political system and on the basis of current legislation. It is interesting that simultaneously a part of the nationally oriented intelligentsia, morally alienated from the existing order, was growing within the Soviet-Party structures. Evidently this was a general trend in the opposition movement.
>
> One must conclude that the members of the URSS aimed to defend their civil rights and demanded respect for the legality of their

---

240 Document no. 2 in ibidem, 34.

intentions from the [Soviet] law-enforcement offices. This was done long before the first groups for the defence of human rights made their appearance in the USSR.[241]

***

As we have seen, after Stalin's death in 1953 the Ukrainian SSR followed Moscow down the road of de-Stalinization. The dictator's demise allowed the strengthening of local powers in the Communist Party as well as in the cultural sphere, and in Ukraine a second Ukrainianization occurred, albeit a weaker one. Khrushchev's denunciation of the Stalin personality cult was seen as the last straw that pushed Party members and regular citizens alike to criticize the Soviet authorities well beyond the limits accepted by the Soviet leadership. Among writers, artists, and university workers, the revelations of the Twentieth CPSU Congress caused a resurgence of national pride and often provoked more troublesome questions about the legitimacy and nature of Soviet power.

The Party leadership was able to contain this limited unrest with measured violence, rebuking nonconformist intellectuals and punishing rebellious students. The Party's hold on intellectual workers was quite firm, as the low number of negative reactions to the 1958 educational reforms indicates. Nevertheless, the Party was conscious that a substantial change was needed in order to recast the terms of the social compromise. The creators of culture were provided with more freedom of expression: many new journals and periodicals were started, and Oles Honchar was appointed the new secretary of the SPU to manage this transformation.

Honchar's difficult task was to govern a new generation of intellectuals that was proving to be a threat to the Soviet establishment. They were writers and artists born in the early 1930s and largely of rural origin. Educated entirely in Soviet institutions, they were convinced of the need to reform the Soviet system, but did not dare to question it. On the contrary, they were often Komsomol activists and strong believers in the justice of Marxism-Leninism. Thoroughly disappointed with the state of Ukrainian culture, they promoted a new universe of values. Attention to the individual and respect for truth were paramount. In their efforts to improve their writings and their art, these intellectuals understood that

---

241 Both quotes from Kas'ianov, *Nezhodni*, 44 and 45.

means of expression and language, particularly the Ukrainian language, played key roles. The movement acquired a specific tone of national consciousness, strictly interconnected with socialist ideals. Innovative writers interacted with each other but still operated as individuals, and it was Les Taniuk's foundation of the Club of Creative Youth (KTM) that provided the young intellectual circles of the capital with a common place to gather. The high cultural affinity of the KTM's members was buttressed by their personal friendships, giving birth to the idea of the *kompaniia*. The KTM was a hybrid — a private group of friends who founded an organization with the objective of addressing the public. This was a fundamental step, for Soviet rhetoric urged youth to play an active role in society. Such civic engagement should be seen as an outcome of Soviet education.

The Soviet establishment vacillated between trying to co-opt the movements into its ranks and file (as the KTM's affiliation with the Komsomol shows) and harbouring a profound distrust of the group's claims of independence. The KTM's strong attractiveness and its capacity to influence resulted in an unexpected widening of the movement, and its mature initiatives took place during the 1960s, thus earning its members the name *shistdesiatnyky*. The *shistdesiatnytstvo* movement acquired new members, new goals, and also internal differences. The dialectic of mutual mistrust and a shared desire for recognition characterizes the behaviour of both the *shistdesiatnyky* and the Soviet authorities. This dialectic is the central question of the next chapter.

Chapter Two

The *Shistdesiatnyky* Address the Nation (1961–68)

> Ось у цьому дусі – в дусі комуністичного інтернаціоналістського світовідчування, в дусі розуміння неповторної цінності кожного національного життя і його невичерпних можливостей, а не в дусі зневажливого і бездумного нехтування ними в ім'я бюрократичного "единообразия" та "передовой русской культуры" – і годиться виховувати молодь нашої країни. Це й тільки це може бути запорукою справжньої дружби рівноправних народів, запорукою збереження і примноження величезних національних багатств, щасливо поєднаних у нашому Союзі, запорукою незрівнянної розмаїтості майбутнього духовного життя в комуністичному світі.*

Ukraine's Union of Writers against Russification

The years following the denunciation of Stalin's personality cult saw the birth of many new Ukrainian newspapers and periodicals—products of the rebirth of cultural debate. However, the growing number of Ukrainian periodicals should not be interpreted as a strengthening of Ukrainian language and culture. Although publications in Ukrainian had increased since the end of Stalinism, their circulation and press runs were

---

* Ivan Dziuba, *Internatsionalizm chy rusyfikatsiia?* (Kyiv, 2005), 82. ["It is in this spirit, in the spirit of a Communist Internationalist world view, in the spirit of comprehension of the unique value of each national life and of its inexhaustible possibilities—and not in the spirit of a disdainful and thoughtless neglect of these values in the name of bureaucratic 'uniformity' and the 'dominant Russian culture'—that the youth of our country should be brought up. This and only this can guarantee genuine friendship between equal peoples, can guarantee the preservation and increase of the immense national values fortunately united in our [Soviet] Union, and guarantee incomparable variety in the future spiritual life of the Communist world" (Ivan Dzyuba, *Internationalism or Russification? A Study in the Soviet Nationality Problem* [New York, 1974], 48–49)].

constantly decreased in favour of analogous Russian publications.¹ Often the same journal was published in separate Ukrainian and Russian editions, with the latter enjoying wider circulation, inducing readers to purchase the Russian version due to its greater availability.² The number of copies of newspapers in Ukrainian per citizen was also well below the standards of other Soviet republics. For example, in 1962 there were 536 such copies for every 1,000 Ukrainian citizens, compared to 757 in Lithuania, 967 in Latvia, and 1,090 in Estonia.³ As Roman Szporluk pointed out, the scarcity of Ukrainian publications, including literary periodicals such as *Literaturna hazeta*, was more acute in regions where demand for them was greater—namely, in rural areas. He argued that this scarcity was a major factor in the Russification of predominantly Ukrainian-speaking peasant population, such as in the Donbas.⁴

In contrast to the institutionalized Russification of publications in Soviet Ukraine, Ukrainian-language periodicals published in the West by Ukrainian émigré intellectuals and organizations were able to function freely without censorship and Russification pressures. Of particular importance was the Munich-based monthly *Suchasnist'* (Contemporaneity, founded in 1961)—one of the most influential Ukrainian cultural and intellectual journals of the twentieth century. *Suchasnist'* occasionally published essays dedicated to the state of the press in Soviet Ukraine, many of them by Pavlo Chernov (the pen name of Roman Szporluk), who used official data to document the ongoing Russification of Ukraine.

In hindsight, among Soviet Ukrainian periodicals of that period a special significance should be assigned to *Ukraïns'ka mova v shkoli* (The Ukrainian Language in the School[s]). Founded in 1951, this journal played an important role in the formalization of Ukrainian orthography and syntax and in the teaching of Ukrainian during the 1950s and 1960s. Its overall impact was positive but mitigated by the overwhelming predominance of Marrism in Ukrainian linguistics. In West Germany, the late Ukrainian émigré linguist Oleksa Horbach (aka Olexa Horbatsch) wrote that Marrism was useful for the Russian Communist Party in its

---

1 Iar Slavutych, "Naklady seriinykh vydan' na Ukraïni," *Suchasnist'*, 1964, no. 5: 68–77.
2 Pavlo Chernov, "Presa URSR za mynule desiatyrichchia," *Suchasnist'*, 1962, no. 3: 73–84.
3 Idem, "Shcho chytaiut' u nas na Ukraïni?" *Suchasnist'*, 1963, no. 11: 57–68.
4 Idem, "Do natsional'nykh vidnosyn v URSR: Misto, mova i presa skhidnikh oblastei," *Suchasnist'*, 1964, no. 6: 73–89.

efforts to cement the multiracial and multilingual conglomerate of peoples that survived the old tsarist empire into one "Soviet people," and also in order to halt the de-Russification of various non-Russian republics. This was due, in part, to Marrism's rejection of the "purists'" struggle against the progressive Russification of the languages of the USSR as a "retrograde" phenomenon.[5]

Soviet Russification also reached the highest levels of academia. According to official data, from 1945 to 1962 all twelve of the dissertations defended in the Ukrainian SSR for the degree of doctor of laws (the highest academic rank in the Soviet system) were written in Russian. As another example, among the 183 candidate of sciences dissertations defended at Lviv State University, only three were in Ukrainian.[6] According to Horbach, the distribution of abstracts to candidate-level dissertations was curtailed, and those that were printed were exclusively in Russian— Ukrainian was used only when the subject was strictly Ukrainian.[7] Only one institution in the Ukrainian SSR, the republic's Academy of Sciences, was permitted to grant the academic qualification of doctor of sciences, and candidates were discouraged from writing in Ukrainian by the fact that the academy's members were extremely conservative. The three doctors of science in Ukrainian philology who received their degrees during the years 1956–60 defended their dissertations in Leningrad and in Moscow.[8]

The backwardness of the Ukrainian cultural environment was further highlighted by strained relations with neighbouring Poland. However, the ten-day celebrations of "Polish Literature in Ukraine" in October 1962 were a great success, judging by the book runs: Poland, with ten million fewer inhabitants than the Ukrainian SSR, published ten million more books than Ukraine, whose 85 million copies were predominantly political and literary "trash" (*makulatura*).[9] A comparison with Ukrainian periodicals abroad points up the Russocentrism of publishing in Soviet

---

5   Horbach, "Pisliavoienni movoznavchi publikatsiï v URSR," 81. Nikolai Marr was a Georgian linguist whose pseudo-scientific Japhetic theory was very popular under Stalinism. See Vladimir M. Alpatov, *Istoriia odnogo mifa: Marr i Marrizm* (Moscow, 1991).
6   Volodymyr P. Stakhiv, "Rusyfikatsiia nauky, literatury, pobutu," *Suchasnist'*, 1965, no. 6: 119–20.
7   The abstracts (*referaty*) of Soviet dissertations were usually twenty pages long and distributed to libraries throughout the USSR.
8   Horbach, *Pisliavoienni movoznavchi publikatsiï v URSR*, 94.
9   Volodymyr P. Stakhiv, "Dekada pol's'koï knyhy na Ukraïni," *Suchasnist'*, 1963, no. 1: 124–26.

Ukraine. The annual almanac *Ukraïns'kyi kalendar* (Cracow) contained far more Ukrainian national content than its counterparts in Ukraine. Its 1963 issue, for example, was dedicated to Ukrainian language issues and included articles about Lenin and Mykola Skrypnyk as promoters of Ukrainian.[10]

These problems were the focus of the Third Plenum of the SPU in Kyiv on 10 and 11 January 1962, which was crowned by a limited victory of its reform-minded members. The meeting was chaired by Platon Voronko (1913–88), a Stalin Prize recipient, who invoked the SPU's benevolence toward the new generation of writers. He praised the younger poets Ivan Drach, Vitalii Korotych, and Mykola Vinhranovsky, calling them *shistdesiatnyky* and noting that they "wrote out loud" and comprised a generation of which one could be proud. He assured those present of the "political reliability" of the *shistdesiatnyky*, stating that they were firmly grounded in Communism.[11]

Another speaker, Ihor Muratov (1912–73), was more skeptical about the new generation. He said: "I read [Ivan] Dziuba's recent pointed essays, and I am rather certain that the discovery of the talented Hryhorii Tiutiunnyk is of much greater importance than [Dziuba's] reviews of witty variations on a theme in some sentimental works he selected."[12] Muratov lamented that after the 1958 educational reforms parents wanted their children to be taught only scientific topics, and only in Russian. He also complained that Ukrainian schools for his children could not be found in Kharkiv.[13] For his part, Pavlo Zahrebelny (1924–2009) lamented the unremitting dullness of Ukrainian literature, while better authors such as Drach and Dziuba faced difficulties in disseminating their works. He noted that although the content of the literary periodicals *Prapor*, *Literaturna hazeta*, and *Dnipro* had improved, they were issued in smaller print runs. He was echoed by the literary scholar and translator Oleksandr Diachenko (1919–84): the annual circulation of Ukrainian books had

---

10   Despite what happened in Soviet Ukraine, throughout the 1960s *Ukraïns'kyi kalendar* continued publishing many submissions by the *shistdesiatnyky*, including pictures of Alla Horska's life-size, stained-glass window portrait of Taras Shevchenko (see below) and poems in both the original Ukrainian and in Polish translation. During my interview of Ivan Dziuba, he affirmed that foreign publications—especially the journal *Duklia* published in Prešov, Slovakia— often helped them to make ends meet.

11   See the minutes of the plenum in TsDAMLMU, f. 590, op. 1, spr. 481, ark. 6–9.

12   Ibidem, ark. 11.

13   Ibidem, ark. 13–14.

decreased from 15,000 to 5,000 copies, and in Moscow Ukrainian literature was unheard of.

The prominent literary critic and scholar Leonid Novychenko (1914–96) also celebrated the talent of the *shistdesiatnyky*. After briefly eulogizing Mykhailo Stelmakh's most recent novel, he praised the new generation, especially Ivan Drach and Lina Kostenko, claiming that she had learned her craft from Taras Shevchenko.

> Speaking generally about the prose and poetry of the new generation, I say that this output, these recent aesthetic achievements for which we have long struggled, is the fruit of an awareness on the part of writers of the role of their own creative "self," of their right to artistic subjectivity, of their right to artistic self-education, to internal artistic freedom—qualities that are lacking in some writers.[14]

Ivan Dziuba was the last to speak at the plenum. There he essentially presented an outline of the psyche of his generation of artists.

> I have tried to keep in mind the high-principled conditions under which my generation grew up. On the one hand, our tempers were fostered by the schools. Their unwavering positions, their lessons—all we came in contact with there—encouraged us to aim for the highest Communist ideals, inspiring us and pushing us away from the passive life of the philistine; [and] school taught us to focus on serving society. But at the same time, the specific conditions at school did not demonstrate with sufficient strength the forms of this social service. Neither school nor university were able to escape the ideological contradictions that had arisen as a result of the [Stalin] cult of personality.
>
> Let's say that we believed, and still believe, in Communist ideals. But at the same time, we have seen how an injustice was committed against us under the cover of Communism. We could not understand why it was so, and our educators were also unable to provide an answer to the question.
>
> Comrades, let us imagine the pristine, high-principled, psychological atmosphere in which our honest youth developed, and we will see in it a wide range of possible activity for the writer. Someone, perhaps, would ask why we are rummaging in these old things, in a time already past. But it is from that past that the present

---

14   Ibidem, ark. 60.

grows. And how can we understand the present if we have not dealt with our past?[15]

Dziuba affirmed the Communist-inspired school educations his generation had received, but, while not repudiating this cultural heritage, he did not refrain from remarking that the contradictions of Soviet society had not been explained to his generation. Ever a Communist, Dziuba addressed this failure as a possible subject for future literature, suggesting that writers should engage with these problems. The writer's duty was to tell the truth:

> When a reader of literature does not see in it the whole truth about life, he will not recognize whatever else is good and just in these writings, as he cannot come to terms with the fact that only a part of the truth has been revealed to him while another part has been hidden. If you hide half of the truth, then the rest will seem false to the reader as well. Therefore, if one adopts this point of view, literature must speak about everything.[16]

Dziuba identified this failure to tell the truth as the cause of the crisis in Ukrainian literature, suggesting that the "false" literature was so dishonest that it drove away readers. The new generation of poets, on the other hand, praised truth above all, and their success could be attributed to their willingness to tackle issues never addressed in Soviet literature since the rise of Stalinism. He added that the international dimension of Communist culture was misunderstood, arguing that promoting internationalism should not mean obliterating national cultures, and encouraged Ukrainian writers to study Ukrainian culture, both in their homeland and abroad. A writer ought not to be dismissed for simply expressing love for his own national culture. Dziuba named Ivan Drach as a poet who could cope with both truth and genuine national belonging.[17] His conclusions were supported by his mentor Andrii Klochchia, who agreed that the Twentieth and Twenty-Second CPSU Congresses had condemned the Stalin personality cult and brought the country back to Leninism. But Klochchia subtly attacked Dziuba for his partiality in

---

15 Ibidem, ark. 99.
16 Ibidem, ark. 103.
17 Ibidem, ark. 105–08.

evaluating the *shistdesiatnyky*, and he reminded him that true Ukrainian literature had also existed before their time.

Then it was Ivan Drach's turn to speak. He celebrated the new atmosphere in literature after its "suffocation" during Stalin's personality cult. Stating that artists now had many more possibilities for expression than they had in the past, he explained the new generation's world view as looking at prior art without the cultural burden of Stalinism. Drach underlined the need to cultivate a recognizable Ukrainian culture, and he identified Panteleimon Kulish and Maksym Rylsky as the best examples of past poetry. He also lamented the fact that Ukrainian culture was not spread throughout Ukraine, while in Paris one could go to the cinema on any given day and see a film by Oleksandr Dovzhenko.[18] Drach promoted the establishment of a research institute of Ukrainian literature similar to the Gorky Institute of World Literature in Moscow, and he expressed regret that contemporary Ukrainian novelists such as Yevhen Hutsalo (1937–95) and Volodymyr Drozd (1939–2003) had not achieved the fame of their Russian counterparts owing to the dearth of Russian translations of Ukrainian literature and to the low press runs of their books. According to Drach, Stalinism had blocked the cultural development of the average Soviet citizen, creating a gap between writers and their readers and undermining the future of literature.[19]

In his speech, the writer Borys Antonenko-Davydovych (1899–1994) addressed the shortcomings of life in the Ukrainian SSR: Ukrainian-speaking children were forced to attend Russian schools, where their performance was worse than that of native Russian speakers; in the collective farms the connection between authority and the Russian language was so strong that local collective-farm directors were compelled to use Russian when speaking to their subordinates; and actors performing in Ukrainian-language theatres often mispronounced words and stressed the wrong syllables because they were primarily, if not solely, Russian speakers. Antonenko-Davydovych believed that the consequences of the Stalin personality cult were still omnipresent, adding that, according to a popular saying, a tyrant's power imposed only hope for bread and fear for life.

---

18   Ibidem, ark. 148.
19   Ibidem, ark. 150.

> Fear for one's life and a hope to earn easy bread through calumny and lies. By lying to Stalin, singing praises to his superhuman quality and persuading him of it, we learned to lie in general. [Noisy applause.] And our lies have transformed themselves into inertia, and even, which is more frightening, into tradition … The Stalin cult of personality deprived literature of many of its functions, reducing it to the writing of odes—but, it seems to me, that is not the worst part: the worst is that only the declamatory functions have remained in literature. Where are its social functions? Where is the voice of literature as a signaler and an accuser?[20]

One of the last speeches was by Dmytro Pavlychko (b. 1929), who presented a more variegated and complex view. Ukrainian literature had lost readers, he argued, because youth were more interested in the West—a consequence of their disenchantment with the Stalin personality cult and ignorance of their own national culture. Pavlychko pointed out the need to publish the forbidden classics of Ukrainian literature, such as Volodymyr Vynnychenko, and reaffirmed the astonishing lack of Ukrainian translations of foreign works, which compelled Ukrainian culture into a forced provincialism. He urged his colleagues to write the true story of Ukrainian rural life, which remained untold. Finally, Yurii Zbanatsky (1914–94) put forward the question of writers' remuneration and its effect on literature: because they were paid according to the number of pages, writers tended to write more pages of lower quality rather than fewer pages of higher quality.[21]

The Oles Honchar's closing speech and the plenum's letter to the CPU expressed appreciation for the greater freedom the SPU was granted since the Party had modified its attitude toward literature and writers. Honchar insisted on strengthening the foundation for Leninist democratization and urged young writers not to isolate themselves but to share their problems with the rest of the community. The plenum's letter affirmed that real art is always internationalist but emerges through the knowledge of one's particular national culture. It encouraged the creation of less standardized and more "individualistic" literary characters.

> Today writers understand—and if they do not understand, they must!—that they, as contemporary men of letters, are expected to

---

20 Ibidem, ark. 156–57.
21 Pavlychko's and Zbanatsky's speeches are in ibidem, ark. 159–90.

provide not illustrations, but profound artistic generalization; not fictional tales about everyday economic actions, but genuine artistic revelation and unprecedented words about individuals. From our prose readers expect meaningful personal characters who are able to embody their epoch.[22]

The third plenum marked the victory of the *shistdesiatnyky*: the SPU acknowledged that their claims and concerns were shared by the entire artistic community. The presence of allusions to the 1932–33 famine in Soviet Ukraine by formerly repressed Antonenko-Davydovych and Pavlychko were signs of an openness to cultural and political revival. Lina Kostenko was proclaimed one of the most talented voices of Ukrainian poetry, and two *shistdesiatnyky*, Ivan Dziuba and Ivan Drach, were given the opportunity to take the podium and bring forward their artistic claims.

Ivan Drach (1936–2018) was born in the village of Telizhyntsi near the border of Kyiv and Vinnytsia Oblasts. He attended a rural school, qualified as a teacher of Russian, and joined the Komsomol. After serving in the Soviet Army (1955–58), he studied philology (1959–63) at Kyiv State University.[23] There he participated in a study group, named in memory of the poet Vasyl Chumak, of aspiring poets that was supposedly mentored by faculty but actually self-organized.[24] Drach achieved overnight fame with the publication of his poem "Knife in the Sun" in *Literaturna hazeta* on 18 June 1961. The poem expressed strong national sentiments and had many powerful scenes, in which Ukraine is portrayed as a mother grieving for her sons.

> And she began to dance.
> The devil wind
> spun around the black table.
> Her three sons wept
> from their bloodstained frames.
> One died near Berlin, one in a snowdrift

---

22   Ibidem, ark. 233.
23   Vasyl' Ovsiienko, "Ivan Fedorovych Drach," in *Mizhnarodnyi biohrafichnyi slovnyk dysydentiv kraïn Tsentral'noï ta Skhidnoï Ievropy i kolyshn'oho SRSR*, vol. 1, *Ukraïna*, part 1, compiled by Ievhen Zakharov and Vasyl' Ovsiienko (Kharkiv, 2006), 229–33.
24   The Borotbist revolutionary and poet Vasyl Chumak (1900–19) was shot by White Guards while trying to escape from custody. The acronym of the poets' study group was SICh (СІЧ), which, presumably intentionally, is a homonym of the Sich, the famous Zaporozhian Cossack stronghold on Khortytsia Island below the Dnipro Rapids in Ukraine's southern steppe. It was razed by Russians troops in 1775.

> somewhere near Warsaw, and the third
> officially by his own hand,
> during the black terror of thirty-seven.
> And their mother danced on the holy straw,
> danced round the planet, round the table:
>
> O sons, little sons,
> precious little cucumbers,
> little mop-headed boys,
> my own little songbirds.
>
> Hitler wanders over Ukraine,
> props a handmill on his knee:
> how can I crush you all
> and still escape from Stalin?²⁵

These lines, which hint at the suicides committed during the Yezhov Terror ("black terror") of 1937, were among the most contentious, along with those dedicated to Taras Shevchenko. After graduating from university, Drach continued writing poetry and took part in the KTM's poetry evenings, which brought him ever-increasing fame and infamy.²⁶

The National Question in the Club of Creative Youth

As Ivan Dziuba recalls, "The usual forms of the KTM's activity were literary-artistic meetings, especially literary evenings,"²⁷ and the star of them was Vasyl Symonenko. "Even during his lifetime Symonenko's poetry was very popular. When he arrived [in Kyiv] from Cherkasy and held open readings, they always caused a great sensation."²⁸ Nonetheless, at least in the beginning, the KTM had to compromise with the political regime.

> The youth were looking for any means for self-organization. As we had already organized many literary evenings, we tried to exploit various literary events and anniversaries to speak in public—at the institute or in factories or libraries. Each time we had to face the

---

25 Ivan Drach, *Orchard Lamps,* ed, Stanley Kunitz (New York, 1978), 61–62.
26 Drach later worked as a literary editor and screenwriter. In 1976 he received the Shevchenko State Prize for one of his poetry collections, and in independent Ukraine he was the first leader of the Popular Movement (Rukh) of Ukraine and a member of the Verkhovna Rada. He died on 19 June 2018.
27 Dziuba, *Spohady i rozdumy na finishnii priamii,* 508.
28 "Tsia knyzhka zminyla use moie zhyttia: : Rozmova z Ivanom Dziuboiu," 112.

consequences, but we were so imbued with passion that we simply looked forward to the next opportunity. On the other hand, the authorities knew that such a movement existed among the youth, and so what else could they think, of course, but that this movement could not be acting alone and that the establishment would have to take the initiative into its own hands, for this was the only way they could control what was happening.[29]

The Komsomol was not uniform in its restriction of the KTM's activities. Indeed, some members of this entity controlled by the political establishment supported the club.

> The first was the secretary of the Komsomol's Central Committee, Yevheniia Ivanivna Chmykhalo. The second was the secretary of the Komsomol's [Kyiv] Oblast Committee, Tamara Vasylivna Hlavak. Yevheniia Ivanivna was a spontaneous person, a genuine Communist and member of the Komsomol, but she also had discovered Ukraine on her own, at least a little bit. When she came across this youth movement, something for her was elucidated and she sincerely supported us. I think that to the depths of her soul she was on our side.[30]

With new members joining the KTM, its initiatives took on an increasingly national character throughout 1962 and 1963. The members proposed a series of public commemorations of Ukrainian writers—of Les Kurbas and Taras Shevchenko in 1962 and Ivan Franko and Lesia Ukrainka in 1963—which became forums for expressing popular discontent toward the regime. For example, the organizers of the May 1962 evening in commemoration of Les Kurbas asked participants to bring red carnations to the event and so honour him as a victim of Stalinism. The meeting lasted six hours, with participants commemorating the victims of the Gulag and attacking Stalin's legacy.[31]

The evening in memory of Lesia Ukrainka on 31 July 1963 was conceived as an alternative to the official celebrations. The KTM had received authorization to use the summer stage of Kyiv's Central Park, but when rumours spread that the meeting was to be an organized protest against the Soviet establishment, the Party revoked the permit.

---

29   Ibidem, 108–109.
30   Ibidem, 109.
31   Kas'ianov, *Nezhodni*, 20.

Nonetheless the commemoration did take place, and Dziuba wrote a memo to the SPU to explain its true intent.

The memo was one of the first *samvydav* documents to achieve renown and is worth analyzing, for "letters to the authorities" would become a common format of future *samvydav* documents. Dziuba explained that the evening was a joint collaboration between the KTM, the park management, the State Philharmonic, and the Theatre Society; and that the KTM was acting together with other state institutions and had obtained official authorization to hold the event. The banning of the meeting, however, was not conveyed through official channels, and although Dziuba had tried repeatedly to get in touch with the responsible authorities, they were all on vacation and thus unavailable. Even the meeting with Yevheniia Chmykhalo was futile, as she was about to resign and being transferred to Moscow. KTM members and some actors decided to hold the event in spite of the prohibition. When park staff turned off the power and did not let them on stage, they continued their performance in a nearby street.

Dziuba was summoned to report what had happened to the SPU. His report shows evidence of the clash between two mentalities—the union's "old" bureaucrats, concerned about the dangerous accusation of "bourgeois-nationalism," and the "young" intellectuals.

> Some union leaders clearly saw a "revolt" in the fact that, for instance, the event participants were biased, all from the same damned group ... One hears about this "group" time and time again, though it exists only in the small-minded imaginations of certain literary men. It is a real pity that the [constructive] ideas of these people are conflated with the aforementioned philistine gossip about "nationalists" and "opposition"; and so engaging with these ideas would not be recommended.[32]

Instead of apologizing, Dziuba illustrated how the KTM would operate, acquiescing to the establishment's requests for compromise as long as the authorities supported the club's initiatives. Even if the establishment refused to endorse or permit club activities, the KTM would continue to hold public meetings regardless of official prohibitions, for they considered such injunctions to be violations of their civil rights. Dziuba's letter shows how an initiative organized by several mainstream

---

32 Ivan Dziuba, "Poiasniuval'na zapyska," *Suchasnist'*, 1968, no. 8: 93.

bodies remained in the hands of the less law-abiding organizations even after it was forbidden, thus prompting the movement's radicalization.

The KTM's activities were not limited to memorial evenings. Les Taniuk staged plays by Mykola Kulish and Bertolt Brecht—both forbidden in the USSR—while Alla Horska and her associates organized exhibits of their artworks. Another KTM member, architectural historian Hryhorii Lohvyn (1910–2001), began organizing field trips to Ukraine's historical places, which soon became very popular. An upshot of these initiatives was the creation of a committee for the study of Stalinist repressions, which caused a sensation with its request to build a monument to victims of Stalinism in the Bykivnia Forest, a site of mass burials on the outskirts of Kyiv.[33]

During 1963 the opinion that KTM activities had become too dangerous began circulating. The club's members feared that it could be shut down, so they began collecting signatures on a petition supporting the existence of the KTM. Two of the most esteemed writers of the previous generation, Maksym Rylsky and Mykhailo Stelmakh, signed the petition, and the KTM was allowed to carry on. Taniuk was forced to resign as head of the KTM, however, and was replaced by the painter Viktor Zaretsky (1925–90), Horska's husband. But Taniuk unofficially continued controlling the KTM until its ultimate closure.[34] Starting in 1962, the KTM's position was increasingly weakened by the connection of several of its members with intellectuals belonging to the Prolisok Youth Club in Lviv.

The Prolisok Youth Club

The birth of the Prolisok Youth Club in Lviv was a direct consequence of the influence of Suchasnyk, its counterpart in Kyiv. In May 1962 Dmytro Pavlychko, Ivan Drach, Mykola Vinhranovsky, and Ivan Dziuba travelled to Lviv to organize several meetings at the city's university, whose then rector (1951–63), geologist Yevhen Lazarenko (1912–79), was an aficionado of Ukrainian poetry. The writers from Kyiv wanted to meet with local young intellectuals who were enthusiastic supporters of the KTM. Such young litterateurs in Lviv had already been meeting at the Young Authors' Room under the guidance of Rostyslav Bratun (1927–95),

---

33 Ibidem, 21; Dziuba, *Spohady i rozdumy na finishnii priamii*, 508; and Les' Taniuk, "Vbytyi talant," in *Alla Hors'ka: Chervona tin' kalyny. Lysty, spohady, statti*, ed. Oleksii Zarets'kyi and Mykola Marychevs'kyi (Kyiv, 1996), 162–63.

34 Dziuba, *Spohady i rozdumy na finishnii priamii*, 510–11.

were favourably impressed by the revelatory writings of the *shistdesiatnyky*,[35] and were as thirsty for new, "forthright" art as their Kyiv colleagues.

> The real education for artistically talented youth was to be obtained through literary-artistic societies. By establishing them in each raion's main town, in each village, at Lviv State University, and on the editorial boards of factory newspapers, I intended to show [the people] artistically talented young novelists, poets, and artists who offered an honest representation of current society, who did not imitate the famous old writers or copy the troubadours of the Communist era, or paint recurring Soviet reality in rosy colours or praise utopian ideals, which could lead Ukrainians into a dead end, to an abyss of impoverishment.[36]

A few months later Ivan Svitlychny went to Lviv to meet with this group in order to discuss the formation of a second club in Ukraine.

> Then, although I met Svitlychny for the first time, we immediately began talking about what actions would prove to be effective in our struggle with the Soviet authorities. While I was in favour of clandestine activity, Svitlychny believed instead that, in a country where denunciations were an element of state policy, only legal activity could produce successful outcomes. His conception of public action reminded me of the activity of our fellow compatriots in 1860.[37]

After this conversation with Svitlychny in Lviv, the brothers Mykhailo and Bohdan Horyn and other local intellectuals decided to establish a club similar to Les Taniuk's KTM. The club was founded in December 1962, while Taniuk and Alla Horska were in Lviv to stage Mykola Kulish's *Myna Mazailo*. According to Mykhailo Kosiv's records, in the days after the show

---

[35] Iurii Zaitsev, "Ti, shcho ne movchaly," in *U vyri shistdesiatnyts'koho rukhu: Pohliad z vidstani chasu*, ed. Volodymyr Kvitnevyi (Lviv, 2003), 79. The best analysis of the cultural evolution of post-World War II Lviv (including portraits of Lazarenko, Bratun, Bohdan Horyn, and others) is William J. Risch, *The Ukrainian West: Cultural and the Fate of Empire in Soviet Lviv* (Cambridge, 2011).
[36] Volodymyr Kvitnevyi, "Lytsari natsional'noho vidrodzhennia," in *U vyri shistdesiatnyts'koho rukhu*, 59.
[37] Mykhailo Horyn', "U nas bula velyka misiia," in *Bunt pokolinnia*, ed. Berdykhovs'ka and Hnatiuk, 201.

some people assembled in the Actors' Building, an offshoot of Lviv's Zankovetska Theatre,[38] with the intention of following in the footsteps of the KTM in order to avoid accusations of illegality. The new group requested and obtained official patronage from the Komsomol through its member, the literary critic Volodymyr Kvitnevy (b 1938). A graduate student in philology at Lviv State University, Mykhailo Kosiv (b. 1934), was elected president of the new Prolisok Youth Club. Its chosen name, derived from the Ukrainian name of the bluebell, invoked imagery of the Khrushchev Thaw and the desire for change. Bohdan Horyn was chosen the club's vice-president, and Kvitnevy took on the duties of secretary, including the difficult task of fostering relations with the Komsomol. Some fifty local literati, including the poet Ihor Kalynets (b. 1939), his wife Iryna Stasiv (1940–2012), the actor Bohdan Kozak (b. 1940), and the archeologist Larysa Krushelnytska (1928–2017) joined the new club, which received premises in the Actors' Building. Prolisok's members had a strong national consciousness because of the particular cultural development of Galicia, which had been incorporated into Soviet Ukraine just two decades earlier during the Second World War, and is reflected in their upbringing. The Horyn brothers serve as a typical illustration.

Mykhailo and Bohdan Horyn were born on 17 June 1930 and 10 February 1936, respectively, in Kniselo, a village southeast of Lviv in Polish-ruled interwar Galicia. One of their grandfathers had participated in the creation of the Western Ukrainian National Republic in 1919, and their father was a member of the OUN underground. Although their relationship with the Polish inhabitants of the village was friendly, Mykhailo remembers that politics was a taboo subject, and that his father used to argue with the Polish director of the local school.[39] Their mother, Stefaniia Hrek, was a cousin of Mykola Lebid, the leader of the OUN's Bandera faction and head of its security and foreign services during the Second World War. The brothers were raised with a strong sense of national awareness in a house where Ukraine's national symbol, the golden trident, hung on a wall. Their lives took a difficult turn when their father was sentenced to death by the Polish government at the start of the war; he managed to escape from prison and his fate only by chance. During the war both brothers received clandestine military from the UPA

---

38   Mykhailo Kosiv, "Prolisky vyrostaiut' z-pid snihu," in *U vyri shistdesiatnyts'koho rukhu*, 71–73.
39   Horyn', "U nas bula velyka misiia," 186–87.

but were not allowed to take part in combat because they were underage. Meanwhile, to avoid arrest and secure a better life for his family, their father abandoned his political activity and went to work in a sugar refinery in the nearby village of Khodoriv.[40] His wife and three sons joined him there after the war.

After graduating from a Soviet high school in 1949, Mykhailo enrolled in the Faculty of Psychology at Lviv State University. He was expelled in 1953 for refusing to join the Komsomol, but after Stalin died he resumed his studies once the university's rector, Yevhen Lazarenko, reinstated him because there was no official act of expulsion. Mykhailo then joined the Komsomol after all, graduated a year later,[41] and worked for the Lviv Oblast Inspectorate of Education until 1961, when he was admitted to the graduate program in psychology at the university.

From 1954 Bohdan Horyn studied philology at the same university. His talents did not go unnoticed, and he became acquainted with many important figures in Lviv's literary circles, such as the literary critic Mykhailo Rudnytsky (1889–1975), who acted as his advisor, and the writers Iryna Vilde (1907–1982) and Mykhailo Yatskiv (1873–1961)[42] After graduation Bohdan was admitted to the graduate program in philology. However, perhaps because he was too influenced by Ivan Franko's writings, and with the prompting from the KGB, he was sent to the Kirovohrad (now Kropyvnytskyi) Pedagogical Institute. Unable to find somewhere to stay there, he appealed to the authorities to allow him to return to Lviv. They did so, and Bohdan began studying art there with the painter Volodymyr Patyk (1926–2016) while contributing literary criticism to the Komsomol newspaper *Molod' Ukraïny*.[43] With the help of Vilde and the writers Dmytro Pavlychko and Rostyslav Bratun, in June 1962 he was hired as a research associate at the Lviv Museum of Ukrainian Art (renamed the National Museum in 1991).

In Lviv the Horyn brothers took part in the establishment of Prolisok and helped to strengthen its relations with intellectuals from Kyiv. Viacheslav Chornovil arrived to work in Lviv in 1963, while Dziuba, who had met his wife-to-be, Marta, on his first trip to Lviv, often returned to

---

40   For a full report on the war years, see ibidem, 190–97.
41   Ibidem, 199–200.
42   Taras Batenko, *Opozytsiina osobystist': Druha polovyna XX st. Politychnyi portret Bohdana Horynia* (Lviv, 1997), 27–34. Yatskiv had been a member of the Moloda Muza group (1906–1909) of Galician Ukrainian modernists and Ivan Franko's friend.
43   Ibidem, 37–43.

visit her there. In the meantime Rostyslav Bratun became the editor-in-chief of the Lviv journal *Zhovten'*, which became one of the most innovative literary periodicals in Ukraine until his dismissal in 1966.[44]

Prolisok's purpose, at least in the beginning, was both artistic and patriotic. It

> included the youth of the Galician *shistdesiatnyky*—a multifaceted world of poetry, music, and song, a patriotic blast of young vitality and the first effort toward a Ukrainian Renaissance. At that point in the 1960s, there was still no [Ukrainian] Helsinki Group or any progressive political party or brotherhood for national culture with courage enough to shake the walls of the hated Stalinist occupational regime.[45]

Aside from the obligatory first evening dedicated to Lenin, all of Prolisok's initiatives were infused with a strong national sentiment. The most successful meetings were in 1963, commemorating the fiftieth anniversary of Lesia Ukrainka's death, and in 1964 on the 150th anniversary of Taras Shevchenko's death. *Samvydav* poetry and political writings circulated widely among the club's members, and soon underground publications were being exchanged between Lviv and Kyiv—a perilous activity.

In May 1964 Prolisok organized a trip to Kaniv to commemorate the date when his remains were brought back to Ukraine and buried in that town. From Kaniv the group intended to continue on to Kyiv, and Mykhailo Horyn had prepared a suitcase full of underground documents to share with the club there. However, at the last minute Horyn decided not to go because his first daughter had just been born. He entrusted the suitcase to Myroslava Zvarychevska (1936–2015), requesting that she pass it on to Ivan Svitlychny. On the way to Kaniv KGB agents stopped the bus carrying Prolisok's members to arrest Horyn, Ivan Hel, and Zvarychevska. Horyn was missing, Hel was detained for several hours, and Volodymyr Kvitnevy, lied to the agents, denying that Zvarychevska was on the bus, and thus making it possible for her to deliver the suitcase to Svitlychny.[46] In observing their methods of disseminating *samvydav* documents, we can identify crucial differences between the Kyiv and Lviv

---

44 Mykhailo Il'nyts'kyi, "Literaturnyi L'viv i shistdesiatnytstvo," in *U vyri shistdesiatnyts'koho rukhu*, 21.
45 Kvitnevyi, "Lytsari natsional'noho vidrodzhennia," 56.
46 Ibidem, 64.

groups. For example, according to Mykhailo Horyn, in 1964 Svitlychny refused to distribute the anonymous document *Prospects and Tasks of the Ukrainian Liberation Movement* in Kyiv, as it was contrary to the spirit of *shistdesiatnytstvo* and likely to attract the attention of the KGB. But in Lviv Horyn himself reproduced the document and distributed and discussed it with his colleagues.[47]

The anxious journey to Kaniv ended with the placing of a wreath made of precious metals at Shevchenko's monument. Prolisok's members were repeatedly stopped at the gravesite by KGB agents and were only able to reach the grave owing to the intervention of several members of the cultural establishment (such as the writer Mykhailo Stelmakh). This demonstration of solidarity is another example of how the movement of the young *shistdesiatnyky* was able to muster the support of many older members of the Soviet Ukrainian literary elite.[48]

The *shistdesiatnyky* had received a dispiriting, heavy blow when, on 14 December 1963, Vasyl Symonenko died of cancer at the age of twenty-eight. His tragic death was blamed on the Soviet regime, which had confined Symonenko in Cherkasy and refused him access to proper medical treatment. A few days after his death the KTM organized a commemorative evening, but the only acknowledgement of Symonenko's passing in the official press was a short paragraph published in *Literaturna Ukraïna*, the SPU's official paper, in which "a group of comrades" remembered him as "sincere, happy, and witty."[49] Members of both the KTM and Prolisok journeyed to Cherkasy to attend their comrade's funeral. There Mykhailo Horyn, Mykhailo Kosiv, and Svitlychny gave brief eulogies, the singer Halyna Menkush (b. 1944) sang traditional songs, and recordings of Symonenko reciting his poetry were played aloud.[50] A delegation also visited Symonenko's mother, who gave Svitlychny her son's archive, including unpublished materials.

---

[47] Horyn', "U nas bula velyka misiia," 206–207. Th author of the document was the dissident Yevhen Proniuk (b. 1936), whose family was active in the OUN and deported to Kazakhstan in the late 1940s. Proniuk disseminated and wrote anti-Soviet, anti-Communist tracts throughout the 1960s and and was a political prisoner from 1972 to 1984. He became a founding member of the Ukrainian Helsinki Association and the Ukrainian Memorial society in 1988, and of the All-Ukrainian Society of Political Prisoners and the Repressed in 1989.

[48] Il'nyts'kyi, "Literaturnyi L'viv i shistdesiatnytstvo," 19–20.

[49] Hrupa tovaryshiv [anonymous group of friends], "Vasyl' Symonenko," *Literaturna Ukraïna*, 19 December 1963, 4.

[50] Kosiv, "Prolisky vyrostaiut' z-pid snihu,"74–75.

The Soviet authorities' composure in the face of Symonenko's death was a sure sign that the political leadership had changed its views about the cultural upheaval in Ukraine. However, the replacements at the head of various secretariats of the Communist Party would introduce policies touching on nationalities that were somewhat ambiguous.

The End of the Thaw, and the Appointment of Petro Shelest

After President John F. Kennedy's triumph on the international stage during Berlin Crisis of 1961 and Cuban Missile Crisis of 1962, the CPSU's General Secretary Khrushchev sought revenge internally. Facing economic disaster and plummeting popularity, "Khrushchev's instinctive inclination, as it had been at the end of 1956, was to crack down on domestic laxity and present himself as a defender of the Soviet state and ideology."[51] Ivan Dziuba, who was present with Ivan Drach and Mykola Vinhranovsky at Khrushchev's second attack on artists, at the House of Unions in March 1963, recalls the vulgarity ("You are faggots! Are you men or not? No, you're not men, you are faggots!") and anti-Semitic tone of Khrushchev's speech there.[52] The fears provoked by this meeting caused a quick upsurge of new artistic orthodoxy in both Ukraine and Russia. An interesting example of this can be found in Leonid Novychenko's article in an April 1963 issue of *Komunist Ukraïny*. Although not a *shistdesiatnyk*, Novychenko was part of the cultural milieu of nonconformist intellectuals and had contributed articles to Bratun's *Zhovten'*. After praising Khrushchev's guidance, Novychenko attacked what he called "formalism" and writers' efforts to exploit the freedoms they had been granted while disregarding their task of supporting the Party in its war against capitalism. He stressed that one of the greatest sources of danger was the influence of Western artistic movements, theorizing on the incommunicability between the cultures of the capitalist West and the Communist world: "The experience of recent years has shown that any effort to mechanically transfer the poetics of Italian neo-realism into representation of the Soviet man and the new world that surrounds him inevitably causes an ideological decadence and the silencing of the main important values of vital truth."[53]

---

51 Zubok, *Zhivago's Children*, p. 209.
52 "Tsia knyzhka zminyla use moie zhyttia: Rozmova z Ivanom Dziuboiu," 114–15.
53 Leonid Novichenko [Novychenko], "Bol'shaia otvetstvennost' khudozhnika pered narodom," *Kommunist Ukraïny*, 1963, no. 4: 68–69.

Despite appeals to embrace a global culture, Communist orthodoxy resulted in the severing of the literary field into two halves: into the new Bolshevist contingent and the old "corrupted capitalist" contingent. Novychenko was quick to identify the culprits of decadence. He denounced the Kyiv-born Russian novelist Viktor Nekrasov (1911–87, one of Ivan Dziuba's closest friends) for depicting the United States too positively in his novel *Both Sides of the Ocean* (originally published in *Novyi mir*). Novychenko also did not spare poets, accusing Ivan Drach, of fostering hostility toward the older generation. He argued that the state of literature spoke to the "necessity of resolute improvement in working with youth and of increased principled criticism among comrades."[54] This was confirmed during the Conference of Members of the Ukrainian Creative Intelligentsia and Party Ideology Officials, held in Kyiv on 8–9 April 1963. There Andrii Skaba attacked the *shistdesiatnyky*, while Drach, Vinhranovsky, and Vitalii Korotych were self-critical.[55] The publication of works by many young poets abroad in the Ukrainian nationalist press in the West had broken the trust of Soviet leaders.[56] In subsequent months the pages of the Soviet Ukrainian press were filled with articles about a new cultural policy. The *shistdesiatnyky* were warned that the regime's past laxity had been abandoned and that concrete actions were about to be taken.

This policy shift was reinforced by several replacements in key political posts who influenced the implementation of the new cultural line. In 1965 Mykola Pidhirny resigned as head of the CPU and left for Moscow to become the chairman of the Presidium of the Supreme Soviet of the USSR. He was succeeded as first secretary of the CPU by Petro Shelest (1908–96), who had been the first secretary of the CPU in Kyiv Oblast since 1957. Volodymyr Shcherbytsky (1918–90), who had headed the Soviet Ukrainian government since 1961, was demoted to the CPU secretary for industry in Dnipropetrovsk Oblast. From Shelest's diaries we know that he helped to organize Khrushchev's removal in favour of Leonid Brezhnev in October 1964 and to dismantle Khrushchev's economic reforms, which had granted slightly more autonomy to Ukrainian enterprises. He was able to present himself to the public both as a champion of Ukrainian needs and to the new leadership in Moscow as a

---

54 Ibidem, 70.
55 Lewytzkyj, *Politics and Society in Soviet Ukraine, 1953–1980*, 61–66.
56 Volodymyr P. Stakhiv, "Kryza 'ideolohichnoï nadbudovy', shcho ïï podolaty ne mozhna," *Suchasnist'*, 1963, no. 8: 74.

dependable comrade.[57] Shelest's personal ties with a handful of Ukrainian intellectuals—particularly his friendship with Oles Honchar—led some to believe that he would protect the Ukrainian cultural revival. As it turned out, this was far from the truth.

The First Clash: From Alla Horska's Shevchenko Window to the Arrests

After the victory of the *shistdesiatnyky* during the 1962 Plenum of the Writer's Union of Ukraine, the CPU leadership decided to respond with ever increasing strength to those questioning its authority. At the beginning it adopted some discouraging measures. Ivan Dziuba was dismissed from his job at *Vitchyzna* in 1962 and had to accept a job as a consultant at the Molod publishing house. A year later publication of Lina Kostenko's fourth book of poems, *Zorianyi intehral*, was forbidden, and Symonenko had to accept a serious bowdlerization of his essays and poems. But even harsher attacks on freedom of expression were still around the corner. Perhaps the most symbolic event was the destruction of the stained-glass window portraying Taras Shevchenko at Kyiv State University (itself named in honour of the bard) in 1964.

The figurative arts in Ukraine were under scrupulous control. If one sought innovative works that distanced themselves from any visual pandering to the regime, one had to visit artists' studios in person, because "revolutionary" painters were not permitted to hold public exhibitions.[58] On the rare occasion that a painting passed official censorship, the stir it created was often so great that the authorities could not help but retire it, as was the case with Viktor Zaretsky's *Portrait of a Girl* in 1958.[59]

In early 1964 the university held a design competition for a stained-glass window in the entrance hall that would be installed on the occasion of the 150th anniversary of Shevchenko's birth. The winning project, proposed by a group headed by Alla Horska, showed Shevchenko comforting a woman, very probably a personification of Ukraine. The window could be interpreted as a denunciation of the poor state of Ukrainian culture, and this was likely the designers' intention. In March

---

57 Lewytzkyj, *Politics and Society in Soviet Ukraine, 1953–1980*, 94–97.
58 Kosiv, *Prolisky vyrostaiut' z-pid snihu*, 74.
59 "The Art of Painting in Soviet Ukraine," *The Ukrainian Review* 6, no. 1 (Spring 1959): 73–74. The "Autumn Exhibition of Works by Kyiv Artists" displayed over one hundred canvases by sixty artists, and Zaretsky was the only representative of the younger generation.

1964 the work was nearing completion when it was inspected by the university's rector, Ivan Shvets, and the secretary of the Kyiv City Committee of the CPU, Vasyl Boichenko, who declared that a commission of the Ukraine's Union of Artists' had been appointed to evaluate the piece. The new commission was supposed to view the window at 10 p.m. the following day, 9 March. But Boichenko called Andrii Skaba, the Ukrainian SSR's minister of higher education, and arranged for the window to be covered. The Union of Artists' commission was therefore unable to view the window. A new date for the inspection was set for 18 March, but Boichenko had the window disassembled and its pieces destroyed before the inspection was to occur. The artists were not informed of the decision and only heard that the window had been destroyed from student witnesses.[60] Afterwards a crowd gathered at the site, including Mykhailo Stelmakh, but the doormen, who were ordered to hide the remnants, herded the people away.

On 13 April 1964 another commission of the Union of Artists convened in a closed session to interview the window's designers. Alla Horska and her colleague Liudmyla Semykina (b. 1924) were expelled from the union, accused of producing a low-quality artwork and using Shevchenko as a weapon against his country.[61] News of the window's destruction reached the West through an article in *Ukraïns'kyi kalendar*, the annual miscellany published in Cracow by the Alliance of Ukrainians in Poland, which contained a photograph of the window, subsequently reproduced, along with a summary of events, in *Suchasnist'*.[62]

On 24 May 1964 a fire broke out at the important Vernadsky Public Library in Kyiv. A significant number of valuable books and documents perished, causing an inestimable loss of Ukraine's historical and artistic patrimony. According to the reports to the CPU, the fire had been set in many different zones of the library, and it destroyed nearly one-third of the library's holdings and jeopardized the building's stability.[63] On 25 May Viktor Pohruzhalsky was arrested on suspicion of setting the fire, a crime to which he confessed. According to the Ukrainian SSR Ministry of

---

60 John Kolasky, *Two Years in Soviet Ukraine* (Toronto, 1970), 90–92.
61 Unofficial minutes of a brief part of the session were published in the fourth issue of *Ukraïns'kyi visnyk*. It is reprinted in V'iacheslav Chornovil, *Tvory v desiaty tomakh*, vol. 3 (Kyiv, 2006), 436–38.
62 "Znyshchennia vitrazhu T. Shevchenka v Kyïvs'komu universyteti," *Suchasnist'*, 1965, no. 6: 104–05.
63 Report, 25 May 1964, in TsDAHOU, f. 1, op. 1, spr. 5925, ark. 75.

Internal Security, Pohruzhalsky was apprehended soon after the incident. He was a librarian and had written repeatedly to the authorities to denounce the poor conditions in which the precious collections were kept. He confessed that he had spent the previous night in Kyiv's National Botanical Garden, where he had divulged his intent to a mysterious girl named Valia (Valentyna), and then returned to the library to set the fire. A woman from the cleaning service reported seeing Pohruzhalsky walk out of the library with a wounded leg around 5 a.m., the time the fire broke out.[64] The official reconstruction of the crime was questionable, largely because a single person could hardly set several fires in different parts of the library simultaneously. Furthermore, the fire destroyed precisely the documents that Pohruzhalsky was trying to protect from neglect by the authorities. Nevertheless he was identified as the only culprit and subsequently tried. The trial sentenced Pohruzhalsky to ten years of imprisonment, painting him as a psychologically unstable person who had set the library on fire out of hatred for the director.

Soon after an anonymous underground pamphlet titled "Concerning the Lawsuit against Pohruzhalsky" was disseminated and rapidly acquiring nationwide notoriety. The author's identity remained unknown until 1991, when the work was universally ascribed to the literary critic and psychologist Yevhen Sverstiuk (1928–2014), who had been a member of the KTM. The text accused the Soviet Ukrainian authorities of Russian chauvinism. It began by underlining some singular coincidences: the library lacked any fire-control system; the fire brigade was unable to do anything for the first two hours because the raion's water mains were not working; and only the floor where Ukrainian materials were stored was set on fire, even though Pohruzhalsky worked in another department. Moreover, the library's catalogue was also lost in the fire, making it impossible to know which and how many books had been destroyed. Finally, Pohruzhalsky's trial placed greater emphasis on the suspect's love life and mental condition than on the actual events on the night of the fire. The document contained a harsh political assessment of the debacle.

> Exterminating millions of Ukrainians in 1933 through famine, torturing the best representatives of our intelligentsia to death, strangling even the smallest effort to think, they have transformed us into obedient slaves. Since we expend our strength and give the

---

64   TsDAHOU, f. 1, op. 1, spr. 5925, ark. 78.

> fruits of our labours to the state, we do not have time to think: who are we? What are we living for? Where are they leading us?
>   This is not the first time they have spat in our faces, yet this year they have spat especially impudently. They have burned the greatest Ukrainian library. They destroyed the small bridge between our past and the present.[65]

The document lamented that Ukrainian students were taught only Russian history and did not know anything about their ancestors. Only a few could go to the library and study Ukrainian historical documents, but the fire obliterated the potential for attaining knowledge that could strengthen and protect the Ukrainian nation. Thus the fire represented a great loss for the future.

> Ukrainians! Do you know what has been burned? They burned a part of your intellect and soul. Not the part that the Stalinist terror hunted, spat all over, made to kneel down, but the part that was supposed to live in our sons and daughters. They burned down the cathedral where the soul resurrects.
>   Russian state chauvinism, like anti-Semitism, has been revived in the colonial empire they call the USSR.[66]

The pamphlet stated that the central Soviet institutions in Moscow supported Russification not only in Ukraine but also in the other national republics, to the detriment of their native cultures. And since the men who occupied the highest posts were chauvinists, there was no hope for justice. Sverstiuk concluded sadly, "We live in a country where one can be ruined like a criminal without a trial just for speaking a word of truth."[67] In such an environment, he argued in closing, for the average Ukrainian Taras Shevchenko was a vivid symbol of national pride, which created fear within Soviet institutions. Sentiments and symbols of national patriotism represented a threat to the Soviet establishment and therefore had to be quashed. The fire at the library was not a coincidence but a premeditated attack. Sverstiuk's pamphlet was distributed throughout Ukraine, especially in the western oblasts, where the Horyn brothers personally saw to its dissemination.[68] It was also distributed widely outside Ukraine,

---

65 "Z pryvodu protsesu nad Pohruzhal's'kym," *Suchasnist'*, 1965, no. 2: 81.
66 Ibidem, 82.
67 Ibidem.
68 Kas'ianov, *Nezhodni*, 94.

with its first foreign publication taking place in *Suchasnist'* in February 1965.

Other *samvydav* documents had a similar success. Despite the official ban on his works, Symonenko's popularity increased in 1964 owing to the underground circulation of his poems and short diary, written between 1962 and 1963, in which he accused the Soviet authorities of censorship and blamed them for his confinement in Cherkasy.[69] The state-approved publication of a collection of his poems, *Zemne tiazhinnia* (Earth's Gravity), in 1964 did not quell the distribution of unofficial versions. In 1965 a collection of Symonenko's writing, including his diary and an anonymous preface, was published in Munich under the title *Bereh chekan'* (The Shore of Expectations), embarrassing Soviet authorities in the international arena. The publisher, Suchasnist, declared that it had tried to assemble a collection that best reflected Symonenko's vision for his output without censorship or alterations. The edition included another anonymous document, titled "Symonenko—ideia" (Symonenko—the Idea), which had been widely circulated in *samvydav*. Decades later it was revealed that it was also penned by Sverstiuk, who prepared it for the commemorative evening at the Institute of Medicine in January 1964.[70] Sverstiuk praised Symonenko as *the* poet of the Ukrainian homeland.

> Symonenko's profound understanding of the meaning of his roots, the constant feeling of strength that comes from one's native land, the feeling of happiness and the bitterness of responsibility toward one's own people—all that was so elementary and strong in his work, as reflected in the words
>
> Without you I am meaningless,
> Like a bird without wings.[71]

Sverstiuk portrayed Symonenko as an extremely talented poet who was able to render a complex internal world of feelings in stunningly simple language without resorting to standardization. There was no hatred toward Russia in his poetry, but just the need to affirm his own

---

69 Wolfgang Strauss, "The Symonenko Case," *The Ukrainian Review* 12, no. 4 (Winter 1965): 35–37.
70 Oles' Obertas, *Ukraïns'kyi samvydav: Literaturna krytyka ta publitsystyka (1960-i – pochatok 1970-kh rokiv)* (Kyiv, 2010), 114.
71 "Symonenko—ideia," in Vasyl' Symonenko, *Bereh chekan'* (Munich, 1973 [1st ed. 1965]), 287.

national belonging. Sverstiuk illustrated this point with an incident at a literary evening with Symonenko.

> But someone who had not sought to understand the verses … adopted a dubious tone and immediately circulated a note intended to frighten [Symonenko]. It read: "What independent Ukraine are you speaking of when you write 'Let the Russians and Americans be silent,' or 'I have the sacred filial right to remain in solitude, with my mother'?" Vasyl calmly, and almost carelessly, read this note and answered: "For me there is only one Ukraine. If the author of the question knows another one, let him say so. We will choose." This was an example of his laconic and genuinely popular simplicity and wisdom.[72]

Sverstiuk's "Symonenko—ideia" illustrated the struggle between the *shistdesiatnyky* and the Soviet leadership for the spiritual heritage of a poet whose popularity was uncontrollable.

In January 1965 the SPU and the Molod publishing house, where Dziuba worked, nominated Symonenko for the Taras Shevchenko State Prize, the highest Ukrainian literary award. At the same time a gathering took place in Kyiv to commemorate Symonenko on the anniversary of his thirtieth birthday, with his mother in attendance. Among the speakers were Dmytro Pavlychko and Ivan Dziuba. In the latter's interpretation of Symonenko's poetry one can find the source of that obligation that the *shistdesiatnyky* felt toward civic duty. Dziuba described Symonenko as a poet of sincerity who "spoke the truth, and the truth alone made him greater and greater," as a "cruelly self-critical" poet conscious of his artistic and political duty and constantly striving toward self-improvement; and, above all, as "a poet of the national idea," inspired by a patriotism that emerged from universal values.

> Symonenko belonged to those who felt the strong connection between a national idea and all the values common to mankind, the concepts of human dignity, honesty, and conscience, concepts of personal and social ethics and justice. These very concepts of dignity, conscience, and justice that led him to the national idea, a renewed understanding of Ukraine.
> … The sovereign Ukraine that Dziuba envisioned would embody a "national contribution toward the general cause of peace,

---

72 Ibidem, 288.

democracy, and socialism. This idea lies at the foundation of Vasyl Symonenko's poetry." Symonenko rejected the "indifference and civic demoralization" of the Stalinist intelligentsia, and he believed that the problems of his society could be boiled down to "the discrepancies between word and deed, theory and practice," which he fought to eradicate.

... Personal adherence to principle, [an] uncompromising stand and calm courage were joined in him with [a] high and binding social consciousness; human dignity and self-respect, human honesty and conscience were to him the main prop of social life. His work reflected the rise of [a] new national awareness among Ukrainian youth, where the shoots of perennial greenery and youth of human dignity, human freedom and independence, invincibility and inexhaustible human spirit are growing through the layers of past ages "that spur the body to the struggle," that call us to stand by our nation and to make it the meaning of our lives.[73]

Dziuba accused Ukraine's general public and high-ranking officials of hypocrisy, and he criticized Leonid Novychenko, who had recently praised Symonenko at the SPU. Dziuba was afraid that the cultural establishment would gain control of Symonenko's image and transform him into an inoffensive ode-writer of the regime. The battle over Symonenko's memory was a battle over the future interpretation of a generation. In this struggle, the Soviet authorities were ultimately defeated by their external enemies. Symonenko's diary was published abroad by a Ukrainian nationalist journal, as was his collection *Bereh chekan'* a few months later.[74] This was the last straw for the Soviet leadership, which sought to retaliate with a firm hand.

In March the KTM was forced to shut down and its archives were destroyed or subsequently lost. On 15 April *Radians'ka Ukraïna* published a letter purportedly written by Symonenko's mother, in which she accused his friends of betraying her son; and an essay by the writer Mykola Nehoda (1928–2008), in which he described Symonenko as a Sovietophile and accused Ivan Svitlychny and the translator Anatol Perepadia (1935–2008) of helping to smuggle his writings abroad. But the letter from Symonenko's "mother" and Nehoda's essay had no effect on

---

73 Ivan Dziuba, "Vasyl Symonenko," *The Ukrainian Review* 14, no. 1 (Spring 1967): 44–47.
74 The first (incomplete) publication of the diary abroad was in *Suchasnist'*, 1965, no. 1 (January): 13–18.

the rapid dissemination of the original text of Symonenko's diary throughout the country.⁷⁵

At this time discontent about Soviet nationality policy in Ukraine was increasing. According to a report commissioned by the CPU's sector for monitoring science and education, in early 1965 Kyiv State University was at the centre of many subversive initiatives. There were several instances of both students and professors questioning the Party's policy on the development of Ukrainian culture and requesting the establishment of an entire program of studies, from elementary school to university, in Ukrainian. A larger movement to form an Association of Defenders of Ukrainian Culture independent of the Party was initiated by Vasyl Lobko (1914–95), then working at the Institute of Hydromechanics of the AN URSR. However, the two university students heading the proposed association's steering committee, Oleksandr Nehrebetsky and Stanislav Drobot, reported the initiative to the KGB and it was quashed. Nonetheless the fact that there was an attempt to create such an association provided the authorities with an alarming insight into the intelligentsia's state of mind.⁷⁶

On 24 August 1965 several KGB agents arrested Ivan Hel (1937–2011), a law student at Lviv State University, a friend of the Horyn brothers, and a founding member of the Prolisok Youth Club who had been actively disseminating *samvydav* literature. In the following days other persons were arrested in Lviv, including the Horyn brothers, the teacher and literary critic Mykhailo Masiutko, and the writer and university lecturer Mykhailo Osadchy (1936–94). Many of those apprehended were connected to Prolisok, whose activities ended abruptly as a consequence of the arrests. In late August and early September the KGB imprisoned other intellectuals in Kyiv and in Volyn, Ternopil, and Ivano-Frankivsk Oblasts. The pretext for the arrests was the distribution of *samvydav* pamphlets such as the "Prospects and Tasks of the Ukrainian Liberation Movement" and "Concerning the Lawsuit against Pohruzhalsky," and because these documents had been smuggled out to the United States by Oksana Smishkevych, Ivan Svitlychny's Ukrainian-American friend.⁷⁷

---

75 They were published together under the title "Everest pidlosti" (The Everest of Despicability) in *Radians'ka Ukraïna*, 15 April 1965, 3. At the time Perepadia was working for Dnipro publishers in Kyiv.
76 See TsDAHOU, f. 1, op. 1, spr. 6003, ark. pp. 17–34.
77 Report to the CC CPU, August–September 1965, in TsDAHOU, f. 1, op. 1, spr. 6160, ark. 26–29.

Among those arrested were Svitlychny and Valentyn Moroz (1936–2019), a history lecturer at the state pedagogical institute in Lutsk. Moroz was sentenced to four years in a Mordovian prison camp, while Svitlychny was released after eight months, being no longer considered dangerous. The two of them, together with Ivan Dziuba, would represent the two extremes of *shistdesiatnytstvo* after 1965, so it is worth briefly examining their lives up to this point.

Svitlychny was born on 20 September 1929 in the village of Polovynkyne, now in Starobilsk Raion, Luhansk Oblast. His mother went to work on a collective farm to help the family survive the famine of 1932–33. In 1943, during the German occupation, Svitlychny lost his fingers on one hand while trying to tear away a German mine. He moved to Kharkiv in 1947 to study Ukrainian philology at state university. After graduating in 1952, he was admitted to the graduate program at the Institute of Literature of the AN URSR in Kyiv, where he began his career as a literary critic. While working at that institute, in 1957 he became the senior editor of literary criticism at the journal Dnipro—a position he was fired from in 1963 for his nonconformist views and his activity in the KTM. Unfortunately Svitlychny did not write any memoirs or keep a diary, so this biographic account is based on his friends' memories.[78]

One of Svitlychny's friends, the literary scholar Mykhailyna Kotsiubynska (1931–2011), provides a powerful portrait of Svitlychny as both the moral and geographic linchpin of the *shistdesiatnyky* movement.

> Ivan Svitlychny was the generator of all of these [*shistdesiatnytstvo's*] ideas. Although he did not have young [Ivan] Dziuba's oratorical skills, he somewhat unnoticeably and subtly found himself at the centre of each cultural activity. It was he who read, as it seemed, all that was worth reading and passed it on to others....
>
> Svitlychny was able to inscribe every notable fact of our artistic legacy and artistic creation into a vitalizing circulation of cultural blood ... [His] little apartment on 35 Umanska Street became the core of an intensive spiritual life, an unofficial Club of Creative Youth. There everyone felt at home—Vasyl Symonenko and Ivan Drach, Opanas Zalyvakha and Alla Horska, Ivan Dziuba and Yurii Badzo,

---

78 See, for example, Bohdan Zakharov and Vasyl' Ovsiienko, "Svitlychnyi, Ivan Oleksiiovych," in *Mizhnarodnyi biohrafichnyi slovnyk dysydentiv kraïn Tsentral'noï ta Skhidn'oï Ievropy i kolyshn'oho SRSR*, vol. 1, part 2, 672–76.

Halyna Sevruk and Vasyl Stus, Ihor Kalynets, and Vasyl Holoborodko.[79]

Svitlychny's centrality to *shistdesiatnytstvo* was not just a matter of providing a meeting place. He would record various events on tape, compiling an impressive oral archive of the movement. He was also dedicated—perhaps more so than his peers—to Ukraine's unification.

> Svitlychny was the living bridge between eastern and western Ukraine, between Kyiv and Lviv. It was he who introduced many colleagues and friends, including me, to the nonconformist artistic circles of Lviv. That is how genuine national-cultural unification was accomplished. Today we take it for granted, but it had to be gradually established. This is Svitlychny's indisputable credit.[80]

Svitlychny was well known as a literary critic. He was particularly famous for the irony he employed to unmask the dull-wittedness of some of his colleagues. In his essay "Harmony and Algebra" he mocked the repetitiveness and ineptness of official Soviet critics of Taras Shevchenko's works.[81] In addition to his literary criticism, Svitlychny's own works echo all of the themes typical of *shistdesiatnytstvo*. "Steel Does Not Rust," first published in *Zhovten'* in 1963 and then in English translation in 1971 (a fact that would contribute to his arrest a year later), was written to commemorate Lesia Ukrainka on the fiftieth anniversary of her death. In it Svitlychny's portrait resounds with the ethos of the 1960s.

> If Lesya [sic] Ukrainka's creative work was the pinnacle of the development of the Ukrainian pre-1917 dramaturgy, this was because she elevated Ukrainian drama from everyday, family, psychological subject matter—at best, spontaneous rebellion and struggle—to the level of conscious politics and open partisanship.... As far as social-democratic partisanship is concerned, she constantly fought for high ethical norms, and her unchangeable motto was the principle "a clean cause demands clean hands."[82]

---

79 Kotsiubyns'ka, *Ivan Svitlychnyi, shistdesiatnyk*, 8.
80 Ibidem, 9.
81 See Ivan Svitlychnyi, "Harmoniia i alhebra," *Dnipro*, 1965, no. 3: 142–50.
82 Idem, "Steel Does Not Rust," *The Ukrainian Review* 18, no. 2 (Summer 1971): 40–41. The full, original version of this essay is "Krytsia ne irzhaviie," *Zhovten'*, 1963, no. 8: 129–35.]

Svitlychny presented Lesia Ukrainka as an advocate of liberated development of the self and of a renewed concept of the relationship between the individual and society as a whole.

> In contrast to this thoroughly pessimistic, thoroughly individualistic philosophy, Lesya Ukrainka placed the ideal of Harmony between individual and society. Supporting a human being's right to an all-development of his personality, and consequently, the principle of high individualization in part, she wrote: "Each man is unique and there is no other one like him in the whole world, there is no one, there was no one and there will be no one like him from now until eternity."... [The key to her creativity was] in the harmonious fusion of the interests of an individual personality with the interests of society, in the development of spiritual forces of man on the basis of collective experience.[83]

According to Svitlychny, for Lesia Ukrainka genuine freedom was synonymous with internal freedom and the ability to subdue our inner censor.

> A slave remains a slave as long as he submits to his slavery; therefore, slavery depends on slaves no less than on slave owners; the destruction of spiritual slavery is the first and the surest guarantee of liberation from physical slavery.[84]

The champions of inner freedom were the paladins of national liberation, but the fulfilment of national destiny went hand in hand with the realization of a socialist, multinational, and democratic state.

> Lesya Ukrainka did not limit herself to the merciless exposure of spiritual slaves and renegades, but also created pictures of internally free, courageous and uncompromising heroes—fighters for national liberation.... Lesya Ukrainka imagined the socialist future, new relations among people, as a community of [the] like-minded, brothers in spirit and in blood. Fighting for the elementary civil rights for [of] an individual, Lesya Ukrainka wrote: "We should see to it at the same time that the rights so achieved will not serve the interests of the ruling nation primarily, but would benefit the whole huge and varied complex of the Russian state; so that political

---

83 Ibidem, 42.
84 Ibidem, 43.

freedom would be regional, national, decentralized, and equally democratic for all."⁸⁵

Development of the self, self-criticism, honesty, and the struggle for national liberation are all recurring themes of the *shistdesiatnytstvo* movement. And if the culture of the 1960s entailed a rediscovery of the value of personal ties, Svitlychny, together with his sister, Nadia, and wife, were the living proof that the family unit of the *shistdesiatnyky* had acquired a renewed importance as a locus of love and sharing. Les Taniuk remembers the Svitlychny family as a community where reciprocal trust was extended to all guests: "The Svitlychnys were a particular nucleus, where each one could rely on the other, and this was why there was a special atmosphere at their place."⁸⁶ In this respect the Svitlychnys were the opposite of the typical Stalinist family, in which mistrust and silence had caused serious social atomization.⁸⁷ With the Svitlychny household at the heart of *shistdesiatnytstvo*, the familial importance that Svitlychny and his sister held extended into this sphere.

Born seven years after her brother, Nadia Svitlychna (1936–2006) studied in the same Kharkiv University faculty as he did. She then worked for several years as a high-school teacher, lecturer, and librarian in the countryside of Luhansk Oblast to be closer to their mother. When she arrived in Kyiv, Svitlychna began working at the Radianska Shkola publishing house, befriended Alla Horska and Mykhailyna Kotsiubynska, and quickly became one of the central figures of the *shistdesiatnyky* by taking on the crucial work of editing, copying, and disseminating *samvydav* documents. In an interview published in the year she died, she confirmed her role in the underground publication of Symonenko's works, Mykhailo Osadchy's novel *Cataract*, and Yevhen Sverstiuk's and Ivan Dziuba's most influential works.⁸⁸ Svitlychna's memories of this period reveal the recurring tensions between the Komsomol—regarded as an arena in which young people could be active—and the Communist Party, the epitome of Soviet conservatism. Although she did not elaborate extensively on this apposition, she said: "I was actually a member of the Komsomol, a very active member at that, despite the fact that I joined late,

---

85 Ibidem, 43-44.
86 Taniuk, *Parastas*, 9.
87 Cfr. Orlando Figes, *The Whisperers: Private Life in Stalin's Russia* (London, 2007).
88 "Interv'iu z Nadiieiu Svitlychnoiu," *Moloda natsiia*, 2006, no. 2: 28–29.

when I was already at university. I did not join the Party—thank God it was possible to avoid it."[89]

Valentyn Moroz's story was very different from Svitlychna's. He was born on 16 April 1936 in the village of Kholoniv, now in Horokhiv Raion, Volyn Oblast. His wife states that "Both his father and mother were nationally aware peasants. I believe that Valentyn received the beginnings of his national education from them."[90] After graduating from high school, in 1954 Moroz moved to Lviv to study history at the state university. The atmosphere in the Faculty of History there was quite nationalistic, and there was constant friction between the university's Russian and Ukrainian speakers. During his second year at the university Moroz met his future wife—Raisa Levterova (Lefteris, b. 1937), a Ukrainian-speaking ethnic Greek from Velykyi Yanisol (now Velyka Novosilka) in Stalino (now Donetsk) Oblast. There his political inclinations did not stand out as particularly heterodox. After graduating in 1958, Moroz taught history at a school in Marianivka in Volyn Oblast. When Raisa joined him there a few years later, she learned he had been labelled a Ukrainian nationalist because of the strong national consciousness he exhibited during the annual commemorations of Taras Shevchenko. Neither Valentyn nor Raisa fit into the small town's mainly Russian-speaking society. In 1963 Moroz worked as a history lecturer at the Lutsk State Pedagogical Institute. There he and his wife became acquainted with the members of a "poetry club" that circulated the writings of Vasyl Symonenko, Ivan Drach, and Lina Kostenko. There they also first learned about Ivan Dziuba, the Horyn brothers, and the clubs of creative youth.[91]

The following year Moroz was not reappointed as a lecturer in Lutsk, and the couple relocated to Ivano-Frankivsk, where both of them were hired as lecturers at the city's pedagogical institute. It was in Ivano-Frankivsk that the Morozes discovered and fell in love with the folk culture of the Hutsuls, a Ukrainian ethnographic group in the Carpathian Mountains, and they shared what they learned about Hutsul folklore with their friends in Lutsk.[92] Besides embracing Ukrainian culture and reading—also likely disseminating—underground literature, Valentyn and Raisa (who was a member of the Komsomol) did not engage in any secret or subversive activity. Nonetheless Moroz was one of the

---

89   Ibidem, 23.
90   Raïsa Moroz, *Proty vitru: Spohady druzhyny ukraïns'koho politv'iaznia* (Lviv, 2005), 45.
91   Ibidem, 49–50.
92   Ibidem, 50–51.

shistdesiatnyky arrested on 1 September 1965 and did not see his family for quite some time. At his trial in January 1966 he was sentenced to five years in a harsh labour camp in the Mordovian ASSR. In his final statement to the judge, he spoke of his dream for an independent Ukraine with the same rights as Poland or Czechoslovakia. He stated that prison made many people into good poets and thinkers and that he wished such a destiny for himself.[93]

Around thirty Ukrainians were arrested between 24 August and 13 November 1965. Some of them were released after a brief incarceration, but twenty were sentenced to terms ranging from six months to eight and a half years in prisons or labour camps. The Soviet authorities hoped that this wave of arrests would be carried out quietly, as had the Jurists' Affair in 1961. This did happen with some of the intellectuals who had fewer ties with the *shistdesiatnytstvo* core. Though they were tried in open court on 25 March 1966, Moroz and his fellow Lutsk lecturer Dmytro Ivashchenko (1919–2004), for example, did not receive help or support from other *shistdesiatnyky* because the latter were not yet acquainted with them.[94] On the other hand, because the other detainees were more or less active members of the clubs of creative youth, their arrests caused an public uproar. The first such protest occurred at the Ukraina movie theatre in Kyiv on 4 September 1965.

Ukrainian Cinema and the Case of *Shadows of Forgotten Ancestors*

By the time the Kyiv community of young intellectuals heard about the arrests, the Suchasnyk Club had already been pre-emptively shut down. Its closure was not so much a premeditated initiative as a hasty reaction to the public protest that took place at the Kyiv premiere of Serhii (Sergei) Paradzhanov's film *Shadows of Forgotten Ancestors*. However, it was not completely accidental that these events coincided.

Ukrainian cinema of the 1960s was also affected by the cultural milieu of the *shistdesiatnytstvo* movement. Young directors, actors, and cameramen strove to translate the values of the new generation into film, giving birth to the so-called Ukrainian poetic cinema of the 1960s. Drawing inspiration from Oleksandr Dovzhenko, the great filmmaker in honour of whom the Kyiv Film Studio was named, these artists transformed the Ukrainian film industry into a worthy competitor of

---

93 Ibidem, 65.
94 See Vyacheslav [V'iacheslav] Chornovil, *The Chornovil Papers* (New York, 1968).

powerhouse Russian productions. As Bohdan Nebesio has noted, "The main impetus behind the Ukrainian Poetic Cinema was the revival of Ukrainian language films or films on so-called 'Ukrainian topics.' While its intentions were quite honourable, the thematic considerations of the movement led to the enforcement of stereotypes and to the narrowing of thematic possibilities."[95] Borrowing plots from Ukrainian literary classics and history, these filmmakers reaffirmed some of the biases surrounding rural Ukraine rather than exploring new forms of expression.

The Communist Party, which exerted control over the film industry as a means of communication, was not happy about many Ukrainian film projects and refused to support them. A report on the Dovzhenko Film Studio dated 7 November 1966 notes that the Committee for Monitoring Cinema was dissatisfied with the output of the Ukrainian film industry. Despite their stated duties, the studio managers did not vet screenwriters, directors, or actors. This lack of control resulted in large amounts of money being spent on films that the Party committee was subsequently forced to censor. The most egregious example was the film *Check Your Watches*, written by Lina Kostenko and Arkadii Dobrovolsky (1911–69). The committee considered this work to be "not a film about Soviet poets who died in mortal conflict with fascism, but a film about our shortcomings, about the imperfection of the social organization of the Soviet country on the eve of the [Great Patriotic W]ar, a film about how this imperfection became a tragedy for the hero-poets of the film."[96] Similar criticisms were launched against the Georgian director Paradzhanov's last film, *Kyivan Frescoes*, "whose examination revealed that it was characterized by distorted and somehow pathological perceptions of actual reality, and showed spiritual failings."[97] The report stated that the studio employed too many actors who barely worked, as they were usually passed over for roles in favour of more famous faces. The committee recommended implementing new contracts that would force directors to repay the costs of any anti-Soviet film. This proposal was not considered seriously, but it is surprising that no effort was made to explain the poor management at the Dovzhenko Studio.

---

95 Bohdan Y. Nebesio, "Questionable Foundations for a National Cinema: Ukrainian Poetic Cinema of the 1960s," *Canadian Slavonic Papers* 42, nos. 1–2 (2000): 40.
96 Report of the Ukrainian Committee for Monitoring Cinema to the CPU's Department of Science and Culture, in TsDAHOU, f. 1, op. 1, spr. 6143, ark. 12.
97 Ibidem, ark. 13.

The director of the studio was Vasyl Tsvirkunov (1917–2000), Lina Kostenko's second husband.[98] Born in a small village in what is now Zaporizhzhia Oblast, he studied at Voroshylovhrad (now Luhansk) State University and worked as a teacher and director of a village school. During the Soviet-Finnish War and the Second World War Tsvirkunov served as a Soviet paratrooper until he was wounded and lost a leg. From 1944 to 1953 he directed the air force school in Voroshylovhrad, became the secretary (1953–55) of that city's Party Committee and the Party's principal journal in Ukraine, *Komunist Ukraïny*, and received a candidate of sciences degree from the CC CPSU's Academy of Social Sciences. In 1962 Tsvirkunov was appointed the director of the Dovzhenko Studio. He held this post until 1973, when he was dismissed for holding unorthodox political views. Nevertheless he remained a member of the CPU until 1991.[99] Tsvirkunov's position at the Dovzhenko Studio arguably contributed to the relatively unproblematic official reception of *Check Your Watches*.

Kostenko and Dobrovolsky's script received an award as the second-best Ukrainian screenplay of 1962, and it was published in the journal *Dnipro* in 1963. It follows the stories of three Ukrainian poets while as they are fighting to liberate their "fatherland" during the Second World War. The rest of the cast offers an unforgiving insight into the meanness of Stalinist society, well summarized by the denunciation one character writes against a protagonist, the head of the Komsomol.

> Secretary Shvindin of the Komsomol defends enemies of the people and spreads doubts about the righteousness of the NKVD's actions. Additionally, Shvindin said that Stalin does not understand the problems of literature and has turned his personal bad taste into an objective criterion of evaluation.[100]

This portrayal of Stalin's cultural policy stemmed from Dobrovolsky's personal experience as a scriptwriter in Stalin's times who was repressed in 1937 and imprisoned in the Gulag in the Soviet Far East North, from which he was allowed returned to Ukraine many years later, in 1959.

---

98 Kostenko and the Polish writer Jerzy Pachlowski had divorced some time after the birth of their daughter, Oksana, in 1956.
99 Lina Kostenko provides a brief biography of Tsvirkunov in "Narodzhenyi pid znakom Stril'tsia," *Kinoteatr* 40, no. 2 (2002): 4–7.
100 Lina Kostenko and Arkadii Dobrovol's'kyi, "Perevirte svoï hodynnyky," *Dnipro*, 1963, no. 2: 14.

Ultimately, the film's biting criticism of the Soviet establishment sealed its fate: it was never shown in theatres, and its footage was destroyed.

Paradzhanov's internationally acclaimed masterpiece, *Shadows of Forgotten Ancestors* (1965), was made at the Dovzhenko Studio despite Party censors' reservations. The screenplay was an adaptation of the famous novel of the same name by the popular Ukrainian modernist author Mykhailo Kotsiubynsky (1864–1913). The exceptional talents of the film's three artists—Paradzhanov (1924–90), his cameraman Yurii Illienko (1936–2010), and the lead actor Ivan Mykolaichuk (1941–87)—contributed to its success. The film tells the sad story of Ivan and his peasant family in a Hutsul village. The Hutsuls (whose folklore had charmed Valentyn and Raisa Moroz) were a perfect subject for those who wished to uncover a seemingly uncontaminated Ukrainian sub-ethnos. Although Georgian by birth, Paradzhanov was, and still is, often considered a Ukrainian director. Speaking of this film, he declared:

"I have always been interested in Ukraine ... But I wanted to render this universe in its primordial beauty, clearing 'popular' opinion of all of the artifices typical of an ethnographic museum."[101]

After failing to render Ukrainian folk culture accurately in his previous films, Paradzhanov approached Kotsiubynsky's story with the intention he states above. Upon visiting the Hutsul region, he became further convinced of its inhabitants' primordial nature and was angered by the Soviet government's attempts to "civilize" them.

> Until today these people have accepted their universe with a childlike freshness as the only possible one. And they are themselves "the only possible ones" in this particular universe. All that they have created was ordered by nature and very rapidly, almost immediately, blended with nature itself. Their wooden churches are inseparable from the architecture of the forests and the mountains, and the voice of their jew's-harps is generated by the echo.... Their fusion with nature, their particularism, has not been killed by history ... The Hutsuls have lived through all of the torments visited upon my Ivan.[102] And despite that they have remained free.... We did not come to discover the Carpathians as ethnographers. Love,

---

101 Serhiej Paradjanov [Paradzhanov], "L'ombra degli avi dimenticati," in *Serhiej Paradjanov*, ed. Antonin J. Liehm (Venice, 1977), 94.
102 "My Ivan" is a reference to the main character of the film.

despair, loneliness, death—these are the frescos of human life that we wanted to create.¹⁰³

In his own way Paradzhanov was a *shistdesiatnyk*, awaiting the renaissance of Ukrainian culture and interested in the private universe of human feelings. His film was released in 1964 and was a great success, thanks both to its theme and to the revolutionary way in which Paradzhanov used colours to express feelings. It was welcomed as a cultural point of reference for the *shistdesiatnyky* and their supporters. For this reason the film's premiere on 4 September, with Paradzhanov in attendance, had a significance that probably motivated the intellectuals to make a public declaration.

Most of Kyiv's *shistdesiatnyky* were at the film's screening in the evening of 5 September. Ivan Dziuba recalls that he attended with his friends Mykhailyna Kotsiubynska and the literary critic Yurii Badzo and that all of them were distressed by the lack of news regarding the recent arrests of their colleagues. During the public discussion that was held at the movie theatre before the film was screened, Dziuba therefore decided to announce the disturbing news to the audience.¹⁰⁴ He knew Paradzhanov personally and had brought a bouquet of flowers to give to one of the actresses. According to the record of the KGB interrogation of Paradzhanov and the theatre's director, Fedir Braichenko, Dziuba came onstage during the speeches, handed the bouquet to the actress, and then took the microphone and addressed the audience. Braichenko remembered Dziuba's words thus:

> This is a momentous occasion for us, but we are also in great grief—the creative youth of Ukraine are being arrested … the mothers of Ukraine are despairing and crying for their sons. Comrades! Mass arrests of the Ukrainian intelligentsia are occurring right now. There have been mass arrests in Lviv and in Kyiv. They are now repeating [the Bolshevik Terror of] 1937. I implore you not to tolerate this ignominy. Shame on the government!¹⁰⁵

---

103 Paradjanov, "L'ombra degli avi dimenticati," 95–96.
104 *Naspravdi bulo tak: Interv'iu Iuriia Zaitseva z Ivanom Dziuboiu*, 63–64.
105 Derzhavnyi arkhiv Sluzhby bezpeky Ukraïny (hereafter DASBU), case 69260 f., vol. 7, ark. 12–20, here ark. 19.

At this point Braichenko came onstage, seized the microphone, and ordered his staff to turn off the lights and start the film. Someone (perhaps Viacheslav Chornovil or Vasyl Stus, according to different sources) shouted "Whoever is against tyranny—stand up!" and up to a third of the audience rose to their feet. Then the house lights were turned down, allowing the key players in this incident to escape. Contrary to expectations, the KGB did not arrest or interrogate them, and they were not questioned about that evening's events for several years—not until after the mass arrests in 1972.

Ivan Dziuba's *Internationalism or Russification?*

Dziuba recalls that after this incident he decided to write a treatise titled "Internationalism or Russification?"[106]

> Already at some point in 1965, maybe earlier, the desire to express my own point of view on this problem [of Soviet nationalities policy] came to the fore; the question certainly existed, but there was no answer. There was a lot of talk about the difficult situation—we talked and wrote a lot ourselves, too—about the abnormal conditions of Ukrainian culture and language, [and] of Ukraine as a whole. But no one could make up their mind to expose in a somewhat broader way exactly what the problem consisted of.[107]

Dziuba would try to express the *shistdesiatnyk* movement's stance on the nationality question. He had three audiences in mind, the first being the Communist Party and Soviet leadership in general. The structure of his essay relied on the classics of Marxism: "It was necessary to speak exactly the same language, from the same position. That is to say, destroying those stereotypes from within, filling them with a certain real, living meaning."[108] The second intended audience was the Russian-speaking intelligentsia.

> To those who asked, "Who is harassing you, who is forbidding you to speak Ukrainian?" I had to show that the violence did not consist of somebody standing with a whip and constantly hitting you on the head, even if it had been this way beforehand. [But] Russification had reached such a level that it was necessary to cast it off. The

---

106 "Tsia knyzhka zminyla use moie zhyttia: Rozmova z Ivanom Dziuboiu," 118.
107 *Naspravdi bulo tak*, 62.
108 Ibidem, 67.

> mechanism worked, you only needed to start and lubricate it. The essence of politics consists of creating such conditions in which a person might voluntarily do what he had to be forced to do before. I wanted to show these conditions, this mechanism of Russification. That is why so many paragraphs were dedicated to my analysis, or to my effort to analyze this mechanism of Russification.[109]

The third audience was Ukraine's young people, who needed to know that they had constitutional rights to defend their own culture. Dziuba managed to finish his treatise by the end of December 1965. It was written in the form of a petition to the republic's highest Soviet authorities, namely, First Secretary of the CPU Petro Shelest and Chairman of the Council of Ministers of the Ukrainian SSR Volodymyr Shcherbytsky. Some scholars have suggested that Dziuba was in contact with Shelest during this time, but Dziuba has denied this. In his preface he voiced his concern that the 1965 arrests might usher in the return of mass terror, and he declared that the accusation of bourgeois nationalism was used against any defender of Ukrainian culture.

> From past and recent history it may be seen that in the Ukraine it was permissible to label as a 'nationalist' anyone possessing an elementary sense of national dignity, or anyone concerned with the fate of Ukrainian culture and language, and often simply anyone who in some way failed to please some Russian chauvinist, some 'Great Russian bully'.[110]

He stated that such labels were not valid, since the people worrying about the future of Ukrainian culture were "good Communists".

> Personally I am firmly convinced that today a Ukrainian who is devoted to the cause of building communism have every reason to be worried about the fate of the nation, and if that is so, nobody in the world has the power to prevent him from speaking out about it.
> I am firmly convinced that the anxiety felt by an ever-widening circle of Ukrainian youth is the inevitable result of grave violations of the Leninist nationalities policy, or more precisely: a total revision of the Leninist nationalities policy of the Party was carried out by

---

109 Ibidem.
110 Dzyuba [Dziuba], *Internationalism or Russification?* 5. In 1968 the Humanities Press and Weidenfeld and Nicolson (London) first published the English translation and Suchasnist (Munich) issued the first edition of the original Ukrainian text.

> Stalin in the 1930s and continued by Khrushchev in the recent decade.
>
> I am firmly convinced that for the cause of building communism, for a future communist society, and for the fate of world communism, it is difficult to find today anything more useful and more indispensable than the restoration of the Leninist policy, since the fate of entire nations lies in the balance.[111]

Dziuba hinted at the lack of Ukrainian population growth under Stalinism but failed to elaborate on its cause. Like the rest of the *shistdesiatnyky*, he lacked either the courage or the information to speak extensively about the 1932–33 famine in Soviet Ukraine, and the reticence of the older generations who survived it might have contributed to the silence on this subject. Veiled allusions such as Dziuba's should be understood as the first ventures toward recovering the memory of the horror that would later be known as the Holodomor. Quoting Alexander Herzen, Marx, Engels, and others, Dziuba illustrated how the nationality question was considered a key issue that needed to be solved on the path to communism. In Marxism-Leninism the national question is subordinated to the social question, but its only possible solution entails the enrichment of nations, not their repression.

In the first chapter of *Internationalism or Russification?* Dziuba argued that crucial mistakes had been made regarding Soviet nationalities policy. He asserted the right to criticize Soviet policy and rejected the notion that the October Revolution had solved the nationality question, arguing that "in Lenin's time the Party did not conceal errors, difficulties and changes in the nationalities policy, did not shun broad and principled discussion of the nationalities question, …but on the contrary, considered such discussion indispensable for the assessment of all the factors …in a nationality situation or in the building of a nation."[112] He believed that this was the spirit that ought to guide the current Soviet leadership.

In his third chapter Dziuba described how Russian chauvinism to reappeared in the USSR during the 1920s despite the countervailing efforts of Soviet Ukrainian political leaders such as Hryhorii Hrynko and Mykola Skrypnyk. While Lenin's ideas continued to be the official ideology in theory, in reality the gap between theory and practice of the nationalities policy started to widen, due to the actions of people such as

---

111 Ibidem, 8.
112 Ibidem, 27.

Christian Rakovsky.[113] Quoting Marx's words against Paul Lafargue, Dziuba attacked the idea of creating a society without different national cultures and argued that Marxist rhetoric obscured the reality of the Russification process and disguised it as the end product of the confluence of nations.

> Lenin defended not assimilation, but the political union of proletarians of all countries, and *in this context* rejected opposition to such a union based on the fear of assimilation....[114]

The champion of this policy of assimilation was Stalin, who inaugurated the theory of the "confluence of nations," then developed by Khrushchev. But this kind of assimilation (on the basis of a single national culture or in some other way except on the basis of universal culture) is identical with colonialism (since it deprives other peoples in advance of the essential condition of equality—the right to an equal contribution to universal culture—and condemns them to cultural dependence, with all its consequences for the psychological nature of individuals belonging to this nation and for their resulting status in society).[115]

Dziuba mentions that Antonio Gramsci deemed "non-national conceptions" to be erroneous. In Ukraine, Stalin betrayed the true nationalities policy by way of a clever ruse to defeat Ukrainization.

> This was done by Stalin notwithstanding the resolutions of the Comintern and the Party Congresses; it was done silently, 'quietly', without public justification, theoretical or political. The resolutions were not carried out, they were not revised or repealed, but were simply put aside and replaced by quite opposite decisions. Even today the concept of 'Ukrainization' is considered odious, and

---

113 Hrynko (1890–1938) was a prominent Borotbist who joined the Bolshevik Party and held held important positions in the Soviet Ukrainian and USSR governments. He fell victim to the Stalinist purges in 1938. Skrypnyk (1872–1933) was an Old Bolshevik, the people's commissar for education in the Ukrainian SSR, and the first supporter of the Ukrainization policy. He committed suicide in 1933. Rakovsky (1873–1941), originally from Bulgaria, was a senior Soviet Ukrainian government figure and Soviet diplomat. In the 1930s he was marginalized for his criticism of and opposition to Stalin, who ordered the NKVD to kill him.
114 Dzyuba, *Internationalism or Russification?* 43.
115 Ibidem, 45.

people are 'ashamed' or afraid to mention it, although, we repeat, it was a Leninist policy, elaborated at Party Congresses and approved by the Comintern. There began a policy of destroying the achievements of the previous period, a policy of physically destroying the Ukrainian nation, especially its intelligentsia. This reversal was indeed one of the greatest tragedies of the Ukrainian people in its entire history.[116]

The absurdity of the situation in Soviet Ukraine is in stark contrast to the autonomy Ukrainians enjoyed in Slovakia. In Ukraine it was a common practice to accuse any supporter of Ukrainian culture of separatism. But Dziuba nonetheless underlines that no one was claiming Ukraine should be independent, even though the Soviet republics all had the right to secede from the USSR. Dziuba's entire seventh chapter focuses on exposing Russian chauvinism in order to demonstrate that Ukrainian "bourgeois nationalism" does not exist, but only opposition to Russification. In his analysis Dziuba uses classic arguments about the socio-national composition of the population: "Today, especially in the large cities, there is a very considerable stratum of Russian petty bourgeoisie which is hopelessly far from being a carrier of communist internationalism and is instead the spiritual heir of 'ten generations of colonizers'."[117] Stalin concealed tsarist imperialism by using socialist rhetoric—a tendency affirmed by the way official Soviet history was studied.

> To satisfy the most absurd tendency of identifying the USSR with the heritage of the former Russian Empire and of 'rehabilitating' the latter, today's historian does not interpret the 'history of the Fatherland' as the history of the Russians, Ukrainians, Georgians, Latvians, etc. respectively, but as the history of the Russian Empire, the master of that 'immense amount of stolen property', failing to distinguish its lawful owners and in fact defending the rights of the robber.[118]

Dziuba notes that the Soviet press attributes the successes of the Soviet Union only to the Russian people, forgetting the fruits of co-operation with other peoples inhabiting that multinational state. This subordination

---

116 Ibidem, 53.
117 Ibidem, 62.
118 Ibidem, 79.

is presented as a microcosm of the greater subordination of all economic activities to Moscow. The Russian capital organizes forced movements of populations to mix different nationalities together so that their individual identities would disappear within a greater Russian community. Regions such as Galicia in western Ukraine, where nationalist sentiments are stronger, are kept in poverty in order to force their inhabitants to migrate and lose their national roots.

Dziuba analyzes the discrimination against the Ukrainian language in publishing and education, noting that the number of publications in Russian is higher than those in Ukrainian, even within the borders of the Ukrainian republic. There is a lack of Ukrainian publications in strategic fields, notably in many of the sciences, resulting in the Russification of the Soviet technical intelligentsia. The Soviet Constitution states that all nationalities are equal, but discrimination is self-evident when only the Russians are protected and given the sole opportunity to speak their language exclusively in the other republics. Members of any other Soviet nationality who move beyond their national borders find themselves in a Russian-speaking environment. In the sphere of education, teaching in Ukrainian is compulsory at university only in Ukrainian literature and history courses, whereas courses on scientific subjects are all taught in Russian. Stalin himself established this mechanism of Russification, of which language is the first field of action.

> And here the national question again develops into a social one: we see that in city life the Ukrainian language is in a certain sense opposed as the language of the "'lower' strata of the population (caretakers, maids, unskilled labourers, newly hired workers [from the village], rank and file workers, especially in the suburbs) to the Russian language as the language of the 'higher', 'more educated' strata of society ('captains of industry', clerks and the intelligentsia). And it is not possible to 'brush aside' this social rift. The language barrier aggravates and exacerbates social divisions.[119]

Dziuba describes the tsarist policies that discriminated against nineteenth-century Ukrainian writers and laments the repression of Rostyslav Bratun and Serhii Paradzhanov. He pinpoints the lack of translators both from and into Ukrainian as a key factor in the cultural stalemate. Isolated from the rest of the world, Ukrainians remains

---

119 Ibidem, 135–36.

unaware of developments in human knowledge and are rendered unproductive by their inability to communicate with other nationalities, even those within the Soviet Union. They are denied their historical memory, since the classic works of Ukrainian literature (e.g., by Ivan Franko) and historiography (e.g., by Mykhailo Hrushevsky and Mykhailo Drahomanov) are published in very small numbers or not published at all, while important Ukrainian literary works (e.g., by Volodymyr Vynnychenko) have been unavailable to Soviet readers since the 1930s.

In Dziuba's book the subchapter "The Language Blockade" constitutes the conceptual core of his treatise. There he argues that the Soviet regime has been denationalizing Ukrainians by marginalizing the use of the Ukrainian language. This policy carries consequences for the development of individuals as well as society, given the importance of language in the acculturation processes.

> Language is so intrinsically linked with the deepest sources and most subtle manifestations of individual and social spiritual life that its renunciation, either by linguistic assimilation or a mass transition to another language, cannot occur without leaving some mark on the individual and on society as a whole. It cannot fail to produce certain dislocations, certain disturbances in the 'alveolar' system of the spiritual 'microstructure', disturbances that may be imperceptible, but can tortuously produce indirect, but none the less, grave consequences and complications. First of all this causes an inevitable impoverishment, a certain drying up and silting up of the springs of the spirit, which may not be noticed immediately, but just as rivers do not run dry immediately after the drying up of forest springs; for with the loss of your native language you lose an unfathomable world of the subconscious, you lose the whole national psychological-spiritual subsoil, all the underground springs and secrets of the great collective soul, of the collective experience of the people.[120]

Dziuba's analysis draws conclusions similar to those of the linguistic turn that was revolutionizing Western historiography at that time. The loss of language corresponds to the loss of an entire culture in the broader anthropological sense. Dziuba attacks the duplicity of the Russians who govern the Soviet Union.

---

120 Ibidem, 152.

> If to rob a people of its language is to kill it, and if this crime is immeasurably greater than any other, what then can we say when such a murderous policy hides behind noble words; when its perpetrators, assuming the role of both judge and jury, declare any instinctive self-defence a crime—including a people's defence of its own language—and are not honest enough to show their faces, but assure us that it is not they who are robbing a people of its mother tongue, but that it is the people itself which is renouncing its language of its own accord?[121]

The "spontaneous" Russification of the Ukrainians was the result of the predominance of Russian in Soviet society, fostered by targeted laws and government practices. Dziuba enumerates the spheres of this predominance: Russian is the compulsory language of all official and formal events; it is the language of the Party, Komsomol, and trade unions; the language governing all economic institutions and administrative bodies, and of the military. Russian is the language of higher education, the most common language used by primary school teachers, even in Ukraine, and the great majority of Soviet publications and materials available in libraries and archives is in Russian. This process has consequences for Russians as well—namely, that the use of Russian by so many non-native Russian-speakers involves the denationalization and bureaucratization of the Russian language, depriving it of many of its colourful nuances. Like other Soviet nationalities, the Russians run the risk of losing the characteristics that made them human, and thus they become a nation of philistines.

> Potebnya, too, rightly said that a nation which assimilated dozens of other nations ceased to be itself and would bring 'the abomination of emptiness' upon itself also. The first signs of this can already be observed today in such things as the Union-wide national vulgarity with its Philistine-bureaucratic cynicism and Volapük which invades present-day variety shows, television, and amateur art in all the Republics and is advancing ever more massively toward all spheres of culture.
> But this is not the only evil. There is another, no smaller than the first. If dozens of nations in the USSR are to lose their languages and nationalities 'voluntarily'—a very great deal of falsehood and injustice will be necessary ... regarding the past history of these

---

121 Ibidem, 154.

> peoples, regarding Marxist-Leninism, regarding the nature of communism, regarding the character of these processes which are taking place before our very eyes, regarding the values of human culture, regarding our needs for the future ... Will the burden of this untruth and injustice not press too heavily upon the shoulders of future generations? Will it be possible then to create that highly humane and moral atmosphere which we inevitably associate with communism? Can we arrive at truth through wrongdoing? These are questions which affect the future of all the nations of the USSR to an equal degree.[122]

Dziuba analyzes the discrepancy between Soviet nationality policy's theory and practice, and, using rhetorical models, he provides many examples of how the Soviet leadership tries to conceal the reality of Russification. He has a clear idea of how a genuine confluence of nations should look.

> The aim of socialism, to repeat Lenin, is not only 'to bring nations closer to each other, but also to merge them'. But this merging is viewed not mechanically as the destruction of differences, but dialectically as their mutual stimulation and cross-fertilization.... Lenin spoke of a spontaneous process of gradual amalgamation which would take place naturally over a long historic period, as a stage of the general evolution of humanity. But what our leaders have in mind is quite different and the exact opposite: a planned and state-managed amalgamation, a clearly outlined process directed from above by appropriate measures, in essence a supplanting of many nationalities, languages and cultures by a single one. What Lenin had in mind was a natural historic evolution of humanity; what is being effected in our country is the artificial Russification and emasculation of dozens of nations, in short, the very thing that Lenin fought against.[123]

Dziuba asserts that the historical blending of nations was the opposite of the "revolution from above" that is typical of Stalin's policy. Dziuba underlines the classic opposition between Ukraine's Russian-speaking cities and the Ukrainian-speaking countryside, and he reflects on the origins of the *shistdesiatnyky*.

---

122 Ibidem, 169–70. Oleksander Potebnya (Potebnia, 1835–91) was a famous Ukrainian linguist at Kharkiv University.
123 Ibidem, 185–86.

> Lenin and the Party always stressed how important it was for the proletariat and for socialist construction to resolve the conflict that exists in Ukraine between the Ukrainian-speaking peasantry and the predominantly Russian-speaking proletariat, between the Ukrainian village and the Russified city. This in particular is the meaning of the policy of Ukrainization. The proletariat, the industrialized city, were to become the active bearers of Ukrainian culture and on this basis to strengthen their alliance with, and their leadership of, the peasantry. Thus the Ukrainian nation should have become a fully-fledged socialist nation in its own right and not some sort of underdeveloped embryo, some ethnographic raw material that carries unforeseen complications for the future. The Ukrainian nation should have unfolded its strength in the proud creation of a socialist statehood ...[124]

But the peasant masses and workers who moved to the cities became Russified instead of Ukrainianized because of the discriminatory policy of Stalinism. Such a situation cannot lead to genuine communism.

> Communism leads to the maximum material and spiritual wealth of humanity, to the development of all its powers and potential, to the preservation and proliferation of all its attainments.... The contrary policy—a policy of squandering, debasing, 'writing off' these riches as scrap, a policy of bureaucratic standardization and 'reduction to a common denominator'—is a crime before communism, and future generations will not forgive such a bankrupted heritage.[125]

According to Dziuba, the *shistdesiatnyky* were struggling against standardization and the progressive homogenization and impoverishment of culture resulting from the attempt to form a single world culture. For them fighting for the preservation of Ukrainian culture meant maintaining the richness of human diversity, a task at the heart of communism. Therefore the Soviet Ukrainian government was as much responsible for betraying real Leninist principles as the USSR government in Moscow.

Dziuba asserts that the Soviet Union should not consider the renaissance of Ukrainian culture as an outbreak of nationalism, for it is a

---

124 Ibidem, 193–94.
125 Ibidem, 196.

spontaneous social process of self-defence aimed at avoiding the obliteration of the Ukrainian people. This blossoming of Ukrainian culture has been brought about by the support of rural Ukraine and its young sons.

> There is an improvement in the material position of the Ukrainian village, which sends forth more and more young people who are no longer downtrodden and crushed by poverty, but fresh, strong and proud, ready to stand up for their national identity.[126]

For Dziuba this is not a matter of demographic pressure but the result of the peasant population's improved cultural understanding through education, with young Ukrainians personifying a hopeful future.

> By thousands of different paths this [peasant] youth has come to an intuition of the Ukraine.
> This socialist national consciousness, this certainty of their right and duty to give a good account of their socialist nation to humanity, this desire to see the socialist Ukraine as truly existing and a genuinely equal country among other socialist countries, to see it as a national reality and not simply as an administrative-geographical term and a bureaucratic stumbling-block—all this is also intensified by a number of universal factors in world history and in the world communist movement.[127]

Dziuba puts forward a proposal to catalyse this utopian merger of socialism and the nation, a joint policy of democratic centralism and voluntary Ukrainianization. Quoting Lenin's work on democratic centralism, he asks:

> Would we not achieve better economic results and would we not win decisively in economic competition with capitalism by adopting a policy of broad economic initiative and independent action on the part of the [Soviet] Republics, a policy which would utilize local resources as much as possible, a policy of healthy social-economic competition between distinctive Republics (unlike the present levelling and depersonalization), a policy based on broad self-government and independent social economic activity of the

---

126 Ibidem, 205.
127 Ibidem, 206.

masses, a policy based on spiritual enthusiasm which would doubtless be awakened by the activization of national-cultural life?[128]

Dziuba's proposal was thoroughly in line with the stream of thought emanating from Eastern Europe in the 1960s that advocated socialism with a human face. The idea of Ukrainianization that Dziuba proposed was inspired by the particular values of the *shistdesiatnyky*.

> And in this matter, the nationalities question, sooner or later we will have to return to truth, we will have to return to Lenin, to Lenin's nobility of mind and sense of justice—to Lenin's nationalities policy....
>
> At the same time, it is a simple matter (and extremely necessary) to avoid that element of administrative coercion and that 'campaign' atmosphere which quite understandably frighten many people in the very word 'Ukraini[ani]zation'. A forced, official Ukraini[ani]zation from above would only compromise Ukrainian culture and language, especially when many people do not understand the need for it....
>
> I propose to counter this coercion with one thing only: *freedom*— freedom for an honest, public discussion of national matters, freedom of national choice, freedom for national self-knowledge, self-awareness and self-development. But first and last come freedom of discussion and disagreement.[129]

Dziuba maintains that justice, truth, freedom, and national awareness are the true principles of Marxism-Leninism and of the *shistdesiatnyky*. Ultimately he reacted to the current repressions in Ukraine aimed at silencing a hitherto artistic and cultural movement, and thus he stepped into politics, revealing the lies at the foundation of the Soviet Union and indicating the path to change. It is no surprise that his treatise was disseminated widely through *samvydav* and transformed Dziuba into the symbol of the *shistdesiatnyky* movement.

Covering the Trials: The Work of Viacheslav Chornovil

The arrests made it clear to the *shistdesiatnyky* that forming an official opposition was necessary and that there were two possible routes for this

---

128 Ibidem, 209.
129 Ibidem, 212–13.

opposition to take. First, they would engage in a fight for information, which meant collecting news about the repressions and disseminating it using underground publications. Second, they would demand that the Soviet security agencies identify exactly which laws had been broken and then contest the verdicts, well aware that none of the detainees had done anything illegal. This tactic also included writing numerous appeals to the Soviet authorities, and these documents were also subsequently distributed in *samvydav*. In pursuing these tasks, the *shistdesiatnyky* showed great solidarity and a sense of community. The common experiences of the clubs of creative youth spurred them to collectively assisting all of the arrested activists as though they were members of their group, even if they had never met. In the spring of 1966 Raisa Moroz was contacted by Ivan Svitlychny, who invited her to Kyiv to investigate what had happened to her husband. Besides Svitlychny's usual hospitality and willingness to help, Raisa found a sense of community there that she had never noticed before. It was as if the *shistdesiatnyky* understood "that the arrest of my husband ... was not the consequence of any forbidden activity but a vexing misunderstanding. We are not violating any laws, but the state is violating its own laws. Without even realizing it, my new friends gave me lessons on civic courage and dignity."[130]

This network of solidarity contributed to a new civic consciousness and provided its members with practical assistance in times of need. Raisa Moroz remembers that when her son became ill, Svitlychny introduced her to Nina Strokata, who offered to house her in Odesa, where her son could benefit from the milder climate.[131]

Although they were unable to attend Valentyn Moroz's and Dmytro Ivashchenko's trials because the regime had filled the courtrooms with soldiers, the *shistdesiatnyky* tried to be present at all of the other trials, including Mykhailo Ozerny's (b. 1929) in Ivano-Frankivsk on 4–7 February 1966, in order to keep unofficial minutes of the trials and then publicize the injustices perpetrated against the detainees. Court officials tried to prevent people from taking notes and ordered the confiscation of any unofficial accounts of the trials. In spite of these obstacles, a portion

---

130 Raïsa Moroz, *Proty vitru*, 69.
131 Ibidem, 85. In Odesa, Nina Strokata, a microbiologist and immunologist, and her husband, the linguist and poet Sviatoslav Karavansky, were among the founders of the Ukrainian Helsinki Group (they are profiled below).

of the minutes of Ozerny's trial was published in *samvydav*, together with his final statement.[132]

Another common form of protest was writing letters to the authorities with requests that the closed and secret trials in Kyiv, Ivano-Frankivsk, Zhytomyr, and Lviv be open and public. Thus the *shistdesiatnyky* demonstrated their ability to mobilize and their rhetoric of dissent, which continuously referred to the concept of justice and the alleged ideals of communism. The seventy-eight intellectuals who signed one of their petitions unanimously opposed the arrests. In another collective letter, signed first of all by Serhii Paradzhanov, the signatories lamented that the arrested persons are forbidden to meet with their families. Its last two paragraphs attest to the spirit of this protest.

> We are worried that this state of affairs will have a negative influence on the conditions of Ukrainian cultural life, especially on the mood of the creative youth.
>
> We also hope that in our time, when the Leninist principles of social democracy have been restored, we will have the right to an open and public examination of this question as a guarantee of justice.[133]

In a telegram to the Presidium of the Twenty-Third Congress of the CPSU, Nadia Svitlychna demanded information about her brother Ivan and directly condemned the Stalinist practices of KGB agents from a neo-Leninist point of view.

> When I was [interrogated by the KGB], when I was trying to communicate the innocence of my brother, the inquisitor of the KGB of Donetsk replied: "They shot too few of your kind in those days!" What is "your kind"? What are "those days"? What for? Is this the justice that I believed in all my life (at school, in the Komsomol, at the university)? With whose benediction is this arbitrariness taking place? Why do you Communists remain silent?

---

132 Some of these documents reached the West and were published in *Ukraïns'ka inteligentsiia pid sudom KGB: Materiialy z protsesiv V. Chornovola, M. Masiutka, M. Ozernoho ta in.* (Munich, 1970).
133 Ibidem, 187–88.

> Desperately I hope that it is possible to find some honest Communist who will not "fix my mind" but will directly and humanely answer my questions.[134]

From 13 to 15 April 1966 the closed trial of Bohdan and Mykhailo Horyn, Mykhailo Osadchy, and Myroslava Zvarychevska took place in Lviv. It was beset with unexpected disturbances from the beginning. Ivan Drach, Lina Kostenko, Viacheslav Chornovil, and the poet Mykola Kholodny travelled to Lviv to attend the proceedings, and Ivan Dziuba joined them after the first day. During the trial, people who had supported the Prolisok Club assembled in the courtroom, where they disparaged the KGB agents and praising the *shistdesiatnyky*. Chornovil refused to give evidence behind closed doors, and after he was allowed to enter the courtroom he strove to record all that he heard.

The atmosphere of the interrogation before the trial is masterfully described in Mykhailo Osadchy's memoir, *Cataract*.[135] The KGB agents were imbued with Russian chauvinism, as Osadchy found out at his first hearing.

> [The agents said] "He even wrote his thesis about one of them—that shitty humorist Vyshnya [Ostap Vyshnia]. Ha-ha, you want to make nationalists famous?"
> I object, I really object to this senseless tirade of sneers and taunts. "But how dare you ... a prominent Ukrainian ... seven volumes of his work about to be published ... nominated for the Lenin Prize ... long since rehabilitated ..."
> "Rehabilitated?" They gape at me as if I have told them of a new Pompeii. They refuse to grant credence to my words and burst into laughter. They actually double up with laughter and point their fingers at me as if I were some sort of freak. Oh, how they laugh![136]

---

134 Ibidem, 190–91.
135 Mykhaylo Osadchy, *Cataract*, trans., ed., and annot. by Marco Carynnyk (New York and London, 1976), xvii–xxii. Osadchy (1936–1994) was born in a village in Sumy Oblast. He studied journalism at Lviv State University and, after graduating in 1958, worked an editor at the regional television station in Lviv. Osadchy also pursued an academic career, writing a candidate of sciences dissertation on irony in Ostap Vyshnia's prose, and became a journalism lecturer at Lviv State University in 1960. Ostap Vyshnia is the pen name of Pavlo Hubenko (1889–1956), a famous Soviet Ukrainian humourist and statirist who was sentenced to ten years in concentration camps in northern Siberia in 1933. In 1943 he was allowed to resume writing and was published again thereafter.
136 Ibidem, 8.

This portrayal casts doubt on whether the Khrushchev Thaw ushered in any real or significant changes in the KGB.

> I talk to him about freedom of speech, about the new concept of dictatorship of the proletariat which, according to the Party Program, "has accomplished its historical mission and from the viewpoint of internal developments ceased to be indispensable in the USSR." I remind him that "the State in the present era has been transformed into a State of all the people, an instrument for expressing the interests and the will of all citizens."...
>
> "There always was and always will be a dictatorship," he remarked with a sly squint.
>
> "Excuse me," I attempt to contradict him, "but I am a young communist, and surely I ought to take the Party's word sooner than yours."
>
> "Communists, even young ones, don't wind up in here," he replies, a smile quivering at the corners of his thin lips. "And as for what you said, I'm not certain whether it was stated by the Party or by Khrushchev."[137]

Under such circumstances, the four accused could not count on the judges' impartiality. The transcript of Mykhailo Horyn's "Last Word" at the trial became a classic of *samvydav* and is the quintessence of *shistdesiatnytstvo* in spirit. In it Horyn begins by contesting the accusations.

> In the final indictment I am accused of holding anti-Soviet nationalistic views. And the state prosecutor allowed himself to compare my activities with those of Ukrainian bourgeois nationalists. I declared and I still declare that nationalistic views are alien to me....
>
> ... I state once more that neither ideology, philosophy, legislation, nor the social and political system of the Soviet state are alien to me. When I criticized, I did not criticize the Soviet legislation, but the violation of that law in everyday life; I did not criticize the Soviet social system, but separate aspects of the socio-political and economic life of our country.[138]

---

137 Ibidem, 11–12.
138 Chornovil, *The Chornovil Papers*, 106–107.

One must assume that Horyn was being forthright, since he had actually declared more than once that his political views had always been anti-Soviet.[139] However, the strength of Horyn's words, expressed when he was already convinced he would be found guilty, demonstrates that Kyiv's *shistdesiatnyky* had influenced his thinking. Unlike Levko Lukianenko's case, however, there is not enough documentation to call Horyn's subsequent declarations into question. His childhood in a nationalistic environment suggests that his statement at the trial was hypocritical. On the other hand, it could be assumed that his political views fluctuated throughout the decades, and that by the mid-1960s, owing to the influence of personalities such as Svitlychny, he was less nationalistic and more of a socialist than he would later admit.

In his "Last Word" Horyn went on to describe Soviet discrimination against Ukrainian culture within and beyond the borders of the Ukrainian SSR. A most interesting passage in his famous speech focuses on Stalinism, the Khrushchev Thaw, and the latter's fundamental shortcomings.

> The third problem that worried me was the losses to Ukrainian culture during Stalin's despotism. I was always revolted by the fact that citizens who had a sense of civic duty and Party members who had a sense of duty towards the Party witnessed crimes and did nothing about it. It was then that the philistine moral philosophy, "This does not concern me", was born. Under the threat of reprisals, the broad masses of workers ceased to take part in the political life of the country. Politics were mainly concocted in the kitchen of Stalin who, according to Lenin, liked "spicy dishes." This moral philosophy was officially elevated to the level of state behaviour by Nikita Khrushchev, who announced at the congress that he knew about Stalin's crimes but was afraid to oppose him openly, fearing that he could have been exterminated and branded as a traitor to his fatherland. This from the leader of the Party and the head of the government! In that case, how could ordinary citizens act? Therefore I stated that remnants of Stalinism still exist in our public and political life, that this spirit ought to be rejected, and that the masses ought to be drawn into political life; the only way we can safeguard ourselves from the repetition of events of the [nineteen] thirties is for every person to have a strong sense of civic duty.[140]

---

139 Horyn', "U nas bula velyka misiia," 188–99.
140 Ibidem, 110–11.

These lines reveal the dissatisfaction that the *shistdesiatnyky* felt toward the politics of the Thaw. The "philistine" philosophy in politics is the opposite of what was called *mishchanstvo* (babbittry) in literary terms.

Horyn concluded his speech by stating his credo for the future.

> And so I declare that the fight against Stalin has only just begun. And the possibility of a revival of Stalin's despotism and lawlessness can be buried forever only when all the people begin to take part in the political life of the country, when a reliable apparatus is established to control the government, and when the elections are, first of all, transformed into an instrument of such control. It will be possible when the instigation for policy changes in the realm of economics and culture comes not just "from the top", but also from the "bottom"; when the change in the material situation of *kolkhoz* members do not depend on the good mood of [Aleksei] Kosygin alone, but is in the hands of the *kolkhoz* peasants themselves; when, finally, a feeling of civic duty in every citizen replaces the feeling of philistinism which is being so widely cultivated.[141]

Mykhailo Horyn was sentenced to six years in prison camps. Meanwhile Soviet security agencies began persecuting those who were trying to keep the public informed about the trials, focusing much of their efforts on the journalist Viacheslav Chornovil. Chornovil's activity was in many ways representative of the renaissance of Soviet journalism during the Thaw—which, driven by the "raison d'être of *honest journalism*"—was "transforming Soviet media into an intermediary between the intelligentsia and the state."[142] However, Chornovil himself attracted more attention from the authorities by pushing these journalistic precepts farther than most of his colleagues dared. Abandoning the official channels of information and dedicating himself to underground journalism, he cast off any form of self-censorship in his pursuit of "honest journalism." His first two pamphlets, "Justice or Revival of Terror?" and "The Misfortune of Intellect," reflect his audacious spirit.

Chornovil was an editor of the Soviet Ukrainian newspaper *Moloda hvardiia* from September 1964 until his dismissal in September 1965, after which he worked for a smaller periodical, *Druh chytacha*, until the

---

141 Ibidem, 112.
142 Zubok, *Zhivago's Children*, 140-49, quote 146.

beginning of the 1965 trials. On 15 September 1965 he resigned from the Komsomol, justifying his decision by arguing that a good communist could not partake in an organization that defied socialist legality.[143] This was a declaration of war against the system, and the authorities interpreted it as such. On 30 September KGB agents searched Chornovil's apartment and seized fifty-five old Ukrainian books, mainly published before the First World War in Habsburg-ruled Galicia; they were never returned to him.[144] Further antagonizing the authorities, he refused to appear as a witness at Mykhailo Osadchy's trial because it was being held behind closed doors. The judge subsequently found him in contempt him for refusing to testify and convicted him of anti-Soviet activity on April 19. In his statement to the judges during one of his appeals, Chornovil recalled his career as a model young communist, including his successes in Soviet schools and the Komsomol, which many other young intellectuals shared.

> And suddenly [these intellectuals] are a bunch of criminals. What is this—a paradox or conformity to the law? If this is a paradoxical case, then how can one explain why nearly twenty people, primarily young and with irreproachable pasts, have been sentenced under article 62? But if this is an instance of conforming to the law, then that is frightening. One does not wish to believe that intelligence, curiosity, and a sense of social justice have led young people to [harbouring] and anti-Soviet sentiment. Instead, perhaps what they call "anti-Sovietism" is just a mixture of [their] innocence and the irreproachability of the Soviet order?[145]

Chornovil was not afraid to point out the KGB's frequent illegal actions and the inconsistency of their accusations, subtly calling the integrity of the judges into question.

> I do not have any illusions about the verdict. You are certainly going to sentence me to the maximum penalty prescribed by this article. But even if you threatened me not only with forced labour and administrative woes but also with prison and drudgery, I would still speak thus. For there is no penalty more frightening than the

---

143 *Ukraïns'ka inteligentsiia pid sudom KGB*, 15–18. On Chornovil see also *Do 70-richchia Viacheslava Chornovola (1937–2007)*, a special issue of *Moloda natsiia* (Kyiv), vol. 50 (2009).
144 *Ukraïns'ka inteligentsiia pid sudom KGB*, 19–39.
145 Ibidem, 49.

tortures of an unclean soul; for there is no higher court than the truth.[146]

Despite his belief that imprisonment was inevitable, Chornovil was exonerated of the charges related to his unwillingness to testify. He documented the ideas he expressed in his courtroom speech as a pamphlet that he disseminated in *samvydav* under the title "Just Trials or Relapses into Terror?" It has is also be referred to by its opening line, "I Ask Nothing of You." This work, a brief essay on the injustices committed during the 1966 trials, was introduced by two letters, the first to the prosecutor general of the Ukrainian SSR, the head of the Supreme Court of the USSR, and the chairman of the KGB in Ukraine; and the second, to First Secretary of CPU Petro Shelest. Although the authorities were known for being "apathetic to human tragedies, to the demoralizing effect of fear, which like a slimy serpent, creeps into the lives of many a Ukrainian family," Chornovil addressed the pamphlet to them in the hope that they would acknowledge the gravity of the injustices: "I am not speaking out because I hope to alleviate the lot of the prisoners and convicts.… But not to disclose today my own attitude towards what is taking place would mean my becoming a taciturn participant in the wanton disregard of socialist legality."[147] The letter addressed to Shelest was notably friendlier in tone, as he was considered a defender of the *shistdesiatnyky*. Placing hope in Shelest as an ally, Chornovil implored the functionary who would first read it not to give the letter to Andrii Skaba (by then an undersecretary of the CC CPU) but directly to Shelest.

In the pamphlet Chornovil examines all of the stages of the 1965–66 repressions, frequently quoting the law directly in order to underline the unjust behaviour of both the KGB and the judges. The main impetus for the wave of repressions was article 62 of the Ukrainian SSR's Criminal Code, which stipulated the prosecution of any anti-Soviet activity. This enabled penalizing those who exercised their right of free expression. A "systematic philistinism," so to speak, thus arose from this law: "What lesson do our citizens learn from Article 62 of the Criminal Code of the Ukr. SSR? They are taught to follow blindly and accurately the tracks of

---

146 Ibidem, 55.
147 Vyacheslav Chornovil, "The Petition of Vyacheslav Chornovil," in *The Chornovil Papers*, 3. I am using this translation, which corresponds most closely to the version in Ukrainian published in Chornovil's *Tvory v desiaty tomakh*, vol. 2 (Kyiv, 2003), 79–155. A slightly different version is in his *Ia nichoho u vas ne proshu* (Toronto, 1968).

the latest trends published by the press; they learn the petty-bourgeois morals—to fear and to look behind."[148] Chornovil describes the illegal ways in which wiretapping, searches and arrests, interrogations, intimidations of witnesses, and trials are conducted. Using many examples drawn from covert minutes of the trials, he highlights the criminal investigators' and judges' Russian chauvinism and their repeated violations of the law. His conclusion is terse: it is the security agents, not the intellectuals, who are undermining Soviet legality.

Chornovil does not stop, however, at identifying defects in the Soviet system. He also attempts to locate their sources. Looking beyond the Stalin regime, he views the Yezhov Terror as the outcome of an earlier terrorist process. Interestingly—perhaps too focused on the history of the Ukrainian intelligentsia—Chornovil fails to include the Soviet Ukrainian Great Famine of 1932–33 in his narrative.

> Somehow, many people associate the beginning of the Stalin terror with the year 1937, when renowned Party leaders were sent to jail. In fact, it all began much earlier, though at first glance the earlier suppressions might have appeared more respectable. In Ukraine, at least, we find that tendencies toward gross violation of socialist legality appeared by the end of the [nineteen] twenties. At first, with the expansion of collectivization, they arrested a part of the intelligentsia (predominantly from the villages), those who had supported the UNR [Ukrainian National Republic] during the revolution but who later became absolutely loyal to the Soviet regime and who enthusiastically welcomed the ukrainization [sic] announced by the Party.[149]

Chornovil draws parallels between the atrocities of Stalin's regime and the events of the present, recalling how Stalin attacked intellectuals outside the Party, contrived the show trial of the fictitious Union for the Liberation of Ukraine (SVU), and removed those who stood firmly against Soviet policies (e.g., Ostap Vyshnia, Les Kurbas, Mykhailo Yalovy, and others).[150] The show trials, the murder in 1934 of Sergei Kirov, head of the

---

148 Chornovil, "The Petition of Vyacheslav Chornovil," 14.
149 Ibidem, 70.
150 The Soviet Ukrainian writer Mykhailo Yalovy (1895-1937, pseud.: Yuliian Shpol) was a leading member of the Borotbist party that merged with the Bolsheviks in Ukraine, and the first president of the Vaplite writers' organization (1925–28). Falsely accused of espionage and terrorism by the NKVD in 1933, he was sentenced to ten years in a labour

Bolshevik Party in Leningrad, and the purges during the Yezhov Terror purges of 1937 were seen as a continuous escalation of violence that would be interrupted only by Stalin's death. Chornovil was afraid that the new secret trials indicated the return of terror as a means of governing. He seems to have believed that at least some Soviet leaders, such as Shelest, were opposed to resurrecting the old NKVD-KGB methods, but the repressions were alarming nonetheless.

> Who is put behind bars in Ukraine today? The authorities are trying mostly young people who grew up under the Soviet regime, who were educated in Soviet schools, Soviet universities, and in the Komsomol. Tried as bourgeois nationalists are people who do not remember the bourgeois system, whose grandfathers or fathers suffered privation in their rich native land. And no one even thought of looking for a deeper reason, instead of talking idly about the influence of the bourgeois ideology and bourgeois nationalism.[151]

Chornovil viewed the detainees not as anti-Soviet activists but as citizens with a human conscience who were trying to face and resolve the problems of Soviet society. It was they who were really fighting against the enemies of the Soviet Union.

> At this point in time, when the condemnation of Stalin's despotism and violence is final and irretrievable (although some not too clever and hopelessly cruel people would like very much to turn back the clock), experiments with the undercutting of roots, experiments with silencing and intimidation, are unfit and historically irresponsible. I will say, with full conviction, that this is essentially an anti-Soviet affair. That is why I write about it.[152]

In his subsequent work, "The Misfortune of Intellect: Portraits of Twenty 'Criminals,'" Chornovil abandoned the pamphlet form for reportage about twenty victims of the 1965–66 repressions. The longest section was about Sviatoslav Karavansky (1920–1916), whose story differs from the others'. He was born in Odesa, where he attended school and the state university. During the Nazi-Soviet War he fought in the Red Army,

---

camp in the Solovets Islands. He was shot and buried in the Sandarmokh forest in Soviet Karelia, as were nine thousand other political prisoners in 1937 and 1938.
151 Chornovil, "The Petition of Vyacheslav Chornovil," 72.
152 Ibidem, 73.

avoided capture by German soldiers, and returned to Odesa in 1942, where he organized a bookshop and joined the OUN. He was arrested in 1944 and sentenced in 1945 to twenty-five years in prison camps in the Far North and Siberia. After being released in December 1960 on the basis of the 1955 amnesty decree, and returned to Odesa, where he worked as a mechanic, translator, and part-time correspondent. He also compiled a dictionary of Ukrainian rhymes, translated English poetry and Charlotte Brontë's *Jane Eyre* into Ukrainian, and contributed articles on language issues to Ukrainian periodicals. However, on 13 November 1965, without a trial, he was sent again incarcerated in a prison camp to serve the remainder of his original sentence,[153] likely to punish him for his activities as a defender of Ukrainian culture, including the writing and dissemination of *samvydav* documents. Karavansky opposed the 1958 education reforms in Soviet Ukraine and had denounced Soviet Ukraine's minister of higher education, Yurii Dadenkov, for not respecting the equality of nations.[154] In "About a Single Political Error" he condemned the official position "against teaching the national tongue [Ukrainian] in the schools. What true internationalist could be worried by the fact a child learns the language of a brother-nation? Only chauvinists can lock their children in narrow national frameworks, hiding behind theories of the exclusiveness of their nationality."[155]

Karavansky claimed that Soviet laws contradicted the Leninist principles of nationality policy and internationalism. Because he was a former member of the OUN, his advocacy of Leninist principles is likely a strategic choice rather than an expression of genuine support for Communism. Karavansky is an example of how the culture of the *shistdesiatnyky* was able to draw other streams of the Ukrainian national movement into their milieu. While he echoed the rhetoric found in the writings of his contemporaries, his originality lay in the attention he devoted to other nationalities. In his petition to the chairman of the Council of Nationalities of the Supreme Soviet of the USSR, Karavansky examined Soviet nationality policy, underlining the persecutions suffered by the Armenians, Crimean Tatars, and other Turkic peoples, Estonians, Jews, Latvians, Lithuanians, and Volga Germans in the USSR, especially after the Second World War; and he condemned the Soviet internal-

---

153 Chornovil, "The Misfortune of Intellect," in *The Chornovil Papers*, 166–70. The essay is also known as "Woe from Wit."
154 See ibidem, 170–74.
155 Ibidem, 178.

passport system of identification as discrimination against rural inhabitants.¹⁵⁶ In another petition, which he wrote in 1966 while in a prison camp in Mordovia, Karavansky requested an investigation of the infamous Katyn mass murder of Polish officers in 1942, which he believed the NKVD had committed.¹⁵⁷ His specific contribution to *shistdesiatnytstvo* was his ability to connect the struggle for Ukrainian culture to the broader problem of Soviet nationalities policy, thereby laying the foundation for an alliance between the Ukrainians and other Soviet nationalities that would take place in the latter years of the 1960s.

Chornovil's "Misfortune of Intellect" painted a portrait of a generation of young, mostly rural-born, scholars concerned with the question of Ukrainian culture, whose efforts to enrich their society were met with repressions by the Soviet state. Unmasking the hypocrisy of Soviet rule, it provoked a strong reaction when it began circulating in *samvydav* in 1967.

On 3 August 1967 Chornovil was arrested, charged with fabricating and disseminating slanderous materials about the Soviet Union. Though he denied having written anything slanderous,¹⁵⁸ he was brought to trial on 15 November 1967. He began his closing statement at the trial by refuting the accusation of being a nationalist and claimed he was simply fulfilling his idea of journalism.

> It seems that I am a nationalist as well. If only it could be established whether [I am] a bourgeois or, maybe, a socialist one? I did not dwell on the nationalities question in my statements. The conclusion [that I am a nationalist] has been drawn solely on the basis of the fact that I wrote about violations of legality committed in the Ukraine. And if I lived in Tambov and wrote something similar, what kind of nationalist would I be then—a Tambovian one?¹⁵⁹

After declaring that he could and should not be indicted for having sent petitions to Soviet officials, as this did not constitute a crime, Chornovil called into question the reason for his trial in order to illustrate the speciousness of the accusations.

---

156 See ibidem, 198–207.
157 See ibidem, 207.
158 See Browne, ed., *Ferment in the Ukraine*, 157–58.
159 Ibidem, 159.

> I consider that my trial is far from being a routine trial, and is even to a certain extent in the nature of a milestone. Because it is not only I as a person who am on trial here; thought is on trial here....
>
> ... If, having carefully studied the works of Lenin, I began to maintain that in theory we subscribed to correct Leninist teachings on the nationalities question, but that in practice we committed deviations from them, and if I based my thesis on Leninist principles and an analysis of concrete data about questions of contemporary cultural construction, economics and so on, what would this represent on my part—a point of view, my convictions, or slander against Soviet reality?...
>
> ... would this, on my part, be [an exercise of] my constitutional right to appeal, with my ideas, to the authorities I have elected or 'the dissemination of slanderous fabrications'?
>
> But even if I was wrong ... and it proves possible to counter my arguments with a series of other arguments which turn out to be more weighty, does this mean that I should be put on trial so that I and everybody in the future would not dare to think at all?[160]

Thus Chornovil demonstrated the authorities' violation of human rights and the substantial injustice of his trial. Although one might have expected an accompanying condemnation of the entire Soviet establishment and its ideology, a sweeping denunciation of this kind was not in keeping with the mentality of the *shistdesiatnyky*. Drawing upon Leninist principles, Chornovil argued that it was the duty of all citizens, and not just designated institutions, to participate in the state's governance and uphold legality.

> When the [October] Revolution triumphed and the construction of a new type of state began, V. I. Lenin constantly insisted that as many citizens as possible should take part in governing the state and society; in this he saw the only guarantee of a successful development of socialism. His famous phrase that a cook should be able to govern the state should obviously not be interpreted in the vulgar sense ... These words should be understood to mean that under socialism each ordinary citizen should be able to think in statesmanlike terms, formulate his point of view even in the most complicated case, and not wait until someone writes the next program into him. As proof of this, one can quote other words of V.

---

160 Ibidem, 162–64.

> I. Lenin's which he uttered during the first months of Soviet rule: "All citizens must take part in the work of the courts and in the government of the country. It is important for us to literally draw all working people into the government of the state. It is a task of tremendous difficulty. But socialism cannot be implemented by a minority, by the Party. It can be implemented only by tens of millions when they have learned to do it themselves."
>
> I tried to act according to these Leninist precepts, and you will now inform me of the result of this attempt.[161]

Indeed it was this adherence to Leninist precepts that informed Chornovil and his generation's way of thinking. Disturbed by the chasm between the theory and practice of socialism, Chornovil's peers attempted to reconcile Leninist principles—or what they believed them to be—and their implementation. The birth of a strong national sentiment in the *shistdesiatnyky* was an extension of this endeavour.

Mykhailyna Kotsiubynska explained it thus:

> In his introduction to Svitlychny's [1990] collection *A Heart for Bullets and Rhymes* Dziuba remarks that he embraced Ukrainian patriotism not out of national sentimentalism or emotion, but out of humanitarian ideals and values common to the whole of humankind. Ivan's "Ukrainianness" was evident in a quiet way, unostentatious. When he translated [Pierre de] Ronsard or Baudelaire, it was aimed at a practical strengthening of the very rich possibilities of the Ukrainian language, without any parenthetical admiration of its much-vaunted "nightingaleness." Patriotism not as a slogan but as work, as breathing.[162]

The national feeling of the *shistdesiatnyky* did not spring from a nationalistic education but from a Soviet education, which, they believed, taught them to love their culture, fight for its full-fledged development, and condemn the discrepancy between theory and praxis.

Chornovil's sentence to three years' imprisonment in a labour camp was quickly commuted to eighteen months. Ivan Dziuba, Lina Kostenko, Ivan Svitlychny, and Nadia Svitlychna sent a letter to the Soviet Ukrainian authorities to denounce the trial—although it had been open, it violated the rights of the defence to examine the contested documents and call

---

161 Ibidem, 165.
162 Kotsiubyns'ka, *Ivan Svitlychnyi, shistdesiatnyk*, 10.

witnesses.[163] Unfortunately, their appeals fell upon deaf ears, and Chornovil was sent to a prison camp in Vinnytsia Oblast, where he would remain until February 1969. He was deliberately kept far apart from the other convicts, as even within the camp's confines the community of intellectuals who were arrested in 1965 had proven capable of substantially changing the Ukrainian national movement.

In and Out of the Mordovian Camp

Almost all those convicted in the 1965 arrests were sent to serve their terms in a prison camp in the Mordovian ASSR southeast of Moscow. This was the same camp where Levko Lukianenko and a large number of former members of the OUN and the UPA were already being held. The arrival of this group of *shistdesiatnyky* in the Mordovian Gulag changed the general environment—a change that would be reflected in the significant transformation of some of the figures themselves.

The best example of the shift in camp atmosphere is Lukianenko, who in his memoirs seized upon the importance of the arrival of three of the *shistdesiatnyky*—Mykhailo Horyn, Valentyn Moroz, and Mykhailo Masiutko. According to Lukianenko, the inmates' discussions in the barracks were dominated by a struggle for supremacy among the egos of the various Ukrainian nationalists. The *shistdesiatnyky* inaugurated what he called "brand new trends."

> In 1966 a new generation of Ukrainian political prisoners arrived. They brought with them a fearless attitude toward the police, aggressive exchanges of opinion in political discussions regarding the administration of the camps, and overtly maintained relationships with the intelligentsia of Kyiv and Lviv and with Ukrainians abroad. These neophytes began collecting evidence of violations of the rights of the political prisoners with the goal of obtaining their release, and their radicalism pushed them also to collect evidence of the illegality of the police persecution of the civilians who were collecting evidence on their behalf. In short, the new generation brought to the zone a new phenomenon of antagonism toward the law-enforcement bodies: the prisoners collected evidence of violations of the law, and the administration fought to keep the letters containing information about said

---

163 The letter is in ibidem, 166–68.

violations from leaving the zone. Since it was our initiative, our ingenuity awarded us the victory in this competition.[164]

The *shistdesiatnyky* brought their methods of battling the Soviet authorities into the prison camps and taught other inmates how to confront the bureaucratic system by using the same techniques. Lukianenko remembers the pride he felt when he first encountered this group. Other nationalities, especially the three Baltic ones, had previously held moral primacy among the prisoners, but now the Ukrainians showed "that Ukraine was not yet dead, that it was fighting for freedom."[165] The victory against the camp's administration can be attributed to the fact that the *shistdesiatnyky* transformed the "battlefield," in a manner of speaking.

> Horyn, Moroz, and Masiutko brought to the zone not only a belief in their rectitude but also the courage to confront other prisoners and officers of the Ministry of Internal Affairs and the KGB, and to publicly demonstrate that they spoke the truth while the authorities lied. They proved, with various examples taken from domestic and foreign policy, that the authorities were wrong and suppressed the truth; for the truth of life differed absolutely from how they [the authorities] represented it. In addition, following the premise that truth always wins in the end, they [the *shistdesiatnyky*] were confident that the truth would prevail this time as well. Within a few days, all of the prisoners and the [camp] administration realized that a new phenomenon had appeared that had not existed before, and that this new phenomenon was establishing a new atmosphere, new relations with the administration, and new dynamics among the prisoners.[166]

The *shistdesiatnyky* in the prison camps continued their struggle so that the truth might prevail over the Soviet government's lies. This destabilized the camp's hierarchy, for their new methods of fighting against Soviet structures were much more effective than those of the previous generation of Ukrainian nationalists. But the prison camps did

---

164 Lukianenko, *Z chasiv nevoli*, bk. 2: 228. "*Zona*" (zone) can mean a prison camp (internment zone), but it also refers to the idea of the entire USSR as a prison camp. In Soviet prisoners' parlance the former is always linked to the latter.
165 Ibidem, 229.
166 Ibidem, 231.

not end the struggle of the *shistdesiatnytstvo* movement, as they had the war between the UPA and the Soviet state.

> Prisoners did not conceal their contacts—on the contrary, they were proud of their friendships with poets, artists, and educated and honest people in general. But even more importantly, relatives and friends did not disown their arrested loved ones and did not blame them, but rather expressed the desire to continue to keep in touch, to write them letters and telegrams, and to send them their regards. Meanwhile the authorities arrested their potential enemies dishonestly. The arrests were not approved of by people who knew the detainees and did not intimidate them; instead, the authorities lost popular support and became isolated from the community.[167]

Lukianenko noticed that the old propaganda employed against Ukrainian nationalists did not work against the *shistdesiatnyky*. A favourite charge that the Soviet Union used to levy against the so-called bourgeois nationalists was that they did not have popular support and were financed during the Second World War by capitalist Germany with the aim of conquering new land in the western regions of the country for fascist exploitation. These old fictions were no longer effective,

> for these young people were born in Soviet Ukraine, received their education in Soviet universities, and spent their youth in the Komsomol and the system of Communist upbringing. Their first steps were the same as those of the police and KGB agents. They did not inherit their parents' state-inspired guilt complex, and they regarded the officers not from below but at the same level. In addition, they held two crucial advantages: first, they could see more profoundly the shortcomings of the Communist system, since they were more educated; and second, they had the courage and bravery to tell the truth that the agents tried to conceal, in this way demonstrating the agents' cowardice.[168]

As genuine products of the Soviet system, the *shistdesiatnyky* were not a foreign body. They felt themselves at home in a home they knew better than anyone else, better even than the watchmen. Their intellectual skills made them more clear-sighted and strengthened their desire for honesty.

---

167 Ibidem, 231.
168 Ibidem, 232.

They differed significantly not only from the KGB agents, who were a legacy of Stalinism, but also from the old nationalists, as Lukianenko was forced to acknowledge. Recounting the discussions among the prisoners and the police who monitored them, Lukianenko remembers that the *shistdesiatnyky* were not as nationalist as the other inmates and that Ukrainian independence was not the primary objective of their struggle. An independent Ukrainian national state was the final outcome, so to speak. But considering the world view of our three *shistdesiatnyky*—Horyn, Moroz, and Masiutko—they had another task after they arrived in the camp. Before and during their investigation and for some time after, they still did not stand up categorically for the independence of Ukraine, nor did they agree with any nationalist declarations. Instead they supported, through their words and their writings, the defence of the Ukrainian language and culture and the freedom of literature and any form of artistic expression.[169]

According to Lukianenko, many of the *shistdesiatnyky* became true nationalists during their incarceration in the prison camp, a process he considered inevitable, but not all of them were thus affected. (The influence of the prison-camp experience on the inmates' psyches will be examined in further detail below.) In the early days, in fact, it was the *shistdesiatnyky* who seemed to exert an influence on their surroundings rather than vice-versa. The most important and significant consequence was the publicity surrounding the Jurists' Affair, as Lukianenko's case would come to be known. It was Mykhailo Horyn who urged Lukianenko to recount his story through official petitions to the Soviet authorities.

> "Oh Levko ... Kyiv's patriotic circles first heard some information about your union as a group of lawyers in 1964. Ivan Svitlychny mentioned it. We have to release information about the other political prisoners."
> "Where did Svitlychny learn about it?"
> "A *chekist* [KGB agent] mentioned it in high-society company. It was only generic information. But it would be interesting to know more. So write about your case in detail for our Kyivan friends. Some honest people will see what you write, and then maybe with luck it will be distributed."[170]

---

169 Ibidem, 232.
170 Ibidem, 235.

With Horyn's encouragement, Lukianenko and his companions decided to write petitions to the Soviet authorities regarding their cases and the conditions they were forced to endure in the camp. Lukianenko, Vasyl Lutskiv, Stepan Virun, and Ivan Kandyba wrote letters about their cases and any incidents illegality or violence they suffered. Some excerpts from these missives are in chapter 1, and several more will be included here to demonstrate how the struggle in which Lukianenko and his companions were engaged in 1966 was the outcome of merging the sentenced Lviv jurists' legal skills with the dissent tactics of the *shistdesiatnyky*. This amalgamation would become a distinctive characteristic of dissent in Ukraine in the following decades. In his letter to Roman Rudenko, procurator general of the USSR, Lukianenko raised the constitutional right of secession to justify the formation of the URSS.

> It is true that in 1959 I spoke with Virun about the desirability of forming an organisation, would not be nationalist but directed at struggling against illegal limitations on democratic freedoms and for the secession of the Ukrainian SSR from the USSR on the basis of Article 17 of the USSR Constitution. And taking advantage of a constitutional right can hardly be regarded as nationalism.[171]

Within the accusations against the KGB agents of acting illegally during the investigations there was an undercurrent of frustration regarding the failures of the philosophical turn of the Twentieth CPSU Congress. Since the agents' behaviour was no different than the NKVD's in Stalin's time, clearly the precepts established at the congress had been disregarded. This is explicitly stated in Virun's appeal to Oles Honchar.

> From the very start the preliminary investigation was conducted by people who, in the course of many long years, had assimilated into their blood and bones methods of conducting investigations now condemned by the Party. The spirit of the new age had not reached them; they did not discard their notorious past experience. Having shut us up in jail, they began to work on us according to all the rules of their art, guided by the well-known adage: if ordered to get a conviction, getting it is merely a technical matter.[172]

---

171 Browne, ed., *Ferment in the Ukraine*, 36.
172 Ibidem, 50.

It is worth noting that the jurists purposely used Marxist ideology as a rhetorical weapon against the state, which ideologically and propagandistically, if not practically, considered itself the embodiment of socialism. For instance, Lukianenko cited the principle of national self-determination in his letter to the chairman of Ukraine's Supreme Soviet to ground his political claims.

> The persecution of people who wish to exercise the constitutional right of secession runs counter to Marxist theory, which has always included the right of nations to self-determination. The right of nations to self-determination has always been an integral part of the Programme of the CPSU. And if an individual is a communist in practice and not just as a matter of form, he cannot oppose the Ukrainian nation's right to self-determination.[173]

The significance of these letters might have been minimal had they been read only by the Soviet authorities, but they became popular pieces of *samvydav* in 1966 thanks to Ivan Svitlychny, who decided to give the previously unknown Jurists' Affair as much visibility as possible. In his preface to Lukianenko's letters Svitlychny explained why he wished to circulate them. Admitting that he had previously known little about the Jurists' Affair, he nonetheless confirmed his conviction that everything in the letters was true. From his own experiences of the 1965 arrests, Svitlychny understood that under physical and psychological pressure people could be forced to confess to crimes they did not commit. He also stressed the detrimental effect of the secret trials, for unlike in 1965–66, in 1961 the Soviet authorities had succeeded in keeping the general public unaware of what was going on. Therefore publishing these letters was an effort at restoring justice.

> That is why, without knowing the actual purpose which prompted the dispatch of these documents from the camp, I still consider it my civic duty to forward them (without correcting any roughnesses, even grammatical or stylistic ones) not only to the addresses given on the letters and statements but also to other civic and cultural personalities, so that this matter should finally receive publicity and not be reviewed yet again by the same instigators …
>
> It is not merely the fate of a number of men which is at stake, however, but equally the affirmation of Soviet legality, our civic

---

173 Ibidem, 90.

conscience, [and] our ideals—for which we must fight with word and deed. Who knows whether these people, who disposed so cruelly of L. H. Lukyanenko [Lukianenko] and his comrades yesterday, are not today doing the same to others? Every injustice and every [kind of] arbitrary action is possible behind closed doors, out of sight of society.[174]

The above quotation clearly elucidates *samvydav*'s function: making facts available to the public that the authorities preferred to keep secret. *Samvydav* did what journalists and other information agencies behind the Iron Curtain failed to do—it attempted to restore Soviet legality. These letters, written under the influence of the *shistdesiatnyky*, were for Lukianenko the ultimate manifestation of the democratic, though not yet nationalistic, dissenting spirit of the 1960s.

In sum, Lukianenko and his companions in the Mordovian prison camp were about to undergo a transformation at the hands of the *shistdesiatnyky*. Lukianenko constantly discussed politics and Ukraine with the other inmates, willingly modifying his own and influencing others' political views. He writes that "The Ukrainian groups of political prisoners arrived in the camp as democrats. In three years they turned into nationalists."[175] The demographic breakdown of the camp facilitated this transformation: "Nearly half the camp consisted of nationalists. Among them were those who fought in the UPA under the command of the OUN against [all foreign] occupiers ... and had fought for the independence of Ukraine; and political prisoners who had been democratic before their arrest became nationalists here."[176]

Although it is difficult to believe that the world view of anyone who was a member of the OUN or the UPA in the 1940s was not based on nationalist ideology, it is easy to see how captivity generated hatred of the Soviet state in the inmates. Lukianenko remembers his fellow inmates' to share their state of mind with new prisoners: "Each insurgent wanted not only to become personally acquainted with me—that happened during the first two to three months after my arrival in the zone—but also wanted to have lengthy conversations about politics, about his own case, and

---

174 Browne, ed., *Ferment in the Ukraine*, 32.
175 Lukianenko, *Z chasiv nevoli: Sosnovka-7*, 472.
176 Ibidem, 475.

about everything in the world; if I refused, they would grumble and accuse me of being conceited toward ordinary riflemen."[177]

Although Lukianenko's memoirs give the impression that he was responsible for the imprisoned UPA members' discovery of genuine Ukrainian nationalism, in reality it was they who educated him, introducing him to the world of classic Ukrainian nationalism, with which he had never been acquainted. The memoirs overflow with conversations in which Lukianenko is introduced to the main elements of Ukrainian nationalist culture, beginning with the "Decalogue" (ten commandments) an OUN member must keep and ending with nationalist anthems.[178] During one such conversation he was presented a derogatory judgment of his past activity: "You exploited Soviet law to cover up your nationalistic activity, but your faith that Communist law might conquer Communist rule and engender political freedom is, frankly speaking, juridical idealism or simply naiveté."[179]

Within the first year of his imprisonment, these prolonged conversations already had a significant effect on Lukianenko. Contacting members of the underground organization Oblast Yednannia (Realm of Unification), he declared:

> I have taken up your struggle, just as you Banderites took up the [earlier Ukrainian independence] movement led by [Symon] Petliura, who stood on the shoulders of the previous fighters for Ukraine's freedom. It is important that the chain not be interrupted. I am not sure that our generation will achieve independence, but if the next generation is able to achieve it, this victory will have been made possible by our struggle. Therefore I must fulfill the mission of my generation. In that I see the meaning of life.[180]

A few years later Lukianenko would declare that he hoped "to do approximately what the Central Leadership of the OUN did in 1943."[181] Yet the OUN's armed resistance during the Second World War had

---

177 Ibidem, 476. Here "insurgent" (*povstanets*) means a soldier of the Ukrainian Insurgent Army.
178 See ibidem, 118-28.
179 Ibidem, 119. This statement indicates that Lukianenko was a supporter of law-abiding struggle for freedom, even if he denied believing in it.
180 Ibidem, 81.
181 Ibidem, 479.

nothing to do with Lukianenko's program of the URSS. It appears that his transformation into a nationalist was complete.

Although Lukianenko's interactions in the camp with the younger generation appeared to be edifying, the *shistdesiatnyky* found their experiences there more taxing. Mykhailo Horyn remembers the difficulties he and his peers had communicating with the older generation.

> The older generation could not understand us, the young. They used to tell us: "What good is all this poetry? We had machine guns, and yet we were not able to achieve anything." It was difficult to explain to them that these "scribbles" of ours were more effective weapons than their machine guns.[182]

But among the old nationalists even the Horyn brothers found a patron—Mykhailo Soroka (1911–71), an OUN member who had been a Soviet political prisoner since 1940 and had also been incarcerated under the interwar Polish republic. Despite their often disparate mindsets, the two contingents of Ukrainian inmates strove to foster a community built around a sense of Ukrainian nationalism. They organized secret events to commemorate famous Ukrainians, such as Taras Shevchenko, and holy days were celebrated as a part of the national culture.[183] This sense of community rendered the prison camps "universities of dissent," to quote Bohdan Horyn.[184] In some cases the prisoners tried to continue the work they had done before their internment. Mykhailo Horyn's wife, for example, was able to deliver to her husband a manuscript copy of Dziuba's *Internationalism or Russification?* by hiding it in the double bottom of a suitcase filled with food. A hostile barrack mate noticed him reading it and informed the camp guards. As a result Horyn, Moroz, and Masiutko were sentenced to several extra years of detention for possessing and disseminating anti-Soviet literature. The three men were not aware that they had been tried in absentia, and they were simply informed of their new sentences by the camp authorities.[185]

---

182   Horyn', *U nas bula velyka misiia*, 221.
183   Batenko, *Opozytsiina osobystist'*, 84. There are only a few mentions of the the role religion played among the *shistdesiatnyky*. Religion seems to have been foreign to most of them, so it is safe to say that the celebration of holy days in the camp was clearly a sign of the influence of the older Ukrainian nationalists.
184   Ibidem, 88.
185   Horyn', *U nas bula velyka misiia*, 218–19.

The Mordovian Gulag was where the *shistdesiatnyky* also became acquainted with other nonconformist intellectuals, including Yulii Daniel and Andrei Siniavsky, who had been arrested in Moscow in September 1965. The two groups were not friendly, perhaps because the Russian *shestidesiatniki* found it difficult to understand the Ukrainians' plight, while the Ukrainians believed that most of the Russian and Russified Jewish inmates were chauvinists.[186] Nevertheless Mykhailo Horyn and his fellow prisoner Aleksandr Ginzburg (1936–2002), a prominent Russian dissident, became good friends.

Life in the camp also had a profound effect on Valentyn Moroz. During his imprisonment in Mordovia, he wrote his famous essay "A Report from the Beria Reservation," which he based on his experiences there. Despite its title, this work was no mere report, but rather an elucidation of Moroz's political beliefs and experiences. It begins with an account of how three Lithuanian prisoners were hunted down and executed by a firing squad for trying to escape from the camp. But then Moroz turns his attention to describing who the prisoners of the camps were and why they had been incarcerated. The theme of injustice emerges from the start with the case of Makhmed Kulmagambetov, a philosophy lecturer at Simferopol State University who was imprisoned after he stopped teaching because he disagreed with the teaching program. His investigator made a surprising admission during his interrogation.

> "Generally speaking, there is nothing even to try you for, but you have *a dangerous way of thinking*." A typical case for the KGB, but unique in the frankness of its disregard for the law. As a rule, the KGB tries to fabricate at least a semblance of "anti-Soviet" *activity*. But in this remote province it did not even consider this necessary and admitted that Kulmagambetov had been *convicted for his views*.[187]

The crime that the average prisoner in the Mordovian Gulag was accused of was "free thought," specifically, in the Ukrainian cases, demanding that the rights stipulated in several documents and in the

---

186 Horyn and Lukianenko shared this opinion. See Horyn', *U nas bula velyka misiia*, 222; and Luk'ianenko, *Z chasiv nevoli: Sosnovka-7*, 472.

187 Valentyn Moroz, "A Report from the Beria Reservation," in his *Boomerang: The Works of Valentyn Moroz*, intro. by Paul L. Gersper, ed. Yaroslav Bihun (Baltimore, 1974), 10–11.

Soviet Constitution be respected. After citing several such cases, Moroz concludes that

> maybe a conclusion can be drawn: people convicted for "anti-Soviet agitation and propaganda" *think differently* or, simply, *think*, and their spiritual world does not fit the Procrustean bed of Stalinist standards which the KGB carefully defends. They have dared to claim the rights proclaimed in the Constitution and raised their voices against the shameful stranglehold of the KGB and the violations of the Constitution.[188]

Responsibility for re-educating the prisoners was the KGB agents', who "defended Stalinist standards" and believed that Stalin, "on the whole, deserves high praise." Moroz was sarcastic about their ability to re-educate him.

> "Well, what did you need? You had a good job, an apartment ..."
> They spent several hours proving that a man has nothing more than a stomach and so many meters of intestines. An idea? Protection of Ukraine from the threat of Russification? Here, as far as my interlocutors were concerned, the discussion definitely left reality and moved into the realm of children's fairy tales.[189]

Moroz's hatred of standardization and his desire for a spiritual life prove that he subscribed to the values of *shistdesiatnytstvo*. Like his contemporaries, he believed that these values could be realized by celebrating individuality.

> The very nature of creativity is rooted in the unprecedented and in the *unrepeatable*, and the carrier of the latter is the individual. Each individual consciousness embraces *one* facet of the all-embracing, boundless existence, an *unrepeatable* facet which can be reflected *only* by this particular individual and by no other. The more of these facets of consciousness there are, the more complete is our picture of the world. Therein lies the value of the individual; with the disappearance of each individual point of view, we *irrevocably* lose one of the possibilities, and at the same time one facet of the million-faceted mosaic of the human spirit stops sparkling.[190]

---

188 Ibidem, 16.
189 Ibidem, 19.
190 Ibidem, 21.

Moroz systematized these elements in his interpretation of Soviet history. For him Stalin was a preserver of order who, having consolidated his power, tried to maintain it by nullifying any source of change. Like other "standardizers" of history, Stalin had tried to destroy this mosaic to keep power through order.

> Since the seed of all changes is hidden in the uniqueness of the individual, they [standardizers] at first try to standardize him, to kill the originality within him. This cannot be achieved completely, but the degree of standardization of the individual has always been the measure of the power of the brake at the disposal of the forces of stagnation.[191]

Convinced that uniformity was the prerequisite for unity, Stalin and his followers tried to destroy individual truths and establish a single, superior truth. This single truth was maintained through censorship and the rule of socialist realism, which pervaded every sphere of individual human expression. As a historian, Moroz observed that standardization had become more pervasive in the last century than before it, and its ubiquity eventually came to define Soviet society.

> The twentieth century has seen the emergence of unprecedented controls over all aspects of community life, even family life. The entire course of a man's life—from the cradle to the grave—is controlled. Even leisure is standardized; evading the roundup for a "cultural excursion" to the museum is proclaimed a sin. Despotic forms become more and more disgusting, and degenerate into Auschwitzes. In this some see regression, "the end of the world." Actually, it proves the opposite: despotism ceases to be the accepted norm of human relationships and must continually assert itself in order to survive.[192]

Unfortunately for dictators, original thinking cannot be physically eradicated, despite what the KGB seemed to believe when they arrested people for possessing anti-Soviet literature. It was not rooted in tangible externalities but rather in the mind, in a spiritual life existing outside the dictator's power. Moroz was told more than once by his investigators,

---

191 Ibidem, 21–22.
192 Ibidem, 25–26.

"Unfortunately we can't see what is in your head," and he victoriously proclaimed:

> You cannot catch a thought and put it behind bars. You cannot even see it. How horrible! Even a thought forced into a man's head does not lie there like an element in an electronic device; it grows and develops (sometimes in the direction opposite from that programmed), and no apparatus can control this process.[193]

This is why despotism requires terror to remain in power, and why violence was so prevalent throughout the Soviet Union. Through these two forms of repression, Stalin was able to build an "Empire of Cogs." This regime was successful until a new generation stood up and had the courage to unmask the real nature of Soviet power. In Ukraine the new generation was able to create a public opinion that reacted angrily to the illegal arrests and trials of 1965–66. The first standard-bearer of this public opinion was Viacheslav Chornovil, who refused to testify against innocent people.

In the final section of his "Report" Moroz cites many violations of Soviet law in the Mordovian camp, focusing on the violence and torture that the prisoners had to endure. Despite its sombre ending, his work is full of hope for the future, inspired by a belief that once the truth is revealed it would be impossible to maintain the system of power built on the single falsehood of Stalinism. Moroz concludes with the statement: "A lie has short legs—that has long been known. But it is only half the truth. Let us not forget: TRUTH HAS LONG ARMS!"[194]

The "Report" immediately became a renowned and widely-circulated *samvydav* work. It did not contain any criticism of Marxism-Leninism, but it treated Soviet history as though it were completely independent from this ideology. The authorities considered Moroz's approach equally condemnable. Although the "Report's" was author anonymous, Moroz was suspected and brought to Kyiv in 1967 to be questioned about whether he was the author. His wife Raisa was also questioned, at which point she discovered that all of their correspondence had been seized and used against her husband. However, the investigators were not able to prove Moroz was the "Report's" *author*, and he was sent back to the prison

---

193 Ibidem, 26–27. Notice the similarity of these lines to the excerpt of Symonenko's poem that is the epigraph in this book.
194 Ibidem, 60.

camp to finish serving his sentence. There, instead of waiting passively for a new verdict, he began writing petitions to various Soviet authorities. In one of them, addressed to Petro Shelest and dated 15 May 1968, Moroz did not deny he was the "Report's" author but questioned how his essay could be considered anti-Soviet or anti-Communist. Compared to other members of the *shistdesiatnyky*, he was less interested in reviving Leninist policy and furthering the cause of world socialism. In one of his petitions he uses the ideological battle between the socialist East and the capitalist West as an argument to persuade Soviet institutions to free him, arguing that

> In the "Report from the BeriaReservation" there is not a single word against Soviet rule or Communist ideology. The document is directed against violations of the legality. It cites crimes. And still the document has been declared not only "anti-Soviet" but even "subversive." It is finally clear: I was not tried for anti-Soviet activities; on the contrary, the violators of the law carried out reprisals against those who expose their crimes.[195]

Moroz stated that the issues of freedom and human rights are at the centre of the ideological battle between the East and the West, and that this battle would be won by the regime that assured more rights for its citizens. According to him this rationale was the reason Lenin supported the policy of Ukrainianization. He asked Shelest: "Will Ukrainian communists today be able to renew at last the Leninist policy of Ukrainianization and declare all-out war on Russian chauvinism in Ukraine? The successful outcome of the ideological conflict with the West depends precisely on this."[196]

Moroz pointed at Czechoslovakia and its reforms as an example to follow, and rhetorically asked Shelest whether Ukraine would be able to do so. He argued that national rebirth, "the most powerful force today," could not be defied, only supported to ensure that it developed correctly. Otherwise the opposing powers would be overthrown.

> The KGB is preparing new reprisals. Basic human rights will again be trampled even as humanity marks the International Year of Human Rights. Again the West will receive a powerful argument in its ideological conflict with Communism.
> Whose interests does this serve?

---

195 Valentyn Moroz, "Statement," in his *Boomerang: The Works of Valentyn Moroz*, 143–44.
196 Ibidem, 146–47.

> Is it possible that once again the Central Committee of the Communist Party of Ukraine will fail to stop those whose actions are undermining the position of Communism?[197]

These lines reveal a new nuance in Moroz's writing. In appealing to Shelest, Moroz was hoping to persuade him to take the side of the *shistdesiatnyky*, those in favour of a renewal of the Soviet regime, just as a part of the socialist leadership had done in Czechoslovakia during the Prague Spring of 1968.

Moroz's proposal to Shelest reflected the emergent trend of broader circles of Ukraine's population, especially intellectuals, becoming involved in the national renaissance and pushing for societal change. The supporters of both scholarly and popular initiatives were questioning the dominance of the Russians and the Kremlin over Ukraine. After the unsuccessful 1966 trials, the Soviet Ukrainian leaders were trying to determine the best way to deal with the demands coming from below. And a privileged spot in the intellectual world was occupied by historical research, which contributed significantly to the debate surrounding Ukraine's right to secede from the Soviet Union.

The Braichevsky Case and the Renaissance of Ukrainian Historiography

The Twentieth CPSU Congress brought about significant reforms within the sphere of historical research. Even before Khrushchev's secret speech, Anastas Mikoyan, the deputy chairman of the USSR's Council of Ministers, had declared the need for new historical research on a number of themes, particularly those pertaining to Ukrainian history: subjects such as Nestor Makhno, Nykyfor (Matvii) Hryhoriiv, the New Economic Policy, the first years of Communist rule, and relationships with other parties needed to be reinterpreted. Mikoyan's call was echoed, somewhat surprisingly, by Anna Pankratova, the staunchly Stalinist historian and editor-in-chief of the prestigious history journal *Voprosy istorii*, who urged her colleagues to revise the interpretation of Soviet nationalities policy.[198] In the following years reinterpretations of certain problematic themes of Ukrainian history in several articles in that journal and in a book by the Soviet Ukrainian historian Mykola Suprunenko prompted new discussions of important and controversial Soviet Ukrainian political and

---

197 Ibidem, 147–48.
198 See Lewytzkyj, *Politics and Society in Soviet Ukraine 1953–1980*, 8–9.

cultural figures and political parties of the 1920s and 1930s, such as Mykola Khvylovy, Oleksander Shumsky, Mykola Skrypnyk, the Ukrainian Communist Party (of Borotbists), and the Communist Party of Western Ukraine (CPWU).[199]

The new era in Ukrainian Soviet historiography was ushered in with the foundation of *Ukraïns'kyi istorychnyi zhurnal* (Ukrainian Historical Journal) in 1957. Its primary objective was to examine the Ukrainian past through a new historiographical lens, distancing itself from the Stalinist interpretations that still dominated the 1953 *Theses on the Tercentenary of Ukraine's Reunification with Russia*.[200] The new journal's editor-in-chief, Fedir Shevchenko (1914–95), was a scholar at the Institute of History of the AN URSR. Born in the village of Dunaivtsi in Podillia and educated at Moscow State University, he had pursued a career in the management of Soviet archives until he was employed by the AN URSR in 1949. In his research he focussed on the Khmelnytsky Uprising of 1648–54 and on Lukian Kobylytsia and the Hutsul uprisings in Bukovyna in the 1840s. Shevchenko and his colleagues Kostiantyn Huslysty (1902–73), Ivan Hurzhii (1915–71), and Volodymyr Holobutsky (1903–93), as well as others, constituted a group of historians who wished to reshape Ukrainian historiography while remaining loyal to the Soviet leadership. In his study of post-Stalin Ukrainian historiography, Vitalii Yaremchuk described the group.

> An "intermediate" category of historians of the Ukrainian SSR was comprised of people whose uncritical acceptance of the existing socio-political order was combined with a love for Ukraine and its

---

199 See ibidem, 15–23; Suprunenko (1900–84) was a well-known Soviet Ukrainian historian, a member of the AN URSR, and the author of many articles and books. Khvylovy, Shumsky, and Skrypnyk are the three key figures of Ukrainian national-communism. See James E. Mace, *Communism and the Dilemmas of National Liberation: National Communism in Soviet Ukraine, 1918–1933* (Cambridge, Mass., 1983). The Borotbists were the leftst faction that broke away from the Ukrainian Party of Socialist Revolutionaries and aspired to become the official Ukrainian Communist Party. Alkthough they merged with the Communist Party (of Bolsheviks) of Ukraine, they were among the favourite targets of the Stalin Terror. The CPWU was active in Polish-ruled Galicia and Volhynia during the interwar years. It was disbanded in 1938, and many of its members were repressed during the 1939–41 Soviet occupation of Western Ukraine.

200 The *Theses* were issued by the CC CPSU in Moscow but written by Soviet Ukrainian historians. They reinstated the Ukrainian nation as a historical actor but postulated the almost indissolubile union between the Ukrainian and Russian peoples. See Yekelchyk, *Stalin's Empire of Memory*, 154–59.

past—whose world view was shaped by loyalty to the regime, to Communist ideology, and to their native land and traditions. This dichotomy, ideological eclecticism, and striving for improvement and change within the framework of the system were the original components of the ideological ferment of the *shistdesiatnyky* movement in its beginning phase; however, these historians of the Ukrainian SSR did not have direct ties with *shistdesiatnytstvo*. By analyzing their fate we see that their probing nature was revealed in their elementary honesty and critical thinking, in their deep roots in the Ukrainian peasantry, in popular culture, and most of all in the tangible personal experience of Stalin's totalitarianism. After the Twentieth CPSU Congress, when the truth was coming to light concerning the previous period of Soviet history, the inhumane nature of this Stalinist experience was confirmed.[201]

Although convinced of the need for a reappraisal of Ukrainian historiography and dedicated to the honest fulfillment of their work, in practice this group of historians did not wish—and perhaps did not dare—to question the entire Soviet system, which they ultimately considered legitimate. Substantially older than the *shistdesiatnyky*, they found it more difficult to radically reinterpret the Stalinist phenomenon, under which they had spent much of their lives. At the same time they had no doubt that a new explanation of that phenomenon was to be found in historical research. This belief emerged in their analyses of articles published in *Ukraïns'kyi istorychnyi zhurnal* (*UIZh*) and from their efforts to defend the authors of new unorthodox theories. Shevchenko and Suprunenko defended the publication in their journal of writings by Oleksandr Karpenko (1921–2013), a historian in Lviv who was studying the revolutionary years in Galicia, the peasant uprisings there in the 1930s, and the CPWU; and by Olena Luhova (b. 1928), whose article in *UIZh* in 1967 about tsarist rule in Ukraine broke every rule, accusing the Russian Empire of colonialism.[202]

This renaissance of historiography in Soviet Ukraine took three lines of development: (1) the recontextualization of Ukrainian history, especially of the medieval and early modern periods, within the broader European milieu in order to affirm the European roots of Ukrainian civilization; (2) the rewriting of the history of the Zaporozhian Sich; and

---

201 Iaremchuk, *Mynule Ukraïny v istorychnii nautsi*, 164.
202 See Oleksandr S. Rubl'ov, "'Ukraïns'kyi istorychnyi zhurnal': Istoriia ofitsiina i zalashtunkova (1957–1988 rr.)," *Ukraïns'kyi istorychnyi zhurnal*, 2007, no. 6: 18–55.

(3) the periodization and state of national consciousness in Ukraine from the Middle Ages to the nineteenth century. These three tasks were often condensed in the study of Cossack civilization as the classic "golden age" of Ukrainian history, when the Ukrainian lands were economically and culturally integrated in the European context and a strong will to constitute an independent state first emerged, but also when the destiny of subjugation by the tsarist empire was determined.[203]

The harbingers of this renaissance were a second group of historians, who were protected by Fedir Shevchenko and his colleagues and differed significantly from his generation. Most of them were ten or more years younger than Shevchenko and had a strong patriotic world view largely unrelated to Soviet ideology. These nonconformist historians, among whom the most distinguished were Mykhailo Braichevsky (1924–2001), Olena Kompan (1916–1986), and Yaroslav Dzyra (1931–2009), had direct relations with the *shistdesiatnyky* and understood their duty toward society in a similar way.

> They all had in their personal libraries, or borrowed from each other, works by the "ubiquitous" Hrushevsky—as they used to call him in the Department of ("Feudal") History [of the Institute of History of the AN URSR]—and other classics of Ukrainian historiography, works which usually were kept in the restricted sections of the libraries. All of them, except the determined anti-Communist Yaroslav Dzyra, were enamoured of the "new interpretations" and the classics of Marxism-Leninism; the then-recent works by revisionists of Marxism such as Palmiro Togliatti and Milovan Đilas also belonged on their reading list. They received news about the real conditions in the country and the world through Western radio programs.[204]

Commitment to their cause was evident in their social initiatives. They gave lectures on Ukrainian history at public meetings (Braichevsky did this at evenings organized by the KTM), and in 1965 they founded the Brotherhood for the Protection of Historical and Cultural Monuments to raise public awareness about the problems of preserving the country's

---

203 On the primacy of the Cossacks in Soviet Ukrainian historiography, see Lev Bilas, "How History Is Written in Soviet Ukraine," *The Ukrainian Review* 5, no. 4 (Winter 1958): 39–47, and Osyp Danko, "Suchasnyi stan ukraïns'koï istorychnoï nauky ta suspil'no-politychnykh dystsyplin," *Suchasnist'*, 1962, no. 12: 58–68.

204 Iaremchuk, *Mynule Ukraïny v istorychnii nautsi*, 182.

historical heritage. To this end Braichevsky wrote essays promoting the protection of the historical centres of Kamianets-Podilskyi and other Ukrainian cities in academic and literary journals.[205] However, the task of engaging the public in this historiographical reappraisal was not without its difficulties. Due to the esoteric nature of historical research, these historians struggled to draw the attention of a wide audience. Furthermore, since all resources for historical research came from the state, even nonconformist historians used mild tones and employed a prudent self-censorship to avoid being excluded from the profession.[206]

In July 1966 Braichevsky sent the editorial board of *UIZh* a manuscript titled "Annexation or Reunification? Critical Reflections on the Underpinnings of an Idea." But the editorial board, despite having solicited this treatise, decided it could not be published. After this rejection, several copies of the manuscript circulated in *samvydav*, transforming Braichevsky into another symbol of *shistdesiatnytstvo*. Braichevsky, however, could hardly be considered a typical *shistdesiatnyk*. Born into to a family of intellectuals in Kyiv in 1924, his studies at Kyiv State University led him to a love of Ukrainian history. After graduating, he worked at the Institutes of Archeology and History of the AN URSR, achieving renown as an expert on the origins of Kyivan Rus' and the Cossacks. His treatise "Annexation or Reunification?" dealt more with defining historical terms than hypothesizing future nationalities policy, but his revolutionary approach, questioning the Stalinist view of Ukrainian history and accusing it of not being Marxist, proved controversial.

Braichevsky challenged the use of the word "reunification" for the outcome of the Treaty of Pereiaslav.[207] In his interpretation, three distinct nations had emerged after the end of the Rus' of Kyiv, so they could not be *re*unified, never having been united in the first place. Braichevsky affirmed that what happened to Ukraine was an *annexation* under the colonial exploitation of Muscovite rule. Therefore, considering the Treaty of Pereiaslav a reunification was both anti-historical and un-Marxist. Braichevsky observed that in the 1930s the treaty had not been viewed in a positive light. Nevertheless, since the end of the 1930s, and particularly after Stalin's criticism of Engels in a 1941 speech, "any criticism of the

---

205 Rubl'ov, "'Ukraïns'kyi istorychnyi zhurnal,'" 31.
206 Iaremchuk, *Mynule Ukraïny v istorychnii nautsi*, 106–53.
207 About the treaty, see chapter, n 3.

imperialistic policy of tsarism has been considered dangerous, capable of causing problems for the friendship of Soviet peoples."[208] Stalin's speech laid the groundwork for a revisionist historiography of the national-liberation movements—one that challenged the Marxist interpretation. In this revised evaluation, all movements directed against Russian primacy, regardless of their historical significance, were considered detrimental. Soviet historiography abandoned the analysis of class conflict and began describing Russian imperial history as a progressive process of the unification of the Russians and their fraternal peoples. The annexation of different national entities by the Russian Empire was explained first by the theory of the lesser evil—that is, it was better to annex these peoples than having them absorbed by other empires—and then by the theory that these peoples could rise to their potential only through unification with the Russians.

For Braichevsky the main concept of Marxism was quite different.

> Marxism-Leninism begins with each nation having the inalienable right to independent historical development, which is recognized to be the normal path of progress. Thence [arises] Vladimir Lenin's formulation of the main principle for solving the nationality question: the right of each nation to self-determination—up to [and including] secession as an independent state. This principle is part of the foundation of our Party's nationality policy; [our] Party and our entire nation are guided by it in dealing with every issue connected with national relations.[209]

Quoting Lenin's famous lines, Braichevsky argued that he supported the liberation movements of oppressed peoples. If the bourgeoisie was the victorious class in these wars, these movements were progressive by definition because, according to Marxist theory, they were contributing to the overthrow of the feudal system. Lenin accused those who opposed such wars of liberation, in Ukraine or in any other land, of chauvinism.

> Thence arises the general political principle of support for the national-liberation movements in colonial and dependent countries, regardless of what social forces are leading those movements at that moment; "in those countries where the national- liberation

---

208 Mykhailo Iu. Braichevs'kyi, *Pryiednannia chy vozz'iednannia? Krytychni zauvahy z pryvodu odniieï kontseptsiï*, preface by Roman Rakhmannyi [Oliinyk] (Toronto, 1972), 13.
209 Ibidem, 21.

movement is led by the bourgeoisie and taking place under the flag of nationalism, the working class supports the activity of national governments directed at defending state sovereignty and at undermining imperialism's positions in economic life.[210]

Braichevsky denounced the turn in historiography caused by Stalin's revision of Soviet nationalities policy. This Stalinist interpretation resulted in the condemnation of national-liberation movements—a position that a directly contradicted Leninism. Yet this was not the only problem: "The unwillingness to abandon the theoretically erroneous idea of a 'union of peoples' within the framework of tsarist Russia has led our historians to willingness to consider the latter as the state of the Russian people!"[211] Braichevsky maintained that considering the tsarist empire and the Soviet Union as two manifestations of a single entity, without respecting their social foundations or the class conflict, was a gross mistake. In no way could the Russian Empire be considered a prelude to the future Soviet state, not even with respect to minority relations within the two multinational states. A Russian chauvinist might accept such an idea, but never would a Communist.

As for the consequences of the Treaty of Pereiaslav, Braichevsky's evaluation of Ukraine's situation was even more severe: "Ukraine, like the other lands seized by tsarism, became the object of colonial plunder, and if general progress nonetheless carved out a road for itself, this happened not because of but despite of her [Ukraine's] dependent existence."[212]

Citing Lenin again, Braichevsky concluded that the Russian domination of Ukraine meant a drastic worsening of its economic and cultural development. Before the Treaty of Pereiaslav the degree of economic exchange between Ukraine and Europe to the west had been great, but it became nearly non-existent under the tsars. The popular revolts in seventeenth-century Ukraine were a sign that Ukraine's social structure was developing toward a more bourgeois economy, but the rise of tsarist autocracy resulted in the transformation of large numbers of free peasants into serfs. Ukrainian culture was prevented from developing normally, and, for the first time in history, Peter I penalized the Kyiv-Mohyla Academy and other Ukrainian higher schools and banned publications in Ukrainian. It is indeed possible that if the Cossack

---

210 Ibidem, 25.
211 Ibidem, 31.
212 Ibidem, 34.

Hetmanate state had chosen a different path instead of the Treaty of Pereiaslav, it might have developed into a full-fledged sovereign state

In sum, Braichevsky rejected the word "reunification" for the annexation of Ukraine, arguing that as a formula for the union of two nations it was not historically justifiable. Political decisions at the time of the treaty were made not on the basis of popular will or benefit, but with the aim of restoring feudalism. "No one thought or asked about the genuine interests of the people (Ukrainian or Russian) either in Moscow or at Pereiaslav—the issue was resolved on a completely different plane."[213]

Braichevsky also condemned the Soviet mythicization of Hetman Bohdan Khmelnytsky as a popular hero. He acknowledged Khmelnytsky's ability to unify the Ukrainian people during the war with Poland of 1648–54, but he argued that Khmelnytsky raised their hopes and then went on to betray them.

> ... we should not forget that B. Khmelnytsky was a typical figure of the feudal class and a spokesman for feudal ideology *in that period when the feudal system had long ago become a reactionary force impeding the way for progress*, [and] therefore considering him a progressive agent is, in accordance with a constructive program, impossible ...
>
> ... As a representative of the feudalized Cossack *starshyna*, from the very beginning B. Khmelnytsky defended the interests of his social group.[214]

Braichevsky rejected the celebration of Khmelnytsky in Soviet historiography as a "champion of the interests of the popular masses," and he claimed that Soviet historians had forgotten the principles of Marxism-Leninism. Analyzing the revolts that followed the annexation of Ukraine by the tsarist empire, he stated: "The chief obstacle is the [Soviet] historians' abandonment of the fundamental Marxist principle of class evaluation of every concrete historical phenomenon."[215]

Braichevsky firmly believed that the official Soviet interpretation of Ukrainian history conceived under Stalinism was false and not based on Marxist-Leninist principles. He had the courage to express this conviction and submit it to an official journal. Clearly the atmosphere in certain

---

213 Ibidem, 59–60.
214 Ibidem, 51–52.
215 Ibidem, 57.

scholarly circles was still relaxed and liberal, despite the trials held several months earlier. As an academic, Braichevsky was a *persona non grata* because of his unorthodox interpretation of the origins of Kyivan Rus', but he did not suffer any particular repression for writing "Annexation or Reunification?" even though it became very popular in *samvydav* literature. The Soviet leadership was inclined to tolerate nonconformity to a degree as long as it remained within the confines of intellectual speculation. The repressions against Braichevsky and the *shistdesiatnyky* came when the actions of these intellectuals crossed over into a decidedly political field.

A New Sense of Community: The *Shistdesiatnyky* and the Construction of a Public Political Space

Between the 1966 trials and 1968, Soviet authorities cracked down on the activities of the *shistdesiatnyky* with what has been called administrative persecution. Because the tactic of direct confrontation proved to be counterproductive because the intellectuals had been scoring victories in their public protests against the repressions, the Soviet leadership decided to penalize the nonconformists by making their lives as difficult as possible. With state or state-related enterprises being the only income sources for the *shistdesiatnyky*, the authorities decided rescind their jobs, expecting that hunger and poverty would silence them. Both Ivan Svitlychny and Ivan Dziuba were fired from their positions at the AN URSR, and Vasyl Stus was expelled from the graduate program at the Institute of Literature of the AN URSR, ostensibly because he took part in the protest at the Ukraina cinema in Kyiv during the premiere of Paradzhanov's film *Shadows of Forgotten Ancestors*. This was not a very effective tactic, however, for the intellectuals settled for humbler jobs yet continued their dissent.

In one case, the milder method of repression proved to be effective. Ivan Drach, attacked for his participation in the protests against the Lviv trials, decided to apologize publicly and submit to the regime. In the 30 May 1966 recantation that he submitted to the CPU, he blandly withdrew his previous statements against Soviet rule, declaring that he was sorry and had gone to Lviv without realizing the political significance of his actions.[216] This letter does not reveal any of Drach's real motivations behind his decision to compromise. He distanced himself further from the

---

216 Drach's letter is in TsDAHOU, f. 1, op. 1, spr. 6160, ark. 63–64.

other *shistdesiatnyky* in his article "Oh, May You Be Cursed Once Again! A Reply to Mr. Kravtsiv and Co." in *Literaturna Ukraïna*. Considered to be the first renunciation of *shistdesiatnytstvo*, in it Drach attacked several of Bohdan Kravtsiv's essays published in *Suchasnist'*. Kravtsiv (1904–75), a postwar émigré and prominent nationalist poet living in the United States, had considered Drach a colleague in the struggle against the USSR. Drach now moved to dispel this belief, reminding readers of Kravtsiv's activities as an "ally of the Nazis." Drach even threatened a nuclear war should the Ukrainian émigré "fascists" dare to return to Ukraine. He affirmed his loyalty to the Soviet Union and quoted several earlier propagandistic poems by Pavlo Tychyna and Maksym Rylsky.[217]

Drach's refutation of his politically risky stances provoked condemnation in the émigré press. Though the Soviet authorities somewhat tolerated nonconformist thinking within Ukraine, they were more concerned when works by a Soviet author were published abroad and used in Western propaganda. Other *shistdesiatnyky* did not consider Drach's article a betrayal, but clearly he had decided to safeguard his position by withdrawing from the civic arena.[218] Drach reaffirmed his loyalty to the Soviet state at a literary round table he took part in in New York in November 1966. When asked there about the arrests and trials, he defended the actions of the Soviet authorities, saying that the arrestees were accused of being Gestapo agents during the Second World War. But he expressed hope that some of his closest friends, such as the painter Opanas Zalyvakha (1925–2007) and the Horyn brothers, would be released.[219]

At this stage of the conflict between the intellectuals and the Communist state, the majority of the *shistdesiatnyky* did not retract their opposition to the Soviet regime. Yevhen Sverstiuk persisted after he was dismissed from *Ukraïns'kyi botanichnyi zhurnal* (The Ukrainian Botanical Journal) in May 1966, as did Mykhailyna Kotsiubynska (1931–2011) when she was expelled from the Party and, two years later, from the Institute of Literature. Kotsiubynska was a reliable distributer of *samvydav* literature; she even typed up the first copies of Dziuba's "Internationalism or Russification?" Born in Vinnytsia, from 1935 she lived with her father and mother—an ethnic Armenian from Crimea who had worked as a teacher

---

217 See Ivan Drach, "O, bud'te prokliati vy shche raz! Vidpovid' panovi Kravtsivu i Ko.," *Literaturna Ukraïna*, 22 December 1966, 2.
218 "Tsia knyzhka zminyla use moie zhyttia: Rozmova z Ivanom Dziuboiu," 126–27.
219 See Browne, ed., *Ferment in the Ukraine*, 177–78.

of Ukrainian (Mykhailo Stelmakh was among her students) in Chernihiv—where they ran a museum dedicated to her father's older brother, the famous writer Mykhailo Kotsiubynsky. Kotsiubynska grew up in an intellectual environment that included the poets Pavlo Tychyna, Maksym Rylsky, and Volodymyr Sosiura. At that time she developed a strong Ukrainian identity but identified as Soviet. She explained this duality when recounting the Nazi occupation of Ukraine during the Second World War.

> I remember that one evening—during the first year of the German occupation of Kyiv—Pavlo Tychyna came to visit us and read his poems "A Mother's Voice" and the recently written "The autumn Night Was Foreboding." In this poem there is a description of occupied Kyiv. Everybody began to cry, including me and Tychyna himself. Everyone felt with particular strength his own isolation from Ukraine, the uncertainty of destiny. This was, perhaps, some sort of Soviet patriotism. I have often debated this with Yevhen Sverstiuk. He believes that something like Soviet patriotism never existed. But I remember quite well how painfully those people who had come to us suffered when Ukraine was under German occupation—they did not want the Germans. And even if I was still a child then, I clearly recorded it in my memory. I will not insist on the term *Soviet patriotism*, for I do not even know what to call those feelings, but I have no doubt that they brought those people together. In that very same instant Tychyna's extraordinary poem "A Friend's Funeral" was born. They were absolutely sincere verses. One could feel that no one imposed them on him.[220]

This sense of Soviet belonging is the reason why Kotsiubynska joined the Komsomol and later the Communist Party, even if she was never particularly active in either. In 1949 she was admitted to Kyiv State University's Faculty of Philology, and in 1954 to graduate studies there. From 1958 to 1968 she was a junior scholarly associate at the Institute of Literature of the AN URSR. There she became acquainted with the *shistdesiatnyky* and began questioning Soviet history and ideology. She eventually became one of the central figures of their movement, collaborating with the KTM on organizing many literary evenings and

---

[220] Mykhailyna Kotsiubyns'ka, "U moemu zhytti bulo tak bahato dobra ...," in *Bunt pokolinnia*, ed. Berdykhovs'ka and Hnatiuk, 158. See also Eleonora Solovei, ed. *"U merekhtinni naidorozhchych lyst": Zaduiuchy Mykhailynu Kotsiubyns'ku* (Kyiv, 2012).

motivating Dziuba to deliver his famous public address at the Ukraina cinema. As a scholar she was a target of the conservative critic Mykola Shamota (1916–84), then the director of the Institute of Literature. She affirmed that her true allegiance was to her mentor, the famous writer and former political prisoner Borys Antonenko-Davydovych. For her he was the "personification of Ukrainianness" and played an important role in transmitting the legacy of the "Executed Renaissance" to the succeeding generations of poets.[221]

Kotsiubynska had an interesting way of explaining the relationship of her generation to the ideals propagated through Soviet education. When she was being expelled from the CPSU in 1966, a member of the commission that questioned her how she would feel the next day. She answered: "You know, when I joined the Party I was very young and green. I believed in ideals. But if have to choose between [these] ideals and [my] Party card, then I am keeping the ideals and handing in the Party card."[222]

Kotsiubynska's words confirm that the *shistdesiatnyky* considered themselves followers, not opponents, of the values they had been taught, albeit with a different cultural background. She was fired in 1968 during the restructuring of the Institute of Philology to eliminate employees deemed disloyal to the regime. However, she managed to land a job as an editor at the Vyshcha Shkola publishing house in Kyiv thanks to the intercession of the Communist Party of Canada, which publicly lamented that Mykhailo Kotsiubynsky's niece and her son had been deprived of an income.[223]

Despite the Communist system's increased efforts to silence the *shistdesiatnyky*, their activities continued and became more dangerous. Deprived of the KTM, which had served as a place of mediation with the government, the *shistdesiatnyky* took a free rein in organizing their future meetings. These initiatives, no longer the products of compromise, promoted the intensification of their revolutionary character. Thus the existence of an opposition within the Soviet regime became increasingly evident. The first such meeting, which would acquire significance in the coming years, was held on 22 May 1966 at the Shevchenko monument in Kyiv, across the street from the university. Led by Ivan Svitlychny and

---

221 Ibidem, 165.
222 Ibidem, 172.
223 Ibidem, 173.

Alla Horska, a group of people gathered to listen to the poetry of Vasyl Symonenko and Lina Kostenko and to sing folk songs. Because the audience was small, this meeting did not worry the Soviet leadership.[224]

Then in September 1966 Ukraine's capital became the centre of attention for the entire whole Soviet Union, as Kyiv's Jews assembled at Babyn Yar ravine (aka Babi Yar, from its Russian name, Babii Yar) to commemorate the victims of the mass murders carried out there by the Nazis there on 29 September 1941. The Holocaust had been removed from Soviet memory after the liquidation of the Soviet Anti-Fascist Committee, and the subject of Nazi persecutions, with the related theme of collaboration by Soviet citizens, was buried under "oblivion from above."[225] But the events of 1941 were recalled in 1960, when Kyiv's Jewish community asked the authorities to build a monument to commemorate the thirtieth anniversary of the massacre. In March 1961, not long after this request was refused, a mudslide ravaged the site of the massacre, drawing the attention of intellectuals in Moscow. The well-known Russian poet Yevgeny Yevtushenko visited Kyiv, where widespread rumours attributed the natural disaster to the revenge of the Nazis' victims. Yevtushenko was struck by the portentous occurrence and wrote his famous poem "Babii Yar," which was published in Moscow in *Literaturnaia gazeta* on 19 September 1961. The Russian composer Dmitrii Shostakovich dedicated his thirteenth symphony to the massacre and planned that the movements should be interspersed with Yevtushenko's verses. The first performances of the symphony were well received in Soviet cultural circles, but the monument was not erected.[226]

In the 1960s official Soviet anti-Semitism did not seem to diminish, although the Communist Party tried to make it appear otherwise. In 1964 the Party's propaganda office published the brochure *Judaism without Embellishments*, whose author(s) argued that anti-Semitism was characteristic of the Western countries but did not exist in the Soviet bloc. The brochure caused an international scandal and was condemned by many Communist parties in the West. This denial of Soviet anti-Semitism

---

224 See the report to the CPU, in TsDAHOU, f. 1, op. 1, spr. 6160, ark. 104.
225 See Shimon Redlich, *War, Holocaust and Stalinism: A Documented Study of the Jewish Anti-Fascist Committee in the USSR* (Luxembourg, 1995); Joshua Rubenstein and Vladimir P. Naumov, eds., *Stalin's Secret Pogrom: The Postwar Inquisition of the Jewish Anti-Fascist Committee* (New Haven, 2001); and Antonella Salomoni, *L'Unione Sovietica e la Shoah: Genocidio, resistenza, rimozione* (Bologna, 2006).
226 See Gian Piero Piretto, *Il radioso avvenire: Mitologie culturali sovietiche* (Turin, 2001), 260–64.

was also published in academic books, adding a troublesome gravity to the Party's false claim.[227]

From August 1966 the Russian journal *Iunost'* serialized the novel *Babii iar* by Anatolii Kuznetsov, a Russian engineer living in Tula. In it he who wrote about his youth in German-occupied Kyiv and recounted the massacre of the city's Jews at Babyn Yar, but Soviet censors had removed all of the passages referring to local collaboration with the Nazis.[228] In 1966 Kyiv's Jewish community, led by the writer Viktor Nekrasov, organized a demonstration to commemorate the victims on the twenty-fifth anniversary of the massacre. At 5:30 p.m. on 29 September 1966 a group comprised mainly of Jews gathered at Babyn Yar; among them were the Soviet Jewish writers Nekrasov and Ilya Ehrenburg and the Ukrainians Ivan Dziuba and Borys Antonenko-Davydovych. Several writers gave speeches about anti-Semitism in Ukraine and expressed their hope for a change in the popular mentality. A Department of Documentary Film team shot the event without official authorization.[229] At the gathering Dziuba delivered the most powerful speech. In it he addressed the problematic relations between Ukrainians and Jews and expressed sorrow for what had happened at Babyn Yar. For Dziuba the mass murders were a crime not only against the Jewish people but against all of humanity.

> Babyn Yar is the tragedy of the whole of mankind, but it took place on Ukrainian soil. And therefore a Ukrainian has no more right to forget about it than a Jew. Babyn Yar is our common tragedy, a tragedy above all of the Jewish and the Ukrainian people. This tragedy was brought to our people by fascism, but at the same time we must remember that fascism did not start with Babyn Yar and does not end with it. Fascism begins with disrespect of the individual and ends with destruction of the individual, the destruction of peoples—but not necessarily with the same type of destruction as in Babyn Yar.[230]

---

227 See Bohdan Osadchuk, "Skandal u Kyievi, abo deshcho pro suchasnyi radians'kyi antysemityzm," *Suchasnist'*, 1964, no. 6: 115–18.
228 In 1968 Kuznetsov fled to Britain, where an uncensored version of his book was published and he worked for Radio Liberty. See A. Anatoli [Kuznetsov's pen name], *Babi Yar: A Document in the Form of a Novel*, trans. David Floyd (New York, 1970). The Russian version appeared in issues 8–10 of *Iunost'*.
229 Report to the CPU, in TsDAHOU, f. 1, op. 1, spr. 6160, ark. 148–51.
230 Ivan Dziuba, "Babyn Yar Continues," in *Revolutionary Voices: Ukrainian Political Prisoners Condemn Russian Colonialism*, ed. Slava Stetsko (Munich, 1969), 56.

Dziuba asserted that Jews and Ukrainians were fraternal nations because they shared a history of tragedies such as Babyn Yar. He interpreted fascism like a *shistdesiatnyk* would, as "disrespect of the individual." His suggestion that people could be destroyed not only physically alluded to the persecution of the Ukrainian nation and prefigured the association of Soviet power with fascism. Such a suggestion was already common in the West but it was unusual for the Communist bloc. This is one instance of a prominent trend in *shistdesiatnytstvo* in 1966, in which the totalitarianism of the Soviet regime was emphasized and associated with fascism. Valentyn Moroz had referred to Soviet totalitarianism in his "Report from the Beria Reservation," more as a rhetorical formula, and he preferred the term *standardization*, which had deep roots in the culture of the *shistdesiatnyky*. While Moroz became more radical in his thought and condemnation of Soviet rule, Dziuba became his polar opposite, typical of those who did not wish to oppose the USSR directly on a political level. However, after the 1966 arrests and trials even Dziuba was ready to switch to the side of the overt dissidents.

After this brief propagandistic digression in his speech, Dziuba returned to the matter of Leninist nationality policy: "It seems that Lenin's instructions on the struggle against anti-Semitism are being forgotten, just as Lenin's instructions on the national development of Ukraine are being forgotten."[231] It was Stalin who began a battle against the free development of Jewish culture within the Soviet Union, and Dziuba believed that the two oppressed nations, the Ukrainian and the Jewish, should seek an alliance against their oppressor. Anti-Semitism was the ideological heritage of the tsarist empire's captive nations. A brotherhood of nations was Dziuba's dream: "We should outlive all hatred toward any human beings, overcome all misunderstandings, and with all our lives bring about true brotherhood."[232]

Dziuba stated that the poets Taras Shevchenko and Lesia Ukrainka had foreseen this brotherhood between the Ukrainian and the Jews. He argued that the two nations should be granted the right to develop their own cultures and study each other's culture: "The road to true brotherhood, not false, lies not in self-oblivion but in self-knowledge. We

---

231 Ibidem.
232 Ibidem, 57.

should not repudiate ourselves adapt ourselves to others, but should be ourselves and respect others."[233]

The struggle for "mutual understanding and friendship" was the duty of all humanity. Dziuba's speech circulated widely in *samvydav* and confirmed his role as the spiritual leader of the *shistdesiatnyky*. Their movement had reached a crossroads and faced finally having to decide whether to continue opposing the Soviet regime or to seek a compromise with it. Instead of making an outright decision, Dziuba oscillated between his desire to maintain a critical position and his hope that the system might still be reformed.

Meanwhile the administrative repressions continued. The literary critic Yurii Badzo (1936–2018) was dismissed from the Institute of Literature and had to seek work in a bread factory, while the campaign against the *shistdesiatnyky* grew even more bitter. Its first target became Dziuba, the author of *Internationalism or Russification?* After its release, he was repeatedly summoned for questioning by various Communist Party organs. One such meeting occurred between Dziuba and the director of the Institute of Party History, Ivan Nazarenko (1908–85). Nazarenko said that Petro Shelest had ordered him to convince Dziuba to write an article distancing himself from the propaganda of the West, where his manuscript was beginning to circulate.

> He talked to me in a very friendly way. The conversation had a conciliatory tone. The Party, he said, sees everything that I have written about, the Party knows about it and does all that is possible to repair these distortions. "Do not interfere, for you can only stand in the way. The Party knows about it better than you and will do all that is necessary, while you can only cause damage. Imagine what will happen when your book ends up abroad. They will transform you into a hero, they will put you on a banner"; and so on.[234]

Dziuba refused any compromises. Although the Western press had not yet published his treatise, an essay in the September 1966 issue of the Soviet satirical journal *Perets'*, "On Mr. Stetsko and the Great Martyred Little Frog" signed with the pen name Vasyl Osadchy—accused Dziuba of conspiring with émigré Ukrainian nationalists. The essay begins with

---

233 Ibidem.
234 "Tsia knyzhka zminyla use moie zhyttia," 124. In this interview Dziuba repeatedly refers to Nazarenko incorrectly as Dmytro Ivanovych instead of Ivan Dmytrovych.

two allegorical stories, one about a frog that fulminated against a river's flow and one about an ephemeral intellectual named Panko Koloda. "Vasyl Osadchy" describes Dziuba as a vain writer who spends his days in some distant sunny locale and who is proud of the scandal the false news of his arrest has caused among Ukrainian nationalists. The last paragraphs clarify what the author sees as Dziuba's real crime.

> Now, when his hypertrophied nihilism and skepticism toward our socialist life has been adopted as a weapon by [Ukrainian] nationalist groups abroad, Ivan Dziuba has suddenly become silent. Until now he has had no voice to express his position on the anti-Soviet campaign happening around him.
>
> And it is necessary to speak. For all sorts of political tales, ideological filth, and many other unpleasant and awkward things are circulating about him. Essentially the name Dziuba is openly exploited for the piloting of a disgusting anti-Soviet campaign.
>
> We have already seen and heard too many of these campaigns, events, speeches, and petitions directed against Soviet Ukraine and its people, which in a brotherly union with all workers of the Country of Soviets is confidently building its new life. Every now and then all sorts of demonstrations, speeches at congresses "for the defence of Ukraine," "weeks of the oppressed nations," and "days for the liberation of Ukraine," etc., are conducted abroad, especially in the USA. But we have not become accustomed to that. We know very well what we are fighting for, [and] who our battle is against.
>
> What side are you on, Ivan Dziuba? [Why a]re you silent? You will have to answer to the Soviet community ...[235]

"Vasyl Osadchy" accused Dziuba of helping to facilitate "fascist" propaganda and failing to speak out against the exploitation of his notoriety in the West. *Internationalism or Russification?* had not yet been published there, but the Soviet authorities, anticipating the furor that his book was going to cause, were trying to implement a preventive condemnation of any anti-Soviet fallout. Linking Dziuba to Nazi collaborators was also an effort to muddy his reputation domestically. The article did not mention that he worked at the AN URSR as a proof-

---

235 Vasyl' Osadchyi, "Pro mistera Stets'ka i velykomuchenyts'ke zhabenia," *Perets'* 40, no. 17 (September 1966): 5. "Mister Stets'ko" refers to Yaroslav Stetsko (1912–86), a prominent member of the OUN in wartime Galicia and the postwar West, and the founding president of the Anti-Bolshevik Bloc of Nations from 1946.

reader—the only job he could find after his dismissal—and that he was in a sanatorium being treated for tuberculosis.

Despite the personal nature of this attack, Dziuba decided not to answer in any way. Instead, a group of journalist friends, led by Viacheslav Chornovil, sent a letter in defence of his reputation to the editorial board of Perets'. The letter was not published, but it circulated in *samvydav*. It dismissed "Vasyl Osadchy's" piece as slander and emphasized the cowardice of the editorial board that had allowed it to be published, particularly since no one had had the courage to own up being the author (or authors).[236]

Nevertheless the Ukrainian intellectual world was waiting for an answer from Dziuba, the first voice of the *shistdesiatnytstvo* movement. In December 1966 a journalist from the Ukrainian-language newspaper *Nove zhyttia* in Prešov, Slovakia, interviewed Dziuba. When he was asked what problems troubled him, Dziuba answered:

> In the first place, I am concerned about the fate of my friends. I am troubled by the complicated and at times contradictory processes that are taking place in our social and national life. I am worried about the problems, disappointments, and aspirations of those of our youth who want to contribute to the processes of creating a fully valued socialist life in practice, not just talk, and think of what they can gain from it subjectively in their search for truth and [the] purpose of life, and what they can give to the nation. A number of broader social and ethical problems could be mentioned. Generally, ethics interest me more than politics, but ethics in a broader sense, as the relation of man to the world and to himself. [237]

Dziuba's diplomatic response that posed more questions than it answered. How broad could the ethics of *shistdesiatnytstvo* be? To what extent were its spokespeople ready to face up to the Soviet regime? Dziuba's vagueness did not satisfy the journalist, who asked whether he would reply to *Perets'*. Dziuba responded: "My answer of any kind would constitute a sanction or legalization of the slanderous allegations, which are beyond all moral and judicial norms. Elementary human contempt will not permit me to pay it any attention."

---

236 The letter was first published in *Suchasnist'*, 1967, no. 11: 53–61; English trans. in *Revolutionary Voices*, 31–36.
237 Both this and the next quote are from "Ivan Dziuba Replies," *The Ukrainian Review* 11, no. 2 (Summer 1967): 20–23. The original in Ukrainian is in *Nove zhyttia*, 14 January 1967.

Dziuba refused to rise to the attack. His field of action was on a higher plane, that of personal conscience. He sidestepped the opportunity to transform the cultural movement he represented into a political one. For the CPU it was a sign that Dziuba was less dangerous than had been anticipated. His unwillingness to engage in a political battle was noted by the Party in a letter to the SPU.[238]

Dziuba confirmed his hesitation to take the helm of the political opposition. He has declared many times that he did not want to be a politician or head the opposition, and that he wrote *Internationalism or Russification?* out of a sense of civic duty. This lack of leadership made it impossible for the *shistdesiatnyky* to achieve some practical success in a peaceful way before the international situation in 1967 caused the CPSU to crack down hard on nonconformism.

The highest point the *shistdesiatnytstvo* movement reached in the construction of a new public space was on 22 May 1967 during the annual gathering at the Shevchenko monument in Kyiv. I agree with Liudmila Alexeyeva, who identifies this incident as being politically central to the movement and places it at the beginning of her account of Ukrainian "dissent."[239] On that day a larger number of citizens had assembled at the monument. Around ten o'clock in the evening several police cars arrived and the police ordered a halt to the demonstration. The crowd ignored them, and the police randomly arrested four men. Then the demonstrators decided to reassemble outside the building of the CC CPU to demand the unconditional release of the arrestees. About three hundred people took part, singing Ukrainian songs and the *Internationale* until they were stopped by a barricade of police cars and Party activists near the CPU building.

Dr. Mykola Plakhotniuk, a former member of the KTM, led the demonstration and the negotiations with the authorities. Only fifty or so people remained until two in the morning, but the protesters obtained the release of the arrestees. There were no further consequences.[240] Although the demonstrators showed great resolve in demanding that the police release the arrestees, not one of the leaders of the *shistdesiatnyky* was at the head of the crowd. Though he had been involved in the KTM since 1963, Plakhotniuk had not written any famous documents, and his political

---

238 Report on Dziuba's activities, in TsDAHOU, f. 1, op. 1, spr. 6313, ark. 33.
239 Ludmila Alexeyeva, *Soviet Dissent: Contemporary Movements for National, Religious, and Human Rights* (Middletown, Conn., 1985), 22–23.
240 Kas'ianov, *Nezhodni*, 70–71.

views differed slightly from those of the other *shistdesiatnyky*.[241] He was active in distributing *samvydav* and was a good friend of Viacheslav Chornovil and Yaroslav Hevrych (b. 1937), a dentistry student and dissident arrested in 1965 and imprisoned for three years in a Mordovian labour camp. Plakhotniuk effectively led the protestors on 22 May. But he lacked the leverage of Dziuba or Chornovil, both of whom had missed this event, the former because he was reluctant to play the role of political leader, the latter because he was confined in Lviv at the time. Recent studies of the *shistdesiatnytstvo* movement affirm that it attracted "wide social circles, including students, workers, and members of other professional groups."[242] But despite the fact that the movement expressed popular discontent with the Soviet regime, the number of people at its demonstrations was not that larger. The 22 May public protest — probably the decade's most successful Ukrainian dissident demonstration — was only attended by around three hundred persons. Only about seventy people attended the commemorations of Taras Shevchenko held in Kyiv in 1968 and 1969.[243] Not many were prepared to occupy public squares and demonstrate against the regime, and thus *shistdesiatnytstvo* remained a primarily an intellectual movement whose elite was unwilling to struggle against the Soviet regime.

That regime was often successful in taking over such events to deprive them of their significance. Although the commemoration of 22 May was considered blatantly anti-Soviet and could not be viewed otherwise, the

---

241 Plakhotniuk (1936–2015) was born in the Kursk region of the Russian SFSR, where his parents had fled during the 1932–33 Great Famine in Soviet Ukraine. They returned to their native village in the Kyiv region in 1942 during the German occupation, where Mykola grew up in a traditional Ukrainian environment. He studied at the Kyiv Medical Institute, which was strongly Russified, and recalled that only two subjects were taught in Ukrainian and the textbooks were only in Russian. Plakhotniuk's interest in literature prompted him to became acquainted with philology students, and from 1963 he began attending the KTM's literary and artistic evenings. His political views were not typical of his generation because of his knowledge of the Holodomor, about which he had learned from his parents. Plakhotniuk never considered himself a communist and was skeptical about the possibilities of reforming the Soviet Union. In our interview on 3 June 2009, he told me that he used to argue with Borys Antonenko-Davydovych about it and that he did not believe in Petro Shelest: "When they told me that Shelest cared about Ukrainian culture, I laughed."
242 Iurii O. Kornusov, *Inakomyslennia v Ukraïni (60-ti – persha polovyna 80-kh rr. XX st.)* (Kyiv, 1994), 81.
243 See the teports to the CPU about unsanctioned demonstrations in Kyiv, in TsDAHOU, f. 1, op. 1, spr. 180, ark. 3–7.

commemorations of the Nazi mass murders at Babyn Yar were taken over by the Soviet authorities from 1968 onward. The rationale was that in taking away the opportunity for a potentially anti-Soviet demonstration, people would be forced to participate in a state-controlled event. This strategy seemed to work well at Babyn Yar, where the number of people who attended the publicized and organized event doubled compared to previous years, when the gathering was spontaneous.[244]

This takeover and its consequences were not evident to observers at the time. Some leaflets advertising the meeting could even have sounded worrisome to Soviet authorities. The sample handed to the Party attacked ongoing Russification as a betrayal of the true nationality policy and called the USSR a "dictatorship of Party bureaucrats".

> Ukrainian-haters took all of the grain from Ukraine. Then, in 1933, a famine was artificially created, causing the death of millions of peasants working in the collective farms.... The Twentieth and Twenty-Second Party Congresses, interpreting the spirit of the time, raised the possibility of establishing a normal life in the USSR. But the popular hopes turned out to be in vain. Party bureaucrats are restoring Stalin's policy. They are trying again to stop the socialist development of society and to restore in the country an atmosphere of fear ... forcing the people to lose personal dignity, renounce independent thought, and reducing them to the status of food consumers.[245]

The leaflet urged the Kyiv's citizens ("comrades") to engage in a "non-standardized way of thinking," seek the reinstatement of a genuine Leninist policy, and gather at the Shevchenko monument regardless of the threat of arrest. The *shistdesiatnytstvo* movement, insisting on its battle against unified thought and against the formation of a standardized consumer society, had not lost its intellectual appeal. Its social criticism prefigures similar critiques of consumer society that Western intellectuals such as Pier Paolo Pasolini would make about ten years later, speaking out against what he considered to be actual totalitarianism.[246]

---

244 See the report about the commemoration on 29 September 1969, in TsDAHOU, f. 1, op. 1, spr. 180, ark. 17–20.
245 Leaflet sent to the CC CPU, in TsDAHOU, f. 1, op. 25, spr. 127, ark. 36.
246 Pasolini elaborated the concept of consumerism as real totalitarianism in articles for the *Corriere della Sera* in the early 1970s. See Pier Paolo Pasolini, *Lettere luterane* (Torino, 1976); English trans.: *Lutheran Letters* (Manchester and Dublin, 1983).

The occasion to express what kind of *hromadskist* (civic-mindedness) the *shistdesiatnyky* had in mind was offered by Oles Honchar, a prominent Soviet Ukrainian writer who could hardly be considered a *shistdesiatnyk*.

The Case of Oles Honchar's *Sobor*

In January 1968 Oles Honchar's novel *Sobor* (The Cathedral) was serialized in the literary monthly journal *Vitchyzna*. Because of his age and involvement in the Soviet *nomenklatura*, Honchar cannot have been a *shistdesiatnyk*. But many historians have suggested that his role within the cultural revival of the 1960s was more significant than previously thought.[247] In any case, *Sobor* is an unusual work for a conformist member of the Soviet establishment. Honchar advocated the integration of the new generation of writers into the SPU in order to prevent open opposition. This strategy had been fully expressed in 1966 at the Fifth Congress of Ukrainian Writers by Petro Shelest himself. He had ascertained that some representatives of the "new generation" had become leading intellectuals and that "this clearly shows once again that those among our intellectual workers who had hoped for a conflict between the generations of Soviet artists experienced a bitter disappointment. Young people of Ukraine have gone, and are still going, the same path as their parents and elders, and no one will ever undermine this unity of our glorious generations." The head of the CPU seemed to offer an escape route to young intellectuals in the wake of the 1965 arrests, adding that those whose works were used in Western propaganda need only to publicly dissociate themselves from them in order to be welcomed back into the official fold.[248]

In his address to the congress, Honchar quoted Lina Kostenko—"On the barricades of revolution our literature, democratic in its essence, is internally ready to apply the revolutionariness and fighting humanitarianism of Lenin's ideas"—and praised her and Vasyl Symonenko. He stressed the importance of developing the Ukrainian language but also knowing other national cultures.[249] He was followed by the much younger poet Vitalii Korotych (b. 1936), who formulated a specific concept of internationalism.

---

[247] Vitalii Koval', "'Sobor' i navkolo n'oho," *Dnipro*, 1988, no. 4: 6–50; the need for further research has been pointed out by Iurii Danyliuk, Oleh Bazhan, *Opozytsiia v Ukraïni (druha polovyna 50-kh – 80-kh rr. XX st.)* (Kyiv, 2000), 28–29.

[248] See the minutes of the 5th Congress of the Union of Writers of Ukraine, TsDAMLMU, f. 590, op. 1, spr. 630, ark. 31–33.

[249] See ibidem, ark. 40 and 85.

> Isolation from the art of other peoples means death, but understanding it creates an even foundation, a revolutionary conception of the world. "Cosmopolitan art" does not exist. Those who claim to be cosmopolitan and without a fatherland are foolish and do not deserve praise from any nation. Therefore there is no difference whether they are in Uruguay, in Ukraine, or in Monaco: any sincere nationalist poet is at the same time internationalist.[250]

Other speeches were dedicated to singling out the future lines for the development of Ukrainian literature. Much older Pavlo Baidebura, a representative figure of the culture of the Donbas, noted that unlike in Russian literature, the theme of the conflict between the "worker-innovator" and the conservative factory director had not been properly explored.[251] The first to touch upon the subject of a specifically Ukrainian cultural inheritance was Korotych's contemporary, the poet Viktor Korzh (b. 1938):

> We live in our world, and everything in it is beloved and holy to us: the beloved monuments of our national culture—from the yellowing page of a manuscript to every detail of an architectural work—and the beloved nature of our native land, whose disfigurement hurts like a sharp pain. Our beloved culture, our language ... We want the Ukrainian language to be always pure, colourful, picturesque, beginning from kindergarten to higher education. Therefore it is very important to teach in the native language in the schools, in the universities ... Being internationalists, we will always remain Ukrainian.[252]

He was supported by the Transcarpathian writer Ivan Chendei (1922–2005), who claimed that restoring old structures, and particularly country churches, was an "internationalist" duty:

> I believe that we writers have to intervene when the protection of national assets, of monuments, is at stake, and if we do not do that in the proper way, then we fail in our duty to the people, to their present, their past, and their future. When we do not do all that is possible to protect the culture of the past, that is the same as writing

---

250 Ibidem, ark. 165.
251 Ibidem, spr. 631, ark. 23.
252 Ibidem, ark. 106.

without using all our talent—writing not in the way a real piece of art should be written.[253]

The congress ended with speeches by the older, conservative Leonid Novychenko, who harshly criticized the Soviet philosopher Akhed Agaev's theory of the predominance of Russian, and by even older Oleksii Poltoratsky, the editor of *Vsesvit*, who hoped that Soviet Ukraine could grant more freedoms to literature and publishing.

Nearly a year after the congress, Honchar's *Sobor* was published. The novel's plot is simple. Volodia Loboda, a Party official, wants to demolish the cathedral at Zachiplianka, an imaginary small city close to Dnipropetrovsk, in order to build a new market in its place. The villagers, who are good Communists and mostly workers at the steel plant in the larger city, rise up in defence of the cathedral. Among them is Mykola Bahlai, an idealized hero. Intelligent, fit, and handsome, he is a university student, a poet, and an inventor, who redeems and wins over Yelka, a country girl being courted by Loboda. Finally, despite interference from local bureaucrats and owing to the intervention of the oblast's Party secretary, the air purifiers Bahlai invented are installed in the steel plant. The cathedral, rescued from demolition, stands as a symbol of the moral integrity of Zachiplianka's inhabitants and is the backdrop for its most meaningful events.

Sobor was published at the beginning of the year that Honchar turned fifty. he presumably thought this novel could become a part of the tradition of stories about innovative inventors and reactionary bureaucrats inaugurated with Ilya Ehrenburg's *Ottepel'* (The Thaw). As Susanne Schattenberg has pointed out,

> This constellation, in which the "bureaucratic" official was pitted against the "democratic" and committed technical specialist, became a common trope of the Khrushchev era … It served as a parable both of Stalin's demise and post-Stalinist political change, and also of the beginning of a new chapter of technical progress and economic growth. But whilst writers and readers were interested in both the former and the latter, the party used the "bureaucrat vs. engineer" formula to try to concentrate public discussion on

---

253 Ibidem, ark. 147.

economic matters, and thereby to distract the public from political debate.²⁵⁴

The institutionally minded Honchar had no revolutionary aspirations. However, like the Ukrainian-born Russian author of the 1956 novel *Not by Bread Alone*, Vladimir Dudintsev (1918–98), Honchar was accused of committing a few "errors." *Sobor*'s Loboda is a Party official but not a simple bureaucrat; he pretends to take care of the people's needs but is mostly concerned with his public image and career. It is he who steals from the cathedral and mocks Bahlai and his project for the air purifiers. Honchar's novel used the opposition of bureaucrats against inventors to attack not the old Stalinist *nomenklatura* but the new post-Stalinist establishment and its philistinism.

In one scene Bahlai discusses the possible demolition of the cathedral with Romtsia, a friend who helped him to develop the purifier project. A matter-of-fact man, Romtsia urges Bahlai to be realistic about people's daily needs.

> "You must be a realist," he lectured Mykola. "Take any one of our hard workers. Give him a television, a motorboat, and a pass to the Red Steelworker's Sanatorium on the Black Sea, and he will brush aside all that which you call spiritual. You're worrying about the cathedral. You think it moves everyone the way it moves you? Shpachykha has been walking all her life past it, do you think she needs those cupolas that much? She never even looks at them! Her basket weighs her down to the ground, give her money! Suggest a choice to her: the cathedral or an indoor market—and she'll be for the market with both hands. What's that cathedral for her life? Or for Fedir, the roller? You cannot be satiated on spiritual things alone, brother. The matter is primordial ..."
>
> "Those soup-eaters probably think the same way. You mentioned walking stomachs yourself."
>
> "Don't take me at my word. Anyway, people have long been tightening their belts, surviving on ration cards, and if now they create a new cult for themselves—call it the cult of the stomach, if you like—then will you condemn them for it?"²⁵⁵

---

254 Susanne Schattenberg, "'Democracy' or 'Despotism'? How the Secret Speech was Translated into Everyday Life," in *The Dilemmas of De-Stalinization: Negotiating Cultural and Social Change in the Khrushchev Era*, ed. Polly Jones (London and New York 2006), 64.

255 Oles Honchar, *The Cathedral: A Novel*, trans. Yuri Tkach and Leonid Rudnytzky (Washington, DC, 1989), 84–85. Shpachykha is an old Communist woman who was

Romtsia's theory of the "cult of the stomach"—a provocative definition for the new political course after the condemnation of the Stalin personality cult—is proven wrong, since even the "stalwart workers" demonstrate their need for "spiritual things" by protesting in defence of their cathedral. But the offensive against cultural legacy was deeper and more dangerous than the introduction of new forms of consumption: it was an attack on the core of popular culture, as demonstrated in Loboda and Bahlai's dialogue. The former, after stressing that "things change, as the philosopher remarked, they change, and how! Now one can't go far on hackneyed dogma. You have to shake up the brain, seek new things," expresses his position on Soviet nationality policy.

> What have you, a young man from a workers' suburb, found in degenerate Yavornytsky? Cathedrals … Cossack sabers … huts! All of that is history legacy, the rubbish of past ages, how can you not understand that? In the space-age these aren't the things that should be troubling us.… You young people support me, and tomorrow, in place of this cathedral, I'll erect a great cafe for the young! With everything! A real darling cafe, they'll only gasp in the provincial center!… Of course you can ask: what about our national heritage? And am I against traditions? Am I some bastard, a passportless tramp? Everything can be designed in Cossack style; on the cafe's facade we can have a Cossack standing with a spear and Cossack Mamay sitting cross-legged with a bandura, both wearing Cossack trousers. Even the cafe can be called Cossack Mamay' or 'Cossack Mamay's Place.' Wouldn't that be great?[256]

Loboda's conception of Ukrainian national heritage is an extension of the Stalinist folk culture of the 1930s. It has a national form but no true national content. It is a Cossack-themed café in place of a real eighteenth-century Cossack cathedral. This "fake" national folklore, allegedly created by the people as a spontaneous form of self-expression, was the ideal means of achieving a fictitious organic unity among Soviet peoples and thus implementing the leading Soviet policy on the nationality question.[257]

---

later a leader of the popular demonstrations.
256 Ibidem, 93–94. "Degenerate Yavornytsky" is a reference to the famous academician and historian of the Zaporozhian Cossacks, Dmytro Yavornytsky (1855–1949).
257 Ivan Koshelivets' wrote that Loboda "brilliantly formulated the Party idea of Ukrainian culture: a kebab house with a Little Russian name." See his article "Pro 'Sobor' Olesia

Honchar's view of the role of writers and of their relationship to power can be considered unorthodox. Through Loboda's thoughts he presents the regime's opinion of intellectuals.

> Loboda immediately became morose: Oh, we know those thinkers. They're not very strong on socialist realism, more on humanism.... Present them with eternal questions, the eternal truths. This cathedral was for them—they'd stand before it all their lives and pray to it. Don't feed them bread, just give them those glorious Cossack times!... Strange people: they had everything, drove about in their own cars, but they still wanted something. They probably didn't know themselves what it was!... No, we've spoiled them! They criticise others and yet don't refuse comforts themselves! They probably didn't set out in buses like this very often ... True enough even though he is in his car, he knows everything, the rogue, hears everything. Just let him get wind of you, should he find out somehow about this story with the cathedral plaque, for instance, he wouldn't pass it by, he'd churn out a whole novel about the cathedral!... What a public! What a despicable people![258]

By describing himself a man who cared about Soviet institutions but is also a strongly humanist intellectual, Honchar was claiming a role in the political debate, perhaps stretching out a hand to the *shistdesiatnyky*. The character of Loboda, who possesses many traits that directly oppose the values of *shistdesiatnytstvo*, is set up as the obvious antagonist. Demonstrating that he is unable to understand what else one should want besides material comforts, he ultimately reveals himself to be nostalgic for Stalinist methods when he threatens a teacher with exile in Siberia.[259] Bahlai, his more sympathetic opponent, provides readers with an interpretation of the novel that is in line with the intellectual *Zeitgeist*. When his friend Hennadii wonders why a physics genius such as Mykola should be enthused by such an "anachronism" as the cathedral, Bahlai explains.

Honchara," *Suchasnist'*, 1968, nos. 7–8: 62–74 (quote 71) and 9: 44–53; and Hoffmann, *Stalinist Values: The Cultural Norms of Soviet Modernity*, 171–72.

258 Honchar, *The Cathedral*, 127.
259 Ibidem, 230–31.

"A cathedral like this doesn't belong to you or me; more correctly stated, it does not belong to us alone. It belongs not only to the nation which created it, but to all the people of the planet!"
"Oh!"
"There is some kind of collective consciousness in people, in mankind—should it be passed on into the future? Should it survive in future memories?... Those who built [the cathedral] were thinking of eternity. It is a peculiarity of people who strive for eternity, to find in it a goal and inspiration for themselves ... I doubt if there's anything more deserving than to perfect one's spirit, to immortalize oneself in work, in one's creations. Or is this a mirage too, according to your way of thinking?"
"But without them, can't ordinary, simple mortals survive?"
"Sure they can. One can survive without the cathedral, and without song, and without Raphael. One can live without everything that is protected and unprotected by plaques. *Anna Karenina* can be read in an abridged form, compressed down to one and a half pages of text. But would we then remain people in the full sense of the word? Wouldn't we then become simply soup-eaters, devourers of shashliks? History's beasts of burden?"[260]

This is not a hymn to a single national culture. The cathedral is an inspiration to all "who strive for eternity." It belongs to humankind, representing a guiding light on the path leading to the perfection of real human nature. These poetics become clearer in the final lines of the dialogue, when Hennadii asks:

"Does modern man become enriched spiritually? and if he does, then how? What exactly does he gain? and what does he lose?"
"That's what you and I must investigate."
"We?"
"If not us, then who?... We're the sons of a nation which has rammed through the old servile world with the armored trains of our hatred; our mothers pass on to us not conceit, not arrogance and greed, but a sense of honour, dignity and love of freedom—that's worth something! The sons of barricaded streets! We're the sons of [Taras] Shevchenko's anger, the sons of [Nikolai] Kibalchich! To erect these cathedrals, these steelworker citadels of the times ... To raise the

---

260 Ibidem, 215.

Titan of revolution over them ... Oh, my friend, this isn't the fruit of subservient brows!"[261]

This last declaration of spiritual freedom as a national inheritance both worried the Soviet authorities and conquered the hearts of the *shistdesiatnyky*. Bahlai claims his generation's right to play a decisive role in this search for a new *raison d'être* through the development of national culture.

Although in no way anti-Soviet, Honchar's novel emphasized the importance of a national legacy and of intellectual freedom, and it contained enough controversial elements to provoke a negative reaction from Leonid Brezhnev's cohort. Nonetheless, the condemnation did not occur immediately.

A few days after the publication of the first part of *Sobor*, the writer and literary critic Marharyta Malynovska proclaimed Honchar's new work a masterpiece. In her long and detailed essay, she concluded:

> The problems [raised in] the novel are not specifically historical, but—we are not afraid to use these words—common to all humankind. It is not just a matter of the attitudes the different characters have toward the cathedral, but, more accurately, the attitudes of a person toward other people mediated through the matter of the cathedral. It is about drawing attention toward those dimensions the cathedral exemplifies, which often lead to the discovery of broader horizons that go beyond the limits of literal meanings. In this sense the cathedral [is] a general artistic symbol.[262]

Before it was attacked politically, the official interpretation of Honchar's novel identified central themes of humanism and a search for the definition and perfection of humankind. The national question was understood as one possible manifestation of a broader problem. Commenting on the first edition of *Sobor* as a separate volume, the writer Oles Lupii (b. 1938) lamented that the 20,000 copies printed were too few

---

261 Ibidem, 219. Kibalchich (1853–81) was a Russian revolutionary of Ukrainian-Serbian origin born in Korop, Chernihiv Guberniia. He was hanged by the tsarist state for his part in the assassination of Alexander II as the main explosive expert for the terrorist group Narodnaia Volia (People's Will).

262 Marharyta Malynovs'ka, "Zhyttia v romani," *Literaturna Ukraïna*, 19 January 1968, 2; Malynovska (1941–83) was a writer, poet, and literary critic. Her support for *Sobor* earned the wrath of the CPSU, of which she was a member.

and added that "first of all *Sobor* should be perceived as the song of a bright cathedral of human souls, as a great epic of our contemporaneity with all its complexity but also its transparency, which is in anyone who loves, preserves, and creates beauty."[263]

The commemorative essays published in celebration of Honchar's birthday on 2 April 1968 followed this line of interpretation, suggesting a division within the Ukrainian cultural establishment. At this point the attacks against him had already begun but they had not yet reached the national press. Therefore any published reviews remained largely positive. Dmytro Pavlychko described Honchar as a "master, a humanist, a lover of truth," while the literary critic Vitalii Donchyk (1932–2017), in an essay meaningfully titled "The Depth of People's Lives," dared to write:

> Oles Honchar is turning fifty, half of his own centenary, as the author of the new novel *Sobor*—a work reflecting on contemporary life, on the problem of Soviet man's responsibility toward his nation today and in the past.... In this work one can sense eternal values such as friendship, honesty, wisdom, love, principles, and persuasion, love of one's mother, love of our native land, memory, beauty. Whoever wants to free himself from any responsibility inevitably becomes an enemy of high human values.[264]

In private, writers were even more explicit. In a well-known letter, the writer Hryhir Tiutiunnyk (1931–80) defined *Sobor* as a "warning bell" that carried a deep and grave significance.

> In our time, allegedly quiet and blessed, you can hear only a snake rustle at your feet ... and suddenly there's *Sobor*! It seemed that "everything is silent because there's prosperity"—TV sets under slate country roofs, pensions for collective-farm workers, collective management, patriotism, formulaic equality for all—and suddenly [there's] *Sobor*! It seemed that normalization was underway—no more cult [of personality], "personal errors," generals standing and applauding when his name is mentioned; bosses' wives and forty-year-old Komsomol members convinced by leading writers that

---

263 Oles' Lupii, "Sobory dush liuds'kykh," *Literaturna Ukraïna*, 29 March 1968, 3.
264 Both articles are in *Literaturna Ukraïna*, 2 April 1968, 2.

1937 was not so criminal, that someone was rightly made to "smoke the last cigarette" — and suddenly there's *Sobor*!²⁶⁵

A young writer like Tiutiunnyk could see in *Sobor* a strong protest against the Brezhnev regime. This did not go unnoticed in Dnipropetrovsk, where its oblast's Party secretary, Oleksii Vatchenko, had already heard of the novel. In that oblast the first review of the novel was quite positive, identifying humanism as the main theme of a work "that embraces nearly all of the immensely vast material of our life."²⁶⁶ But on 28 March, a day before the meeting of the Plenum of the CPU, Vatchenko called Petro Shelest to denounce the unorthodox ideology of Honchar's novel, lamenting that he recognized himself in Loboda.²⁶⁷

Honchar had once written to Vatchenko in 1965, asking him to improve the poor storage conditions at the history museum in Dnipropetrovsk.²⁶⁸ According to the testimony of a Mr. Dobryk, when Honchar had visited rural Dnipropetrovsk Oblast in 1967 as the Party secretary in Dniprodzerzhynsk, he had deplored the overuse of Russian on public street signs and in everyday communication.²⁶⁹ Perhaps these incidents had been an incentive to choose this oblast as the setting for the novel, but there is no indication that Honchar wanted to attack Vatchenko in his novel. In Shelest's words, Vatchenko shared similarities with Loboda: "Vatchenko's father is in a seniors' home. Vatchenko is rude, uneducated, angry, so it seems as though he hates all of humankind. In the end this is what set Vatchenko off against Honchar."²⁷⁰ At the Plenum on 29 March Vatchenko attacked Honchar, saying "Comrades, we have to admit that among us sometimes one can find people who, willy-nilly, help bourgeois propaganda by criticizing our Soviet works ... This novel is against people who work, against those simple people who in fifty years under the wise direction of the Communist Party have achieved a previously unseen

---

265 Letter published in Oles' Honchar, *Tronka – Sobor* (Kyiv, 2005), 520–21.
266 Petr Symonenko, "Iz pravdy i krasoty," *Industrial'noe Zaporozh'e*, 21 February 1968, reprinted now in *Ternystym shliakhom do khramu: Oles' Honchar v suspil'no-politychnomu zhytti Ukraïny 60–80-i rr. XX st.*, ed. Petro T. Tron'ko, Oleh H. Bazhan, and Iurii Z. Danyliuk (Kyiv, 1999), 79–83.
267 Petr Shelest, *Da ne sudimy budete: Dnevnikovye zapisi, vospominaniia chlena Politbiuro TsK KPSS* (Moscow, 1994), 303.
268 Letter published in *Ternystym shliakhom do khramu*, 50.
269 Minutes of the CPU's Steering Committee for Dnipropetrovsk Oblast, in TsDAHOU, f. 1, op. 54, spr. 50, ark. 9–10.
270 Shelest, *Da ne sudimy budete*, 302.

growth of economy, science, culture, and literature."[271] Shelest, who had not read the novel, defended Honchar in a general way, suggesting that it was up to readers to judge the novel's contents.

Honchar had an opportunity to defend himself at his public birthday celebration. There he gave a short speech, which later circulated in *samvydav*, to reaffirm the probity of his work. After paying lip service to the Russian guests "with whom we are united in one single great brotherhood," he sketched a scenario in which young writers devoted to the truth opposed those who were still somehow linked to the past.[272] Honchar stated that he was working on the development of Ukrainian culture together with the "knights of creativity." His opponents were devils "who sometimes even now, at night with the smoke of incense burners, try to slander our new works with old outmoded labels." He claimed that *Sobor* was no less patriotic than any other of his novels and that he had written it from a "Leninist" point of view combining the Soviet patriotism of Ukrainian literature with its humanitarian aid. Honchar's job consisted of "writing the truth, a deeply perceived truth, maybe even a painful truth in all its dimensions and insistence."[273]

Trusting in the support of Shelest, who was attending the birthday party, Honchar decided not to indulge in self-criticism and launched a tirade against the guardians of the "old order." The same arguments were used by his older colleague Andrii Holovko (1897–1972), who believed *Sobor* was "wonderful" and naturally attractive to the younger generations.[274]

On the same day as Honchar's party, *Literaturna hazeta* published the essay "How Much We are Losing." Signed by many Ukrainian personalities, the article echoed *Sobor*'s themes by speaking of the need to preserve Ukraine's architectonic legacy.[275] A report on *Sobor* prepared for Shelest by the Communist Party's propaganda and culture departments contained moderate criticisms but stressed Honchar's good intentions,

---

271 Minutes of the Plenum of the Communist Party of Ukraine, 29 March 1968, TsDAHOU, f. 1, op. 1, spr. 2058, ark. 85–86.
272 Oles' Honchar, "Slovo na vechori 3 kvitnia 1968 roku," *Journal of Ukrainian Studies* 1, no. 1 (Fall 1976): 48–50 (here 48).
273 Ibidem, 49–50.
274 TsDAMLMU, f. 18, op. 3, spr. 27, ark. 2–10.
275 *Literaturna Ukraïna*, 3 April 1968, 3.

concluding that "the author's generous aspirations and breaking of rules deserve varied support."[276]

Meanwhile, the campaign against *Sobor* was underway in Dnipropetrovsk Oblast. Communist Party cells there organized meetings to involve ordinary people in the attacks. A point of contention for the Party and workers alike was Honchar's description of the daily life of workers as a dark reality—a generalization that discounted the alleged political richness of the industrial suburbs: "As far as we metallurgical workers are concerned, nearly everything is depicted by the author in a distorted way without any knowledge of working conditions and workers' psychology, their quests, their needs. Where did the author see those people 'oppressed' by work?"[277] Oleksii Vatchenko reported to Shelest about this supposed popular dissatisfaction with *Sobor*,[278] seeking to convince Shelest there was a popular movement against the novel. In reality the KGB had registered angry reactions against the negative reviews of the novel, but Vatchenko was wary of informing Shelest about them.[279]

The local press engaged in intimidation tactics, sending negative reviews directly to Honchar.[280] Further attacks followed in *Vitchyzna*—the SPU's monthly journal—and the daily newspaper of the CC CPU, *Radians'ka Ukraïna*, proving that Vatchenko's qualms had found some supporters among conservative intellectuals. The Party's literary critic Mykola Shamota attacked *Sobor* as a symbol of the past, since "that 'sixth sense,' which turns a writer into an expert on people and society, is the ability to feel history in the present, to evaluate the present from tomorrow's point of view, and support the motivating power of

---

276 TsDAHOU, f. 1, op. 31, spr. 3447, ark. 54.
277 Letter by workers of the Dniprospetsstal Plant, titled "No, This Novel Is Not about Us," originally published in the newspaper *Zaporiz'ka pravda*, in *Ternystym shliakhom do khramu*, 108.
278 Vatchenko's report, dated 15 May 1968, in TsDAHOU, f. 1, op. 25, spr. 20, ark. 23–31.
279 See the KGB report to Vatchenko, 15 May 1968, in *Ternystym shliakhom do khramu*, 143. In reaction to this discontent, local authorities persecuted intellectuals, culminating with the arrest of the poet Ivan Sokulsky, who wrote the "Letter of Creative Youth of Dnipropetrovsk (see Chapter Three). According to Leonid Boiko, Leonid Brezhnev and the KGB supported Vatchenko. See "Vid'oms'ki poliuvannia na 'Vatchyni,'" *Vitchyzna* 1999, nos. 11–12: 111–25.
280 Honchar's wife began sending back these reviews because she thought they were "not worth reading," as happened with a copy of the Kryvyi Rih newspaper *Chervonyi hirnyk*, in TsDAHOU, f. 1, op. 25, spr. 20, ark. 33–37.

progress."[281] To contradict Honchar's characterization of the writer and revolutionary populist Pavlo Hrabovsky (1864–1902) in *Sobor*, the 18 May 1968 issue of *Radians'ka osvita*—the official newspaper of Soviet Ukraine's Ministries of Education and Higher and Secondary Specialized Education—published an article by Oleksandr Mazurkevych (1913–95), a prominent specialist on the history and methodology of pedagogy in Ukraine, in which he quoted letters by the Ukrainian poet and revolutionary populist Pavlo Hrabovsky in which the latter rejected the idea of an independent Ukraine.[282] Another condemnation of *Sobor* in *Izvestiia*, the major newspaper of the USSR government, indicated that the central powers in Moscow disapproved of the novel.[283]

This official censure of *Sobor* prompted Petro Shelest to meet privately with Honchar around 18 April in order to advise him to treat the promotion of his novel with caution so as to prevent its exploitation by foreign propaganda.[284] A few days later, commenting on a 15 April report about the novel, Shelest concluded: "Honchar's *Sobor* is a serious and unfortunate misstep for the author, and we hope that the author of this novel finds the courage to soberly judge his work and those shortcomings within it that the press is writing about, and especially to address the metallurgical workers and make amends for this work."[285] Despite this critique, Shelest nevertheless remained supportive of his favourite writer.

During this time a group of *shistdesiatnyky* began disseminating a "Letter of the 139," addressed to the highest Ukrainian officials and defending Ukrainian intellectuals, particularly Chornovil. In response, as noted in a letter to the CC CPSU in Moscow dated 4 June, Shelest met with the leaders of the SPU—among them Honchar, Mykola Bazhan, Leonid Novychenko, Pavlo Zahrebelny, Dmytro Pavlychko, and Vitalii

---

281 See Mykola Shamota, "Realizm i pochuttia istoriï," *Radians'ka Ukraïna*, 16 May 1968, 2–4 (quote on p. 4).See also Viktor Ivanysenko, "Tvortsi i brakon'iery," *Vitchyzna*, April 1968, 139–48; and M. Yurchuk and F. Lebedenko (unidentified pseudonyms), "Pered lytsem diisnosti," *Radians'ka Ukraïna*, 26 April 1968, 3–4 an attack on the positive reviews published in *Literaturna Ukraïna*.
282 Oleksandr Mazurkevych, "Fiktsiia suproty nauky," *Radians'ka shkola*, 1968, no. 39: 2–3. Mazurkevych is the author of a textbook on teaching Hrabovsky's works in Soviet schools.
283 Nikolai Fed', "Dostoinstvo iskusstva," *Izvestiia*, 13 June 1968, 4.
284 Shelest, *Da ne sudimy budete*, 306.
285 *Ternystym shliakhom do khramu*, 125–26.

Korotych—and Fedir Ovcharenko[286] to address "some recent problematic trends in Ukrainian literature." Among the criticisms voiced at the meeting was the appearance of "ideologically and artistically weak pieces of work, substandard theoretical levels of literary criticism, the tendency toward subjective and biased evaluation of works, and the proliferation of individualism and political philistinism in young writers." Furthermore, in some cases "politically imprecise" writings by Ukrainian writers, including Mykola Bazhan, Ivan Dziuba, Ivan Drach, Lina Kostenko, and Yevhen Hutsalo, had been exploited by the émigré nationalist press. "During the meeting a radical change of mind about the future development of Ukrainian literature took place ... The writers indignantly judged the literary figures who had signed the letter to the CC CPSU."[287]

On the same day, 4 June, Oleksii Vatchenko gave Shelest a letter that further worsened Honchar's position. It was supposedly written by a group of Kyiv writers, who claimed that "when in 1959 Honchar became the head of the SPU, he immediately began surrounding himself with undeserving and dishonest people." The letter's anonymous authors accused Honchar's allies, especially Zahrebelny, Pavlychko, and Yurii Zbanatsky, of being nationalists and Nazi collaborators. They also declared that Honchar had written *Sobor* to influence Western public opinion and that they were therefore turning to Vatchenko for support and assistance.[288] On 9 July Vatchenko received another, similar letter, which he also forwarded to Shelest.[289]

When an article attacking Honchar, titled "What Certain 'Humanists' Defend" was eventually published in *Literaturna Ukraïna* in July 1968, it was of a political rather than a literary nature. In it Honchar was not even mentioned by name. Because of the recent publication of Viacheslav Chornovil's writings in the West, the article's author, *Vsesvit*'s editor in chief Oleksii Poltoratsky, expressed concern about the condemnation of Chornovil and Sviatoslav Karavansky, who in his opinion were Western imperialist puppets. The goal of the essay was to show that Western appeals to humanitarianism were a rhetorical stratagem to conceal bourgeois nationalism, which Poltoratsky attempted to prove by attacking

---

286 Ovcharenko, Shelest's ally, had replaced Andrii Skaba as head of the CPU's Department of Propaganda on 29 March 1968 and was entrusted with the task of ensuring that the arrested Ukrainian dissidents would not become political martyrs.
287 The record of the meeting is in TsDAHOU, f. 1, op. 25, spr. 20, ark. 44–48.
288 The record of the meeting is in TsDAHOU, f. 1, op. 25, spr. 20, ark. 44–48.
289 The letter is in ibidem, ark. 47–48.

Honchar, whom he counted as a defender of Chornovil and Karavansky. After reminding readers that Karavansky had been convicted for his wartime involvement in the OUN, he addressed Honchar, who was a known Red Army veteran.

> You, for instance—a talented writer (I do not name you as I am convinced that you deeply regret your action), the author of one of the best books on the [Great] Patriotic War—what will you say now that you have learned what 'talented" journalists' you defend? You and I fought shoulder to shoulder at the fronts of the Great Patriotic War. What would we have done then if we had caught [people] such as Chornovil with his exhortations or Karavans'ky with the revolver, three grenades and forged documents?... Why then do you now play at 'humanitarianism' and defend him who betrayed, and is betraying, the Fatherland [and] our people?
> ... You see how you—you honorable 'humanitarians"—have by your thoughtless actions served the enemies—the ideologists of imperialism and their assistants, the bourgeois nationalists![290]

In other words, humanitarianism was but another Trojan horse invented by Western propaganda to spread dissent. Honchar was guilty of forgetting where the front line lay and of unwittingly helping the enemy. Poltoratsky's diatribe generated a letter of protest cosigned by Ivan Dziuba, Yevhen Sverstiuk, Mykhailyna Kotsiubynska, Lina Kostenko, and Viktor Nekrasov, who defended their two imprisoned colleagues. Though they did not Meanwhile Petro Shelest was likely more concerned with the international situation, particularly the Prague Spring and the resulting crisis in Czechoslovakia. Although he publicly declared that the revolt could not affect the Ukrainian intelligentsia, he was aware of the many links between the two nations. Two Czech journals had even intervened in defence of Honchar's novel, regarding it as "a search for humanitarianism in Ukrainian culture." Shelest took part in all of the meetings on the Czechoslovak crisis and was a strong supporter of a Soviet military invasion to present the spread of the revolt into his republic.[291] In the first days of August, afraid that the cultural unrest *Sobor*

---

290 Oleksii Poltorats'kyi, "Kym opikuiut'sia deiaki 'humanisty,'" *Literaturna Ukraïna*, 7 July 1968, 2; English translation in *Ferment in the Ukraine*, 200–204, here 203–204.
291 See Grey Hodnett and Peter J. Potichnyj, *The Ukraine and the Czechoslovak Crisis* (Canberra, 1970), 63–85. In 1968 a few *samvydav* documents urged Honchar and the SPU

had might lead to a general revolt, he decided to communicate with Moscow to find a solution. *Izvestiia*'s editor Lev Tolkunov called Shelest and suggested publishing "an article about ... *Sobor* in *Izvestiia* by a specialist ... [they] decided that if a central newspaper intervened with an objective, well-qualified review, then slander and lack of objectivity in the evaluation of *Sobor* would come to an end." Tolkunov vowed to "support him [Honchar] in any case." Nikolai Podgorny (Mykola Pidhirny), the chairman of the Presidium of the USSR's Supreme Soviet, also gave his agreement.[292] The delicacy of the operation required Shelest to read the draft of the article and spot any weaknesses.[293] However, the outbreak of the Czechoslovak crisis and the Soviet invasion blocked any opportunity of reprinting Honchar's work, and both the review in *Izvestiia* and the Russian translation of *Sobor* went unpublished.

While Honchar's attempt to integrate the more revolutionary voices of Ukrainian literature into the Soviet cultural sphere had faltered because of strong internal opposition, the Czechoslovakia crisis ensured its ultimate failure. According to Dziuba,[294] despite the expectations *Sobor* had created, the *shistdesiatnyky* lost all hope of reform once the Soviet invasion of Czechoslovakia occurred.

The World View of the *Shistdesiatnyky*

Although Communist Party bureaucrats gave *Sobor* a frosty reception, Honchar's novel immediately gained favour among the *shistdesiatnyky*. In April 1968 the sculptor, painter, and ethnographer Ivan Honchar (1911–93; no relation to the writer), who had dedicated his life to collecting Ukrainian artifacts, wrote a letter to *Zoria*, the Dnipropetrovsk newspaper that had ruthlessly attacked *Sobor*. He defined *Sobor* "a patriotic hymn to the eternal beauty of the spirit of freedom-loving people."[295] Meanwhile Mykhailyna Kotsiubynska, after her expulsion from the Institute of Philology for signing the "Letter of the 139," declared to the Orthodox bishop of Chernivtsi that "the Ukrainian intelligentsia understands life and contemporary reality in a new way; proof of this is that Honchar

---

to follow their Czechoslovak colleagues on the path of liberalization. See "Lyst do Olesia Honchara i sekretariv SPU," *Suchasnist'*, 1968, no. 12: 50–60.

292 Shelest, *Da ne sudimy budete*, 316–17.
293 Draft of the article reviewed by Shelest, in TsDAHOU, f. 1, op. 25, spr. 3447, ark. 72–73.
294 During my interview of him on 13 June 2009.
295 The article was reprinted in *Ternystym shliakhom do khramu*, 134–38.

wrote *Sobor.*"²⁹⁶ The novel appealed to the *shistdesiatnyky* not because it spoke to the "bourgeois nationalist cause," but rather because it proposed a new formula for promoting belonging to the Ukrainian nation.

The most conscientious defence of Honchar's novel appeared in *samvydav* and was signed by the literary critic Yevhen Sverstiuk.²⁹⁷ His essay "A Cathedral in Scaffolding" was conceived as a reply to *Sobor*'s negative reviews, and its political, intellectual, and spiritual considerations are an enlightening example of the mentality of the *shistdesiatnyky*.²⁹⁸ Because he was one of the less Sovietized *shistdesiatnyky*, Sverstiuk had the ability to transform the concept of Soviet internationalism into an idealized humanism in that essay.

"A Cathedral in Scaffolding" begins with Sverstiuk's reflection upon human destiny in the contemporary world. According to Sverstiuk, the

---

296 See Ovcharenko's letter about punishing the signatories of the "Letter of the 139," TsDAHOU, f. 1, op. 25, spr. 127, ark. 70–71; and the report to the Party about Kotsiubynska, in TsDAHOU, f. 1, op. 25, spr. 20, ark. 201.

297 Sverstiuk's intellectual path was unique: he was born on 12 December 1928 in a village in Volhynia, then occupied by Poland. His was a well-off peasant family that lived in a half-Ukrainian, half-Jewish village; his schooling was in Polish. Sverstiuk's family survived the Second World War without losses because their village was not touched by the German-Soviet conflict or the brutal Ukrainian-Polish hostilities in Volhynia. During the Soviet reoccupation Yevhen's older brother was arrested for his involvement in the OUN, and there was a risk that the family's ir property would be confiscated. But Sverstiuk was able to continue his studies. From 1947 to 1952 he studied psychology at Lviv State University (he actually wanted to study English literature). During his university years Sverstiuk began expressing his skepticism toward Soviet rule, but he was overlooked during the purge of 1949 began working as a teacher of Ukrainian in Pochaiv in 1952. In 1953 he was accepted into graduate program at the Scientific Research Institute of Psychology of theMinistry of Education of the Ukrainian SSR in Kyiv. After defending his candiate's dissertation, Sverstiuk taught Ukrainian literature at the Poltava Pedagogical Institute (1956–59); was a senior associate of the Institute of Psychology (1959–60, 1962–65); headed the prose department (1961–62) of the SPU's journal *Vitchyzna*; and was the managing secretary of the *Ukrainian Botanical Journal* (1965–72).While studying and working in Kyiv he became acquainted with Ivan Dziuba, Ivan Svitlychny, and the other *shistdesiatnyky*. In addition to his nonconformist research in psychology (e.g., he questioned Ivan Pavlov's theories), Sverstiuk became a literary critic. He was the courageous author of the *samvydav* exposé of the officially sanctioned arson and fire at the Vernadsky State Public Library (now the National Library of Ukraine) in Kyiv in 1964. See Ievhen Sverstiuk, "My vybraly zhyttia," in *Bunt pokolinnia*, ed. Berdykhovs'ka and Hnatiuk, 33–71.

298 The essay was first published in the West in Sverstiuk's collection of *samvydav* essays *Sobor u ryshtovanni* (Paris and Baltimore, 1970). The cathedral in *Sobor* was enclosed in scaffolding because Loboda proposed "concealing" it thus because no funds were available for to restoring it.

development of society had provided people with too many "divertissements Pascaliens" that distracted them from their true aim and forced them to homogenize. The world was undergoing an unheroic phase in its history, and anyone who struggled for self-realization and against conformism was considered either a hero or a Don Quixote. Sverstiuk understood Honchar's novel as an invitation to "creating one's own *individuality as a part of one's nation*, as a hopeful basis for cultural and spiritual life."[299] He believed "The basic meaning of Honchar's novel is the search for spiritual foundations, the search for living sources of humanness, the deciphering of national traditions and values to which a nation can hold to save its own being and character in the shaky world of standardization."[300]

This was driving force of Honchar's Bahlai—longing for a spiritual foundation and a search for an augmented human condition, both of which united Kant, Marx, Dostoevsky, and Tolstoy in a single intellectual tradition. The meaning of the cathedral, a symbol of national culture, is explained through Lenin's actions: "When Lenin, even during the revolution, wrote about the preservation of monuments and about taking over all of the cultural riches created by mankind in the course of history, he meant, of course, first of all, the spirit of preservation and creativeness, as well as the rescue of the foundations on which the spiritual aspirations and needs of man rest."[301] The polar opposite of Lenin was Stalin, who violated legality and enacted a counter-revolution that the Communist Party lacked the courage to admit it.

In a ten-page section Sverstiuk surveys Ukraine's history, quoting the medieval chronicles, Taras Shevchenko, Hetman Bohdan Khmelnytsky, and the Cossacks, and laments Russia's constant attempts to destroy Ukrainian culture. He stresses the importance of Bahlai, a hero of our times who "*seeks his heritage*, aware that 'if not us—then who?'"[302] Loboda, Sverstiuk reiterates, is only concerned with his own success and had forgotten the principles of Marxist doctrine. One of Marx's most important goals was the struggle against alienation, and alienation was the greatest danger confronting Ukrainians in everyday life.

---

299 Ievhen Sverstiuk, "A Cathedral in Scaffolding," in his *Clandestine Essays*, trans., with an intro., by George S. N. Luckyj (Cambridge, Mass., 1976), 18.
300 Ibidem, 24.
301 Ibidem, 25.
302 Ibidem, 39.

> A man of our time has gone through a whole revolution of alienations. The peasants have not yet recovered from the chain effect of the decay of the old forms of life and the almost Biblical tribulations in our recent history. Alienation from the land. Alienation from the products of their labor. Alienation from religion, customs, and beliefs. Alienation from language, which in the press, radio, and the universities has come to mean something else—some kind of parallel reality to everyday life. Alienation from conscience, which is now the responsibility of government, whose directives become duties (the Hutsuls would not of their own free will destroy their church). Finally, alienation from oneself. A man who managed his own affairs in the past is today merely a function of a great economic mechanism—a driver, a tractor driver, a brigade leader, a milkmaid, a chairman, a team leader....
>
> ... It is well known that Marx considered alienation to be the greatest curse inflicted by private property and saw a solution in "human communism" (carefully distinguishing it from "despotic" or "coarse" communism, which represents "an expression of the evils of private property, which wants to be confirmed as positive collectivism").[303]

This statement is an irrefutable condemnation of the Soviet Union and its attempt to control every of its inhabitants' actions. Sverstiuk accuses the USSR of practicing despotic communism instead of human communism. Although the *shistdesiatnyky* constantly reinterpreted Marx and Lenin, the call to Marxism was not just lip service to political orthodoxy, especially not in Sverstiuk's *samvydav* essay.

Sverstiuk could see this process of alienation occurring in the young Ukrainians who came to the city order to study at university, "driven by a longing to reach what they find in books—spirituality, beauty, honor, decency, art, and people who assume duties and responsibilities for matters that are of concern to the nation and to humanity. "But these students would be rejected by the urban environment unless "they take over the 'city language.'... That is, when they may become completely severed from those roots which alone guarantee organic growth."[304] By using the expression "city language," Sverstiuk suggests more than a national, Ukrainian vs. Russian, antagonism, but also a cultural one—rural Ukrainian individuality vs. urban Soviet homogenization.

---

303 Ibidem, 49–50.
304 Ibidem, 50.

In his conclusion, Sverstiuk reaffirms that Honchar sought to bring about a discussion on serious issues, including pollution. He stresses not only the need for state employees to be being able to reject bad decisions handed down from above, but also the importance of public opinion and *samvydav*'s influence on it. Anxious about the consequences of a possible nuclear war, Sverstiuk declares his hope for an international human alliance.

> ... Today's bombs can destroy everything but they can save nothing.
>
> The spiritual unity of mankind, toward which we are, after all, progressing becomes willy-nilly and, however slowly, an obvious necessity. But in order to achieve this unity we must elevate our language, raise our human criteria, safeguard our undeniable moral authority.[...]
>
> ... We must learn once more to call things with their right names in order to be understood in the world and to find new friends there. In the modern world one must unite with others, revealing in oneself all the better qualities, which will shine on the market of world values....
>
> We must change so as to respect ourselves, learn to respect others, and thus earn the respect of others. What else can an international association of people of good will, regardless of creed, conviction, race or nationality mean? It means that the concept of good will is a common denominator of human morality—of people who are united in their desire to create order and peace in their own house.[305]

Like *Sobor*'s early critics, Sverstiuk supports its innovative spirit, but the scope of his review exceeds the novel's parameters. He unflinchingly denounces the Soviet Union as the outcome of Stalin's counter-revolution, though his denunciation does not extend to Marxist ideology. Sverstiuk deems the national question a major problem in contemporary Soviet policy, but he presents it within a framework that juxtaposes national riches and Soviet standardization rather than Ukrainian and Russian nationalism. Sverstiuk believed that an international pacifist alliance of humans was the only way to avoid a future of war and deathly pollution. Such a "spiritual unity of mankind" had to be realized regardless of differences, but it could only be achieved by respecting these differences.

---

305 Ibidem, 63–64.

This mentality informing Sverstiuk's interpretation of Ukrainian literature is present in another of his famous *samvydav* essays, "Ivan Kotliarevs'kyi Is Laughing," about irony in the works of the founder of modern Ukrainian literature.

> ... In *Eneïda*, and especially in *Natalka Poltavka* and *Moskal'-charivnyk* (The Soldier-Sorcerer), he [Kotliarevs'kyi] confirmed this *deep feeling of human dignity*, both human and national, without which it is impossible to think of the rebirth of a subjugated, colonized country.
>
> This well-developed feeling became the spine of the new Ukrainian literature which always, more or less sharply and openly, defended the reputation and good name of Ukraine.[306]

With Sverstiuk, *shistdesiatnytstvo* affirmed the centrality in society of the human element, which had to be protected from any threat. Incompatible as it was with Soviet orthodoxy, Sverstiuk's proposal belonged to the realm of political utopia rather than political action. Honchar's attempt to integrate these aspirations into Soviet official culture was a lost cause, because the *shistdesiatnyky*, like Sverstiuk, would never be able to accept a compromise with a power they considered illegitimate and counter-revolutionary.

The Scandal Peters Out

Although Honchar suffered an onslaught of criticism because of *Sobor*, he was not the only one to be attacked. After receiving other anonymous denunciatory letters, Ivan Hrushetsky (1904–82), a member of the CC CPSU and head of its Cultural Commission, began compiling information about Dmytro Pavlychko.[307] In two reports dated December 1968 he provided various materials against Honchar's ally: documents regarding Pavlychko's arrest during the Second World War under the suspicion of being an UPA member, his compromising declarations about Francisco Franco, and many statements by his colleagues that he was an immoral careerist. Hrushetsky stressed Pavlychko's acquaintance with Ivan Drach, Ivan Dziuba, and Lina Kostenko, and he reported that during

---

306 Ievhen Sverstiuk, "Ivan Kotliarevs'kyi Is Laughing," in his *Clandestine Essays*, 87.
307 Hrushetsky supported Vatchenko's position that there had been a popular uprising by Dnipropetrovsk's citizens against *Sobor*. See Tron'ko, Bazhan, and Danyliuk, eds., *Ternystym shliakhom do khramu*, 156–63.

a SPU meeting that year Pavlychko had declared "I'm an independent writer and I judge myself" and proclaimed that *Sobor* was a great masterpiece.[308] Hrushetsky attacked Pavlychko's poetry, which in his opinion had always been bourgeois nationalist, criticizing many of his works, from one of his first books, *Pravda klyche* (Truth is Calling, 1959), to his latest collection, *Hranoslov* (The Wordsmith, 1968). The latter contained equivocal verses such as "I'm your tree," "O Ukraine," "Friendly forward," and "Dummies." The poem "In Lenin's Office" quoted the words of an old, Russian-speaking black man in a famous poem by Vladimir Mayakovsky but turned him into a defender of his native language (and consequently into a Ukrainian against Russification).[309]

> But I think to myself:
> communism is a polyglot,
> today it can speak
> all languages.
> I recall a black demonstration,
> 'an elderly one'
> who had studied Russian
> in Cuba,
> and yet his language
> he is ready to defend
> from the whip
> and the vile bullet.

In early January 1969 Petro Shelest received Honchar, who protested against Hrushetsky's rudeness and his attacks against Pavlychko and Yurii Zbanatsky. Shelest noted in his diary that Honchar had learned a lesson from the *Sobor* case. Regarding the next plenum of the SPU, he suggested to Honchar that he "ponder carefully all questions and organize everything in order to avoid bullying, especially by persons such as Hrushetsky and Vatchenko."[310]

---

308 See Hrushetsky's two reports, dated 30 December 1968 and 9 January 1969, in TsDAHOU, f. 1, op. 25, spr. 217, ark. 2–20.
309 "In Lenin's Cabinet" by Dmytro Pavlychko, *Hranoslov* (Kyiv, 1968), 120. In his poem "Our Youth" (1927), Mayakovsky wrote: "And if I were / an old black man / then, / without sorrow and laziness, / I would study Russian / only because / it was / spoken by Lenin."
310 Shelest, *Da ne sudimy budete*, 417.

Honchar heeded Shelest's warnings, and the plenum took place without any scandal. It was opened on 13 January by Leonid Novychenko, who reassessed the commitment of Ukrainian writers to the search for a new humanism, but attacked those Czechoslovak intellectuals who he felt had fallen into the trap of Western propaganda. As for *Sobor*, he restricted himself to saying only that time itself would be the judge.[311] Honchar gave a general speech, focusing on Lenin's friendship toward Ukraine and the need for more Leninism in literary criticism. The other speakers took Honchar's side, defending *Sobor*. The literary critic Mykhailo Ostryk (1927–87) received the loudest applause when he made the following observation: "Professional critics became divided in reviewing [*Sobor*]. This happens. We have to resolve similar conflicts in artistic debate, despite the fact that they might involve some individuals whose understanding of literature is similar to that of Chinese grammar."[312] Nothing was said about Pavlychko or the possibility of replacing Honchar as head of the SPU.

Honchar seemed to be the victor in the debate surrounding his novel, but his political standing was discredited, since the Czechoslovakia crisis had changed the scene. The fear that intellectual ferment could lead to political turmoil convinced Soviet politicians of the need to clamp down on culture. The spokesman for this new line was the novelist Pavlo Zahrebelny. At the plenum of the SPU on 15 January 1970 he recalled Brezhnev's condemnation of those intellectuals whose writings had been published abroad, and he attacked Dziuba's *Internationalism or Russification?*[313] Honchar, who in 1966 had refused to take part in the commission that examined Dziuba's book,[314] could now do nothing but listen. At the Fourth Writers' Congress on 18 May 1971, Zahrebelny criticized *Literaturna Ukraïna* and stressed that more attention should be paid to Ukrainian writers who write in Russian.[315] Conciliation with the dissenting *shistdesiatnyky* was no longer possible, and Honchar's strategy had become futile. Three days later he resigned as secretary of the SPU on

---

311 On Novychenko's reaction, see TsDAMLMU, f. 590, op. 1, spr. 739, ark. 1–25.
312 Minutes of the Plenum TsDAMLMU, f. 590, op. 1. spr. 738, ark. 113.
313 See the minutes of the plenum, in TsDAMLMU, f. 590. op. 1, spr. 775, ark. 30–35.
314 See Honchar's 20 January 1966 letter to Petro Shelest, in *Literaturna Ukraïna*, 3 April 1988, 3.
315 See the minutes of the congress, in TsDAMLMU, f. 590, op. 1, spr. 832, ark. 62.

the grounds that he needed more time for writing.³¹⁶ In his diary he wrote that he left the union "undefeated" even though he had been defeated.³¹⁷

* * *

Developments in Soviet international policy determined the outcome of Honchar's political efforts in *Sobor*. In the early 1960s *shistdesiatnytstvo* was a legal stream of Ukrainian cultural life that seemed able to influence the Communist Party's strategy. After winning the support of the SPU, the *shistdesiatnyky* tried to realize a plan for the formation of a new national and individual consciousness. All of the public demonstrations were nothing but tesserae in the mosaic of a new civic involvement and Ukrainian identity, both personal and collective. Neither the *shistdesiatnyky* nor the Soviet regime were willing to initiate an open conflict. Nevertheless the movement grew, broadening its range of activities, attempting to build a network of clubs, and deliberately nourishing an underground distribution network. This latter initiative proved to be the most dangerous for the Soviet regime, for it constituted an alternative source of information to the official press and included materials written both in Ukraine and abroad.

The real first episode of conflict was the battle over Vasyl Symonenko's legacy. Because the *shistdesiatnyky* perceived his death as the consequence of his exile to Cherkasy, any efforts by the Soviet authorities to incorporate him into the canon of officially approved literature were considered to be a desecration of his memory. Next, the public design competition for the stained-glass Shevchenko window installed at Kyiv State University, which a project considered anti-Soviet won, underlines that the Soviet regime lacked a clear political line. Yevhen Sverstiuk, commenting on his being hired at *Vitchyzna*, stated that in the first half of the 1960s the KGB was not particularly interested in cultural dissent because it was still focused on finding and neutralizing members of the OUN Bandera faction underground. The decision in 1965 to arrest some of the *shistdesiatnyky* considered more politically dangerous was a turning point. On the one hand, this prompted the movement to become more politically inclined. On the other hand, the incarceration of these already nationally conscious figures in the same prison camps as the "old school"

---

316 See *Ternystym shliakhom do khramu*, 201–207.
317 See Oles' Honchar, *Shchodennyky*, vol. 2, *1968–1983* (Kyiv, 2008), 89–91.

nationalists of the OUN and UPA brought about a slow change that will be thoroughly analyzed in the next chapter.

However, *shistdesiatnytstvo* was not yet a completely political movement. Although its members were trying to mobilize the civic consciousness of Ukraine's citizens, they lacked a real political leadership. Sometimes explicitly, the *shistdesiatnyky* had hope a politician would rise to harvest the intellectual ferment they had caused and transform it into a force for political change. The letters and appeals that circulated in *samvydav* were not addressed to Soviet authorities for rhetorical reasons, but rather in the hope that thus they might really find such a person. But the response they sought never came from the Soviet leadership. The slight interest Petro Shelest showed in Ivan Dziuba's and Oles Honchar's cases should not be seen as a willingness to take on a role different from the one he already played. Shelest's political attitudes will also be more thoroughly investigated in the next chapter.

If they wanted to carry out a political struggle, the *shistdesiatnyky* had to produce their own leader. After the arrests and administrative persecutions, Dziuba came to the regarded as a possible leader for any further political moves. But despite his great intellectual skills, he was not the man for that role. Yevhen Sverstiuk that

> Dziuba was not a person with the same nature as Chornovil, a person who seeks greatness and fame. Dziuba never aspired to that. He was a sensitive person. Dziuba went as far as he did because he was honest. Therefore nearly all of the time Dziuba did what he had to do. And when he went too far in this action, then already in the late 1960s he began to step back. After being detained by the KGB, he began revealing [his] dissatisfaction that the significance of his personality had been exaggerated and he had been ascribed a social role he did not want to perform. A certain mistake was hiding in such a way of thinking. A great mistake. But there was also no hypocrisy. Dziuba never wanted to be a political leader.[318]

Although Ukraine had its own Ludvík Vakulík, it lacked an Alexander Dubček. This stalemate could still have continued for a long time, for the Soviet regime was able to withstand a certain amount of dissent in intellectual circles. The situation in Ukraine was, however, strictly intertwined with international policy in two ways. The first was

---

318 Sverstiuk, *My vybraly zhyttia*, 89.

Ukraine's indisputable commonality with the Prague Spring in Czechoslovakia. In response to the liberalization of Czechoslovakia, the Soviet authorities had intervened with a military invasion, which engendered a belief in official circles that a lack of surveillance and control over intellectual life could lead to similar, ill-fated consequences in Ukraine. Secondly, the most politically dangerous *samvydav* writings had already reached the Ukrainian diaspora and were set to be published. This would embarrass the Soviet regime in the international arena, for Ukraine not a small peripheral region of the USSR but one of core constituents. The dissident idea that the Soviet Union was founded on a primal act of imperialism instead of solidarity among nations could harm the Soviet myth and had to be firmly silenced.

Chapter Three

Repressions and Dissent (1968–73)

> Запитання: Де знаходиться перша частина фотокопії книжки "Технология власти"?
> Відповідь: Мені відомо, що перша частина ... знаходиться в КДБ при РМ УРСР*

The Spring Torch: Smoloskyp and the Prague Connection

Throughout 1967 Chornovil's writings were broadcast by Western radio transmissions to the Soviet Union and published in both the Ukrainian émigré and mainstream press in the West.[1] In 1966 Osyp Zinkevych founded the publishing house Smoloskyp (The Torch) in Baltimore. He was a nationalist who had founded the journal *Smoloskyp* in Paris in 1952, first as a supplement to the newspaper *Ukraïns'ke slovo* and from 1956 as an independent paper concerned with Soviet Ukraine and the Ukrainian diaspora. The goal of the publishing house was to make important texts about Ukrainian cultural life available to the community abroad. Smoloskyp's first publication was a short essay by Zinkevych himself, *Svitlychny and Dziuba: Ukrainian Writers under Fire*, followed a year later by a longer work in Ukrainian titled *From the Generation of Innovators: Svitlychny and Dziuba. At the Sources of Modern Ukrainian [Literary] Criticism*.[2] In the following years Smoloskyp published Oles Honchar's *Sobor* (1968), a collection of Lina Kostenko's poems (1969), and Yevhen Sverstiuk's *Sobor u ryshtovanni* (A Cathedral in Scaffolding, 1970), and he also established an information service to transmit news about Soviet Ukraine to the West.

Smoloskyp was not the only publishing house that endeavoured to increase the availability of Ukrainian dissident documents. In 1968 Prolog, the Munich-based publisher of the journal *Suchasnist'*, founded and

---

*   "Question: Where is the first part of the photocopies of the book *The Technology of Power*? Answer: I know that the first part ... is at the KGB [office] at the [building of] Council of Ministers of the Ukrainian SSR." From the interrogation of Nadia Svitlychna on 14 April 1969, in DASBU, spr. 58114fp, vol. 1, ark. 31.

1   Kas'ianov, *Nezhodni*, 105.

2   Osyp Zinkevych, *Svitlychny and Dziuba: Ukrainian Writers under Fire* (Baltimore–Toronto, 1966) and idem, *Z generatsiï novatoriv: Svitlychnyi i Dziuba. U dzherel modernoï ukraïns'koï krytyky* (Baltimore and Toronto, 1967).

directed by Ivan Koshelivets, printed a collection of letters by Levko Lukianenko and his companions titled *Ukrainian Jurists under Trial by the KGB*, the Ukrainian text of Ivan Dziuba's *Internationalism or Russification?*, and two years later a compilation of documents concerning the 1965–67 arrests titled *The Ukrainian Intelligentsia under Trial by the KGB*.[3] In 1968 the Paris-based First Ukrainian Press in France published the Ukrainian text of Viacheslav Chornovil's "Woe from Wit."[4]

Through these publishing initiatives the major *samvydav* texts became available to readers in the capitalist world. The influx of such publications could not help but garner attention and resulted in the translation and publication of nearly all of these writings in English, French, and other languages, sometimes within the same year as their publication in Ukrainian.[5] The spread of these works exacerbated the Soviet Union's battle with world public opinion. Andrei Sakharov's *Progress, Coexistence, and Intellectual Freedom*, published abroad in 1968, had caused a great sensation, underlining the rupture between the Soviet leadership and the intelligentsia. The Soviet government was worried about Moscow's international reputation, and its concerns about Ukraine heightened as the Czechoslovakia crisis progressed. The decision to intervene there was motivated in part by the fear that Prague's social unrest could spread into the USSR—particularly into the Baltic republics, Moldavia, Georgia, and Ukraine—and cause an upheaval. The invasion of Czechoslovakia was the tangible beginning of the Brezhnev Doctrine, which involved a significant tightening of internal discipline.

> The invasion of Czechoslovakia ushered in the mature phase of the Brezhnev era in the USSR, which would be brought to a close after twelve years by events in Poland and the invasion of Afghanistan. It was dominated by an almost obsessive fear of reforms and change: as Pichoia has observed, if before Prague one could wonder how wide-raging the reforms could be, after the invasion the reforms became a taboo no one dared to break until the beginning of the 1980s. Czech events had practically demonstrated to the Soviet leaders that reforms and socialism were irreconcilable, and that they

---

[3] *Ukraïns'ki iurysty pid sudom KGB* (Munich, 1968); *Ukraïns'ka intelihentsiia pid sudom KGB Materialy z protsesiv V. Chornovola, M. Masiutka, M. Ozernoho ta in.* (Munich, 1970).

[4] V'iacheslav Chornovil, *Lykho z rozumu* (Paris, 1968).

[5] Dziuba's *Internationalism or Russification?* and Chornovil's "Woe from Wit" and "Justice of Revival of Terror?," in *The Chornovil Papers*, were first published in English translation in 1968.

had to choose between them. This is how what has been called "creeping re-Stalinization" began, which should be more properly analyzed as a search for order and stability at all costs, realized through repressive measures against any source of interference and through the imposition of a pall of conformism.[6]

Czechoslovakia and Ukraine had deep cultural ties, including a network of friendship societies and the publication in Czech periodicals of writing that could not be published in the USSR. Ukrainians living in Ukraine's western oblasts gleaned information about events abroad from the Czechoslovak radio broadcast in Ukrainian, "Prešov Radio," which was uncensored for several months during the Prague Spring. Although it is impossible to determine to what extent the Ukrainian population was influenced by these events, the Ukrainian intelligentsia looked upon the Czechoslovak reforms with hope. In a May 1968 letter from the prison camp to his friends, Chornovil wrote:

> I categorically state, contrary to all illogical assertions (such for example as: 'The Mel'nykites are writing about him abroad, [and] therefore he is tarred with the same brush') that I have always firmly adhered to the principles of socialism and continue to do so. But not of that socialism which tries to regiment not merely the actions but also the thoughts of the individual. I cannot imagine *true* socialism without guaranteed democratic freedoms, without the widest political and economic self-government of all the cells of the state organism down to and including the smallest, without a real guarantee—and not merely a paper one—of the rights of all nations within a multinational state.
>
> Historical experience shows that two paths have become discernible in socialism: that along which Yugoslavia, and now Czechoslovakia, are feeling their way, and that of Stalin and Mao Tse-tung. Centralism is a very shaky and uncertain position which must inevitably lean towards one of these two paths, throwing the masses off their bearings by its wavering and undermining their faith in any ideals, except that of a more or less secure and neutrally peaceful vegetation.[7]

---

6   Andrea Graziosi, *L'Urss dal trionfo al degrado: Storia dell'Unione Sovietica, 1945–1991* (Bologna, 2008), 359–60.
7   Browne, ed., *Ferment in the Ukraine*, 171.

In this prophetic letter, Chornovil announced his support for the socialism with a human face that was emerging from Dubček's reforms. He reaffirmed his intention to fight for this socialism, distancing himself not only from more nationalist positions but also from the search for a middle position, from "neutrally peaceful vegetation."

Petro Shelest was concerned about the repercussions that the developments in Czechoslovakia could have in Ukraine and seized every opportunity to condemn the Prague Spring, vehemently speaking out against Dubček in a speech he gave on 5 July commemorating the fiftieth anniversary of the foundation of the Communist Party of Ukraine. Shelest supported military invasion as an option, setting himself in opposition to Volodymyr Shcherbytsky, chairman of the Council of Ministers of the Ukrainian SSR, who feared such a move would have a negative effect on the Ukrainian economy.[8]

The Soviet authorities' new attitude toward nonconformist thought emerged in April 1968 during the affair of the "Letter of the 139." This document represents a turning point in the history of *shistdesiatnytstvo*, for it included two fundamentally novel elements. At the heart of this letter is the testimony of Mykhailo Biletsky (b. 1935), a Ukrainian mathematician who had studied and worked for fifteen years in Yerevan and Moscow before returning to Kyiv in 1965. He felt the difference in atmosphere between the Union capital and the Ukraine's capital: "In Moscow these events [illegal arrests of nonconformists] troubled wide circles of intellectuals and were discussed in each intellectual's home, while in Kyiv almost no one, except for a restricted group of elite humanists, knew about the very same arrests."[9] In 1965–68 he travelled frequently between the two cities, trying to put Moscow's and Kyiv's groups of intellectuals in touch with each other. Around November or December 1967 he joined forces with Dziuba, Ivan Svitlychny, the physicists Yurii Tsekhmistrenko and his wife Iryna Zaslavska (1928–76), and the cyberneticist Viktor Bondarchuk (b. 1932), who collectively decided to write an appeal against the trials in Ukraine and generally in the Soviet Union. Biletsky was the connection between the Ukrainians and the historian Petr Yakir (1923–82), one of the leading figures among Moscow's *shestidesiatniki*. The letter mentions the 1965–66 trials in Ukraine, particularly of Chornovil, but also of the Russian dissidents Yurii Galanskov, Aleksandr Ginzburg, Vera

---

8   Hodnett and Potichnyj, *The Ukraine and the Czechoslovak Crisis*, 81–83.
9   Mykhailo Bilets'kyi, "Iak hotuvavsia 'Kyïvs'kyi lyst,'" *Suchasnist'*, 1999, no. 1: 91.

Lashkova, and Aleksei Dobrovolsky, which was causing a stir in Moscow.[10]

In the documents of the *shistdesiatnyky*, references to their Russian colleagues and events in Moscow are rare, and their mention in this letter reflects the desire to establish links between the two movements at a moment when the Soviet leadership seemed weakened by the Czechoslovakia crisis. The attempt to make a play at the all-Union level was clear: the addressees were Leonid Brezhnev, Aleksei Kosygin, and Nikolai Podgorny, who occupied the highest Soviet offices and were not like the usual Ukrainian functionaries. The second novelty was that, in a swelling "euphoria" (in Biletsky's words), the five authors collected as many signatures as possible—not only of nonconformist intellectuals but also of members of the scientific intelligentsia. By encouraging members of the mainstream Soviet intellectual elite to sign the letter, the authors intended to bring them to the side of the *shistdesiatnyky*. Ultimately they hoped to confront the Soviet establishment with the defection of a significant segment of the country's technical cadres.[11]

However, while the *shistdesiatnyky* were ready to face strong repressions, often other intellectuals were not. This time the Soviet regime was convinced of the need to act firmly. *Literaturna Ukraïna* and other newspapers accused a small group of the anti-Soviet contingent of forging a number of signatures, unbeknownst to the supposed signatories.[12] The signatories were summoned to appear at private and public meetings and threatened with expulsion from the Communist Party or the Komsomol and dismissal from their jobs if they failed to confess. Only a few recanted, and while the great majority did not back down and faced the consequences, overall the signatories were not prepared to react as a united group. Judging from the testimonies given to *Suchasnist'* in 1999, they were not a homogeneous group; each one had signed for a particular reason—memory of the 1933 famine, hope for socialism with a human face, belief in Ukrainian nationalism, and so on—unlike the more unified smaller group of *shistdesiatnyky*.[13] But even distribution of the appeal in Russian samizdat failed to bring about the success of this attempt to form

---

10   Zubok, *Zhivago's Children*, 293–95.
11   Bilets'kyi, "Iak hotuvavsia 'Kyïvs'kyi lyst,'" pp. 92–94.
12   See Browne, ed., *Ferment in the Ukraine*, 197–98.
13   Short explanations by nine of the signatories were published in *Suchasnist'*, 1999, no. 1: 99–109.

a larger and more united front of Ukrainian intellectuals against Soviet political hegemony.

The consequences of the "Letter of the 139" became entangled with the polemics against Chornovil and Honchar, spearheaded by Oleksii Poltoratsky's "Whom Do Certain Humanists Protect?" In this article he attacked the letter's authors and tried to prove that they were defending traitors and criminals. Poltoratsky focused on Sviatoslav Karavansky and Chornovil, accusing the former of being an OUN agent during the Second World War (and falsifying some events) and slandering the latter as harbouring anti-Soviet views. Poltoratsky's article contained so many fabricated facts that it was impossible for the *shistdesiatnyky* not to issue a response. Ivan Dziuba, Lina Kostenko, Yevhen Sverstiuk, Mykhailyna Kotsiubynska, and Viktor Nekrasov sent a letter of protest to the editorial board of *Literaturna Ukraïna* disputing Poltoratsky's claims. They stressed that Karavansky was not even mentioned in the "Letter of the 139," which was not trying to defend the accused but rather to assert their right to a fair trial. Dziuba and his colleagues challenged Poltoratsky to provide documents supporting his facts, especially regarding the life of Chornovil, who was considered to be an honest Soviet citizen.

> The aim of such a falsification of V. Chornovil's life history and creative personality, and particularly of concealing the fact that he had only recently been a Komsomol activist, becomes obvious when one reads O. Poltorats'ky's most shameless and foul fabrication. He attributes wild and meaningless words to V. Chornovil which are altogether inconceivable on the lips of any young man brought up in a Soviet family and a Soviet school where all young people without exception belong to the Komsomol: [according to Poltoratsky, Chornovil had stated]: 'This is a completely unnecessary organisation which should be liquidated—even physically might not be out of place. Once the kulaks used to rip open the [Communist] activists' bellies and stuff them with wheat, and now the same activists should have their bellies stuffed with their Programmes and lunatic slogans.'
>
> This 'statement', which O. Poltorats'ky puts into quotation marks as though it came from V. Chornovil, thoroughly stinks of the spirit and turn of phrase used by those murderous troglodytes who made up 'admissions' and 'confessions' for various 'terrorists' and 'enemies of the people' at the notorious trials of the [nineteen] thirties.

> We demand from O. Poltorats'ky that he should give documented proof for attributing these words to V. Chornovil or publicly apologise for libel.[14]

The fact that anyone might doubt their genuine Soviet origins was a sore spot for the *shistdesiatnyky,* and their response to such doubts was decidedly combative. The protest letter ended with a threat that hinted at the information battle being waged through *samvydav*.

> We ask the editors of 'Literaturna Ukraina' to publish this letter. Otherwise we shall be forced to convey its content to the readers of 'Literaturna Ukraina' by every means [at our disposal]. If need be, we shall spare neither the time nor the effort to copy this forty thousand times by hand and send it to each subscriber of 'Literaturna Ukraina' so that the miasma of cannibalism and the atmosphere of lies and impunity may at least be partially dispelled.[15]

This protest letter was not published, nor was it circulated via the usual *samvydav* channels. The Soviet authorities, already busy with the administrative repression of the signatories of the "Letter of the 139," were also preparing much harsher countermeasures. The initiative in this matter was taken by Dnipropetrovsk Oblast's Party secretary Oleksii Vatchenko, following the example he had taken in the case of Oles Honchar's *Sobor*.

The "Letter from Creative Youth" and the Suppression of Dissent in Dnipropetrovsk

In Dnipropetrovsk Oblast, the *Sobor* case was more than a literary affair. In response to the attacks against the novel's author Oles Honchar, an anonymous "Open Letter of the Creative Youth of Dnipropetrovsk" (here shortened to the "Letter from Creative Youth") began circulating in *samvydav* during the second half of 1968. Addressed to First Secretary of the CPU Volodymyr Shcherbytsky, the CPU's Politburo member Fedir Ovcharenko, and the SPU's secretary Dmytro Pavlychko, the letter drew their attention to what it defined as the "savage and absurd persecution of honest Ukrainian citizens devoted to the cause of the construction of communism"[16] and demonstrated how Vatchenko had initiated a diatribe

---

14 Browne, ed., *Ferment in the Ukraine,* 206. The Ukrainian text of this letter was first published abroad in *Suchasnist'*, 1969, no. 2: 86–88.
15 Ibidem, 206–207.
16 "The Witches' Sabbath of the Chauvinists: Open Letter from Young Creative

against Honchar to get rid of the honest intellectuals working in Dnipropetrovsk Oblast's cultural institutions. The authors provided the names and circumstances of the purges and denounced the crimes committed by Komsomol and Party members, who escaped punishment because of their political ties. Such a situation corresponded to an overturning of Leninist legality: principled Communists were being expelled "so that some people could continue to speculate, drink hard and mock Party standards and Soviet laws."[17] Commenting on the case of a university professor who had tried to rape a student and succeeded in avoiding a trial, the authors accused the local Party leaders of having forgiven these crimes because "such people will support any campaign, if only the odds are on its side, without ever giving it a thought whether it is in agreement with the Party line and with the Soviet laws."[18]

The letter's authors also addressed the national question, arguing that real communists should seek to rectify the violations of Lenin's precepts in matters of nationality policy and denounce the banning of Ukrainian from public life as the language of uneducated people. The local authorities devoted no resources to preserving the cultural heritage of the oblast, and the "creative youth" wanted to call the Party to account for this. Their statement reflects both communist thought and Ukrainian culture.

> We, the *avant-garde Ukrainian* youth, have been educated in Soviet schools and higher educational establishments on the works of Marx, Lenin, [Taras] Shevchenko and [Nikolai] Dobrolyubov, and we realize that history is an uninterrupted psychological development of mankind, and everything which is advanced and progressive in this development is worthy of study, respect and esteem of future generations.... Therefore we hold dear both the Zaporozhian Sich which Karl Marx described as a Cossack Republic in his *Chronological Notes*, and the monuments of the past, even [a] building of church architecture or a Cossack hut, for the preservation of which Honchar's *Sobor* fights so significantly.[19]

The polemic around *Sobor* was the tip of the iceberg of enforced Russification in Dnipropetrovsk Oblast. The letter referenced the

---

Intellectuals of Dnipropetrovsk," *The Ukrainian Review* 16, no. 3 (Autumn 1969): 46.
17   Ibidem, 49.
18   Ibidem.
19   Ibidem, 51; Dobrolyubov was a Russian literary critic and revolutionary democrat.

demolition of a church and a Cossack fortress "under the slogan of *the fight against religion.*" But its authors did not urge rebellion, demanding instead that Soviet officials keep close watch over the local authorities.

> We, the creative youth of Dnipropetrovsk, demand that they and all those who stage brutal Ukrainophobe campaigns—witches, sabbaths in the field of Ukrainian culture who persecute honest people dedicated to their nation, only because they want to be themselves and no one else, because they want to educate their children in Ukrainian kindergartens, schools, technical colleges and higher educational establishments—we demand that those persecutors be made to answer.[20]

The authors denounced the cases of imposed Russification by way of the purging of Ukrainian cultural institutions, and they expressed hope that higher management of institutions would react positively to their fight for freedom. (Unfortunately their hope would not be realized.) In the following months the émigré Ukrainian journals *Suchasnist'*, *Visnyk*, and *Ukraïns'ki visti* published the letter, and it was also broadcast by Radio Liberty.

The resulting international outcry forced the Soviet authorities to intervene. On 17 June 1969 the KGB arrested the poet Ivan Sokulsky (1940–92), accusing him of authoring the "Letter from Creative Youth." Sokulsky, who was born into a poor family, had studied at Lviv State University and then in Dnipropetrovsk, where he was expelled "for behaviour unsuitable for a Soviet student," possibly because of his active role in the Prolisok club in Lviv. While at university he had denounced the Russification in Dnipropetrovsk Oblast and wrote an article with several others that was printed in *Literaturna Ukraïna* about the scarcity of Ukrainian-language publications in Dnipropetrovsk's bookshops.[21] Sokulsky worked as an editor of the local periodical *Enerhetyk* until he was dismissed during the *Sobor* campaign. Shortly after his arrest, agents searched his home and found *samvydav* materials there. Arrested along with Sokulsky were Mykola Kulchynsky (b. 1947), a twenty-two-year-old student from Novomoskovsk (originally from Dubno), and Viktor

---

20 Ibidem, 52.
21 Oleksandr Vodolazhchenko, Oleksandr Zavhorodnii, and Ivan Sokul's'kyi, "Iakshcho bazhaty i vmity …," *Literaturna Ukraïna*, 9 February 1965, 2. I thank Roman Szporluk for giving me this article.

Savchenko (1938–2016), an assistant at the Dnipropetrovsk Metallurgical Institute. All three were charged with anti-Soviet activity.[22] At their in camera trial in Dnipropetrovsk, held on 19–27 January 1970, they were accused of writing and disseminating illegal material, including Sokulsky's verses. The court sentenced Sokulsky, who admitted writing the letter but refused to define himself as being anti-Soviet, to four and a half years imprisonment. Kulchynsky was sentenced to two and a half years, and Savchenko to two years.[23]

In early 1970 three essays by local journalists condemning the authors of the "Letter" were published: "The Mask and the Face of Slanderers" by Fedir Tsukanov (7 February in *Zoria*, the Party's newspaper in Dnipropetrovsk Oblast), Larisa Viblaia's "Yes, This Is Treason" (7 February in *Prapor iunosti*, the Komsomol newspaper in Dnipropetrovsk Oblast), and Ivan Shylo's "Poisoned Pens" (8 February in the oblast's weekly paper, *Dneprovskaia pravda*).[24] Their goal was to discredit the "Letter," each one using a different strategy. Tsukanov asserted that the Ukrainian question was invented by imperialist powers in order to divide the Soviet peoples: "Today, Russification is the most cunning fabrication invented by our enemies. It is the bait on the hooks of ideological saboteurs aiming to revive nationalist remnants in Ukraine and in other fraternal republics."[25] Viblaia accused the letter's authors of not being Marxist: "The authors ... have the impudence to say 'We are Marxists' and other absurd inventions, such as 'national dignity, national esteem.' What impudence! What a wondrous contortion of meaning!" And Shylo tried to demonstrate that there was no Russification in Ukraine by forging citations from the "Letter."[26] Meanwhile persecutions continued, including of the former OUN member and Gulag inmate Oleksandr Kuzmenko (1926–99), who was castigated at a "workers' trial" for "ideologically destructive behaviour" and attacked in the oblast newspaper.[27]

---

22 See "Represiï na Dnipropetrovshcyni," *Ukraïns'kyi visnyk: Vypusk I–II, sichen' 1970 – traven' 1970* (Paris and Baltimore, 1971), 37–39.
23 See ibidem, 129–30; and *Khronika tekushchikh sobytii*, issue 12 (28 February 1970): 15–16.
24 These articles were also published in the West in *Molod' Dnipropetrovs'ka v borot'bi proty rusyfikatsiï* (Munich, 1971).
25 Fedir Tsukanov, "The Mask and the Face of Slanderers," *Digest of the Soviet Ukrainian Press*, October 1970, 3.
26 *Digest of the Soviet Ukrainian Press*, October 1970, 33 and 40.
27 See *Ukraïns'kyi visnyk: Vypusk III, zhovten' 1970* (Winnipeg and Baltimore, 1971), 68–69.

The "Letter from Creative Youth" condemned the arrests that occurred during the annual ceremonies in Kyiv in memory of Taras Shevchenko, which led to a public protest headed led by Dr. Mykola Plakhotniuk. The doctor was subsequently summoned to answer questions about his relationship with those arrested in Dnipropetrovsk, but he refused to give any testimony and was fired from the Kyiv Medical Institute.[28] Many documents regarding the repressions in Dnipropetrovsk were published in the newly formed underground bulletin *Ukraïns'kyi visnyk*.[29] After publishing the "Letter" and a brief account of the facts, the bulletin's second issue reported widely on the repressions against Sokulsky. It included Plakhotniuk's essay "Truth Is behind Us," in which, using sardonic humour, he replied to the attacks against him that appeared in the press. His piece disproved the accusations in three Tsukanov's, Viblaia's, and Shylo's essays with meticulous detail, pointing out every place where Sokulsky's words had been misinterpreted. The difference between the three journalists and the Ukrainian intellectuals consisted of the fact that

> [While] Loving their [native] language and Fatherland, such people as I. Sokulsky and M. Kulchynsky also know the Russian language and culture [and] take all the best from this culture.... You [journalists] are defending not the language of the neighbouring people with whom we live in one state, but the language of Russian bureaucrats and chauvinists, whom V. I. Lenin condemned for their vile grovelling before the powerful and their violence against underlings. Such a slave, wrote Lenin, "for example, calls the suppression of Poland, Ukraine, and so on 'defence of the fatherland' of the Great Russians. Such a slave is a toady and a lout who provokes a legitimate feeling of indignation, scorn, and disgust."[30]

Once again, a *shistdesiatnyk* affirmed that there was no tolerance for hatred of other national cultures, the Russian included, but only a desire to protect the Ukrainian language. The essay quotes Lenin's statements about the danger of Russian chauvinism and calls everyone to respect the new political line adopted after Stalin's death. Condemning

---

28 "Sudovyi protses u Dnipropetrovs'ku," *Ukraïns'kyi visnyk: Vypusk I–II*, 132.
29 *Ukraïns'kyi visnyk*'s foundation and publication are discussed below.
30 Mykola Plakhtoniuk [Plakhotniuk], "Za namy — pravda (vidpovid' naklepnykam)," *Ukraïns'kyi visnyk: vypusk I–II*, 139.

Tsukanov, who insisted that Sokulsky's father was purged in Stalin's time, Plakhotniuk commented, "This is so disgusting and amoral: relying on Stalinist sentencings of the parents in order to compromise the sons for people! Did we not have the Twentieth and Twenty-Second Party Congresses, [and] was it then only for show that the 'cult of personality and its consequences' was talked about?"[31]

In that issue of *Ukraïns'kyi visnyk* Plakhotniuk's essay preceded selected poems by Sokulsky and Kulchynsky. Sokulsky's poem "Spartacus" raises particularly interesting questions regarding language choice. The Thracian rebel was a favourite historical figure in the USSR, whom schoolchildren there were taught to worship. The fact that Sokulsky had dedicated verses to this ancient "working-class" hero was not a crime, but because he wrote them in Ukrainian and they contained inferences that Ukrainians had been enslaved by the tsarist empire, the following lines probably sounded threatening to the Soviet censor.

> The slave's brand shouts into my soul,
> The slave's brand shouts into my brain:
> "Do I really have to die a slave,
> Mute, nobody's?!"[32]

This verse exemplifies how Soviet myths were fundamental to the *shistdesiatnyky* and their opposition, and why they perceived themselves as the most truthful interpreters of Soviet culture. This idea, however, was not positively received. Despite Plakhotniuk's efforts, the local press exploited the polemic around the "Letter from Creative Youth" to provoke public protests and to continue the purges, especially within the Komsomol.[33] The general atmosphere was ripe for further attacks on the core group of the *shistdesiatnyky*.

Attacks in the Stalinist Mould

Apart from astonishing Ukraine's intellectuals, the Soviet invasion of Czechoslovakia did not provoke popular protests in Ukraine. Even if many disapproved of the military option, they did not manifest their resentment toward Brezhnev's and Shelest's choices. In fact, the Prague crisis only served to strengthen Brezhnevism. After the resolution of the

---

31 Ibidem, 146.
32 Ivan Sokul's'kyi, "Spartak," ibidem, 150.
33 *Ukraïns'kyi visnyk: vypusk IV, sichen' 1971* (Winnipeg and Baltimore, 1971), 154–56.

Czechoslovakia problem, Shelest focused on Brezhnevist policies in conducting internal affairs. On 7 January 1969 the Central Committees of both the CPSU and the CPU approved a resolution that Heorhii Kasianov has described as "a qualitative turn toward re-Stalinization of [the country's] spiritual life."[34] The resolution, which condoned "increasing the responsibility of leading organs of the press, radio, television, cinematography, and institutions of culture and art for the political-ideological level of published materials," effectively prevented independent thinkers from accessing any official means of communication. Honchar's *Sobor* was withdrawn from libraries, and many periodicals and newspapers were reprimanded for their previous liberality.

The strict control that the authorities exerted on the press meant that certain political incidents were kept quiet. One such event that was ignored by the media was the death of Vasyl Makukh (1927–68), who had been captured as an UPA soldier in his native Lviv Oblast in 1946 and imprisoned for ten years in the Gulag by the Stalin regime. On 5 November 1968 he showed up from Dnipropetrovsk on Khreshchatyk Boulevard, Kyiv's central street, and after delivering a brief speech there about the oppression of Ukraine, shouted out "Long live a free Ukraine!," doused himself with gasoline, and set himself on fire. Makukh died a few days later from his self-inflicted injuries.[35] His politically motivated suicide occurred almost two and a half months before the similar Jan Palach's self-immolation in Prague, but the Soviet authorities censored the news throughout the entire Soviet bloc. Their sensitivity to incidents of dissent around this time was surely exacerbated by the imminent release of a group of *shistdesiatnyky*, including Viacheslav Chornovil, Valentyn Moroz, and Mykhailo Horyn, from the prison camps.

Because the central figure of the movement was Ivan Dziuba, it is no surprise that the next attack in the official press was against him. On 5 August 1969 *Literaturna Ukraïna* published an essay by Liubomyr Dmyterko titled "A Place in Battle—About a Literary Man Who Found Himself on the Other Side of the Barricade."[36] In it he reiterated the danger

---

[34] Kas'ianov, *Nezhodni*, 81. "Spiritual" in the non-religious sense, that is, affecting the human spirit.

[35] "'Ukraïns'kyi visnyk', vypusk I (sichen' 1970)," in V'iacheslav Chornovil, *Tvory v desiaty tomakh*, vol. 3, *Ukraïns'kyi visnyk, vypusky I–VI* (Kyiv, 2006), 63.

[36] Liubomyr Dmyterko, "Mistse v boiu—Pro literatora, iakyi opynyvsia po toi bik barykady," *Literaturna Ukraïna*, 5 August 1969, 5. Dmyterko (1911–85) was born near

posed by Ukrainian nationalist propaganda from abroad and alleged that it manipulated every detail of Soviet life so as to paint the USSR in a negative light. Dmyterko suggested that Ukrainian nationalists abroad had been involved with the Nazis and stated that Dziuba's error was allowing himself to be exploited by this propaganda, regardless of the harm that it could cause the Soviet motherland. Dmyterko claimed that the reason for Dziuba's popularity among Ukrainian nationalists was his use of Marxist ideology to attack the USSR, and that Dziuba was not a real Marxist anymore but a "revisionist," or even worse:

> Before our eyes, not just a falsification of Marxism-Leninism but actually a cynical blasphemy is taking place....
> Taking advantage of the natural and fruitful process of liquidating the [Stalin] personality cult and its consequences, of democratizing all aspects of Soviet life, of returning to Leninist norms, and of preserving Soviet legality, Dziuba has decided not only to reveal the shortcomings and fight against them, but also to completely revise the Party line, to deprecate it, to discredit it.[37]

According to Dmyterko, even if Dziuba was not aware of the extent to which his writings were being exploited in the West, he was guilty of not distancing himself from such propaganda and of continuing to write revisionist articles, which were published only in the émigré nationalist press. Dmyterko described the Komsomol's fiftieth-anniversary celebrations, attended by many heroes of the Second World War. His angle was to defend these veterans while placing Dziuba on the side of the OUN activists. (The favourite strategy of Soviet propaganda was to accuse the internal opposition of being on the side of capitalism and fascism.) In reality, while Dziuba's interpretation of Leninist thought could hardly be considered canonical, it shared nothing with fascist ideology.

Vasyl Stus was the first to respond to Dmyterko's essay. In a letter disseminated in *samvydav* titled "A Place in Battle or in Reprisal?" Stus, who had known Dziuba since their years in Donetsk, turned Dmyterko's

---

Lviv but moved with his parents to Kamianets-Podilskyi in Soviet Ukraine in 1919. He studied there and in Kyiv, graduated from the Kyiv Institute of Cinematography, and became a known writer and screenwriter. From 1962 he was the editor in chief of the Kyiv literary journal *Vitchyzna*. In his memoirs Dziuba wrote that when he worked at this journal, his relationship with Dmyterko was formal but not fraught.

37 Ibidem

rhetoric against him, stating that the right side of the barricades is always that of the people rising up.

> Barricades have only one side, and it is not yours, Dmyterko, not yours! Your constant place has been on the other side of the barricades. There you have a reserved spot forever. So advance in the ranks of reaction, prove your artistic individuality! Remain faithful to yourself.[38]

Stus denounced the censorship against the most talented writers in Ukrainian culture and declared that the attacks against Dziuba were organized by a single centre.

> Now this dark little man [hiding behind people like Dmyterko] is preparing to do battle with a person who is bound hand and foot, [and] deprived of the natural right of [self-]defence. He is using your [Dmyterko's] services in order to create the semblance of an honest duel. But in reality he is preparing a reprisal. Why do you need this place in the reprisal? Against whom? Against the most honourable knight of our culture, a [literary] critic whose equal Soviet Ukrainian literature has barely known during its fifty years [of existence]![39]

Stus announced his wish for the fighter on the barricades to succeed against people such as Dmyterko and for the construction of "cathedrals of honesty." By attacking the "dark little man," Stus also hinted at another diatribe against Dziuba published in 1969. Written by "Bohdan Stenchuk," a collective pseudonym of a group of authors unidentified to this day, titled *What I. Dziuba Is Defending and How,* and edited by the Kyiv-based Society for Cultural Relations with Ukrainians Abroad, this booklet obliquely underlined the importance the international Ukrainian community had for the Soviet authorities. Furthermore, "Bohdan Stenchuk's" introduction revealed the reasons why Dziuba was the object of such consternation: *Internationalism or Russification?* had been presented in the Western press as a Marxist work that demonstrated how the Soviet Union had neglected the Leninist principles that it claimed to hold as fundamental. The primacy of Soviet Communist ideology had been contested from within by a single intellectual who was touted in the West

---

38 Vasyl' Stus, "Mistse v boiu chy rozpravi? Z pryvodu statti L. Dmyterka 'Mistse v boiu," — pro literatora, iakyi opynyvsia po toi bik barykady)," *Ukraïns'kyi visnyk: Vypusk I–II,* 17.
39 Ibidem, 18.

as the genuine voice of Leninism. This interpretation was regarded as extremely dangerous, and "Bohdan Stenchuk's" task was to show that Dziuba was not an expert of Marxist ideology but a bourgeois nationalist.

At the beginning of the first section, "Bohdan Stenchuk" argued that

> It is known that scientific communism considers the nation to be a product of historical development. This is why there is not one common type but two historically determined kinds of nations: the bourgeois nation and the socialist nation. Therefore when the question is, for example, about the Ukrainian nation or its development, it is necessary to discern its character before and after the victory of the socialist revolution.[40]

This statement suggested that it was impossible to judge the development of a nation *after* the socialist revolution using *pre-revolutionary* values, and that in each national movement there were good (socialist) as well as bad (bourgeois) elements. According to "Bohdan Stenchuk", Dziuba willfully ignored the development of nations within the Soviet Union.[41]

> Ivan Dziuba does not want to acknowledge that after half a century of Soviet history some new socialist national feelings were born in the representatives of each nationality of the USSR, were developed and consolidated—feelings of ardent Soviet patriotism, of wholehearted love of the socialist Fatherland, of the immutable friendship of peoples, and of proletarian internationalism.[42]

Dziuba was accused of wanting a national culture both in form and content, while, according to the Stalinist formula, a Soviet republic should be "national in form but socialist in content." In the second section "Bohdan Stenchuk" tried to show that Dziuba adulterated his quotes by comparing them with the originals, although the fact that "Bohdan Stenchuk" resorted to typographic tricks to make Dziuba's quotes look shorter than they actually were suggests that his efforts were not overly successful.[43] The third section stated that during its fifty years of existence

---

40 Bohdan Stenchuk, *Shcho i iak obstoiuie I. Dziuba: Shche raz pro knyhu "Internatsionalizm chy rusyfikatsiia?"* (Kyiv, 1969), 7.
41 Ibidem, 9–11.
42 Ibidem, 14.
43 Ibidem, 58–59.

rule Soviet Ukraine had undergone successful development in every aspect of national life. But this statement was blatantly historical false. Several examples were particularly egregious. First, "Bohdan Stenchuk" denied that the forced Soviet displacement of populations was a significant element of national repression in the USSR.

> Dziuba distorts the facts of mass migrations. Here again, to say it gently, he shows sloppiness and a lack of information. The migration of populations has always been, and will be, one of the natural processes of social development.... Different from the population migrations in capitalist countries, which are caused by poverty and unemployment, this process takes place in an organized way subject to conditions in socialist industry and strictly following the principle of voluntariness.[44]

Stenchuk also denied the demographic losses cause by the 1932–33 man-made famine in Soviet Ukraine: "Except for the two horrible [world] wars,... in the last seventy years the specific concentration of Ukrainians on their ethnic territories has constantly increased (and not decreased, as Dziuba writes)."[45] Stenchuk reaffirmed that in spite of some mistakes, Stalin was right to oppose the Ukrainianization policy that Oleksander Shumsky and Mykola Khvylovy proposed and that the process of "merging of nations" was proper in the socialist environment.

> Because of his shortsightedness and arrogance, Ivan Dziuba cannot understand that what is occurring is a natural process of the integration of economic life, [and of] the internationalization of culture, a process that involves the entire contemporary world. But while internationalization of the economy under capitalism not only fails to solve international conflicts but actually increases antagonism between nations, under socialism this trend is a factor in *corroborating* the friendship of peoples and overcoming national alienation and national prejudices.[46]

"Bohdan Stenchuk" argued that in spite of his statements, Dziuba was not a Marxist, that he tried to hide his nationalism under false pretenses,

---

44 Ibidem, 68.
45 Ibidem, 69.
46 Ibidem, 92.

and that this is why Western propagandists liked him—merely as a Trojan horse to reconquer the Soviet masses and avert them from their mandate.

> Both bourgeois ideologues and contemporary revisionists find in this plan a common ground: together with I. Dziuba they pay lip service to Marxism-Leninism, when in fact they are against proletarian internationalism and against the USSR, [and] rather in favour of its confinement within national borders at the beginning and of its eventual disintegration, with the final goal of restoring capitalism. In general this is the main danger of this 'new' nationalism and of Dziuba's book in particular: that they operate under false pretenses, under the mask of solicitous defenders of high values—and thus, according to the anti-communists' plans, they expect to influence a significant part of the [Soviet] workers.[47]

Dziuba's *Internationalism or Russification?* seriously embarrassed Soviet authorities internationally. They feared that those within the international left who did not regard themselves as part of the Soviet-backed Communist movement could use this book as a weapon to destabilize the primacy of the Communist Parties in the Western world. In Italy, for example, Dziuba's book was printed by Samonà e Savelli, a publisher affiliated with Giangiacomo Feltrinelli's extra-parliamentary, militant leftist forces.[48]

In the meantime Dziuba had to defend himself in order to avoid expulsion from the SPU. When his case was discussed in the autumn of 1969, the support of many of his colleagues, Dmytro Pavlychko included, allowed him to remain in the Writers' Union. Dziuba was then compelled to find a compromise and avoid engaging in battle against the political establishment, which was looking for a reason to silence him. To avoid conflict, Dziuba partly revised his position, which was published in the 6 January 1970 issue of *Literaturna Ukraïna* with a preamble that defined it as "a first step toward the correction of improper and unacceptable artistic conduct." Dziuba distanced himself from the exploitation of his works in the West, saying that he would not take part in any measure that was anti-Soviet in spirit. Worried about the accusations that he was a member of a secret society, he stated:

---

47 Ibidem, 162.
48 Ivan Dziuba, *L'oppressione delle nazionalità in URSS* (Roma, 1971). On the cultural ferment in Italy, see Nanni Balestrini and Primo Moroni, eds., *L'orda d'oro, 1968–1977: La grande ondata rivoluzionaria e creativa, politica ed esistenziale* (Milan, 2005).

> I believe it is necessary to recall that as a Soviet literary person I was and am of a socialist persuasion, a persuasion that does not share anything with the ideology of Ukrainian bourgeois nationalism or with any other misanthropic concept hostile to the people. I have always dealt with nationality issues (as well as any other kind of question) from the point of view of the principles of scientific communism and of the study of Marx, Engels, and Lenin, considering the perspectives of their successful solutions along with the fulfilment of Lenin's will and the construction of communism.[49]

While distancing himself from so-called bourgeois nationalism, Dziuba also rejected the label of "nationalist" for himself, for he believed the term connoted hatred of other peoples and of internationalist friendship.

> I do not accept the denomination of "nationalist," regardless of the meaning one may give it, for I relate with the deepest respect to every people and do not conceive of any patriotism outside the ideals of friendship and mutual understanding among peoples or outside the problems and values that are
> common to all humankind.[50]

Dziuba rejected nationalism's values from the perspective of the *shistdesiatnytstvo* movement's ethics. However, the interpretation of his statement in *Literaturna Ukraïna* made it seem like a betrayal of the movement. This and the conflicted reactions of the other *shistdesiatnyky* are well described by Chornovil:

> The [nationally] conscious Ukrainian community evaluated I. Dziuba's statement to the Presidium of [Ukraine's] Union of Writers in different ways. Some believed that Dziuba's action was right because, without recanting his work or views, he contrived to remain in the Union of Writers: maybe he will now be able to publish, to maintain an officially weightier position, etc. Others, especially the young, condemned Dziuba's statement, believing that his authority as a literary critic and highly principled and steady civil activist did not, under the present Ukrainian conditions, even grant him the right to such a compromise. They believed that he did

---

49 *Shyroke more Ukraïny: Dokumenty samvydavu z Ukraïny* (Paris and Baltimore, 1972), 130.
50 Ibidem.

not gain anything except the conditional retention of his union-member's card, believed that the union is going to demand further concessions from him, and believed that in attacking "nationalism" Dziuba forgot that he himself is called a nationalist—as are those who think like him, both at large and in prison—and completely ignored their Marxist position, and that in certain situations it is not ethical to attack those with whom one does not agree in principle.[51]

The "conscious" Ukrainian intelligentsia was divided between those who thought Dziuba should not burn any bridges with official Soviet cultural circles and those who were leaning toward an open conflict with the political authorities. Dziuba's condemnation of nationalism was a weapon in the hands of Soviet officials, to be used against the other members of the movement.

After the publication of Dziuba's statement, another *samvydav* pamphlet was circulated in March 1970, rather deliberately titled "What Bohdan Stenchuk Defends and How He Does It." The author was Viacheslav Chornovil, who believed that Dziuba was not completely wrong in trying to defend his position in the SPU. But he also felt that "Bohdan Stenchuk's" accusations had to be addressed, so he took up the task because Dziuba was not able to do so. Chornovil's document, subtitled "Sixty-six Questions and Comments to an 'Internationalist,'" consists of sixty-six quotes from the original piece, which he disproves in order to show the pretentiousness of the attacks on Dziuba. After declaring that the ideas expressed in *Internationalism or Russification?* would survive even if its author recanted, Chornovil thoroughly examined "Bohdan Stenchuk's" polemic using irony and logic. He even demonstrated that it incorrectly interpreted Lenin.

> 41. The essence of the matter, however, lies not in this. Even before the Revolution V. I. Lenin wrote in the article "Cultural National Autonomy": "as long as different nations live in a single state, they are bound to one another by thousands and millions of economic, legal and social bonds ... If the various nations living in a single state are bound by economic ties, then any attempt to separate them permanently in 'cultural,' particularly educational, matters would be absurd and reactionary. On the contrary, efforts should be made to *unite* the nations in educational matters, so that the schools become a preparation for what is realized in real life ... One cannot

---

51   Editorial comments in *Ukraïns'kyi visnyk: Vypusk I–II. Sichen' 1970 – traven' 1970*, 20.

> be a democrat and at the same time advocate the principle of segregating the schools according to nationality" (Lenin, *Collected Works*, vol. XIX, pp. 444–45) (B. Stenchuk, pp. 103–104).
>
> By manipulating Lenin's idea in such a way, you have really bared your chauvinistic teeth! You admitted that you are striving to liquidate all non-Russian language schools in order not to "segregate the schools according to nationality" within the boundaries of a single state (in fact, you forget that Ukraine is a sovereign state, according to its Constitution, and that these words can also be interpreted as a demand to liquidate all Russian-language schools in Ukraine, just as was done with Ukrainian-language schools in the Russian S.F.S.R.!).
>
> If it was previously possible to think that you misunderstood some of Lenin's ideas ... I now have all the evidence to contend that you distort Lenin's ideas deliberately and maliciously. You quote out of context a phrase addressed to the Austrian Social Democrats and Federalists, who favored the establishment of "cultural and national autonomy" of the proletariat (and not the territorial autonomy of the entire population) within the boundaries of a bourgeois state. Besides, you ignore everything Lenin wrote about the building of language (including educational questions) in the sovereign Soviet republics after the victory of the socialist revolution.[52]

Chornovil did not limit himself to philological criticism. He contested "Bohdan Stenchuk's" data about the flourishing of Ukrainian culture, arguing that higher education was nearly completely Russified and demonstrating that "Bohdan Stenchuk" had provided false data.

> Even in the figures which you give, despite the cunning in giving the number of titles and not the size and edition (as if a slim propaganda brochure in the Yakut language in an edition of, say, 500 or 1,000 copies were comparable to a weighty Russian tome in an edition of 300,000!). Again you hark back to Nicholas II and impress the reader with percentages. The percentages are, in fact, grandiose and "striking" (1,055 per cent!, 4,278 per cent!!!), but they are not difficult to arrive at if one begins counting almost from zero.

---

52 Vyacheslav Chornovil, "What Bohdan Stenchuk Defends and How He Does It: Sixty-Six Questions and Comments to an 'Internationalist,'" in *The Ukrainian Herald, Issue 6: Dissent in Ukraine. An Underground Journal from Soviet Ukraine*, intro by Yaroslav Bilinsky, trans. Lesya Jones and Bohdan Yasen (Baltimore, Paris, and Toronto, 1977), 27–28.

Let's look at the ratio of Russian and non-Russian (or "national," as you now write, since the Russian language is obviously already considered "international") publications. Even according to the titles for 1958 (by the way, why are your figures so outdated?) almost 73 per cent of books and 68 per cent of newspapers were published in Russian, while in the languages of other nationalities, 27 per cent and 32 per cent respectively. But, according to the 1959 census, Russians comprised 54.6 per cent of the population.[53]

Chornovil concluded his pamphlet by ironically addressing "Bohdan Stenchuk's" anonymity, inviting him/them for a coffee to further discuss the matter. Regardless of the fact that Chornovil disputed "the weakening of Dziuba, his decision to modify his positions, the incurable crisis of whole generations of the *shistdesiatnyky*,"[54] the movement had definitely suffered a great blow. And as Dziuba was criticized by other *shistdesiatnyky*, more fractures became visible among its members.

Valentyn Moroz and Ivan Dziuba: Rivalry and Solidarity among the *Shistdesiatnyky*

In the summer of 1969 Raisa Moroz prepared to welcome her husband home after he had completed his prison term in Mordovia. A few days before he was due to arrive in early September, she was summoned by the rector of the institute where she was working and asked to vacate her room in the dormitory. Evidently he wanted to prevent Raisa's husband from having a bad influence on the students once he had returned. Raisa accepted this demand in order to preserve her job—her only source of income, 120 rubles per month—and tried to find other accommodations. The search turned out to be difficult, as even the lowest rent proved to be beyond her means. Viacheslav Chornovil, who had returned from prison in February 1969, insisted that she take a small apartment in a co-operative building, where the first rent installment was 1,800 rubles. On the first day of that payment Chornovil arrived with the money, saying that he had collected it among "sympathizers" who wanted to help the Morozes.[55]

Over the years a system of solidarity had developed among the *shistdesiatnyky*. As Mykola Plakhotniuk noted during my interview of him,

---

53   Ibidem, 31.
54   Viacheslav Chornovil, "Iak i shcho obstoiuie Bohdan Stenchuk," in Viacheslav Chornovil, *Tvory v desiaty tomakh*, vol. 3 (Kyiv, 2006), 699.
55   Raïsa Moroz, *Proty vitru*, 92.

the KTM's members used to organized lotteries to raise money for Ukrainian students with financial problems, especially those who did not receive government subsidies despite their good marks. After the 1965 arrests Alla Horska tried to organize more formal fundraising initiatives in aid of those who had been arrested, often leaving their families without any income and facing many expenses, including legal and travel costs. In the following years many *shistdesiatnyky* devoted themselves to collecting funds from fellow intellectuals or people who supported their movement. Important sources of assistance were the sporadic donations received from given diaspora Ukrainians visiting their relatives in the Ukrainian SSR.

The most important fundraiser was Ivan Svitlychny, whose apartment attracted many supporters of cultural life in Ukraine.[56] When questioned by the KGB about this "common fund" after 1972, Svitlychny denied that the fund-raising had an organized character; he said instead that it was a way to help those victimized by the repressions. The people who delivered the money were never the ones who had donated it so as not to embarrass the recipients, and the donated sums never exceeded a hundred rubles. Svitlychny added that these operations were supervised by Zynoviia Franko, Ivan Franko's niece, after All Horska's death. The donations were sometimes used to pay for trial costs and lawyers' fees.[57] Although the funds raised never amounted to great sums, they were a significant boon to those who were impacted by the administrative repressions.

While stopping in Kyiv on his way home, Valentyn Moroz was convinced by fellow *shistdesiatnyky* that he should also find a place to stay there, and he made a monetary arrangement to be registered in a woman's apartment. However, despite the difficulties that Raisa Moroz had faced, by the time her husband arrived home the rector had seemingly forgotten his qualms about the couple occupying the dormitory room. But then they discovered that the rector's forgetfulness was not accidental: their room was bugged, and their incoming mail and their telephone calls were monitored by the dormitory "concierge." Moreover, a friend of the Morozes, a certain "P." who brought money to Valentyn to help him after his release from prison, confessed that he was collaborating with the KGB and had the task of reporting everything he knew about Moroz's activity.[58]

---

56 My interview with Mykola Plakhotniuk, 3 June 2009.
57 Proceedings of the interrogation of Ivan Svitlychny on 13 April 1972, in DASBU, spr. 68805fp, vol. 3a, pp. 146–50.
58 Raïsa Moroz, *Proty vitru*, 94.

The Soviet authorities had changed their disposition toward unorthodox intellectuals and were keeping Moroz under strict surveillance.

Nevertheless the surveillance did not stop Moroz from writing, and one of his first acts was to respond to Ivan Dziuba's apparent betrayal. In February 1970 Moroz wrote the *samvydav* essay "Amid the Snows," in which he commented on Dziuba's statement and urged him to recant it. As a historian, Moroz framed his considerations within an interpretation of the significance of the *shistdesiatnytstvo* movement for Ukrainian history. In his essay he assessed the legacy of Stalinism: "Devaluation of the word is the underlying moral problem left over from the Stalinist period."[59] According to Moroz, Stalinism had caused a deep rupture between everyday reality and the propaganda of socialist realist art. This feature of Soviet society, the duplicity, was the origin of moral decadence and of the incredulity of the average Soviet citizen.

> No one believed in the existence of reality, nor in the obligations accepted by the collective farm manager, nor in the critic's review of a new poem. Two worlds evolved, one diametrically opposed to the other. One world was mundane, lacking not only in heroism but even in basic decency. The other world existed in cinema and books, where Young Guardists sang arias before the mine shaft into which they would be thrown five minutes later. The Young Guardists—as everything else in this exaggerated world—were also bound to become unreal.[60]

Among the concepts that became "fictitious" were those of nation, motherland, and patriotism, all frozen in the spiritual nihilism of Soviet culture. Salvation came with the renaissance of *shistdesiatnytstvo*.

> Into these cold ruins, wind-swept of ashes long ago, came the poets of the sixties—"[Vasyl] Symonenko's generation." Not all of their first works were invaluable and profound; yet, their arrival was an *epoch*. They restored *meaning* to words and concepts, and they renewed the faith of the people in the *reality* of the spiritual world. Theirs was a genuine feat: to have faith in an atmosphere of complete nihilism, and rekindle that faith in others.[61]

---

59 "Amid the Snows," in *Boomerang: The Works of Valentyn Moroz*, 64.
60 Ibidem. The Young Guard was an underground Komsomol organization during the Second World War that was later mythologized in the USSR.
61 Ibidem, 65.

For Moroz, Symonenko and Dziuba were like the first Christian believers who had revitalized the spiritually exhausted Roman world with their enthusiasm. This ability to inspire others did not depend on the level of their knowledge, for the Roman philosophers were much more sage and educated, but on "the degree of emotionality" with which they had welcomed their "truth": the truth transformed itself into a "revelation," the warmth of which was able to melt the snow of nihilism. Moroz called this warm feeling an "obsession," quoting Lesia Ukrainka, writing that "that was the mission of the 'poets of the sixties'—to bring the spark of obsession into the frozen reality of Ukraine."[62] According to Moroz, the strength of the *shistdesiatnyky* was so great that the Soviet authorities understood they could not impede them by imprisonment, for the people they repressed were soon transformed into martyrs, some of whom, for example Svitlychny, the Soviet leadership was forced to release. The only way to defeat *shistdesiatnytstvo* was through discreditation and disillusionment. After a great deal of effort, the authorities succeeded in convincing Ivan Drach to recant: "*It was necessary to kill the legend about the poets of the sixties*—a new brand of man—to show that there was nothing new about them, to show that Drach could write the same diatribes about "nationalists" as could Taras Myhal."[63] That was why Dziuba's concession in order to remain in the SPU was so alarming: it dashed the hopes in Ukraine's "flower that grew amid the snows," faith in the *shistdesiatnyky*. To those who defended Dziuba and accused the others of Quixotism, Moroz answered:

> A person's moral stand today is more important than his word. Words are no longer believed, they have been terribly devalued. One's word must be backed by one's position. We live at a time when both Sverstyuk [Yevhen Sverstiuk] and [Mykola Shamota speak the same words about [Taras] Shevchenko: both call him a genius. They differ not in word but in position.[64]

Throughout his essay Moroz often quoted Dziuba to prove that his thoughts were directly influenced by Dziuba's. Moroz despised those who

---

62 Ibidem, 67.
63 Ibidem, 68; Myhal (1920–82) was a Soviet journalist known for his essays denouncing the Ukrainian "bourgeois nationalists."
64 Ibidem, 73–74.

pretended to help Ukraine from within Soviet institutions, such as Dmytro Pavlychko.

> There has never been a shortage of people who wanted to love Ukraine a little and still retain a little comfort. There has never been a need to specially cultivate a Pavlychko—he always grows by himself.[65]

According to Moroz, people like Pavlychko were motivated by a "common, ordinary fear" that made them believe they were martyrs even as they retreated before the threats of the powerful. For Moroz this "Pavlychkoism is an aggressive phenomenon. Psychologists know it well: he who finds himself in a quagmire wants (for most part, subconsciously) to also drag in the one who stands on dry land. This desire makes Pavlychko dangerous. It was on their whispered counsel that Drach wrote his article, and now Dzyuba [Dziuba] his statement."[66]

Moroz pointed out the problematic crux of Dziuba's situation: after having written *Internationalism or Russification?* he had stopped being just a simple citizen.

> He became a symbol. He became an example—and he himself spoke to us about the importance of an example. An ideal is not enough; alone, it is bare and dry; what is needed is its living embodiment. The truth is known; what is lacking is *faith*. The poor Ukrainian fate has chosen Ivan Dzyuba; it has placed upon his shoulders the *burden of being the symbol*. To throw it underfoot, would not be honorable.[67]

In Moroz's view, Dziuba bore a responsibility toward the nation and thus had to consider the effect his actions had on the rest of Ukraine. It was because Dziuba had become a symbol that the Soviet state had decided to target him, hoping that the attacks would weaken the faith that people had in Dziuba and in his movement. Moroz was sure that Dziuba's statement was the first of many tributes that the Soviet authorities would henceforth ask Dziuba to pay, as recent articles in the press seemed to anticipate. In encouraging Dziuba not to surrender to the Soviet logic, Moroz set forth a serious withdrawal from Marxist theory.

---

65 Ibidem, 75.
66 Ibidem, 77.
67 Ibidem, 78.

> The Ukrainian rebirth needs *people of a different quality—aristocrats of spirit*. We laugh at the word "nobility," having forgotten that "noble" comes from the same root. It is the greatest tragedy for Ukraine that endless bad times have made us a *nation of plebeians*. But the *constructive*, selective qualities are found only in the aristocrat. This was well known ... Stalin assured us that the motive force of history was the "proletariat," but, for some reason, he destroyed our intelligentsia, our elite.[68]

Moroz belief that the intelligentsia should play a fundamental role in the awakening of the nation—which he shared with the classic ideologue of Ukrainian nationalism, Dmytro Dontsov—was a defining aspect of his political thought.[69] Moroz regretted Dziuba's condemnation of nationalism as a whole, largely because the *shistdesiatnyky* had long been labelled "nationalist" by Soviet propaganda. Therefore, in attacking nationalists it appeared that Dziuba had attacked his own friends. The rejection of nationalism was contrary both to Leninist principles and Dziuba's own thoughts, which he had put forward in his famous treatise.

> Absolute rejection of nationalism "regardless of the meaning one may give it" is a *Stalinist* and not a Leninist thesis. Lenin would not accept this. Lenin, as is known, viewed nationalism of an oppressed nation as something positive. Dzyuba differs here not only from Lenin, but ... from himself.[70]

Moroz argued that those who were now defending Dziuba had not read his book carefully enough, and he quoted several different authors published in the USSR—Sukarno, Jawaharlal Nehru, and Sun Yat-sen, among others—who affirmed the positive effect of the emergence of nationalism in the development of their countries. According to Moroz, those who loved Dziuba had the duty to tell him when he was wrong, and to exhort him to recant his misguided statement and return to the right path.

---

68   Ibidem, 81.
69   I will discuss Moroz's interpretations further below. See also Dmytro Dontsov, *Natsionalizm* (Vinnytsia, 2006), 187–91. Heorhii Kasianov also asserts that these lines echo Dontsov's thought. See his *Nezhodni*, 108–109.
70   Moroz, "Amid the Snows," 82.

No one is passing "a death sentence" on Dzyuba, as he states in his letter. People do not die from truth. They die from "realism," from the cold skepticism which gave birth to Dzyuba's statement. We do not want Dzyuba to die. We want Dzyuba to rekindle with *pure flames of obsession* — for this is the greatest asset of the presently *frozen* Ukraine.[71]

Moroz extolled the values of *shistdesiatnytstvo*, which Dziuba's statement had markedly betrayed. He also reaffirmed another typical value of his generation: the sense of duty toward society and the spirit of sacrifice of the real *shistdesiatnyky*. It lay in the strictness of Symonenko's self-criticism, together with the consciousness that, as Lina Kostenko wrote, "there has not been an epoch for poets, but poets for the epochs."

In the first months of 1970 Moroz wrote two other short essays. The first was a response to an essay in *Literaturnaia gazeta* by the Belarusian writer Evdokiia Los, in which she stated that her love for Russia overcame her sense of belonging to Belarus. Moroz's reply was based on the consideration that it is impossible to feel genuine friendship for a foreign people and culture if this feeling originates from a sense of inferiority. But there he did not provide a detailed account of his position on the national idea. He did so, however, in his "Chronicle of Resistance," inspired by an incident in which the so-called Dovbush Church in Kosmach[72] (a traditional Hutsul village in the Carpathian Mountains) loaned Paradzhanov its valuable iconostasis for the filming of *Shadows of Forgotten Ancestors* in Kyiv. Despite the agreements in place, Soviet authorities decided that the iconostasis should not be returned to the Dovbush Church but be permanently displayed in the museum in Kosiv. Moroz vehemently condemned this act and accused Paradzhanov of being a thief.

Moroz used this incident to elucidate a broader concept of the meaning of national culture and ongoing cultural processes around the

---

71   Ibidem, 89; a partial English translation is in Valentyn Moroz, "Moses and Dathan," in Id., *Boomerang: The Works of Valentyn Moroz*, 125–128; a complete Ukrainian version is in *Sobranie dokumentov samizdata: Arkhiv samizdata: Ukrainskii samizdat* (Miukhen, 1973), 980.

72   Oleksa Dovbush was an eighteenth-century Hutsul rebel, famous for stealing from the rich and giving to the poor. In 1740 he donated a significant sum toward the building of an Orthodox church in Kosmach (in those years, Hutsuls actively opposed the Ruthenian Uniate Church, whose presence some interpreted as a sign of the extent of Polish Catholic penetration. In order to understand Moroz's reasoning fully (and, in my opinion, his misapprehension), note that the Uniate Church subsequently became a constituent part of Hutsul culture.

world. He described the Hutsuls' opposition to the efforts of various historical rulers to assimilate them and their culture. The Hutsuls had been able to preserve their unique identity, even when the Soviet Union engaged in the material destruction of their artistic patrimony and starved them out, forcing them to find jobs outside their native land. As one of the most distinctive subgroups of the Ukrainian nation, they showed that in order to preserve one's own culture they should adopt only those novelties that fit into their original cultural framework without disrupting it.

> Therein lies the art of national self-preservation: to accept the new without destroying the old, to incorporate the new into old-age structure. Otherwise, the soul of a nation will be built on fragments and be based practically on nothing....
> The ability to preserve—therein lies the secret of Hutsul identity....
> But the illiterate Hutsul understood that behind the dogmatic discussions between the Uniates and the Orthodox stood something more basic: on one side—the fangs of "Polonization" which had already devoured the cities, and on the other side stood Resistance of the Ukrainians. His descendants also understand that the fight for the iconostasis ... is *Resistance!* Resistance to the leveling, dehumanizing force that strips a man of his national and cultural identity and makes him a working machine of one-half horsepower.[73]

Moroz saw this struggle for culture against dehumanization as a connection between the eighteenth-century Hutsuls and twentieth-century Ukrainians. Not only were other cultures threatening Ukraine, but they were also a force that led to homogenization and mediocrity.

> First came the trial by tourists—esthetes and epicureans of art. They smothered more than one flame of originality in many parts of the world. They were followed by the spirit of commercialism; the climate of the unrepeatable was lost[,] as was that certain aura. Artists began to produce on order from wealthy connoisseurs. Their work deteriorated into mediocrity. Kosmach lived through and withstood this.[74]

---

73 "A Chronicle of Resistance," in *Boomerang: The Works of Valentyn Moroz*, 105–107.
74 Ibidem, 108.

Stalin, who hated the Ukrainians but was not able to deport all of them, tried to employ the strategy of assimilation to weaken their resistance.

> Stalin borrowed a method proved successful by the Romans.... Their secret was intermixing.... The son of an Iberian and a Frank born in Sicily became a Roman just as the son of a Byelorussian and Chuvash born in the virgin lands becomes a Russian.[75]

Imposed internationalization was a weapon that the Soviet Union used to Russify the captive nations of its empire. However, the Hutsuls did not dissolve into the broader sea of the Soviet landscape but returned to their villages to revive their culture. Moroz attributed the lack of respect for their culture, as demonstrated in the theft of the iconostasis of the church in Kosmach, to the concept of "quasi-education."

> "Semi-education was the misfortune of Old Russia; it is the misfortune of Soviet Russia, as well," wrote Masaryk.
> *Semi-education* results when a person is first deprived of his traditions and then educated. *Semi-education* results when culture does not develop naturally, but is stuffed into a person according to a Five-Year-Plan, or some other accelerated program. *Semi-education* is manifest when people recognize the value of the Kosmach icons but see no wrong in stealing them.[76]

Here Moroz introduced a more general consideration about the struggle of cultures in the world, including America. The two world powers, which so sharply differed from one another in other fields, had a common strategy to enslave other peoples.

> America is a chaotic mixture of many cultures. America is the deculturalization of all elements who find themselves in its melting pot. Russia, which is so unlike the United States in all other respects, here goes hand-in-hand with it. Russia is also eclectic.... As in the United States, so also in Russia, a person with no roots does not consider himself lacking in respectability; on the contrary, he is proud of his detachment from tradition and "openmindedness." A person who is attached to some definite traditions, both here and

---

75 Ibidem, 109.
76 Ibidem, 111.

there, is considered "backward." The sooner an Italian immigrant becomes Americanized (in other words, forgets his language and traditions), the greater are his chances of being considered "respectable." And so it is here: if you want to prove that you are "progressive," you should forget your ancestry and become a "universal" person (in effect, a Russian).[77]

Moroz interpreted the world as a place where two concurrent processes of cultural homogenization were occurring, neither of which he considered beneficial. There is a certain fear of cultural contamination in his words, and his idea of culture is fixed and static. As Roman Szporluk has convincingly argued,

> Moroz, whose ideas on this subject bear close similarity to those of Solzhenitsyn, considers "deculturation, alienation, dehumanization and rootlessness" to be symptoms of mass culture.... Moroz does not oppose progress, but he calls for a cultural and spiritual revival to accompany technological change. The nation must turn to its own traditional resources, such as those in Kosmach, says Moroz, if it is to counteract the "unprecedented ruin of traditional Ukrainian structures" caused by collectivization, de-Christianization, industrialization, and mass migration.[78]

Moroz might not have been frightened of technological change, but his acknowledgement of cultural evolution gave way to a strong conception of nation and of the duty to preserve it as untouched as possible. His reasoning did not incorporate principles of Marxism-Leninism—an uncommon characteristic among the *shistdesiatnyky*, who regarded Moroz as the standard-bearer of the more nationalist stream of the movement. The sentence where he attacked Paradzhanov, urging Ukrainian intellectuals to rise up in defence of their cultural patrimony, is striking: "I wonder whether the Armenians would let a Ukrainian film director (even if he were a genius!) get away with stealing their icons from Echmiadzin or the Tatev Monastery?" The subconscious accusation against Paradzhanov was that he was not a Ukrainian. According to Moroz, people like Paradzhanov "never really felt Ukraine. To them, an icon from Dovbush's Church "will always be an *artifact*, but never a

---

77 Ibidem, 112.
78 Roman Szporluk, "Valentyn Moroz: His Political Ideas in Historical Perspective," *Canadian Slavonic Papers* 18, no. 1 (March 1976): 88.

*relic."*⁷⁹ But for Moroz national culture was a relic, worthy of nearly religious reverence.

Moroz denounced the Soviet policy of centralization, which damaged Ukraine both on a small scale, with the decision to keep the Kosmach iconostasis in the museum of a bigger city, and on a larger scale, with de-Christianization, collectivization, and industrialization in measures seen to favour the Moscow-directed economy. He lamented that festivities such as Christmas had lost their meaning, that the Soviet Union had reduced them to pure commercialism, and progressive impoverishment of the repertoire of Ukrainian songs. For Moroz the Hutsuls were an example for the rest of the nation to emulate.

> These people will never be destroyed by materialism. Materialism was never important to them—neither when they built homes, when they became *opryshky*, nor when they go for seasonal work into distant lands. The people in these mountains exhibit a tremendous ability to give spiritual value to everything around them.[80]

For Moroz, Hutsul popular culture was the antidote to society's "materialism," that is, consumerism, not the materialism that had anything to do with Marxist theory. The importance of the individual and, on the level of society, of a unitary national culture was a central value of the *shistdesiatnytstvo* movement. However, as some of Moroz's commentators noted,[81] in his writings he abandoned what Harvey Fireside defined as the "optimism" of "A Report from the Beria Reserve" and instead embraced a mistrust of the dominant culture. Moroz fiercely attacked Soviet institutions as agents of de-Ukrainianization, and his new inclinations resounded with concepts typical of nationalist ideology, particularly of Dmytro Dontsov's writings. Moroz had not had an opportunity to read Dontsov, however, and it is quite probable that he had become acquainted with that ideologue's concepts in the Mordovian prison camp. Except for the aforementioned lines, there is no other proof of an ideological bow to Dontsov on Moroz's part, and it would be incorrect to define Moroz as purely an old-school nationalist. The primacy

---

79 Moroz, "A Chronicle of Resistance," 113, 114.
80 Ibidem, 120–21. *Opryshky* were eighteenth-century Hutsul brigands.
81 See George S. N. Luckyj, "Polarity in Ukrainian Intellectual Dissent," *Canadian Slavonic Papers* 14, no. 2 (June 1972): 269–79; and Harvey Fireside, "Valentyn Moroz: Individualist in Jeopardy," *Survey* 22, no. 1 (Winter 1976): 132–40.

Moroz attributed to the nation was received coolly by other *shistdesiatnyky*, including Ivan Dziuba, Viacheslav Chornovil, and Ivan Svitlychny, who respected his positions but did not share them.[82]

Moroz's biting criticism of Paradzhanov inevitably caught the attention of the Soviet authorities, who had found a gallant opponent in Moroz. The first attempt to arrest him occurred during Easter in April 1970, while Moroz was in Kosmach taping ritual Paschal songs at the request of the local community. Three men tried to apprehend him, including a local school director and a member of the village's Party committee, but he was defended by the people attending the ceremony. After this incident, Moroz's lodgings as well as those of other *shistdesiatnyky* were searched. The KGB had grown more violent and disrespectful of basic civil rights, and physical harassment and illegal confiscation of written works had become the norm.[83]

After another search of Moroz's room, he was arrested on 1 June 1970, his wife was notified that she had been fired from the institute where she worked, and the co-operative where they planned to rent an apartment rejected their request, despite having already accepted their deposit. Raisa Moroz was forced to leave her son in the care of her husband's grandparents so that she could accompany her husband.[84] A handful of people in Kosmach were also searched and arrested.

The *shistdesiatnyky* reacted in unison to Moroz's arrest, presenting themselves as a single unit in defence of their members. The high number of letters of protest sent to the authorities suggests that perhaps this was a new strategy of putting pressure on the Soviet leadership. The reaction of the *shistdesiatnyky* caused a great impression and attracted the attention of both domestic and international public opinion. Despite the tactical considerations, the letters revealed that the *shistdesiatnyky* still believed that a part of the Soviet establishment would come to their defence. This is communicated in many of the missives written to Oles Honchar as the head of the SPU, especially one signed by Dziuba, Svitlychny, Chornovil, Yevhen Sverstiuk, and Zynoviia Franko.

---

82 Heorhii Kas'ianov, *Nezhodni*, 110–11; Oles' Obertas, *Ukraïns'kyi samvydav*, 139; and my interview with Dziuba, 13 June 2009.
83 The circumstances leading to Moroz's arrest are described in various issues of *Ukraïns'kyi visnyk* and in *Boomerang: The Works of Valentyn Moroz*, 165–75.
84 Raïsa Moroz, *Proty vitru*, 99–114.

> We are appealing to you, Oles Terentiyovych, to raise the question of the fate of Valentyn Moroz with appropriate authorities and to help ensure that it is decided in accordance with the needs of our society. What we need today are wholesome and honest forces capable of perception and with the civic courage to raise pertinent questions, who become unselfishly involved in today's issues of national importance.[85]

Unfortunately the hopes of the *shistdesiatnyky* were misplaced, for Honchar was weak and about to resign from his post. Similar sentiments were evident in Vasyl Stus's letter to the CC CPU and the KGB, in which he expressed his hope that renewed dialogue with the authorities would put an end to the need for *samvydav*.

> In normal circumstances it would have been possible and necessary to argue with him. But how unconscionable such arguments would be now, when Valentyn Moroz is being summarily persecuted.
> He is being dealt with by people least capable of honest and open discussion!
> In my opinion, to demand that the charges against Valentyn Moroz be dropped is a matter of conscience and honor for every human being in the USSR who values the good name of his society, his country, his native soil.[86]

No response came from the Soviet authorities, and after a few months of investigation Moroz was tried in camera on 17 and 18 November 1970. His colleagues were not allowed to enter the courtroom except for four witnesses—Dziuba, Chornovil, Borys Antonenko-Davydovych, and Babiak from Kosmach, all four of whom refused to answer any questions. Moroz's skilful final statement to the court began with the words

> I shall not attempt to prove my innocence by citing articles of the Criminal Code. As you well know, I am not being tried for any crime. I am being tried for my role in a movement of which you disapprove.[87]

---

85 The letter is in *Boomerang: The Works of Valentyn Moroz*, 178–79.
86 Ibidem, 186.
87 "Instead of a Last Word," in *Boomerang: The Works of Valentyn Moroz*, 1.

The rest of his speech was a summary of his ideas about nations and the repression Ukrainians were suffering under the Soviet Union. He affirmed his intention never to surrender.

> Moroz would be *extremely useful* to you as a penitent author of a repudiating confession that would undermine the movement. But you will *never* see that day. Were you seriously hoping to create a vacuum in the movement by jailing me? When will you understand? *There will never be a vacuum.* The spiritual potential of Ukraine has grown enough to fill any vacuum, to replace any activist who leaves the movement on his own or by way of prison.[88]

Moroz's conviction that the USSR would suffer a final defeat gave him the courage to challenge the judges even though he knew he was going to lose his case. The severe sentence he received—fourteen years in a labour camp—was symbolic and disproportionate to his "crime": it was not only a ruling against Moroz but a condemnation of the *shistdesiatnytstvo* movement as a whole. More letters of protest, requesting a reduction of Moroz's sentence or permission to appeal it, were sent to the authorities.[89] Moroz's own request for an appeal was rejected, and he was attacked in the paper *Radians'ka osvita*, provoking a new wave of protest letters.[90] The Soviet authorities seemed determined to engage in a direct clash with the *shistdesiatnyky*, which the case of Alla Horska's murder also suggests.

The Murder of Alla Horska

In the early morning of 28 November 1970, Alla Horska travelled from Kyiv to the town of Vasylkiv to pick up a sewing machine from the house of her father-in-law, Ivan Zaretsky. When she did not return the next day, her husband Viktor Zaretsky, a former director of the KTM, began to worry. He was unable to contact Alla or his father, or even to enter his father's house, which was locked. The local police were not helpful. On 2 December, after Viktor suffered a nervous breakdown in Kyiv, Nadia Svitlychna and Yevhen Sverstiuk forced the police to break into Ivan Zaretsky's house. In the cellar they found Horska's body—she had been violently murdered. The police initially accused Viktor of the homicide

---

88 Ibidem, 3.
89 See *Boomerang: The Works of Valentyn Moroz*, 210–24.
90 See ibidem, 234–48.

until the body of his father was found on nearby railway tracks. The case was then quickly ruled a double murder-suicide.

This ruling was immediately problematic, given that the family history was anything but tense. Viktor Zaretsky and Horska had let his parents to live with them in previous months while his mother was dying. After his wife's death, Ivan Zaretsky was depressed and physically debilitated, and it is unlikely that he would have had the strength to kill his daughter-in-law, who was a tall and strong woman. Adding mystery to the case, the train that had allegedly struck and killed Zaretsky was never found. The *shistdesiatnyky* had no proof that Soviet authorities were involved in the murder, but Horska's overtly patriotic activity and the unwillingness of the police to investigate her death any further suggest that she was a victim of the Communist regime. After 1991 Les Taniuk raised the matter in the Ukrainian parliament, but no further light was shed on Horska's murder.[91]

Alla Horska was born on 18 September 1929 in Yalta to a Russified family. Her father, Oleksandr Valentynovych, was a key figure in Soviet cinematography. Horska spent most of her childhood in Leningrad, where she survived the first two winters of the city's siege by the German military. Her older brother fought against the Germans as a Soviet partisan and was killed during the Second World War. Horska's family was active in the Soviet artistic community, and after moving to Kyiv in 1946 she enrolled in the painting faculty of the Kyiv State Art Institute.[92] There she met a fellow student, the painter Viktor Zaretsky, whom she married in 1953, and a year later she gave birth to their son. Their apartment was slightly larger than usual, giving them room to work on their art, and it soon became a meeting place for Kyiv's young artists.

After the two joined the KTM, Horska played a central organizing role, and their apartment became its informal headquarters. Her friend Iryna Levytska recalls that Horska was also active in the Komsomol and as a cell secretary took advantage of this position for the KTM's benefit.[93] Horska was instrumental in organizing KTM excursions in Kyiv and

---

91 My account is based on the testimony of Horska's son, Oleksii Zarets'kyi, "Moia maty – Alla Hors'ka," in *Alla Hors'ka*, ed. Zarets'kyi and Marychevs'kyi, 126–34. A powerful portrait of Horska also emerges in the testimonies published in Liudmyla Ohnieva, ed., *Alla Hors'ka: Dusha ukraïns'koho shistdesiatnytstva* (Kyiv, 2015).
92 See Zarets'kyi, "Moia maty – Alla Hors'ka," pp. 115–25; and Serhii Bilokin', "Zhyttia i smert' Ally Hors'koï," in *Alla Hors'ka*, ed. Zarets'kyi and Marychevs'kyi, 197–98.
93 Iryna Levyts'ka, "Neofitka," in *Alla Hors'ka*, ed. Zarets'kyi and Marychevs'kyi, 144.

around Ukraine to study the country's artistic patrimony. She recruited the historians Mykhailo Braichevsky and Hryhorii Lohvyn as guides, and obtained permission from Oleg Antonov, the famous aircraft designer, to use his factory bus for the trips.[94] Les Taniuk has written that Horska was interested in researching Stalinist repressions and that, together with him and Vasyl Symonenko, she was a proponent of the trips to the Bykivnia Forest near Kyiv when mass graves were discovered there, and of the petitions requesting a commemorative monument to be built there.[95]

Horska had many artistic talents, not only as a painter but also as a crafter of mosaics and stained-glass windows. Both she and Opanas Zalyvakha, the artist also condemned in 1966 for the Shevchenko mural at Kyiv State University, were students of Hryhorii Synytsia (1908–96), and they often corresponded to discuss their approaches to art.[96] In one of Horska's letters to Zalyvakha she draws attention to their respective interpretations of the themes of *shistdesiatnytstvo*—namely, how one person's expressiveness can be intertwined with the national content of art. Speaking of the role of the individual artist in common work, Horska commented on what Zalyvakha wrote.

> It is not that you "could not," but you did not want to step over your own proud "I." Here you are! You considered yourself [in this matter] only an executor, and you were deeply wrong. Monumental art is the art of the collective. Like a sea, which springs up from rivers of "I's." When one of these rivers turns away and flows on, then it loses its strength and the sea gets shallower too. In our monumental art there are no executors, for each executor is an artist. Consider the mosaics of [Kyiv's] St. Michael's [Golden-Domed] Cathedral [the mosaics survived after the Bolsheviks blew up the cathedral in 1936]. There's a golden background, which surrounds the figures and flowers, arranged in a general arc. [If you consider] any individual snippet, it's nondescript, for everything is subordinated to the overall image.
>
> Given that, now I turn to this statement of yours: "I do not believe that [Mykhailo] Boichuk laid the foundations of a new Ukrainian art, especially monumental art. His principles for determining themes

---

94 See Halyna Zubchenko, "A bulo tse tak," and Hryhorii Lohvyn, "Podorozhuiuchy Ukraïnoiu," in ibidem, 153 and 179.
95 Les Taniuk, "*Vbytyi talant*," in ibidem, 162.
96 Synytsia was a follower of Mykailo Boichuk (1882–1937), the founder of the modern Ukrainian school of monumental art.

proceed through human figures, the form of the person; the dominant element is the person ... But there is also a higher level—it is the Boichuk school, the school of contemporary national and social art." Where is your argumentation that Boichuk is a school? Where is your argumentation that Boichuk is a national school?... Okay, let's say there is a Boichuk school, an artistic school in Ukraine. It was a new event in art, whose founders and followers—especially through colour—transferred the principles of the early Renaissance wholesale into our times.... Colour, as a primal element in painting (and, of course, also in monumental art), represents a national category in popular art.[97]

Horska's internationalism was grounded in her study of Indian, Japanese, Chinese, and Mexican art, which inspired her. On the other hand, she perceived a lack of communicability with Russian artists. Zalyvakha remembers that when they were in Moscow visiting Russian artists in their studios,

> They received us politely, as you do with rural hicks. Having seen some figurative art, Alla asked whether they knew the works of [Alexander] Archipenko (one of the pieces showed his influence). "No, we've not heard of him," was the answer. [She said:] "In vain we have spent our time, Panas. We know them, but they do not want to know us. Therefore 'Away from Moscow!,' as Khvylovy said. We have our [own] path. Moscow, like ancient Rome, sucks up the juice of its provinces and exercises arrogance. But we have our own concerns!"[98]

The scant interest of Moscow's artistic circles in the goings-on elsewhere in the USSR was a matter of fact, at least until 1968, and it seemed to corroborate the view the *shistdesiatnyky* had of the impossibility of collaborating with anyone in the all-Soviet capital. Dziuba had written *Internationalism or Russification?* in an attempt to inspire dialogue with Russian and Russophone intellectuals, but the results were insignificant. Horska attempted something similar, to a worse end.

---

97 Horska's undated letter (presumably written in 1965) to Zalyvakha, in *Alla Hors'ka*, ed. Zarets'kyi and Marychevs'kyi, 50–51. Zalyvakha's letter is on 45–46.
98 Panas Zalyvakha, "Uznesinnia," in ibidem, 166. Alexander Archipenko (Oleksander Arkhypenko, 1887–1964) was a famous Ukrainian cubist sculptor who moved to Paris in 1908 and subsequently lived in Italy, Sweden, Germany, Czechoslovakia, and the United State. He died in New York City.

After the 1965 arrests Horska played a central role in organizing the movement of solidarity with the arrestees, and in lieu of an official space to meet, her and Viktor Zaretsky's apartment was a haven for nonconformist intellectuals. In the last years of her life, Horska's ideas about the national question became more radical. In 1969 and 1970 she sided with Moroz and supported his criticisms of Dziuba.[99] Summoned as a witness in the investigations of Moroz in 1969, she refused to give testimony and mocked the KGB agent who questioned her. On the night before her murder, Horska and her husband had hosted a group of men, including Danylo Shumuk, a former Communist and a dissident who served many years of imprisonment under the second Polish republic, during the Nazi occupation of Ukraine, and for many years under the Soviet regime.[100] Shumuk had written memoirs that were distributed in the *samvydav* network.[101] Because the *shistdesiatnyky* proclaimed freedom of expression for everyone, reading Shumuk's book or showing him hospitality was not equated with supporting his ideological views. But the Soviet police perceived his presence at Horska's home as a dangerous rapprochement of two streams of Ukrainian nationalism.

Horska's murder in November 1970 and the unwillingness of the police to investigate it seemed like a threat to the entire *shistdesiatnytstvo* movement. Despite difficulties thrown up by the Soviet authorities and several postponements, her funeral, organized by her friends, took place on 7 December 1970, with 150 to 200 people taking part.[102] Disregarding the official ban, four people gave eulogies. Oleksandr Serhiienko (1932–2016), a friend of Horska's from Dnipropetrovsk and later a Soviet political prisoner, said a few words to open the commemoration. Then Yevhen Sverstiuk delivered a longer eulogy, in which he reminded the attendees of Horska's activity as a *shistdesiatnyk*, especially within the KTM, described the meaning of her art and civil engagement as "research for Truth," and spoke of her matchless commitment to helping others. The next speaker was Ivan Hel from Lviv. Although Viacheslav Chornovil

---

99   This is what Chornovil wrote in *Ukraïns'kyi visnyk*, issue IV (January 1971), republished in his *Tvory*, 3: 442.
100 Zarets'kyi, "Moia maty – Alla Hors'ka," 131–32.
101 Shumuk (1914–2004) was allowed to emigrate in 1987 and lived in Canada until 2002. His writings were first published as *Za skhidnim obriiem: Spomyny. Peredruk samvydavnoho tvoru z Ukraïny* (Paris, 1974). Translations and other works of his were later published in both English and Ukrainian.
102 "Ukraïns'kyi visnyk," issue 4 (January 1971), in Chornovil, *Tvory*, 3: 444.

later argued that Hel's words could not be interpreted as an accusation that someone inside the *shistdesiatnytstvo* movement had murdered Horska—a rumour probably spread by the KGB[103]—the imprisonment of some of the *shistdesiatnyky* marked a fracture within the movement. After lamenting the repression of its members, Chornovil stated:

> If these losses are not physical but born in indifference and cowardice regarding those ideals that reunite us, it is a pity and a great anguish. But immeasurably more difficult are tragedies such as the demise of the unforgettable Vasyl Symonenko and this fresh grave [of Alla Horska], which has been dug not only in the long-suffering Ukrainian land but also in each of our hearts.

Hel also extolled Horska as a *shistdesiatnyk* who did not accept any compromise, and thereby he indirectly accused Dziuba of the opposite.

> Alla has remained for us a model of a Person and an Artist who does not bow before an adverse situation and does not believe in "good" or "bad" times, but on the contrary persistently looks for the only way, for each one his own way, to better serve Ukraine.[104]

The last eulogy was given by Vasyl Stus, who read a poem he wrote for the occasion. With Horska's death *shistdesiatnytstvo* suffered a serious blow. Another central figure was gone forever, and the movement seemed anything but united in the face of its ongoing misfortune. The only bright spot in this dark period was the underground *Ukraïns'kyi visnyk*, which managed to follow and report on events in Ukraine almost in real time. This periodical was the fruit of one person's labour in particular—Viacheslav Chornovil's.

The Founding of *Ukraïns'kyi visnyk*

After Chornovil was released in February 1969, his first public project was initiated in response to "Bohdan Stenchuk's" pamphlet. While Chornovil was still in prison, he had started to consider establishing an unofficial means of disseminating information in order to reach a broader readership. When he arrived in Kyiv, he found that the general environment had changed since his arrest. "Many writers had stopped

---

103 See ibidem, 445.
104 Both quotes are from Ivan Hel', "Vystup na pokhoroni Ally Hors'koï," in Chornovil, "Ukraïns'kyi visnyk, vypusk IV (sichen' 1971)," 451.

publishing; society was gripped by a moral fear. It occurred to me that *shistdesiatnytstvo* had changed. Apparently in such conditions [they felt that] engaging in underground activities was counterproductive; it was better to restrict themselves to the literary field and wait for better times."[105]

Despite this shift in the atmosphere, Chornovil was not deterred from establishing an underground newsletter. He chose to follow the example of the *Chronicle of Current Events* issued since 1968 in Moscow.[106] Upon obtaining the support of his closest friends, Chornovil began working on the newsletter, named *Ukraïns'kyi visnyk* (The Ukrainian Herald), with a few collaborators, such as Atena Pashko, Liudmyla Sheremetieva, Yaroslav Kendzor, and Mykhailo Kosiv. Mykola Plakhotniuk was most involved in the editorial work: he collected the materials and distributed the journal in Kyiv.[107] But Chornovil did the greatest amount of the work himself. The "Tasks" of the newsletter, which began appearing in January 1970, were published in its first six issues. They began with the words

> The appearance of such an uncensored publication in Ukraine has long been overdue. There exist many problems of general interest and concern to wide circles of the Ukrainian public that are not covered by the official press. And when, under the pressure of circumstances, the press does occasionally address these problems, issues, it resorts to deliberate falsifications.[108]

Ukraïns'kyi visnyk was dedicated to satisfying the widespread need for truth by those Ukrainians who were convinced that censorship and falsifications were hindering honest information. The newsletter's "Tasks" stated that it would report on violations of freedom of speech and other democratic rights, especially any violation of Ukraine's national sovereignty and repressions against those who defended the Ukrainians' constitutional rights; that it would republish many documents that had already appeared in *samvydav* and were of public interest; and a commitment to maintaining a relative distance from authors' views,

---

105 Chornovil's interview quoted in "Vid uporiadnyka," in Chornovil, *Tvory*, 3: 24.
106 Zubok, *Zhivago's Children*, 300.
107 Pashko (1931–2012) was Chornovil's wife. Sheremetieva (1946–2005, the wife of historian Yaroslav Dashkevych) and Kendzor (b. 1941) were *shistdesiatnyky* living in Lviv.
108 "The Assigment of *The Ukrainian Herald*," in *The Ukrainian Herald*, Issue 6, 13.

because the newsletter was intended to be a free arena of discussion and debate.

> The *Ukrainian Herald* is in no way an anti-Soviet or an anti-communist publication. Its contents and objectives are entirely legal and constitutional....
>
> The abnormal circumstances under which the *Ukrainian Herald* appears are explained exclusively by the fact that violations of the constitutional guarantees and illegal persecutions of civically active persons occur frequently in our society.
>
> The *Herald* is not an organ of any particular organization, group, program, or other organizational unit, and will, therefore, reproduce *samvydav* materials which express various points of view.[109]

The goal of *Ukraïns'kyi visnyk* was to inform without censorship, and the editorial board declared its intent to publish a variety of writings, even those with which they did not agree.

> The task of the *Herald* is to present only objective information about the concealed processes and phenomena in Ukrainian civic life. For this reason the *Ukrainian Herald* will not include any material which was specially written for it and which has not been previously circulated. It will not reproduce documents which are anti-Soviet (as a rule anonymous), that is, those which oppose the democratically elected soviets [councils] as a form of citizens' participation in governing the country; nor will it publish documents which are anti-communist, that is, those which reject communist ideology, as such, in its entirety.[110]

The promise to present objective information was linked with the rejection of anti-communism, which was a defining characteristic of Chornovil's thought. The bulletin's objectives urged readers to support and disseminate it, but also to publicize and react to "every anti-democratic and anti-Ukrainian act." The success of this initiative depended on the level of its readers' social engagement. The first five issues of *Ukraïns'kyi visnyk* came out under Chornovil's editorial supervision, in January, May, and October 1970 and January and May 1971. After his arrest, the sixth issue, dated March 1972, was released by a

---

109 Ibidem, 13–14.
110 Ibidem, 14.

group of Kyiv dissidents. Significantly, the newsletter included all of the main *samvydav* documents produced in Ukraine. Every important instance of repression was documented, and the editorial articles strove to report on everyone who was arrested or repressed, including the charges and types of persecution. The newsletter also contained the texts of new documents written by *shistdesiatnyky* and strove to preserve the memory of the past. This included publishing speeches and writings commemorating Vasyl Symonenko written between 1963 and 1965, when the *Ukraïns'kyi visnyk* did not yet exist.

From the beginning, *Ukraïns'kyi visnyk* played an unprecedented role in transmitting important *samvydav* texts to the West and informing the international public of Soviet repressions. The first two issues, which recounted the crackdown in Dnipropetrovsk and the Karavansky affair, were published in the West by Smoloskyp in 1971, less than a year after the reports circulated in Soviet Ukraine. In the third issue, a short piece titled "A Conversation with the Reader" described the reaction to the newsletter. Generally it had been favourably received, but the editorial board also addressed several criticisms from readers. The first such criticism expressed disapproval of the obvious bias in the editorial about the Dziuba case and his statement to the SPU. Chornovil promised to be more objective in subsequent issues, but he denied the criticism's validity. In the same way he responded to criticisms of the inclusion of a contentious, strongly worded letter to the procurator-general of the USSR by the Ukrainian Greek Catholic clergyman Herman (Hryhorii) Budzynsky, which he had written in 1966 lamenting the Soviet suppression of the Greek Catholic Church in Galicia.[111] Chornovil wrote:

> Religious repression—including the arbitrary liquidation of the Greek Catholic Church implemented by the Brezhnevists—is illegal and anti-constitutional, and therefore *UV* will report on it with the same attention as it has given to similar actions.[112]

Chornovil admitted that Fr. Budzynsky's letter was biased but reminded readers that the data he provides about religious persecutions was collected by an atheist. Furthermore, it was in line with the bulletin's

---

111 Budzinsky (1905–95) had been a prisoner of conscience (1946–56, 1957–59) in Siberia and Mordovia for refusing to join the Russian Orthodox Church and belonging to the underground Greek Catholic Church. The letter is in *Ukraïns'kyi visnyk, Vypusk I – II*, 64–71.
112 [V'iacheslav Chornovil], "Rozmova z chytachem," in his *Tvory*, 3: 428.

mandate to publish letters from other churches that illuminated various opinions about religion. Even if the religious dimension was virtually absent from the set of values that animated the *shistdesiatnyky*, the movement's belief in mutual respect and democracy meant that repressions of the Church and clerics should not be ignored and should be reported as an injustice perpetrated against a fellow Soviet citizen. Finally, the "Conversation" reaffirmed *Ukraïns'kyi visnyk*'s intent not to publish writings compiled specifically for it, but only those "proven through *samvydav*."[113] Therefore the bulletin's real editorial board consisted of the readers and distributers of *samvydav* who independently judged whether a piece of writing was worth reading and distributing, thus determining its success and appearance. In this way *Ukraïns'kyi visnyk* it operated as an extraordinary sounding board for ensuring that the best products emerged from the direct democracy of *samvydav*.

Ukraïns'kyi visnyk paid much attention to the questions of the Ukrainian language and the continued Russification of schools and universities in Ukraine. In the same third issue it recounted the debate that Borys Antonenko-Davydovych's essay in the 4 November 1969 issue of *Literaturna Ukraïna* had sparked. In it he demanded that the authorities reinstate the Ukrainian letter "ґ" ("g"), which had been abolished in Stalin's time, in the Ukrainian alphabet.[114] The debate was soon silenced in the official press but continued in *samvydav* and was summarized in *Ukraïns'kyi visnyk*.

This matter, which at first glance might appear to be an esoteric obsession among linguists, was in reality an important factor in the Russification of the Ukrainian language. Ukrainian possesses the glottal fricative sound ɦ and the velar plosive g, which before the Stalinist orthographic reform of the 1930s were written respectively as "г" and "ґ." The Russian language does not possess the glottal fricative sound but only the velar plosive, which is written using "г," like the Ukrainian glottal fricative. Therefore excision of "ґ" allowed Russian-speakers to ignore the difference between the two sounds when speaking Ukrainian, and this resulted in the orthographic substitution of the velar plosive g with the fricative ɦ. The demand for the restoration of the letter "ґ" was a

---

113 Ibidem, 430.
114 Ibidem, 373. The essay is titled "Litera, za iakoiu tuzhat'" (The Letter That Is Pined For). On the history of the Russification of the Ukrainian language, see George Y. Shevelov, *The Ukrainian Language in the First Half of the Twentieth Century (1900–1941): Its State and Status* (Cambridge, Mass., 1989), especially 131–40.

representative battle for the preservation of one of the most distinctive particularities of the phonetics of the Ukrainian language—a battle that *Ukraïns'kyi visnyk* presented as a decisive factor for the survival of Ukrainian culture.

The Moscow *shestidesiatniki* and Leonid Pliushch

The *shistdesiatnyky* remained close-knit when under frontal attack, but their sense of unity fell apart when faced with the task of developing and executing a political strategy. The problems began with Ivan Dziuba's 1970 statement to the SPU and Moroz's condemnation of it, which split the movement into three factions. In fact, even today the protagonists of those factions are unwilling to discuss this internal debate in their interviews and memoirs. However, the transcripts of the interrogations that followed the 1972 arrests have proven to be surprisingly good sources of information on this point. The questioning revealed the conflicts within the *shistdesiatnytstvo* movement, including about Ukrainian intellectuals' relations with the nonconformist intelligentsia in Moscow and the possibility of joining forces to form a single, united protest movement.

According to Viktor Bondarchuk, one of the five authors of the "Letter of the 139," that important document was conceived as a response by the *shistdesiatnyky* to what they saw as indifference on the part of intellectuals in Moscow toward the repressions in Ukraine. The Ukrainian intellectuals who signed the "Letter" distanced themselves from their Russian counterparts and simultaneously challenged them.[115] Most of the intelligentsia in Kyiv, and more generally in Soviet Ukraine, seemed to be quite isolated from the overall intellectual ferment in the USSR during the 1960s. George Luckyj pointed out that most of the Russian intelligentsia were disinterested in what was going on in Ukraine. There were, of course, exceptions. In *Progress, Coexistence, and Intellectual Freedom*, Andrei Sakharov noted Stalin's Ukrainophobia (apparently the first such mention), and Aleksandr Tvardovsky published several of Dziuba's essays in the Moscow literary journal *Novyi mir* when Dziuba was blacklisted in Ukraine after 1968. But the greatest impact was made by Andrei Amalrik's *Will the Soviet Union Survive until 1984?* (circulated in samizdat in 1969 and published in the West in 1970), whose appearance

---

115 Transcript of Bondarchuk's interrogation, DASBU, spr. 69260fp, vol. 6, ark. 214–19.

confirmed that in the preceding decades Russian intellectual circles had been largely unaware of the turmoil and dissent in Ukraine.[116]

In Moscow the Ukrainian intellectuals' unofficial headquarters was the apartment of General Petr Grigorenko (Petro Hryhorenko, 1907–87), a retired Soviet general and a dissident born in Borysivka, now in Zaporizhzhia Oblast near the Sea of Azov, who had been actively promoting a return to Lenin's principles since 1961. Grigorenko kept contact with Ukrainian intellectuals and granted hospitality to those who travelled from Ukraine on their way to prison camps. This is how Viacheslav Chornovil became acquainted with the Russian dissident Petr Yakir in early 1969 while accompanying Nina Strokata during her trip to visit her husband, Sviatoslav Karavansky, in the Vladimir prison near Moscow. Yakir, a friend of Mykhailo Biletsky, met Strokata and Chornovil while they were staying with Grigorenko and then asked Chornovil about the situation in Ukraine.

> I had heard before from people I knew about so-called Ukrainian philological nationalism, and in my conversation with Chornovil I asked what he knew about it. Chornovil said that in Kyiv Oblast and Ukraine's other oblasts (except the western ones) "Ukrainian philological nationalism" actually existed, and as examples he named the Kyivans [Ivan] Dziuba and [Ivan] Svitlychny. Chornovil explained that proponents of this nationalism speak out against the ongoing Russification of Ukraine and fight for more Ukrainian schools, for teaching in Ukrainian at universities, and for increased publication of Ukrainian literature. He then also claimed that in Ukraine's western oblasts, especially in rural areas, one can observe a genuine Ukrainian nationalism that derives from [Symon] Petliura and thirsts for an "independent, free" [quotes these two words in Ukrainian] Ukraine, i.e., its secession from the USSR. When I asked him to which of these two forms of nationalism Chornovil himself belonged, he essentially did not answer, replying, "I am a journalist." With this our discussion ended.[117]

During the remainder of his interrogation on 23 October 1972, Yakir denied knowing anything more about the activities of this "Ukrainian philological nationalism" and specified that he had briefly met Dziuba

---

116 See Luckyj, "Polarity in Ukrainian Intellectual Dissent," 270.
117 Transcript of Yakir's interrogation on 23 October 1972, DASBU, spr. 69260fp, vol. 6, ark. 232–34.

only on two occasions but had not spoken to him. Yakir confirmed that in May 1969, thanks to the efforts of the Russian human rights activist Liudmila Alekseeva, Chornovil was contacted in order to sign a petition to the United Nations. Chornovil's involvement in the activities of the Russian *shestidesiatniki*, which served in part as a formal excuse to visit them in Moscow, was greater than Yakir wanted to admit to the KGB.

Chornovil and the Ukrainian mathematician Leonid Pliushch (1938–2015) were among the founders of the first Initiative Group for the Defence of Human Rights in the USSR in 1969.[118] This likely proves that the main authors of *Ukraïns'kyi visnyk* and *Khronika tekushchikh sobytii* were in contact and possibly coordinated their efforts. Both Chornovil and Pliushch signed the group's petition, which stated that "We are addressing the UN because our protests and complaints, sent over many years to the highest [Soviet] state and legal bodies, have not received a single reply. The hope that our voices would be heard, that the government would cease the illegalities we reported, this hope has ceased to exist." The Initiative Group hoped that the UN could force the USSR to discuss its protests and complaints in an international debate. The petition included a list of illegal trials in the Soviet Union and may be considered as a first attempt to reconcile the various streams in the civil-rights movement there. It quoted the 1966 trials and Chornovil's, demonstrating that an alliance with the intellectuals in Moscow could lead to the demands of the *shistdesiatnytstvo* movement being included within the broader, Union-wide movement.[119]

Chornovil's activity was animatedly discussed at an evening gathering at Vasyl Stus's apartment in April 1970, to which Stus had invited Chornovil, Dziuba, and Svitlychny to discuss future plans. The atmosphere there was quite unsettled because Valentin Moroz had recently written his critique of Dziuba's "Amid the Snows." When questioned about this on 20 October 1972, Chornovil stated that

> On the topic of the essay *Amid the Snows*, we all reacted with disapproval, although no one, of course, defined it as "anti-Soviet." I observed that I had argued a lot with Moroz and that Moroz's essay was directed not only against Dziuba but to a certain extent against

---

118 Marco Clementi, *Storia del dissenso sovietico* (Roma, 2007), 106.
119 Quote from the Ukrainian translation of the letter published in *Suchasnist'*, 1969, no. 6: 117–21.

me and the others. But I absolutely did not advocate increased *political* activity on the part of Ivan Dziuba or anyone else.[120]

Chornovil adroitly avoided naming individuals, simply adding that the Soviet authorities were attempting to prove that Dziuba was contradicting his previous positions on the nationality question so they could use Dziuba's statement as a weapon against the *shistdesiatnyky*. In Chornovil's opinion, it was important to emphasize Dziuba's alignment with the Soviet world view.

> [Dziuba] absolutely did not say, as he is testifying now, that we need to "return to Soviet positions." I only said that we have to dissociate ourselves from accusations of being anti-Soviet, and stress more emphatically that we are Soviet people and that we live for the interests of Soviet society ... I said that concepts such as "anti-Soviet" and "nationalist" in our situation have been unluckily deprived of any concreteness and are officially attributed any meaning that is convenient. For example, I have always maintained a Soviet position and still do, but it has not prevented them [the authorities] from calling me (as well as Dziuba) anti-Soviet, nationalist, and so on.[121]

Chornovil's stance was motivated by his refusal to admit to ever having an anti-Soviet position, but his insistence on the Soviet nature of his convictions is in fact coherent with the rest of his activity and writing, including his letters from the prison camp and the "Tasks" of *Ukraïns'kyi visnyk*. During his interrogation Chornovil also hinted at other topics and future actions that the group discussed at the gathering at Stus's apartment, which he claimed was a meeting of literate people who were discussing better ways to interest their readers and to help their friends who had been fired from their jobs. Svitlychny's deposition is slightly more detailed, as it explains the reasons for the disagreement between Chornovil and the others.

> Viacheslav Chornovil also reproached us (perhaps under the influence of Moroz's essay "Amid the Snows" or perhaps on his own) about the fact that we—that is to say, Ivan Dziuba, Yevhen Sverstiuk, and I—had become inactive and hardly worked.

---

120 Chornovil's interrogation on 20 October 1972, DASBU, spr. 69260fp, vol. 4, ark. 221.
121 Ibidem, ark. 226.

> However, Chornovil did not specify exactly what he had in mind when speaking of activity and inactivity, and each of us interpreted these words in his own way. I remember that not one of those who were taking part in the conversation considered Chornovil's reproaches opportune, and we all showed that each of us was working according to his strength and potential and that it was not our responsibility if our work output did not reach broad circles of the community. It is even possible that the different opinions on the activeness or passivity of each of us were partly linked to the fact that we each had in mind different spheres of activity, but we thought we were speaking of the same subject.[122]

According to Svitlychny, Chornovil attacked the central figures of the *shistdesiatnytstvo* movement in Kyiv, urging them to find new forms of protest, as he was doing with *Ukraïns'kyi visnyk*. Svitlychny did not specify the reasons behind the disagreement with Chornovil, but from Chornovil's subsequent actions and from other interrogations it emerges that the main point of contention was the organization of the group and its relationship with other groups that were coming into existence in other regions of the Soviet Union.

This question of organization became complicated when a document titled "Program of the U-Communists" was disseminated in *samvydav* in 1971. Its author was Vasyl Ruban (1942–2017), the founder of a "Ukrainian National Communist Party." In spite of its title, the program document analyzed Ukrainian history from a nationalist point of view, promoted Ukraine's secession from the USSR, and accused the Soviet state of being responsible for the 1932–33 Great Famine in Ukraine.[123] Although this document's spirit was extraneous to the values of *shistdesiatnytstvo*, the exposure it received in the underground milieu induced some *shistdesiatnyky* to wonder whether they should also produce such a program. When Dziuba was arrested in 1972, he was accused of being the author of the "Program of the U-Communists." He was released only after a long investigation. Questioned about these facts, Svitlychny confirmed that after that document was disseminated many people approached him enquiring whether there was a programmatic document of the

---

122 Svitlychny's interrogation on 4 October 1972, DASBU, spr. 68805fp, vol. 3, ark. 25–26.
123 This document and the movement are examined in Anatolii Rusnachenko, *Rozdumom i sertsem*, 204–11.

shistdesiatnytstvo movement. But such an initiative was contrary to his, Dziuba's, and Chornovil's beliefs.

> When I spoke about the unsuitability and perniciousness of creating documents of a programmatic nature, I stressed two points. First, under today's conditions any activity performed by an organization with a program would inevitably lead to repression of the intelligentsia, meaning that it would negatively affect cultural development—because that was the most fundamental activity to which we were able to contribute. Second, I drew attention to the fact that editing and disseminating documents of a programmatic nature would involve implicating people in an organized activity putting them in serious jeopardy, and whoever did that was going to bear a great responsibility toward the others.[124]

Svitlychny added that the experience of the Lukianenko group (and of a recent failed attempt to hijack an airplane in Leningrad) should serve as a warning against establishing secret organizations.

During my interview of Dziuba on 13 June 2009, he confirmed that the central point in their reasoning was: editing such a constitution-type document would imply the existence of an alternative organization to the Communist Party, which would mean that their movement, always careful to remain on the side of legality, would be violating the law. Such a document would contradict the values of *shistdesiatnytstvo*, and because the movement considered itself to be a Soviet one, they must not form a secret society within the socialist state.

To what extent the *shistdesiatnyky* were able to organize their own future was a question that was debated throughout 1971. In her interrogation on 27 January 1973, Zynoviia Franko stated that around 20 December 1971 Moroz confided in her his intention to form a committee for the defence of Nina Strokata. As reported in the sixth issue of *Ukraïns'kyi visnyk*, Strokata (1926–1998) was a physician at the Odesa Medical Institute who had married Sviatoslav Karavansky in 1961, after he returned from prison camp. When he was incarcerated again in 1965, Strokata dedicated herself to defending her husband. In 1969 a new trial began against Karavansky, who was accused of having written the *samvydav* essays included in Chornovil's *Woe from Wit*. At the same time,

---

124 Svitlychny's interrogation on 29 August 1972, DASBU, spr. 68805fp, vol. 3, ark. 315–16.

the Medical Institute where Strokata was working denounced her for failing to renounce her husband. Her reaction was firm.

> Nina Strokata pointed out that it was a wife's moral duty to defend her husband's interests, and that the demands that she condemn and publicly renounce him were immoral. She drew an analogy between her present plight and that of the wives of political prisoners during Stalin's time.[125]

In May 1971 Strokata was dismissed from the Odesa Medical Institute. She then moved to Nalchik, the centre of Kabardino-Balkaria in the Caucasus, where she worked as an instructor at a medical school. On 8 December 1971 she was arrested there, allegedly for anti-Soviet activity although the official reasons were not publicized. Members of the *shistdesiatnyky* wanted to speak out against her illegal detainment, but (according to her own testimony) Zynoviia Franko disagreed with Mykhailyna Kotsiubynska, Ivan Svitlychny, and Ivan Dziuba on the makeup of an ad hoc committee. They did agree that because the Committee on Human Rights in the USSR established in 1970 by Andrei Sakharov and others in Moscow was not interested in defending the rights of Ukrainian activists, a Ukrainian committee for the defence of human rights akin to Sakharov's should be founded.[126] However, they did not have the means to establish it.

The initiative was instead taken by Chornovil, who on 21 December 1971 proclaimed the establishment of the Committee for the Defence of Nina Strokata. He named Leonid Tymchuk, Iryna Stasiv, Vasyl Stus, and Petr Yakir as its founders, with the latter as the liaison with the Moscow committee.[127] In a novel departure from previous initiatives, the Ukrainian committee—following the lead of the Committee on Human Rights—was determined to appeal to the highest institution for the defence of human

---

125 [V'iacheslav Chornovil], "Who is Nina Strokata (Karavanska)?" in *The Ukrainian Herald*, issue 6, 146.
126 Zynoviia Franko's interrogation, DASBU, spr. 69260fp, vol. 3, ark. 61–65.
127 Iryna Stasiv (1940–2012) was born in Lviv to a family with ties to the OUN. She began her dissident activity in 1968 as a result of her friendship with Chornovil. Stasiv married the poet Ihor Kalynets (b 1939), who was also active in the civil-rights movement from the end of the 1960s. Both of them were arrested in 1972 and sentenced to six years in labour camps and three years' exile. Leonid Tymchuk (b. 1935) was a former Soviet sailor who worked on tugs in Odesa's port. An active dissident in Odesa from the mid-1960s, he met Nina Strokata in 1968 and joined the committee for her defence in 1972.

rights—the United Nations. The members had ascertained that the very fact of an arrest of a Soviet citizen for expressing their beliefs contradicted the *Universal Declaration of Human Rights* and the *International Covenant on Civil and Political Rights* adopted by the United Nations General Assembly and ratified by the government of the USSR.

> We have come to the conclusion that it is imperative, particularly in serious individual cases, to conduct organized actions in defense of the citizens of the U.S.S.R. who are persecuted for political reasons....
>
> Should all these measures fail to bring the desired results, we will be forced to appeal to the United Nations Commission on Human Rights. The activities of the Committee will continue for the duration of Nina Strokata's imprisonment. The Committee will dissolve upon her release.[128]

Appealing to international public opinion had become an important weapon of the *shistdesiatnyky*. However, their cause was weakened by the fact that they remained incapable of uniting under a single initiative. This divisiveness was highlighted by the fact that the Committee for the Defence of Nina Strokata comprised only five members—a paltry number compared to the signatories of the "Letter of the 139."

The Strokata defence committee developed a strategy first mentioned in a letter to the UN Human Rights Commission in June 1969 from Mykhailo Horyn, Ivan Kandyba, and Levko Lukianenko. In it they described the significant deterioration of their conditions as inmates in the hard-labour prison camp and accused its management of adding chemicals to the prisoners' food.

> In the camp also poison is added to the food. We have conducted a number of experiments and ascertained this. The symptoms of poisoning are as follows: ten to fifteen minutes after the consumption of food a slight pressure appears in the temples which afterwards turns into an intolerable headache. It is difficult to concentrate on anything, even on writing a letter home. When reading a paragraph one forgets by the end what was written at the beginning. In order to return to a normal condition one must fast for

---

128 "A Statement Regarding the Formation of a Citizens' Committee for the Defense of Nina Strokata," in *The Ukrainian Herald*, Issue 6, 141, 143.

24 hours. Thus, we alternate days of fasting with days of poisoned food.[129]

The symptoms had worsened with time, and the three inmates, fearing the possible loss of their cognitive abilities, were appealing for help. The poisoning in the prison camps foreshadowed the KGB's later method of silencing dissidents by incarcerating and poisoning them in psychiatric hospitals for the criminally insane. Among the *shistdesiatnyky* the most famous victim of such repression was Leonid Pliushch, a singular figure with a unique history.

An insight into Pliushch's personality can be gleaned from his memoirs, which he wrote in the late 1970s after being exiled from the Soviet Union in 1976 and settling in France. Despite all that he had been made to suffer in the USSR, Pliushch continued to be a staunch believer in Marxism, and his memoirs were written in its spirit. His introduction elucidates his state of mind and suggests how to approach his book.

> ... [T]he book before you is neither a confession nor a literary autobiography. It is an account of one more road to freedom, a description of how the Soviet Union appears in the eyes of a citizen whose fanatical faith in the Soviet system gave way to a struggle to free himself of its illusions, slavery, and terror. I have tried to show what my comrades in the Soviet Union are fighting for and how they are persecuted.
>
> I should not want my testimony about the reality of "socialism" to serve as a moral justification for all sorts of fascist scum, because my enemy's enemy is not necessarily my friend. Barbarity is barbarity no matter what its ideological hue....
>
> Here in the "free West" (the Western reader knows that its freedom is qualified), I see only one duty for myself: to testify, as if in court, about the Marxist hell that I, a Marxist, have witnessed in my mother Ukraine and stepmother Russia, as well as in other republics of the USSR. By doing so I hope to combat inhuman actions by all governments in the West and the East.[130]

---

129 Browne, ed., *Ferment in the Ukraine*, 216.
130 Leonid Plyushch [Pliushch], "Preface," in his *History's Carnival: A Dissident's Autobiography*, trans. Marco Carynnyk (New York and London, 1979), xvi. The French translation was published two years earlier as Léonide Pliouchtch, *Dans le carnaval de l'histoire: Mémoires* (Paris: Seuil, 1977), with some differences in paragraph order. Pliushch wrote his memoirs in Russian.

The spirit of *shistdesiatnytstvo* is present in the moral tension that drives the author's actions. His memoirs are dedicated to his fellow "humanitarians" in the hope that they will win their battle. Pliushch was a Marxist fighting against the Soviet Union, a son of Ukraine adopted by Russia who wanted to testify against the "illusion, slavery, and terror" that had marked his life. He arrived at this point via a particular route. He was born on 26 April 1939 into a Ukrainian family in Naryn, a city in the Kirghiz republic. His father was killed in battle against the Germans in 1941, and, together with his sister and mother, young Leonid returned to Ukraine to live with his grandmother in the town of Borzna, Chernihiv Oblast. Pliushch had a typical Soviet childhood and adolescence. Although his grandmother had imbued him with religion, long-term treatment in a sanatorium for tuberculosis of the bones jump-started his Soviet education, whose first step was becoming an atheist owing to the influence of a Communist Party propagandist. Pliushch subsequently attended schools in Frunze (today Bishkek) and Odesa. Together with faith in the principles of Marxism-Leninism, he picked up the worst that a Russian-chauvinist education had to offer.

> In school we were required to study the Kirghiz language. At first I proudly refused. I despised the Kirghiz teacher and had no use for the language. Then I started to study the language and make fun of the Kirghiz children.... No one was deliberately bringing me up to hate the natives, but prejudice was in the air. The Kirghiz and Uzbeks were not yet called "animals," but already half the population [in the republic] was Russian and Ukrainian. (The Ukrainians were dispossessed kulaks who tended to live on the outskirts.) The whites [i.e., Slavs] were better educated and had better jobs. They were the bearers of everything progressive and cultured.
>
> This, too, I hold against the [Soviet] regime: inculcating children with chauvinism, anti-Semitism, and KGBism. It took me, a Ukrainian boy, and made me a Russian chauvinist, an oppressor of Chechens, Kurds, and Kirghizians, a white racist blinded by his mission as a *Kulturträger*.[131]

This kind of chauvinist inculcation continued in Odesa, where many people despised the Jews because they were the richest stratum of the population. Under these circumstances Pliushch found "It was natural to

---

131 Ibidem, 8–9.

become an anti-Semite." He joined the Komsomol and briefly a brigade of voluntary popular militia aiding the Soviet police. Pliushch's severity and zeal in combating crime led to a job offer from the KGB. But his extensive reading alerted him to the "glaring contradictions" between Soviet society's ideals and daily reality. Pliushch's desire to express his opinions sometimes caused problems with the authorities. The first, decisive blow to his Soviet infatuation was dealt by Khrushchev's public refutation of Stalinism.

> A close friend came up to me after classes one day. The daughter of a border-guard officer, she was my "comrade in arms" in various Komsomol projects. She had an important secret to tell me: Khrushchev had made a speech at the Twentieth Party Congress, denouncing Stalin for his crimes. My friend told me less than a tenth of what Khrushchev had said, but even this was enough to shake the foundations of my ideology—faith in Comrade Stalin's brilliance and endless kindness toward workers.
> I walked the streets till evening in extreme agitation, then called on a friend and told him what I had heard. I could tell him everything, I felt, because he, too, had high ideals. We wandered about all night, discussing the revelations from every possible angle and concluding "they're all scoundrels." If our leaders knew what Stalin had done but remained silent, they were cowards and not Communists. We also decided that if Stalin was a blackguard, his wrongdoings should be corrected without public discussion. Later I met many adult imbeciles who took the same position.[132]

This self-deception allowed Pliushch to remain in the Komsomol while studying mathematics at Odesa State University. Although his comrades were committing every crime from embezzlement to rape, Pliushch was still convinced that it was possible to improve the system from within. After a brief period working as a teacher in the countryside, he married Tania Zhitnikova in 1961 and moved to Kyiv to complete the fourth year of his mathematics studies. In Kyiv the quality of education was higher, and it inspired Pliushch to expand his knowledge. He began studying parapsychology and cybernetics and read the classics of Marxism, which increased his skepticism toward the Communist Party. After the Twenty-Second Congress of the CPSU, Pliushch understood that the official interpretations of Soviet history were not true.

---

132 Ibidem, 12.

> The "cult of personality," as Stalinism was officially called, seemed a thoroughly un-Marxist concept. Stalinism cannot be explained in terms of the leader's personal qualities or by such "objective" reasons as isolation of the country and the need to struggle against the opposition. Stalinism was obviously not simply a cult, but a rebirth of autocracy on a new class basis. It was necessary to study the class roots of the degeneration of the Revolution instead of placing the blame on "individual distortions" in the leadership of the party and the country. Guarantees that the [Soviet] Constitution would be observed were needed, and the principles of a new constitution had to be developed.
>
> The [CPSU] Congress declared that the USSR was no longer a dictatorship of the proletariat, but, rather, a state of all the people. In terms of classical Leninism this was nonsense, and a Marxist analysis of this new concept was needed. After all, the state is a machine that one class uses to oppress other classes. A state of all the people would be equivalent to a round square.[133]

Dissatisfied with the official explanations, Pliushch tried to form his own interpretative scheme of Soviet history. John-Paul Himka has pointed out that Pliushch's interpretations of Stalinism ("state capitalism," "abstract capitalism," "an ideocracy that has become an idolocracy") were nonetheless unsatisfactory, sometimes contradicting Marxist terms or obscuring them altogether, for Pliushch relied mainly on Marx's early and more ethics-inspired writings.[134] What matters is that Pliushch's faith in Marxism-Leninism and strong longing for the affirmation of moral values was indeed shared by the other *shistdesiatnyky*. This connection is interesting because—apart from a passing interest in the Ukrainian famine of 1932–33 inspired by reading Admiral Fedor Raskolnikov's letter to Stalin—Pliushch's reading in those years was typical of Moscow's intellectual circles and did not include the *shistdesiatnyky*. His interpretation of what he read (from Leo Tolstoy and Antoine de Saint-Exupery to Vladimir Dudintsev, Aleksandr Solzhenitsyn, Ilya Ehrenburg, and, of course, the journal *Novyi mir*) was based on ethical evaluation and was typical of the moral background of intellectual circles in the entire Soviet Union. For example, commenting on Aleksandr Solzhenitsyn's

---

133 Ibidem, 40.
134 See John-Paul Himka, "Leonid Plyushch: The Ukrainian Marxist Resurgent," *Journal of Ukrainian Studies* 5, no. 2 (Fall 1980): 61–65.

Cancer Ward, Pliushch wrote: "One reason for the defeat of the October Revolution was an ethical one. The contempt for ethical values that resulted from the absolutization of class led to an ethical relativism in theory and a barbarity in practice."[135]

Ironically, it was after Khrushchev's condemnation of the formalism of Ukrainian poetry in 1963 that Pliushch and his wife began reading works of the *shistdesiatnyky*, particularly of Ivan Drach, whom Pliushch considered to be more talented than Yevgeny Yevtushenko. The discovery of Ukrainian literature induced him to read earlier Ukrainian authors such as Pavlo Tychyna and Lesia Ukrainka, which resulted in a spontaneous process of self-re-Ukrainianization. He began socializing with the *shistdesiatnyky*, and after the 1965 arrests he attended several of the trials that took place in Kyiv. Nonetheless he continued speaking Russian, which was frowned upon by some members of the movement. In response Pliushch used to say that what was important was the fight for civil rights, not that he should speak Ukrainian. Dziuba agreed with him.

But it was in fact Dziuba's *Internationalism or Russification?* that contributed decisively to Pliushch's Ukrainianization.

> Tychyna, Kulish, and the Ukrainian artists of the 1920's wedged open for me the door to the potential riches of Ukrainian culture, but I continued by inertia to think of myself as a Russian. Shortly after the trials of 1966, however, Ivan Dzyuba's *Internationalism or Russification?* began to circulate clandestinely in Ukraine. Until we read it, Tanya and I had believed that except for fostering anti-Semitism and deporting small nations the party was conducting a correct policy toward the nationalities. Now we learned that Lenin had spoken about "Ukrainianizing the Ukrainian cities."...
>
> Other facts cited by Dzyuba seemed to us at first to be exaggerated, for example, his claim that a person who speaks Ukrainian will be told to speak "human"—that is, Russian. But then, under the influence of Dzyuba's book, I began to speak my native language. At first it was difficult, because my active vocabulary was limited and everyone around me was speaking Russian. One day in a shop I asked a young man, in Ukrainian, to hand me a book. "Can't you speak human?" he snarled. The blood rushed to my head, and right then I became a Ukrainian once and for all, the way Soviet Jews fully

---

135 Plyushch, *History's Carnival*, 113–14.

realize that they are Jews when they are barraged with "anticosmopolitan" or "anti-Zionist" propaganda.[136]

As had happened to Lina Kostenko, Russian chauvinism and discrimination against Ukrainian played a significant role in the consolidation of a Ukrainian identity in an individual who had hitherto felt no resentment toward Russia and did not conceive of the two cultures as distinct. Though he admired Dziuba, Pliushch was convinced that he was not the right man for Ukraine. Recalling their first encounter, Pliushch wrote:

> I went to visit Dzyuba and met an intelligent and modest man who by inclination was indifferent to politics. This disturbed me. We needed "politicians," people who would disseminate *samizdat* and deliberately spread information.[137]

This mindset dictated Pliushch's activity within the movement. Thanks to his research in parapsychology, telepathy, and yoga, Pliushch travelled frequently and enjoyed close relationships with intellectuals in various cities, above all Moscow, where he stayed for an entire month in 1961. There he befriended Petr Yakir and became acquainted with the milieu in which samizdat circulated. After 1966 Pliushch decided to dedicate himself to the dissemination of samizdat and *samvydav* documents in Ukraine and Russia, and he served as a liaison between their intellectual communities. Pliushch and his wife, who was half-Jewish and half-Russian, rediscovered his Ukrainian roots during the latter 1960s. Together they travelled around Ukraine, visiting the Carpathians in search of Hutsul culture, and Galicia, where they became interested in the Second World War and the UPA.

This love for Ukrainian culture did not hinder Pliushch's admiration for those Russians who demonstrated moral and political values — including the Yakir family, who had suffered repeated persecution. It was in writing about them that he expressed his admiration for those who, despite repression, were able to put their entire world view under critical examination, to separate the practical mistakes from just ideas, and to emerge from the traumatic experiences of questioning and imprisonment

---

136 Ibidem, 113–14.
137 Ibidem, 75.

still resolute in their convictions. Pliushch compared the experience of Sara Yakir, Petr's mother, to other elderly female dissidents.

> Why do I mention Sara Yakir when I write about Olitskaya? I have always compared the honest Old Bolsheviks to Olitskaya, Surovtseva, and Andreyeva. Almost all the Old Bolsheviks were to some extent broken, and not because they were weaker than their opponents. The Bolsheviks were defeated first morally and then politically. Olitskaya, Surovtseva, and Andreyeva were politically defeated and tortured, but their moral victory is indisputable. It is easier to resist an enemy than fellow party members, particularly when they have the party leadership and the "people" behind them. When Sara and Iona Yakir were interrogated and tortured, they had only themselves to rely on: the ideal for which they had fought had been defeated, and their entire struggle before, during, and after the October Revolution was in question. How much spiritual strength is needed to avoid giving in to one's torturers! People find succor either in fanaticism or in an unusual strength of mind which permitted them to re-examine their lives, to find the mistakes they, their comrades, and their leaders had committed, and to uphold the ideas that survived this merciless criticism.[138]

In celebrating the spiritual strength of these three women, Pliushch was trying to explain his own position as a Communist who, while acknowledging the injustices of Soviet society, still believed in Marxism and fought for its realization. Just before he was sent to prison, Pliuschch and his wife re-examined their lives.

> Tanya and I went over the last four years. Yes, they were worth going to prison for. If we had not joined the opposition movement, we should never have come to know Olitskaya, Surovtseva, Grigorenko, Svitlychny, Sverstiuk, Dzyuba, and dozens of other splendid people. We had been happy these four years; we had been able to respect ourselves. I was going to prison not for the sake of abstract ideas, but for the sake of respect toward myself and others.[139]

---

138 Ibidem, 156–57. Ekaterina Olitskaya was a Russian dissident; Nadia Surovtseva was a Ukrainian activist since Stalin's time; and Zoia Andreyeva was Surovtseva's anarchist friend from Sevastopol. They all were arrested and imprisoned in the Gulag in Stalin's time and were living together when Pliushch went to Uman to meet them in 1968.
139 Ibidem, 259.

It was this respect for the individual that bolstered their commitment to the struggle for civil and political rights. As envisioned by Pliushch and the *shishtdesiatnyky*, the inclusion of the national question in these rights was not dissonant.

Pliushch and his wife suffered various forms of administrative repressions, including dismissal from their jobs. Then he was arrested in 1972 and imprisoned in a KGB-run psychiatric institution. Interestingly, in 1980 Himka identified Pliushch's self-respect as one of the reasons for this sentence, which he termed a "defeat."

> The politics of self-respect encourages an abdication from the most difficult of political tasks—organizing an effective opposition—in favour of acts of protest that demonstrate one's oppositional virtue, but disregard effectiveness. The Soviet opposition has engaged in many honourable, courageous, self-defeating acts, but it is high time that it concentrated on honourable, courageous acts that lead to victory. For a Marxist it should be clear what these are: acts that expand the social base of the opposition movement, in particular enlisting the working class to fight for its own interests.[140]

The main problems of the *shistdesiatnytstvo* movement were organizational: lack of a leader, lack of a unified political program, internal fragmentation, and—at least for some of the central figures—the predominance of artistic and ethical dimensions over the political one. These were reasons that precluded the *shistdesiatnyky* from developing in the direction of a more powerful social movement. Further complicating matters, the Soviet authorities were growing more convinced of the need to quell any glimmer of independent initiatives.

Silencing Broader Cultural Initiatives

There is no *shistdesiatnyk* who has not cited popular songs as being a key factor in the formation of their cultural identity. From Levko Lukianenko to Lina Kostenko, from Les Taniuk to Mykola Plakhotniuk, they all remember having listened in their childhood to traditional Ukrainian songs, sung either by family members or on public occasions, including in church and at wedding celebrations. Pliushch wrote an account of a

---

140 Himka, "Leonid Plyushch," 78.

concert of folk songs that was staged for a traditional marriage that he attended during a trip to Lviv to visit the Chornovil and Kalynets families.

> That evening, when folk songs were sung in honor of the newlyweds, I discovered something profoundly Ukrainian in those Ukrainian songs. A Ukrainian may call himself a Russian, not know the language, and despise the people, but if he spent his childhood in Ukraine, he becomes a Ukrainian again in song. In eastern Ukraine folk songs have been turned into propaganda by the radio, and no new ones are being written. In Lviv, however, I heard both religious songs and new folk songs. And my friends did not sing them in loud, drunken voices, as Eastern Ukrainian peasants do.[141]

The repositories of different values extant in the popular songs were, in Pliushch's mind, important for the revival of Ukrainian identity. To illustrate this point, he noted the way these songs presented the relationship between men and women.

> I sensed in these songs an extremely tender and respectful attitude toward women. The feminism expressed in them sharply distinguishes Ukrainians from Russians: Ukrainian songs show no sign of the contempt or the exaggerated courtly respect in which Russians hold women, or of that pathological deification of the flesh which is mixed with a sense of woman's sinfulness and corruption. Ukrainian culture does not share the Russians' hysterical condemnation of women. The Ukrainian peasant woman may appear obedient in the presence of the guests, but she will tell her husband exactly what she thinks when they are alone. She is the mistress of her house.[142]

Pliushch went on to suggest that Ihor and Iryna Kalynets, who lived in harmony despite writing two completely different styles of poetry, were a living example of the concordant relationships recounted in the songs.[143]

Pliushch's feminist interpretation of Ukrainian popular songs was echoed in Dziuba's *samvydav* essay "'Sex,' 'Sex,' and a Bit of 'Anti-Sex' (The Female Ideal in Poetry)," which addresses the taboo theme of women

---

141 Plyushch, *History's Carnival*, 187.
142 Ibidem.
143 For an introduction to Kalynets's poetry, see Danylo Husar Struk, "The Summing-Up of Silence: The Poetry of Ihor Kalynets," *Slavic Review* 38, no, 1 (March 1979), 17–29.

and intimacy. As Obertas has pointed out, there Dziuba argued that love's and women's roles were treated completely differently in the poems of the *shistdesiatnyky* than in Soviet literature: "For these poets, Dziuba demonstrates, the theme of the woman is addressed on two levels: the objective (the reproduction of life and the state of women in society) and the subjective (in the experience of their own intimate feelings, in the search for their own spiritual ideal)."[144] In opposition to sexophobia in the USSR, Dziuba wanted to show that, albeit in an artistically still imperfect way, the *shistdesiatnyky* promoted a unique concept of humanity that entailed respect for women as individuals.

Ukrainian folk songs have functioned as a vehicle for the communication of values, possessing a ubiquity that was instrumental in promoting group cohesiveness. The songs have usually been choral pieces, and audiences can join in singing them with the performers in what becomes acts of cultural belonging. The Soviet authorities tried to repress this communal participation, which was most famously practiced by Kyiv's Homin (Echo) choir.

Throughout the 1960s many amateur choirs were established, revitalizing the Ukrainian tradition of sing-alongs in town and village squares on days of rest. The authorities regarded these initiatives with suspicion and hindered them in various ways, sometimes forcibly dissolving the choirs. Homin was formed in Kyiv in the late 1960s from an amalgamation of a number of different choirs. Since none of the members had professional training, they asked the Kyiv composer and ethnomusicologist Leopold Yashchenko (1928–2016) to conduct Homin. That choir "differed from other ensembles in that it did not plan the usual stage concerts; instead, it held its performances of *vesnyanky* or *Kupalo* songs outdoors, in the natural environment of such works. When outsiders joined in the games[,] the festivals became mass participation affairs."[145] Because the songs' content was not nationalistic, the interpretation of such initiatives could change, depending on the context and the political situation. Homin's birth was welcomed by the local authorities, who allowed Yashchenko to use a hall for rehearsals in the

---

144 Obertas, *Ukraïns'kyi samvydav*, 154. Dziuba's essay "'Seks,' 'seks' … i trokhy 'antyseksu' (Zhinochyi ideal u poeziï)" is in *Shyroke more Ukraïny*, 133–46.

145 *The Ukrainian Herald*, Issue 6, 131. *Vesnianky* are folk songs celebrating the beginning of spring (Ukrainian: *vesna*); the feast of Ivan Kupalo, a figure in Slavic folklore, marks the summer solstice, which the Christian tradition linked to the feast day of Saint John the Baptist.

Kharchovyk Palace of Culture of the Trade Union of Food-Industry Workers (a distinctive building in Kyiv's Podil district that later housed the Slavutych Children's Musical Theatre.

As the KGB's scrutiny intensified at the beginning of the 1970s, the choir's activities caught its KGB's attention. In a report dated January 1970, Yashchenko's activities were defined as "bourgeois-nationalist," and Kyiv's Party committee decided to impose stricter control.[146] The Union of Composers of Ukraine met on 20 January and 1 February to discuss the Homin case. Yashchenko stated that the choir's objective was to revitalize the Ukrainian folk-song tradition, and he explained that he had created some new arrangements and "people themselves can be creators of their own rituals." The Union of Composers' leaders and Yashchenko seemed willing to find a compromise: Yashchenko condemned some of the choir's "nationalistic" acts, and the union admitted that his goal was just but recommended that he include more "Soviet content."[147] The inquiry ended with the choir being given more time to conform. In December 1970 the authorities tried to replace Yashchenko with a "more loyal" director (on the grounds that he was not a trained conductor), but the singers refused to work with the new director and Yashchenko was reinstated.[148]

On 22 May 1971 a crowd assembled at Taras Shevchenko's monument in Kyiv for the annual commemoration of the relocation of the poet's remains (a historic procession from St. Petersburg, where he died in 1861, to Ukraine near Kaniv, where he had requested to be buried). Among the nearly 350 participants, many were members of Homin. But Yashchenko was not present. The commemoration was led by Anatolii Lupynis (1937–2000), who had been arrested in 1956 for anti-Soviet agitation and sentenced to ten years' imprisonment, which he served in Mordovian camps and then in the Vladimir Prison. When he was released in 1967, he was physically disabled. His application to study at Kyiv State University was denied, but he was hired as the administrator of the Kyiv Concert and Choir Society. At the 22 May gathering he read a poem about his imprisonment and the destiny of Ukraine, while other attendees sang folk songs. Because there was a large crowd, the political fallout was greater

---

146 Report of Kyiv's Party Committee to the CC CPU, in TsDAHOU, f. 1, op. 25, spr. 359, ark. 1–3.
147 Report of the Kyiv City Committee [of the CPU] to the CC CPU, 4 February 1970, TsDAHOU, f. 1, op. 25, spr. 359, ark. 4–8.
148 Report of the Kyiv City Committee [of the CPU] to the CC CPU, TsDAHOU, f. 1, op. 25, spr. 359, ark. 10–14.

than could have been expected. At that time people also participated in the 22 May "Kyiv spring" events, about which the KGB reported that the large number of participants consisted primarily of onlookers who were curious about the disturbances.[149]

In the following days the KGB identified many of the participants. Lupynis was arrested 28 May, and many Homin choristers became the targets of administrative repressions.[150] Nonetheless, Homin's activities began increasing in number and significance. Throughout the summer its members gathered in public places and sang without authorization.[151] On 5 August 1971 they assembled outside a city theatre where a touring Ukrainian-Canadian choir was giving a concert, and their joint street performance lasted well into the night. On 20 September, however, Homin was disbanded, and 28 September Yashchenko was expelled from the Composers' Union.[152] The choir's members were offered a chance to continue singing as a different ethnographic choir, but none of them did.[153]

In early the 1970s, the Soviet authorities thus defended their cultural monopoly in the USSR, forbidding any unofficial initiatives out of fear they could become a source of anti-Soviet activity. The artist and ethnographer Ivan Honchar had amassed one of the largest existing collections of Ukrainian folk art in his Kyiv apartment (7,000 items—icons, paintings, costumes and embroideries, pottery, tiles, wooden sculptures, musical instruments, toys, metal objects—and 20,000 photographs). By the latter half of the 1960s the growing number of Ukrainians and foreigners who visited his private museum and the gatherings of *shistdesiatnyky* held there convinced the authorities to get hold of the collection. Starting in 1969, he received many proposals to donate his collection to a public institution, including an offer to display the items at the museum in the nearby Monastery of the Caves.[154] But he turned down all of them. Then, 6 November 1970, Ukraine's Union of Artists forbade Honchar to accept visitors to his museum. Fearing that his collection would be confiscated,

---

149 Report from the CC CPU to the CC CPSU, in TsDAHOU, f. 1, op. 25, spr. 546, ark. 103–107.
150 Report of the Kyiv City Committee [of the CPU] to the CC CPU, TsDAHOU, f. 1, op. 25, spr. 546, ark. 114–16; some of the measures taken against Homin's members and Lupynis are described in *The Ukrainian Herald, Issue 6*, 130–38 and 149–53.
151 Report of the CPU's Kyiv City Committee to the CC CPU, in TsDAHOU, f. 1, op. 25, spr. 359, ark. 26–29.
152 Report from the CC CPU to the CC CPSU, in TsDAHOU, f. 1, op. 25, spr. 513, ark. 43–55.
153 *The Ukrainian Herald, Issue 6*, 136–37.
154 See the reports to the CC CPU, in TsDAHOU, f. 1, op. 25, spr. 183, ark. 77 and 109.

he complied with the order.¹⁵⁵ His museum remained closed to the public but intact until he was allowed to reopen it in the 1980s.

From other police reports sent to Petro Shelest, we know that a group called Vatra (Bonfire) with fifteen musicians, three of them bandurysts, was disbanded in October 1971 because of their "suspect" repertoire. Furthermore, censorship in the Ukrainian press also grew stricter, with bans on the publication of Ihor Kalynets's poetry and the prose of Volodymyr Drozd, and the Party's reprimands of the editorial boards of *Literaturna Ukraïna* and the literary journals *Dnipro* and *Vitchyzna*.¹⁵⁶

According to a KGB report, from January 1967 to June 1971 the KGB investigated over six thousand people and prosecuted eighty-seven of them. Among those convicted, sixty-seven per cent were Ukrainians and ninety-two per cent were under the age of forty-five. Six were Party members, and thirteen had joined the Komsomol; twenty-six had studied at university and forty had finished secondary school; and thirty-three (nearly thirty-eight per cent) were prosecuted for nationalism. These data indicate that discontent in Ukraine was especially felt within the younger and more educated generation. Anti-Soviet propaganda consisted mainly of leaflets promoting Ukraine's independence, and one of the most popular issues was Valentyn Moroz's arrest, trial, and imprisonment. Commenting on Moroz's and Ivan Sokulsky's cases, the report affirmed that the preferred form of anti-Soviet ideology was "pseudo-socialism," which was a "special form of the restoration of capitalism."¹⁵⁷ The most harrowing statistics were those concerning the number of dissidents sentenced to undergo psychiatric treatment: among those sentenced, forty-six were institutionalized in mental hospitals. Among the others apprehended by the KGB, 117 were imprisoned without trial because they had been declared mentally ill, and another sixty-four were forcibly administered drugs.¹⁵⁸

In March, a few months before the release of this report, the KGB suggested to the CPU that it publish an article with documents linking

---

155 Letter of the Union of the Artists of Ukraine to the CC CPU, in TsDAHOU, f. 1, op. 25, spr. 183, ark. 112. On Honchar see Natalka Poklad, ed., *Master, abo terny i lavry Ivana Honchara* (Kyiv, 2007).
156 See the letters and reports sent to Petro Shelest, in TsDAHOU, f. 1, op. 25, spr. 515, ark. 1–40.
157 Report, 2 November 1971, in TsDAHOU, f. 1, op. 25, spr. 546, ark. 75–81. The definition of anti-Soviet ideology is on ark. 78.
158 Ibidem, ark. 79.

Moroz to other *shistdesiatnyky* still at large—Ivan Dziuba, Viacheslav Chornovil, and Borys Antonenko-Davydovych—so as to discredit them.[159] Despite a letter of protest from the Canadian Embassy in Kyiv denouncing the illegality of Moroz's trial,[160] the KGB ignored such international pressure and had prepared propagandistic and practical instruments for a new wave of repressions.

The 1972 Pogrom

Starting on 12 January 1972, a series of arrests swept through the Soviet Union. In Ukraine many intellectuals were subjected to home searches and arrested, some of which were connected to the 4 January arrest of Yaroslav Dobosh, a Belgian citizen of Ukrainian descent, was detained at the Ukrainian-Czechoslovakian border and accused of smuggling anti-Soviet materials and being an agent of a capitalist country. Among those arrested were Leonid Pliushch, Mykola Plakhotniuk, Vasyl Stus, Ivan Svitlychny, Yevhen Sverstiuk, Danylo Shumuk, Viacheslav Chornovil, Mykhailo Osadchy, Ivan Hel, and Iryna Stasiv. Others, like Ivan Dziuba and Zynoviia Franko, were initially only searched, but the KGB subsequently detained and intensively interrogated them.[161] News about the arrests spread throughout the *samvydav* network. As soon as the Reuters news agency broke the news in the West, both the Ukrainian community abroad and the international press reacted strongly.[162] But the Soviet authorities did not desist from continuing their repressions, which lasted through all of 1972. Included in these operations was Nadia Svitlychna's arrest, which resulted in the placement of her two-year-old son in an orphanage.[163]

The KGB had been monitoring those they would arrest in 1972 for some time. In March 1969 Svitlychna was searched as she was leaving a library and was found in possession of samizdat copies of Abdurakhman

---

159 Letter, 25 March 1971, from Pavlo Fedchenko, head of the CC CPU's Department of Agitation and Propaganda, to the CC CPU about the KGB's proposal, in TsDAHOU, f. 1, op. 25, spr. 546, ark. 82–83.
160 Also preserved in this file on ark. 84–92.
161 The first information on the arrests was given by *Ukraïns'kyi visnyk*, see *The Ukrainian Herald*, issue 6, *Dissent in Ukraine: An Underground Journal from Soviet Ukraine*, 15–20.
162 See Rostyslav L. Khom'iak, "Sichnevi areshty ta reaktsiia svitu" and the open letter signed by Ukrainian émigré intellectuals, "Vidozva v spravi ostannikh podii na Ukraïni," *Suchasnist'*, 1972, no. 3: 113–22; and "Lystivka z Ukraïny pro areshty diiachiv ukraïns'koï kul'tury," *Suchasnist'*, 1972, no. 9: 108–109.
163 "'Khronika potochykh podii' pro represiï na Ukraïni," *Suchasnist'*, 1972, no. 9: 121.

Avtorkhanov's *Tekhnologiia vlasti*.[164] She was interrogated along with many of her friends and acquaintances. Viktor Bondarchuk revealed many details about the life of the Kyiv and Moscow nonconformist circles, but no one was arrested.[165] The KGB compiled materials that would provide an outline of the activities of the *shistdesiatnyky* and allow the secret police to anticipate their movements and strike them hard in the next few years. The *shistdesiatnyky* were psychologically prepared for their impending arrests: as this chapter's epigraph shows, they did not react with fear but courageously confronted their fate. Many, like Mykhailyna Kotsiubynska, refused to supply any information about their friends, and all of them demanded that the authorities respect legality.

On 20 January 1972, Ivan Svitlychny lectured the KGB agents interrogating him about his political views in an unusually long discourse. In his confession he documented his position. The knowledge that they would certainly be convicted seemed to hearten the victims of this political pogrom, and they decided they might as well use the opportunity to declare their beliefs. Svitlychny's statement on *shistdesiatnytstvo* is an extraordinary document that is worth quoting nearly in its entirety.

> Answering the question "In what sense is the broadening and deepening of democracy considered possible and desirable?"—a question that concerns my comrades who call themselves democrats—is more or less thoroughly difficult, but under the conditions of imprisonment it is completely impossible....
>
> If democracy has to be widened and deepened, it means that the people who believe this has to be done think that democracy is in a poor and inadequate condition in relation to [Soviet] society's present state and needs. In my circle of friends this [view] is common, and sometimes I would even agree....

---

164 Avtorkhanov (1908–97) was a Chechen Soviet historian who fell victim to the Yezhov Terror in 1937. He was released in 1942 by the NKVD and sent to Chechnia to infiltrate the anti-Soviet Chechen circles. There he immediately defected to the Germans, and after the Second World War he emigrated to the United States. He worked at the US Army Russian Institute and participated in the establishment of Radio Liberty and the Institute for the Study of the USSR in Munich. *Stalin and the Soviet Communist Party: A Study in the Technology of Power* (New York, 1959), a translation of Avtorkhanov's *Tekhnologiia vlasti*, which circulated in samizdat, is an extraordinary source of information about Stalin's rule.

165 The first file about the Svitlychnys was begun in 1969, starting with the interrogation of Nadia Svitlychna about Avtorkhanov's book. See DASBU, spr. 58114fp, vol. 1, ark. 1–235.

When founding the Soviet state, Lenin stressed particularly that, contrary to the bourgeois [state], which is substantially a representative democracy, the Soviet government must establish, develop, and cultivate various forms of "direct democracy"—that is, a democracy where the masses could express their will and decide on the state's most important issues not through their representatives but by themselves, in person. This would be accomplished through referendums or plebiscites, which are called to resolve problems of the state through polling either the entire population of the country [the USSR] or a single republic, territory, or oblast.

Of course, at the beginning of the formation of the Soviet state we could not yet talk about a broad development of direct democracy, because the exploiting classes had just been pushed out of power; they still significantly influenced the life of the country, [however], and in case [there had been] a referendum they could have seriously warped the will of the people. Therefore Lenin, speaking about the necessity of developing forms of direct democracy, considered their full development would happen in the future.

But after Lenin's death the forms of direct democracy did not undergo the development they were supposed to have had under the system of Soviet power. They have not been developed even since Stalin's death. After the Twentieth CPSU Congress many reforms were made in our country, but none of them concerned direct democracy. Even the economic reform that is being carried out now gives great rights to institutions and their organizations, but only in the person of their directors and leaders; the rights of the workers themselves have changed negligibly. In order to understand how poorly the forms of direct democracy are developed in each country, one has to consider this fact: after the war our country experienced a series of historical turning points; in its sociopolitical life important and cardinal changes took place that affected everyone's direct interests. But during all this time not a single referendum was carried out, not a single plebiscite that would reveal the will of the people directly.

All of the most important decisions have been made by the government, by the Supreme Soviets—which are representative organs. The population, in the best of cases, only took part in the *discussion* of any given question (and not even in an inclusive way but only through representatives), and it was never given the opportunity to deal with these problems directly....

Direct democracy is poorly developed even in the workers' assemblies. Generally, the [Party] meetings of factories, institutions, or organizations (which could make crucial decisions in many ways) consider questions of only secondary importance: daily conditions, training for the collective, and so on; in very rare cases they decide about implementation of a plan, but the plan is already written down, not devised by them. On questions of organizational structure, leadership, and other important issues, they do not have a decisive word, and the leadership does not take them into account.

Such a state of direct democracy is, in my opinion, a serious obstacle to the development of true Soviet power in our country, and this concerns me and my friends. The governance and development of direct democracy is an ideal that we lean toward, and in the realization of which we would all like to assist.

But the concept of direct democracy is much less than the concept of democracy overall in the USSR. Direct democracy cannot replace representative democracy; the fact is that both forms of democracy—direct and representative—await [integration] as never before, and both have to be developed to the highest degree. At this time, the organs of representative democracy such as the soviets, from the rural ones to the Supreme Soviet, are also not as developed as the present level of sociopolitical development of the people of the soviets, who elect them "democratically" only in the sense that all electors have the same rights. But, at the same time, the electors all lack some essential rights. The word "elections" itself [in Ukrainian: *vybory*, from *vybyraty* 'to choose'] means that the electors can *choose* among some candidates. As it stands, it is clear that in elections of state organs only one candidate is running; therefore, there is no choice, and the electors *vote but do not choose*. The election of deputies from among a few candidates, or at least between two, would corroborate the power of the soviets, for the deputy chosen in such a way would better represent all of the people, but for some reason that is not done. This profoundly concerns those people to whom I belong and who call themselves democrats and see the development of Soviet society in this way: the necessity of corroborating the legitimate foundations of the bodies of authority.

Moreover, against the background of such serious contraction and restriction of various forms of democracy in the USSR, centralizing tendencies have been manifested excessively in all spheres of state, society, and community life. The current constitution today, sometimes deliberately contrary to the Stalinist constitution, differs significantly in this respect from the constitution adopted during Lenin's lifetime. At the time of that first Soviet constitution, the Soviet republics had sufficiently broad competencies (especially for those times), which expressed the Leninist idea of a Soviet *federation* of socialist republics. But after Lenin's death, Stalin turned to his own idea of "autonomization," kept secret from Lenin, and thus in the "Stalinist" constitution the republics' competencies were seriously degraded and reduced.... Still, in the first half of the 1960s the Soviet and Party activists ascertained the inadequacy of the new constitution, given the unequal levels of the country's sociopolitical development, and formed a constitutional committee led by Nikita Khrushchev. The committee was continued by Brezhnev, but to date we have not seen any outcome of its work, even though it has existed for nearly ten years. And in practical life there is no sign that any step has been taken toward substantial decentralization—or toward the development of democratization—of our country's social system. And this really holds back the masses' initiative, grassroots control, and social independence.

In addition, it seems that many clauses even of this, in many respects, aged constitution are not being implemented. For example, an important achievement of the Soviet government is the inclusion in the constitution of freedom of expression to each citizen of the USSR. At the same time, however, the criminal code and the practice of Soviet society often bring this freedom to naught.

Freedom of expression means that everyone can say anything they believe in, about whomever or whatever fact. Do the citizens of the USSR have this right? Can anyone say publicly that one of our state workers (it does not matter who) does not carry out his duties and has to be replaced? Of course not. Such acts are qualified in our society as anti-Soviet propaganda and agitation, and whoever says something like that is severely punished. One can seriously disagree with what [Valentyn] Moroz has written, but do not even think of considering his works anti-Soviet propaganda and agitation when freedom of expression is guaranteed by the constitution. I have no doubt that even these notes—which I am writing now as though I were writing in completely different conditions—are going to be evaluated as anti-Soviet propaganda and agitation (and that maybe even these last words will be so considered); nonetheless, in writing them I naturally do not have any anti-Soviet mission.

... Dmytro Dontsov's ideology is fascist, and I do not sympathize with it. But I want to know about it. And to know it, one has to read his writings. But if I ask for his works from somebody, I put the person who gives them to me under a great threat, for it is called "distribution of anti-Soviet literature" and severely punished as anti-Soviet propaganda and agitation—independently from who reads it or supplies it, [or] whether he approves of or condemns what he reads. In my case, this situation is happening regarding the

> article "Word of the Nation." At the same time, according to freedom of expression as citizens of the USSR, we should be able to read such literature freely, as well as any other literature of this kind, and maybe even study it at university, as they now study idealistic philosophy even if it contradicts Marxist philosophy.
>
> Under the concept of "anti-Soviet, "slanderous,"and so on (concepts that have come into use in contemporary [Soviet] society) one can subsume, and often is subsumed, much that not only undermines but also [even] abrogates the freedom of speech, [and] declares restrictions on Soviet democracy, and with painful hearts the circle of my friends discuss this and strive to do what they can to affirm the constitutional right of freedom of expression.
>
> I do not want to name the comrades with whom I have discussed these questions, for even that could be considered anti-Soviet propaganda and agitation and they could be severely punished.[166]

Svitlychny was broadly a supporter of democracy, both direct and representative. He was convinced that the lack of democracy was the reason for the narrowing of the Soviet Union's social base, and that Lenin had promoted a proper democracy, which Stalin corrupted. He condemned Stalin and his successors for not being able to put the principles of Marxism-Leninism into practice, and he lamented the Soviet state's violations of freedom of expression. For Svitlychny the practice of accusing those who expressed their own free thoughts of anti-Soviet propaganda was one of the most dangerous restrictions to democracy, and it hindered the possibility of criticizing the Soviet *nomenklatura* that was not carrying out its duty of serving the state and society. Svitlychny disagreed with the views of Valentyn Moroz and Dmytro Dontsov, but he defended their right to express their thoughts. Ultimately he did not utter a word against the Soviet Union or its ideology, and he declared he was a loyal Soviet citizen.

Although he had not been arrested yet, one of the greatest victims of this so-called political pogrom was Ivan Dziuba. During his interrogation in January 1972 he tried to explain why he wrote *Internationalism or Russification?*

> There was a general feeling that we needed some sort of explanation or statement on [the national] question. The official sources were silent. Among those who widely disagreed with the state's

---

166 Svitlychny's interrogation on 20 January 1972, DASBU, spr. 68805fp, vol. 1, ark. 299–309.

nationality policy, it was hard also find someone who also wanted to make a principled statement openly and address the question in depth. Therefore it fell to me to do it—not because I considered myself someone who was particularly prepared for the task. On the contrary, I strongly wished and waited for someone else to take on this task ... That is how *Internationalism or Russification?* arose.

In this work I wanted to present [my] understanding of facts that troubled a significant part of Ukrainian society; I wanted to explain why my friends and I—[and] why many other, absolutely different people, independently from one another, in various regions of Ukraine—consider the state of Ukrainian language and culture to be unsatisfactory and believe that serious changes are needed in the implementation of nationality policy and that it is necessary to bring the practice into line with theory, because sometimes in our [country] fine Leninist principles are proclaimed in theory but nothing of the sort is done in reality.[167]

After 1991 Dziuba would reiterate these reasons. The *shistdesiatnyky* continued telling the truth, even when questioned by the KGB, for they were convinced that they had not committed any crime. Dziuba did not limit himself to stating that the Soviet nationality policy was inadequate; he wanted to say that all of the abnormalities in that policy originated not from the principles communism and Leninism but from the violations and distortions of these principles.[168]

Dziuba believed that the only real problem with his treatise was the fact that it had been published in the West and had been exploited by anti-Soviet propaganda, which he in no way endorsed. He stated that after the publicity about his painful expulsion from the SPU, he had tried to return to his work. But because there was an official ban on publishing him, he was unable to refute the misinterpretations of his thoughts. He insisted that none of the materials confiscated from his apartment could be considered anti-Soviet.

> But in any case I remain a Soviet citizen—a person who believes in the basic elements of our life and in the ideals of communism, but also a person who does not tolerate deviation from these elements, distortion of these principles, who does not say yes to everything unscrupulously; [I remain] a person who has his own opinion on

---

167 Dziuba's interrogation on 15 January 1972, DASBU, spr. 69260fp, tom. 1, ark. 203–204.
168 Ibidem, ark. 207.

issues and their circumstances; [and] a person concerned not with his own welfare but with the common good, with the welfare of his people.¹⁶⁹

Dziuba reclaimed a different, genuine way of being a Soviet citizen by highlighting his concern for the common good. By professing his Soviet identity, he was accusing the authorities of ignoring the principles of communism.

Meanwhile the Soviet authorities were preparing a decisive condemnation of the *shistdesiatnytstvo* movement. A commission led by Andrii Skaba and comprising the critics Yurii Zbanatsky and Mykola Shamota, among others, analyzed *Internationalism or Russification?* and reached conclusions similar to those in "Bohdan Stenchuk's" pamphlet, denouncing Dziuba as a "bourgeois nationalist" and an enemy of the Soviet Union.¹⁷⁰ The commission's task was made easier by some *shistdesiatnyky* who capitulated under the pressure of their interrogations. The first to do so was Zynoviia Franko in January, who provided details about the others' activities. She was interrogated with a special focus on the relations the *shistdesiatnyky* had with foreigners, and she informed on many of their friends in the Ukrainian diaspora. One such case was that of the Vira Selianska (aka Wira Selansky, pseud.: Vira Vovk), a Ukrainian émigré poet and literary scholar at the Catholic University of Rio de Janeiro who had strong ties with Ivan Svitlychny.¹⁷¹ Franko was questioned about how the *shistdesiatnyky* produced and sent *samvydav* materials abroad. She revealed that she had lent Dziuba her printing machine and that he had given a copy of *Internationalism or Russification?* to Mykola Mushynka (b. 1936), a Ukrainian graduate student from Slovakia at Kyiv State University who was searched and had the manuscript confiscated at the Soviet-Slovak border.¹⁷²

The authorities needed a recantation for their victory to be complete, so they forced Franko to write an open letter that was published in *Radians'ka Ukraïna* on 2 March 1972. In this letter she claimed she had

---

169 Ibidem, ark. 219.
170 The report is included in the file on Dziuba in DASBU, spr. 69260fp, vol. 1, ark. 104–19, which was published in Dziuba, *Internatsionalizm chy rusyfikatsiia?*, 284–99.
171 See Franko's interrogations in DASBU, spr. 69260fp, vol. 3, ark. 45–60.
172 Ibidem, ark. 72–125. After over two decades of political persection in Czechoslovakia, Mushynka (in Slovak: Mikuláš Mušinka) became a professor at Prešov University in 1990. He is a renowned scholar of Ukrainian folklore, literature, and art.

realized that she had committed a crime and caused harm to the Soviet motherland. Franko disparaged the Western press that claimed the wave of arrests was unjust.

> I understand entirely my guilt and deeply condemn all my actions, which caused harm to my fatherland.
> I also understood why the enemies of the [Soviet] Ukrainian people fixated on my family name, Franko, why they needed me. They were trying to exploit in an anti-Soviet way the surname of my great-grandfather—the ardent internationalist, the revolutionary democrat Ivan Franko.[173]

In her public recantation Franko urged everyone who cared about the fate of the Soviet Union to realize their faults and take the proper side. Although she was not an important writer of *samvydav*, she was an important *shistdesiatnyk*. Her confession was a great defeat for the *shistdesiatnytstvo* movement.

On the same day that Franko's letter was published, Dziuba was summoned to appear before the SPU's leadership and discovered that the union's presidium was again putting forward a motion to expel him. All of the presidium's members condemned Dziuba's activity as anti-Soviet. Even Dmytro Pavlychko did not dare to defend him, which he had in the past, and condemned Dziuba's unwillingness to distance himself from his treatise. Their main accusation was: after Dziuba made his 1970 statement, he had not kept his promise to return to the fold and had not written anything publishable since then. When Dziuba protested, saying that publishers had rejected all of his submissions, he was told that he could not expect a Soviet periodical to publish anything by an author of anti-Soviet books published in the West. Commenting on Dziuba's expulsion from the SPU, Liubomyr Dmyterko told him:

> The fact that you will not be a member of the Union does not mean that all is lost. You still will be a literary man, and you will publish, but first you have to dissociate yourself from your work and from your supporters abroad.[174]

---

173 The letter was published in *Suchasnist'*, 1972, no. 5: 86–87. Ivan Franko (1856–1916) was a prominent and influential Galician Ukrainian writer, journalist, scholar, and socialist who lived for most of his life in Lviv.
174 The minutes of Dziuba's meeting with the SPU's presidium are in Dziuba, *Internatsionalizm chy rusyfikatsiia?*, 300–320. Dmyterko's words are on 312.

Dziuba's expulsion from the SPU was a necessary step in facilitating his imminent arrest, which took place on 18 April 1972 after he had been weakened by nearly three months of continuous interrogation. From that point on he was kept in prison, where his tuberculosis worsened every day.

Throughout 1972 and 1973 the trials of *shistdesiatnyky* proved to be a great success for the Soviet authorities. Nadia Svitlychna was sentenced to four years in prison; Plakhotniuk and Vasyl Stus, to five years in prison and three in a labour camp; Iryna Stasiv-Kalynets, to six years in prison and three in a labour camp; Ihor Kalynets, Mykhailo Osadchy, and Viacheslav Chornovil, to seven years in prison and three in a labour camp; Yevhen Sverstiuk, to seven years in prison and five in a labour camp; and Ivan Hel, to ten years in prison camps in Mordovia and Perm Oblast and five years' exile in the Komi ASSR.[175] During the next five years a purge ensued that affected many Ukrainian cultural and academic institutions and resulted in the dismissal of thousands of staffers and cultural figures. [176] The Soviet authorities had decided that internal opposition would not be allowed to flourish the way it had during the 1960s.

Dziuba was sentenced to five years in prison and five years' exile. But as he related to me, in October 1973 the worsening of his tuberculosis, his complete isolation from the outside world, and the impossibility of knowing what was happening in the Soviet Union defeated him. He petitioned the Soviet authorities for mercy, who demanded that he make a public statement. In our interview, Dziuba confirmed that he was motivated by the conviction that he could better serve the cause of change as a free man rather than an imprisoned one. He also said:

> I came to the conclusion that I would do more if I went back to my work. I also hoped that my friends would see I repented not out of conformism but to do something important, and therefore that they would, at least to a certain extent, understand my action.[177]

---

175 The details of these and other sentences are in *The Ukrainian Herald, Issue 7–8: Ethnocide of Ukrainians in the U.S.S.R., Spring 1974. An Underground Journal from Soviet Ukraine*, comp. Maksym Sahaydak, intro. by Robert Conquest, trans. and ed. Olena Saciuk and Bohdan Yasen (Baltimore, Paris, and Toronto, 1976), 138–40.
176 Ibidem, 141–51.
177 "Tsia knyzhka zminyla use moie zhyttia: Rozmova z Ivanom Dziuboiu," 149.

Dziuba was released and worked as a copy-editor at the Antonov Plant in Kyiv. His recantation was published on 9 November 1973 in *Literaturna Ukraïna*. In it he stated:

> Now I clearly understand that for many years, painfully reacting to single shortcomings or complex events, approaching them one-sidedly, I displayed an incorrect understanding of the present state of national relations in the USSR ...
>
> [*Internationalism or Russification?*] contained a profoundly inaccurate interpretation of a series of national problems, of the internationalist nature of our socialist society, and treated them in a distorted way, and [it] was in fact an attack on the Party's nationality policy.[178]

Dziuba announced that he had begun studying the nationality question again during his imprisonment and that he was going to write a book to highlight all of the errors he had previously committed. He declared that he wanted to distance himself from bourgeois nationalism and all those who had exploited his work in the West.

> The Dziuba who had allowed others to make him the talk of the town, and who wasted years of his life in political circumlocutions, does not exist anymore and will not exist again. Instead there is a person who is suffering from the awareness of his clumsy mistakes and of the time wasted, who wants and thinks of one thing only: to work and work, in order to compensate at least partially for the losses and rectify the mistakes.[179]

At the end Dziuba expressed his desire to find employment alongside representatives of the working class in order to feel the atmosphere of a labour collective. According to recantation, the old Dziuba had ceased to exist and had been replaced by "orthodox" Soviet Dziuba. His recantation was considered a betrayal by the other *shistdesiatnyky*, and it actually became the final act of *shistdesiatnytstvo* as a social phenomenon. Dziuba's statement represented the victory of Soviet repressions over the attempts of the *shistdesiatnyky* to convince the Soviet authorities of the need for

---

178 Ivan Dziuba, "Do redaktsiï hazety 'Liternaturna Ukraïna': Zaiava," *Literaturna Ukraïna*, 9 November 1973.
179 Ibidem

change. The victory was temporary, however, for the Soviet Union did not survive, but the question of why Dziuba recanted lingered.

Bohdan Nahaylo examined Dziuba's *Internationalism or Russification?* to verify whether Dziuba's interpretation of Lenin's thinking was correct. Nahaylo posited that "in his [Dziuba's] study Lenin is presented in a biased, idealized manner, as a sort of unblemished, omniscient hero. Moreover, several of Dziuba's statements about Lenin are based on very flimsy supporting evidence or are factually misleading."[180] Apart from the impossibility of conducting free research in the Soviet Union, Nahaylo provides Dziuba with another justification for his superficial treatment of Lenin's ideology: "it is plausible that in this study [*Internationalism or Russification?*], by means of irony, insinuation, and the drawing of particular historical parallels, Dziuba is delivering a veiled criticism."[181] According to Nahaylo, Dziuba was somehow trying to suggest that "Lenin's statements remained only declarative" and to emphasize the "historical continuity of Russian chauvinism and concomitant Russification." There is no question about the second of these two points, as the parallel between tsarist Russia and the Soviet Union is clearly stated in Dziuba's book. What Nahaylo seeks to discover is whether Dziuba sincerely believed in Marxism-Leninism or was trying to use Leninism as a rhetorical weapon. In my opinion, both answers are true. In his interviews he gave after 1991 (including to me), Dziuba justified his adherence to the principles of Marxism-Leninism as an adherence to ideals of justice and equality that were denied in the reality of the Soviet Union. But to the direct question of whether he was a Communist he replied "No, only in the sense…[etc.]."

Unfortunately, I was not able to ask this question in the 1960s, but someone else was. Roman Serbyn, having read Dziuba's book and being tormented by this same question, was determined to ask Dziuba during his visit to Kyiv in 1970 whether he sincerely believed in the Ukrainophile Lenin of his book, or whether he had used him as a rhetorical device. When asked if he believed that "Lenin really acknowledged the right of the nations to self-determination, Dziuba answered positively and, for instance, cited Finland."[182] But Serbyn persisted in his questioning, giving

---

180 Bohdan P. Nahaylo, "Dziuba's *Internationalism or Russification?* Revisited: A Reappraisal of Dziuba's Treatment of Leninist Nationalities Policy," *Journal of Ukrainian Graduate Studies* 2, no. 2 (Fall 1977): 32.
181 Ibidem, 51.
182 Roman Serbyn, "Moia persha zustrich z Ivanov Dziuboiu," *Suchasnist'*, 2001, nos. 7–8, 125.

Dziuba the opportunity to express the complexity of his thoughts. Dziuba admitted "with a wistful smile" that Lenin would "likely not" have granted independence to Ukraine.[183]

As Yurii Shapoval has noted, when Dziuba acknowledged on 10 January 1973 that *Internationalism or Russification?* "objectively had an anti-Soviet significance and has been exploited by anti-Soviet propaganda," he had been broken down by years of interrogations and nine months in prison. During this time he had to defend himself from the accusation of authoring a truly nationalistic piece, the "Program of the U-Communists," which led him to write a 312-page treatise to prove the accusation wrong.[184]

Dziuba was an educated and intelligent Soviet citizen who questioned his world view in his search for the truth. *Internationalism or Russification?* and his subsequent statements should not be seen as the final product of his search but, instead, as an intermediate stage the painful process of an entire generation questioning the principles of the society in which it had been brought up. The condemnation of the crimes of the Soviet Union and the doubts about the righteousness of Marxism-Leninism existed alongside the hope that the USSR could realize the ideals it declared that it followed and that taught to its youth. For Dziuba in 1973, this process had not yet been completed.

Dziuba's recantation in 1972 reinforced his continued unwillingness to play a political role in the *shistdesiatnytstvo* movement. He realized that most of the reasons for his imprisonment were linked with the political exploitation of his writings. As a literary man in a serious personal intellectual and political crisis, Dziuba sought a way to shed his political persona and took refuge in his literary work. Although he embraced his role as the intellectual voice of *shistdesiatnytstvo*, he never aspired to be its political leader. Hence he did not conceive of his 1973 statement as a betrayal of the movement, for he had never agreed to be its leader. By his statement Dziuba voluntarily signed his own sentence to remain silent as the condition for his release. His silence would last until the early 1980s and would be broken more by the disintegration of the Soviet regime than by the dissidents' activity. Ukraine did not have its own Dubček, but it became clear that it would also not have its own Václav Havel after 1991.

---

183 Ibidem.
184 Iurii Shapoval, "Internatsionalizm iak rusyfikatsiia, abo Shcho i iak obstoiuvav Ivan Dziuba 40 rokiv tomu," in Dziuba, *Internatsionalizm chy rusyfikatsiia?*, 25–26.

The Repression of Minds

During the late 1960s and early 1970s the KGB developed a new method of repression and imprisonment: hospitalization of intellectuals in psychiatric institutions and forced "medication" with substances that debilitated mental faculties. The best-known victim of this form of torture among the *shistdesiatnyky* was Leonid Pliushch—who, not coincidentally, in the last few years before he was deprived of his freedom, had begun studying psychology and parapsychology and dared to challenge official Soviet psychological research. Mykola Plakhotniuk and Anatolii Lupynis were also incarcerated for considerable periods in the "special" mental hospital in Dnipropetrovsk.

A comprehensive analysis of the punitive psychiatry conducted at Soviet mental hospitals is difficult because of the nature and scarcity of relevant records. The "special" mental hospitals where dissidents were hospitalized in Ukraine were run by the republic's Ministry of the Interior, which employed common criminals as paramedics and KGB personnel in the medical posts. This situation favoured obscurity, because none of these employees had an interest in the preservation of memory.[185] Therefore the main source of information about the repressions committed in those institutions is the memories of those who were incarcerated—memories that are undoubtedly limited by the prisoners' weakened mental faculties because they had been forcibly injected with various debilitating drugs and had recovered their faculties only after they had been released.

Unlike the intellectuals arrested in the first wave of Soviet repressions in 1965, the *shistdesiatnyky* imprisoned in 1972 mobilized and developed a strategy that focused on forcing KGB agents to follow the letter of the law and on exploiting any opportunity to publicly monitor investigations as prescribed by legislation. This was why Pliushch and his wife, one day before being arrested, had gone to witness Dziuba's apartment being searched. To punish them for this interference, Tania Pliushch was subjected to a personal search that included an inspection of her mouth and of the linings of her clothes. Through its invasive tactics, the KGB was trying to undermine the dignity of the *shistdesiatnyky*.

> Tanya returned furious. "The bitch slit my panties," she whispered. "She cut her finger and dirtied me with her blood." We realized that

---

185 Clementi, *Storia del dissenso sovietico*, 158–60.

they wanted to degrade us and to goad us into a hysterical outburst.[186]

But the Pliushches did not lose their temper. That night, once they had returned to their apartment, they selected and burned part of their collection of *samvydav* documents, destroying the pieces that could be used against other *shistdesiatnyky*. Leonid sardonically described the search of their apartment that took place the following morning.

> An impatient, insolent ringing at the door awakened me. The agents rushed in like bandits with frightened expressions. Why were they always frightened? No one was throwing bombs at them yet. Were they pumping themselves up with courage for their dangerous work?[187]

The Soviet police seemed more afraid than the person they were seeking to arrest. As is clear from the exchange of words between Pliushch and the head of the search team, the fear of raising a scandal in Western public opinion was omnipresent: "That's all right, Leonid Ivanovych. We're not afraid of the West."[188] Pliushch's composure was not affected by the hints dropped about his probable condemnation and committal to a mental hospital.

> "Are you trying to ascribe megalomania to me and to lock me up in a *psikhushka*?" I asked.
> "How can you say that, Leonid Ivanovych? We don't send people to mental institutions. Only psychiatrists do that. And you're perfectly normal."

---

186 Plyushch, *History's Carnival*, 254.
187 Ibidem, 256. The irony of these lines is better understood if compared with Solzhenitsyn's famous description of his arrest: "That's all there is to it! You are arrested! And you'll find nothing better to respond with than a lamblike bleat: 'Me? What for?' That's what arrest is: it's a blinding flash and a blow which shifts the present instantly into the past and the impossible into omnipotent actuality.... The sharp nighttime ring or the rude knock at the door. The insolent entrance of the unwiped jackboots of the unsleeping State Security Operatives"(Aleksandr I. Solzhenitsyn, *The Gulag Archipelago, 1918–1956: An Experiment in Literary Investigation, I–II*, trans. Thomas P. Whitney [Boulder, 1991], 4).
188 Plyushch, *History's Carnival*, 257. Pliushch noted the false ring of this expression of self-confidence. Commenting on the international pressure for his release, he wrote: "And yet they were afraid when they blackmailed Tanya and then begged her not to inform the West [about] when and how I would be released" (Ibidem).

> I remembered that it was KGB men, not psychiatrists, who had diagnosed me as schizophrenic in 1969, when Oleg Bakhtiarov's case was under investigation.[189]

This threat would crop up again in Pliushch's mind on the third day of his arrest when he was awaiting his first interrogation and thinking of his and his family's destinies.

> By evening I realized that things would go badly for me if I didn't develop a psychological method for dealing with life in prison. My fear for my family and friends could become irrational. I had to think about the past instead. I also had to avoid thinking about the future. I had already decided that I would either be given the maximum sentence in a labor camp or be sent to a *psikhushka*.... Later I discovered that my ideas about the *psikhushka*s had been all wrong. The patients were not interesting psychologically, because their behavior was distorted by drugs, and the neuroleptics I was given prevented me from carrying out observations.
>
> Having prepared myself for the very worst, I almost stopped thinking about it.[190]

The Soviet regime had developed one of the most frightful instruments to reduce intellectuals' opposition to silence, striking those faculties that made intellectuals who they were and allowed them to take part in civil life. The intelligentsia feared that being medicated would prevent them from carrying out their role as a nationally conscious vanguard, which was their defining characteristic.

The interrogations and psychiatric forensic tests relied heavily on fear-mongering tactics. The agent questioning Pliushch "immediately set about intimidating me: I'd get a stiff sentence, my wife would go to prison, and all my friends would be arrested."[191] Friendly proposals, such as writing a letter to his wife, sparked Pliushch's suspicion: "They're trying to extract something from the letter, I thought. Or perhaps they want to make me homesick and upset my balance."[192]

---

[189] Ibidem, 256. Bakhtiarov (b. 1948) is a Russian psychologist who studied in Kyiv and was castigated for his innovative techniques.
[190] Ibidem, 261.
[191] Ibidem, 266.
[192] Ibidem, 265.

It was the inevitability of being imprisoned in a psychiatric institution that encouraged Pliushch not to betray his ideals and his friends, for he considered his impending fate to be less difficult than the loss of his principles.

> When it became clear to me that I was sure to be sent to a *psikhushka*, I tried to face the problem honestly. On the one hand there was the danger of losing my mind from the confinement with mental patients and the treatment. Going mad, losing my wife and children was terrible. But what would happen if I betrayed my principles? I might gain my freedom, at a relatively small price. I could even avoid testifying against my friends and simply write a letter of repentance to a newspaper, repudiating my views and accusing myself of hostility toward the people. And then what? I'd lose my wife's and my friends' respect. Even the loyal subjects of the regime would despise me. Only alcoholism or a bullet in the brain would be left. In the end I would lose more than if I went mad in a *psikhushka*. My fear of the consequences of betrayal far outweighed my fear of confinement in a psychiatric prison.[193]

These lines, even if they were not conceived as such, sound like a reprimand of those who did surrender to the authorities. Pliushch's fear of losing his loved ones' respect won out over the instinctive, primordial fear of punishment. During the psychiatric forensic test, he sensed that this anxiety was not only felt by victims of repression, but also harboured by Soviet institutions toward their citizens. He said to the doctor examining him,

> How strange—the bourgeois countries are not afraid of their Communist parties, of Lenin's writings, or of *Pravda*. But in our country everything is feared. What sort of ideology is it that is afraid of other ideologies? And yet it boasts that it is invincible! More than fifty-five years have passed since the Revolution, and yet there's still a fear that the people will side with capitalism if they read the writings of a bourgeois thinker.[194]

Imprisoning dissidents in special psychiatric hospitals was a convenient means of diminishing this fear. It was not possible to

---

193 Ibidem, 271.
194 Ibidem, 296.

acknowledge these figures as dissidents, for that would be too destabilizing for the Communist regime, but labelling them as insane provided a neat solution.[195]

Pliushch's self-confidence abandoned him as soon as he arrived at the psychiatric hospital in Dnipropetrovsk. Inside that *psikhushka* the terror regime had the opportunity to exercise its draconian methods of drug therapy. Its favourite tool was injecting dissidents with haloperidol, an antipsychotic drug that causes many painful and harmful effects. This strategy was effective from the beginning, and Pliushch, who had evaded torture to this point, admitted to being terrified.[196]

After the start of such "treatments," Pliushch's recollections of his time in the "madhouse" became shorter and more confused: of the 379 pages in his "Dissident Autobiography," only twenty-six are dedicated to describing his three-year stay there. His description of an average day therein is one of widespread abuse.

> [the orderlies] also amused themselves by taunting patients who wanted to go to the lavatory....
>
> When the orderlies had tired of that game, they would goad two patients to fight. "He said that you're a queen!" "And he's a stinking faggot!" the other would retort. An exchange of obscenities would take place; someone would take a swipe, and the fight would be on. Sulphur would be ordered: the patients had "got excited."[197]

Sulphur injections were a key ingredient of the hospital's fear strategy.

> Sulphur was regarded as the worst punishment. After an injection of sulphur the patient's temperature would rise to 40° C; the site of the injection would be painful, and the patient could neither walk around nor lie down. Many patients developed hemorrhoids as a result of sulphur injections. The doses would gradually be increased, then decreased. In Section 12, a course of treatment with sulphur usually involved ten to fifteen injections. Everyone spoke with fear about Section 9: the doses there were larger and a course involved twenty to twenty-five injections.[198]

---

195 *Psychiatric Abuse of Political Prisoners in the Soviet Union: Testimony by Leonid Plyushch* (Washington, 1976), 16.
196 Tatiana Khodorovich, ed., *Istoriia bolezni Leonida Pliushcha* (Amsterdam, 1974), 29.
197 Plyushch, *History's Carnival*, 321.
198 Ibidem, 309.

At the top of the terror pyramid were the doctors. Pliushch provides an acerbic description of the first doctor he encountered.

> The inmates called [Ella] Kamenetskaya "Ilse Koch" or "Ellochka the Cannibal." The height of her cynicism occurred when she sat on the head of a patient who had called her "Ilse Koch." She laughed at the nickname—"You see how the men are afraid of me!" She desperately wanted to be thought of as an intelligent person ...[199]

After a short time, Pliushch was moved to Section 9, where he became acquainted with the terror methods of another doctor.

> Although the orderlies gave fewer beatings in Section 9, this was only because Nina Nikolayevna Bochkovskaya, the director of the section, held everyone in her iron grip. She is the one who should have been called Ilse Koch. Her voice was calm and assured, and her refined, cold face would light up occasionally with a contemptuous smile. By comparison with Bochkovskaya, Ellochka the Cannibal was simply a sexually obsessed hysteric.
>
> [Nina] Bochkovskaya refused to get involved in discussions with patients. She would dash into a ward and announce in a lifeless voice, "Petrov, you've been cursing the nurse again. Sulphur! Ivanov, I hear you've been masturbating. Haloperidol!" When an inmate complained about the pain, she replied, "That's all right. You'll stop and think about the sulphur before raping a girl again. You came here to be treated, not for a rest cure." To a patient who asked when he would recover she answered, "When I retire and you stop masturbating!" And to another inmate she said, "Your treatment is our business. We're paid for this. The sulphur will help you. Yes, it will hurt, but you're a man. You'll have to bear it. After all, you're being treated."[200]

Although the tortures and resulting lethargy did not alleviate Pliushch's fears, they did not force him to surrender. He continued rejecting the constant pressure to write a memo of self-condemnation. But drugs took a serious toll on his health.

---

199 Ibidem, 308. Ilse Koch was the wife of Karl Koch, the commander of the Buchenwald and Majdanek Nazi concentration camps. She was infamous for her passion for collecting patches of prisoners' tattooed skin.
200 Ibidem, 317.

> Although I tried to spit the drugs out when I could, they were killing my desire to read or think, and the mere idea of politics became thoroughly nauseating. My memory was slipping away, and my speech became jerky and abrupt. I was overcome by autism and misanthropy, and for days on end I lay on my bed and tried to sleep. The only thoughts that remained concerned smoking and bribing the orderlies for an extra trip to the lavatory. I even dreaded the visits I had longed for so desperately, because I was worried that Tanya might mention new arrests, and I did not want her to see my apathy and sleepiness or the dropsical swelling and convulsions that the drugs brought on. Visits from the children were particularly painful: I had to force a smile and try to make jokes.
>
> I was increasingly afraid that my deterioration was irreversible and that I might help my torturers by going mad. Despair at the thought that there might be no end to this hell led many healthy patients to contemplate suicide. I, too, was losing my will to live. I maintained a grip on myself only by saying over and over: I must not become embittered; I must not forget; I must not give up![201]

Reduced to a shadow of his former self, Pliushch experienced the Soviet regime's attempt to deprive him of his reason, yet he still refused to surrender completely. He was ultimately rescued from these tortures thanks to an international defence campaign on his behalf. Together with his family, he was allowed to emigrate to France in 1976.

Misplaced Hopes

Throughout the course of their activity, the *shistdesiatnyky* hoped that a member of the Soviet political establishment would side with them in their struggle. Many of them believed it would be Petro Shelest. Shelest's dismissal as first secretary of the CPU in May 1972 and the condemnation of his book *Our Soviet Ukraine* in April 1973 have been interpreted as evidence that he was a supporter of the Ukrainian national cause. Traces of this rather benevolent evaluation of Shelest's actions are present even in serious research, such as Yurii Shapoval's introduction to the Ukrainian edition of Shelest's memoirs: "[Shelest] identified his transfer to Moscow as 'the darkest day' of his life. That is how much Ukraine meant to him."[202]

---

201 Ibidem, 325.
202 Iurii Shapoval. "Petro Shelest u konteksti politychnoï istoriï Ukraïny XX stolittia," in Petro Shelest, *"Spravzhnii sud istoriï shche poperedu": Spohady, shchodennyky, dokumenty,*

Shapoval seems to attribute Shelest's sadness to his imposed departure from Ukraine, disregarding that he had already worked in Russia from 1946 to 1950. The reason behind Shelest's misery was likely far less sentimental: the transfer effectively marked the end of his political career, a fact that Shelest understood implicitly.

Shapoval clarifies that Shelest's removal did not in any way indicate that he had voiced discontent concerning the repressions of *shistdesiatnyky*. Rather, it was the result of a disagreement over economic policy between Shelest and Leonid Brezhnev—namely, the aspiration of the former to gain ever-increasing control over this domain: "Shelest's line was based on an original double loyalty—all-Union and republican, continuously maneuvering between two political discourses—centralizing and decentralizing.... Clearly, against the background of Brezhnevite hyper-centralism, the line of unification, and the policy of Russification, this activity on Shelest's part could quite easily be considered 'dangerous.'"[203] Could the *shistdesiatnyky* have believed that they could shoehorn their objectives into Shelest's vacillating policy in order to achieve some political result? Can the harsh criticism of Shelest's book be interpreted as a condemnation of a milder line toward the *shistdesiatnyky*?

Answering these questions would require a thorough examination of Shelest's activity, which is beyond the scope of this study. Nonetheless, some considerations can be discussed here, especially regarding the meaning of his contested book. Shelest was born in 1908 to a peasant family in Kharkiv gubernia and was a representative of the new ruling class promoted by the social transformations of Stalinism. He joined the Communist Party as a worker in 1928 and was recruited to study at Kharkiv's Communist University and the Kharkiv Engineering and Economics Institute. In the 1930s he served an engineer, manager, and director in metallurgical plants in Mariupol and Kharkiv and was the secretary of Kharkiv's Party Committee responsible for the defence industry in 1940 and 1941. In 1954 he was nominated second secretary of the CPU's city and oblast committees in Kyiv, and from February 1957 he served as first secretary of the oblast committee in recognition of his involvement in the oblast's rehabilitation commission. In July 1963 Shelest succeeded Mykola Pidhirny (Russian name: Nikolai Podgorny), who had

---

materialy (Kyiv, 2003), 6.
203 Ibidem, 11–12.

been appointed chairman of the Presidium of the Supreme Soviet in Moscow, as the CPU's first secretary. Despite his engagement in the rehabilitation commission, Shelest was a staunch Stalinist. Commenting on Stalin's death, he wrote in his diary:

> A genuinely devoted Leninist, principled and demanding with himself and his comrades-in-arms, a guide of the Party and the state. Modest in his manners, laconic, experienced in political and economic affairs. An authority, and not a "cult," as they made him afterwards. The civil war, the period of the restoration of the economy of the country, the first five-year plan, the difficult and complex period of the collectivization of agriculture—the first and decisive realization of Lenin's agricultural policy. The victory in the Great Patriotic War and the period of the reconstruction of our national economy—all that and a lot more are tied to the Leninist Communist Party, to the name of Stalin.[204]

Nothing could be more distant than this assessment from the world view of the *shistdesiatnyky*. Even if Shelest described himself in his diary as having fortuitously achieved posts of responsibility, he was a major figure of Soviet policy in the 1960s. He was the central agent in the attack on Nikita Khrushchev in 1964, the first supporter of the military intervention in Czechoslovakia in 1968, and gave a green light to both the 1965–66 and 1972–73 repressions against the *shistdesiatnyky*.

Referring to Zionism and to the multinational reality of Soviet Ukraine in the early 1950s, Shelest wrote:

> Among the ordinary working people the nationality question never had any particular importance. The disagreements and hostilities among nations and religions were invented by the acolytes of religious cults and later by political intriguers and assiduous ideologues.[205]

In March 1973, while defending *Our Soviet Ukraine* in a conversation with Brezhnev, Shelest's positions were slightly different: "With regard to nationalities policy I have always been and am an internationalist, but I do not renounce my people, my national belonging, their culture and

---

204 Shelest, "*Spravzhnii sud istoriï shche poperedu,*" 104.
205 Ibidem, 107.

history."²⁰⁶ It seems plausible that his sense of national belonging could be typical of Stalin's time, "national in form and socialist in content"—that is what emerges from the analysis of his nationalities policy. Even the best-disposed accounts cannot find any accomplishment other than his folkloristic recovery of the Cossack tradition through the founding of a museum in Zaporizhzhia, his support for the publication of works such as the official, multivolume *History of Ukraine's Cities and Villages* and *Ukrainian Soviet Encyclopedia*, a few speeches in favour of using the Ukrainian language, and a *pro forma* defence of Oles Honchar and several nonconformist writers.²⁰⁷

Our Soviet Ukraine was not the first book in which Shelest made his views on the nationality question explicit. He also wrote *Youth's Historical Calling* (1968), a history of the Komsomol, where he suggested that the question of Ukrainian nationality policy had been solved once and for all by the Soviet cultural revolution.

> Acknowledging the cultural revolution, the Party consequently implemented the Leninist nationalities policy, a policy of equality and unbreakable friendship of the peoples of our country. The cultural revolution in Ukraine, as in all other countries, not only put an end to the hatred of the past once and for all, but even led the workers of the republic along the way to an unprecedented blossoming of their national socialist culture. In schools, in technical institutes, and at universities the teaching was conducted in the native Ukrainian language, which was not admitted [to exist] yet persecuted by Tsarism. As a consequence of the Communist Party's great concern, the Ukrainian language came out from the sphere of everyday communication by the people to conquer the sphere of state government, science, culture, and public life.²⁰⁸

Such a successful solution of the national question would form the basis of a new kind of patriotism—"socialist patriotism."

> Socialist patriotism is the highest form of patriotism. In it, woven together inextricably are the warming love of the fatherland and the

---

206 Ibidem, 405.
207 Viktor I. Ocheretianko, "Petro Iukhymovych Shelest i ukraïns'ka kul'tura," in *Istoriia Ukraïny: Malovidomi imena, podiï, fakty* 28, ed. Petro T. Tron'ko (Kyiv, Khmelnytskyi, and Kamianets-Podilskyi, 2004), 237–47.
208 Petr E. [Petro Iu.] Shelest, *Istoricheskoe prizvanie molodezhi* (Moscow, 1968), 54.

> national traditions of the Soviet peoples, self-sacrificing work for the victory of communism, and selfless, genuine, and brotherly support for peoples fighting against imperialism, reaction, [and] social and national oppression.[209]

According to Shelest, under Soviet rule Ukrainian culture had developed fully, and the only sources of national discontent were the Ukrainian bourgeois-nationalist plots.

> Exploiting the remnants of the Ukrainian counter-revolutionary bourgeois-nationalist emigration, the imperialists are trying to inflate the remnants of capitalism in the people's consciousness, first of all with the national question. In every possible way they are heating up the slightest manifestations of national selfishness and isolation, trying to use the misanthropic ideology of chauvinism and nationalism, of national discord and war, to oppose the progress of the ideology of proletarian internationalism and friendship of peoples, the ideology of peace, democracy, and socialism.[210]

The integration of Ukrainians into new socialist patriotism was so effective that in the following pages there was no further mention of Ukrainians, but only of "the inhabitants of Ukraine."[211]

It is unlikely that Shelest modified this view of the national question. A hundred thousand copies of *Our Soviet Ukraine* were published in 1970 and quickly sold out, so some chapters of it were even disseminated through *samvydav*. This handbook on Ukraine for the masses has two parts. The first is an account of Ukrainian history and the successes of Ukrainian development since the establishment of Soviet rule, while the second consists of short paragraphs describing all of Ukraine's oblasts. The first part would prove particularly contentious and fell under attack in April 1973. In it, Shelest argued that the only possible way to achieve the free and rich development of Ukraine was comprehensive unification with the fraternal Russian people. In the chapter dedicated to pre-Soviet history this thesis is repeated up to three times per page, and in the other sections it appears up at least once on every other page. In this regard, Shelest's opinion was opposite to everything the *shistdesiatnyky* had asserted about the national question.

---

209   Ibidem, 184.
210   Ibidem, 215.
211   Ibidem, 256.

Our Soviet Ukraine became widely unpopular and was harshly criticised. Shapoval has clarified that the anonymous review of Shelest's book that appeared in *Komunist Ukraïny* originated in a letter from the Party-sanctioned literary critic Mykyta Shamota to the CC CPU dated 12 September 1972. Shelest was already in Moscow, for he had been dismissed from his post in Kyiv nearly four months earlier, on 25 May, four months earlier. The content of Shamota's letter was approved by the CPU leadership, which also wrote a review of Shelest's book. The Politburo of the CPSU approved the review on 20 February 1973. In April 1973, in conjunction with the publication of the review in Ukraine, Shelest was expelled from the Politburo and pensioned off. Shelest's replacement was Volodymyr Shcherbytsky, a faithful follower of Leonid Brezhnev who held the book's condemnation against Shelest for at least a decade.[212] The review highlighted a few shortcomings of the book.

> The author idealizes the Cossacks and the Zaporozhian Sich to a considerable extent, presenting them as a homogenous, classless society. In the book nothing is mentioned about class stratification among the Cossacks, about the transformation of the Cossack leaders into virtual feudal lords, or about the class struggle among the Cossacks, especially in the Zaporozhian Sich.[213]

It was the same criticism that Mykhailo Braichevsky made of official Soviet historiography in his treatise *Annexation or Reunification?* but unlike Braichevsky, the Party's reviewer(s) accused Shelest of improperly emphasizing the various phases through which Russia's and Ukraine's working classes arrived at their long-awaited reunion. In his 1975 analysis of some contemporary history textbooks, Lowell Tillett argued that Shelest failed to interpret the Pereiaslav Treaty of 1654 as the outcome of the oppressed peasantry's struggle against the feudal yoke.[214] All of the other condemnations of Shelest's book pointed out how he had treated the development of Ukraine in isolation, without illuminating its co-operation with the Russian people.

---

212 Iurii Shapoval, "Iednist' i borot'ba dvokh neprotylezhnostei iak dzerkalo suchasnoï Ukraïny," in his *Nevyhadani istoriï* (Kyiv, 2004), 266–88.
213 "Pro seriozni nedoliky ta pomylky odniieï knyhy," in *Za shcho i iak usunuly Shelesta? Dokumenty* (Munich, 1973), 77–78.
214 Lowell Tillett, "Ukrainian Nationalism and the Fall of Shelest," *Slavic Review* 34, no. 4 (Winter 1975): 758–61.

The question of the development of revolutionary thought in the country is treated [by Shelest] in the same way. The author passes over the incontrovertible fact that the development of advanced social thought, literature, and art in Saint Petersburg and other centres of the country had a great influence on the destiny of all of the peoples of tsarist Russia.[215]

Among the pages Shelest dedicated to this subject, the following passage is especially revealing

> The Kobzar [Taras Shevchenko] was an associate and comrade-in-arms of an assemblage of Russian revolutionaries/democrats, the progressive people of his time—Alexander Herzen, Nikolai Chernyshevsky, Nikolai Dobroliubov—who by angrily stigmatizing the harsh, reactionary policy of tsarism and fighting against it evoked the friendship of all the peoples of Russia and resolutely defended the Ukrainians' rights.... Together with the Russian revolutionary democrats, this fiery advocate of friendship between the Russian and Ukrainian peoples Taras Shevchenko exhorted the masses to bring down tsarist autocracy and serfdom, to build a new life without serfs or lords, and to establish a great, free family of peoples.[216]

The attacks on Shelest's book were largely unfounded. The book's lack of a deep analysis was a small shortcoming, not expected by the book's not particularly educated mass readership. Tillett convincingly argues that the majority of the criticism was invalid.

> Most of the other specific faults which the critics find in Shelest's history are inconsequential and seem undeserved. Shelest is "correct" in his interpretation and coverage, but is not sufficiently explicit or emphatic for purposes of Soviet nationality policy. The book cannot be faulted (except by the bored reader) for a lack of references to Russian-Ukrainian friendship, military and cultural cooperation, and recitations of their "progressive consequences."[217]

The attacks on Shelest's book were baseless and largely motivated by the desire to preclude his return to power. This explains Shcherbytsky's

---

215 "Pro seriozni nedoliky ta pomylky odniieï knyhy," 79.
216 Shelest, *Ukraïno nasha Radians'ka*, 35–36.
217 Tillett, "Ukrainian Nationalism and the Fall of Shelest," 762.

insistence on Shelest's faults. Furthermore, it is not coincidental that the promoter of the review was Shamota, the director of the Institute of Literature and senior bureaucrat at the AN URSR who had already denounced various *shistdesiatnyky*. The review addressed the Party's relations with Ukraine's literati, stating that the book's superficiality was evident in Shelest's comments on the foundation of Soviet literature and art: to him, this process appeared simple and easy. In his book there was no word, for example, about the fact that not all Ukrainian writers immediately accepted the "Great October" narrative; that in the writings of many writers and artists the events of the Revolution, the civil war, and the first years of Soviet rule were not always properly treated; or that with regard to the national question certain writers and artists of the 1920s and early 1930s had wavered and some of them began struggling against the Party's policy.

The review stated that by passing over such questions Shelest diminishes the role of the Communist Party, its ideas and activities regarding the problems of constructing socialism, the Marxist-Leninist education of the intelligentsia, and attracting the latter to take an active part in the consolidation of communist ideals.[218]

The review also condemned of the rehabilitation process with which the Khrushchev Thaw had begun, signalling that the reviewer(s) wanted to put an end to tolerance toward those intellectuals who had dared to question the Party line in literature and other arts in Soviet Ukraine. It stressed Shelest's mistakes, but its positive re-evaluation of Stalinism was a warning to the intelligentsia.

***

The Prague Spring had taught Brezhnev and his comrades a lesson: it was dangerous to allow civil society to express its opinions. Shelest's concern about the situation in Ukraine was justified, because Honchar's novel could be interpreted as a sign that the *shistdesiatnyky* were gaining support among the Soviet establishment. The vast diaspora of Ukrainians throughout the world meant that an international movement was willing to implement a political change. Therefore, starting in 1968, the Soviet authorities organized the meticulously planned repressions of its nonconformist intellectuals. Taking their cues from what had happened

---

218 "Pro seriozni nedoliky ta pomylky odniieï knyhy," 79.

in Czechoslovakia, Soviet leaders were careful to avoid creating any sensation around the persecutions. The KGB imprisoned and condemned those individuals who seemed too dangerous and unwilling to compromise, such as Ivan Sokulsky and Valentyn Moroz. Administrative repressions made the lives of the remaining *shistdesiatnyky* as difficult as possible as the secret police collected materials for a concentrated attack. Ivan Dziuba's recantation after his imprisonment in Kyiv provided the Soviet authorities with the ammunition they needed to deliver their final blow. Ultimately they were able to defeat the political threat the *shistdesiatnyky* represented. But what were the reasons for their defeat?

Shistdesiatnytstvo was born as an artistic movement among a group of friends who were able to form a cultural association, the Club of Creative Youth (KTM), where they could bring their proposals and initiatives to life. From 1961 the movement's values and cultural norms conflicted with those of official Soviet culture in a number of important areas, namely, regarding freedom of expression and the nationalities policy. The Initially benevolent Soviet leadership decided to repress the group, shutting down its opportunity for expression within institutions. This group of private citizens, although formalized in an association, had to decide either to retreat or to address the broader public. The latter option seemed close to realization in 1965, when, thanks to the personal initiatives of Ivan Dziuba and others, the *shistdesiatnyky* tried to break the silence about their activities and involve the Ukrainian people in their movement. The *shistdesiatnyky* were also very concerned with the future of their entire country and its inhabitants, and their cultural proposal was aimed at engaging the entire nation and not restricted only to the intellectual elite. From 1965 to 1968 the movement of *shistdesiatnytstvo*, though somewhat disjointed and unorganized, seemed capable of addressing the nation. Unsanctioned public meetings and *samvydav* disseminated the still indefinite political message of the *shistdesiatnyky* for several years. Their mainly literary and historical *samvydav* writings were enough to create a cultural and political climate theoretically favourable to political change within the educated echelons of society. In this sense *shistdesiatnytstvo* was partly successful, for it resulted in the creation of a new sense of *hromadskist*, but it needed a political interlocutor to reach its full potential.

After the Soviet invasion of Czechoslovakia in 1968, it was clear that no member of the social and political establishments was willing to take up *shistdesiatnytstvo*'s political proposal. If it wanted to survive, the movement had to evolve further. *Shistdesiatnytstvo* needed two things if it was to become a political movement—organization and an ideological set of values and tasks. However, the *shistdesiatnyky* were unable to agree on both points.

In terms of creating a formal organization, the willingness of a group of *shistdesiatnyky* led by Viacheslav Chornovil to do so was stymied by the adamant opposition of the movement's three most prestigious and central figures—Ivan Dziuba, Ivan Svitlychny, and Yevhen Sverstiuk. The fear that such an organization would provoke a firm crackdown from the Soviet authorities held these three leaders back from establishing an alternative to the Communist Party, and they were convinced of the need to look for other forms of opposition.

While failing somewhat as an organized movement, the *shistdesiatnyky* continued working very well as a group of friends. The group's solidarity in economic and political terms never weakened, even when open conflicts such as the disagreement between Valentyn Moroz and Dziuba broke out. This solidarity spread beyond the group of friends to any victims of the Soviet system, whom they sought to assist according to the *shistdesiatnytstvo*'s general human values. This willingness to help persisted even when the victims did not share their values, as was the case of Ukrainian nationalists and religious activists. Similarly, a variety of opinions were given voice on the pages of Chornovil's *Ukraïns'kyi visnyk*. Hosting different points of view in the periodical was the logical consequence of *shistdesiatnytstvo*'s principles, but the idea of creating an equal opportunity for expression was not what the movement needed to survive. Rather, the *shistdesiatnyky* needed a tribune that would foster and disseminate the movement's own values. But the honest attempt to create an impartial newspaper was beyond *Ukraïns'kyi visnyk*'s ability, for the fear of repression prevented Chornovil from publishing any anti-Soviet article.

The psychological limitations of some of the *shistdesiatnyky* can be said to have been partially responsible for the movement's failures. Moreover, the indifference of Moscow's intellectuals to the Ukrainian question prompted Dziuba to propose founding an analogous group in Ukraine instead of joining the Moscow-based Committee on Human Rights in the USSR, as Chornovil and Leonid Pliushch had. Joining a bigger group would have brought about several positive consequences, namely, being part of a broader network of political and intellectual exchange, as well as the opportunity to bring the Ukrainian question to the centre of the Soviet system, where it could gain more visibility not only inside the USSR, but beyond its borders. But these opportunities were lost.

In terms of ideology, the situation was even worse. The conflict between Valentyn Moroz and Dziuba prefigured the increasing opposition between those who gave absolute pre-eminence to the national question and those adherents of more general human values who considered the nationality issue just one of the many manifestations of the lack of democracy in the Soviet Union. There was no ideological consensus among the *shistdesiatnyky*, meaning that they lacked the crucial element for the success of any political initiative. The ideological burden of *shistdesiatnytstvo* was even more decisive. Because they had been raised in the Soviet Union, the *shistdesiatnyky* firmly believed in Soviet propaganda and that they were on the right side of the worldwide conflict between capitalism and socialism. Once they had ascertained that the Soviet system was worse than it overtly acknowledged, or even that it contradicted its own values, the *shistdesiatnyky* had to go through a long and painful process of self-criticism to break away ideologically from the Soviet Union. Even by the end of the 1960s very few of them could bring themselves to take this step, and many of those who were prepared to do so, such as Moroz, were, not coincidentally, swiftly imprisoned. Chornovil's unwillingness to include anti-Soviet writings in *Ukraïns'kyi visnyk* and the universal incapability of openly dissociating themselves from the Soviet Union, to condemn it as betraying the values it ought to defend, were signs that the *shistdesiatnyky* could not bring their criticism of Soviet reality to its extreme but inescapable conclusions.

The transformation of *shistdesiatnytstvo* from a cultural elite made up of friends into a political group able to exert influence on the country's political country ultimately failed owing to the lack of organization and of a common set of values and tasks. The *shistdesiatnyky* could object that they did not want to become a political movement. Indeed, Dziuba continued to try to find another way to influence policy through his status as an intellectual. It is true that an intellectual can affect the course of politics through his writings, sometimes even deeply, and without founding his own political movement. But this can only occur in countries where freedom of expression is guaranteed. In the Soviet Union there was no way for intellectuals to have a free voice using the official means of communication. Dziuba and many others who were unwilling to engage in open conflict with the Soviet Union were condemned to remain silent until new political dynamics readmitted them into the public arena in the early 1980s.

Epilogue

> Пошли мені, Боже, хоч ворога
> коли друга послати жаль.*

What Remained of the Friendships

Vasyl Stus was among those who were arrested on 12 December 1972. On the ninth day of his confinement he wrote the following lines.

> How good it is that I am not afraid of death
> and that I do not wonder if my cross is heavy....
> Oh, my people, I will come back to you
> and turn my death into life ...[1]

This poem was an eerie premonition. After his release in August 1979, Stus enjoyed less than a year of freedom. In May 1980 he was again arrested for his involvement in the Ukrainian Helsinki Group and sentenced to ten years' imprisonment. Denied the right to see his family and with his health deteriorating, he died in the morning of 4 September 1985 in a strict-regime prison camp in Perm Oblast. Stus's death became a symbol of the brutality of the Soviet regime toward the dissidents of the 1970s, just as he himself had been a symbol of *shistdesiatnytstvo* when he was alive.[2] Communicating themes of love, often for his family, and notable for its lyrical composition, Stus's poetry expressed many ideals of

---

* "Oh God! At least send me a foe, / if you don't want to send me a friend" ("Solitude," in Symonenko, *Hranitni obelisky*, 42–43).

1 Vasyl' Stus, *Zibrannia tvoriv u dvanadtsiaty tomakh*, vol. 3, *Chas tvorchosti / Dichtenszeit* (Kyiv, 2008), 13.

2 Stus's engagement as a civic-rights activist began earlier. He was born on 8 January 1938 in Rakhnivka, a village in Haisyn raion, Vinnytsia oblast, southwest of Kyiv. Even though it was during a time of war, Stus remembered his childhood as happy in the Russified city of Stalino (renamed Donetsk in 1961), where he graduated from the city's pedagogical institute in 1959. After three months as a teacher in Kirovohrad Oblast and two years of compulsory military service in the Urals, he returned to Donetsk, where he worked as an editor for the newspaper *Sotsialistychnyi Donbas* for three years. In 1963 *Dnipro* published a collection of Stus's poems, and in 1964 he was accepted as a graduate student by the Institute of Literature of the AN URSR in Kyiv. He married in 1965, and his son, Dmytro, was born in 1966. See Jaropolk Lassowsky, "Vasyl Stus," in Vasyl Stus, *Selected Poems*, trans. and ed. Jaropolk Lassowsky (Munich and New York, 1987), 150–51; and Marko Carynnyk, "Vasyl Stus," *Journal of Ukrainian Graduate Studies* 1, no. 1 (Fall 1976): 62–67.

shistdesiatnytstvo.[3] Other themes, such as expressing the truth, were also not alien to him. In 1963 he wrote:

> So much truth in the throat, so much suffering—
> a night is too short to tell it all.
> A mournful rattle in the empty forest,
> a prickly whistling of the birds.
> Leaves are falling.
> Where can a butterfly alight?
> ("Leaves are Falling," in Stus, *Selected Poems*, 20–21) [4]

In March 1965 he wrote about his native land and the fundamental value of friendship:

> Friends know
> that you're a friend,
> even if you should be a great sinner.
> They will accept you even as such.
> Even as such they will accept you.
> After all, don't you, knowing each one of them,
> absolve, as God the Lord,
> each one's sins,
> when you see
> how smiles the severe mouth,
> just like shined shoes,
> of a sloppy teacher of ethics,
> how gently discourses yesterday's Judas,
> how, besotted, the drunkard stands firmly on his feet,
> hiding his face into an open Pravda. (Stus, *Selected Poems*, 62–63).

Stus became one of the central figures of the movement. He was present at the pivotal public protest at the Ukraina movie theatre in Kyiv, wrote and signed many different letters of protest, composed a famous poem for Alla Horska's funeral, and organized meetings with Chornovil, Dziuba, Svitlychny, and Sverstiuk. Because of his involvement in the protest at the Ukraina movie theatre, Stus was expelled from the Institute of Literature of the AN URSR. Although he managed to get hired as an

---

3   See, for example, "To V. P.," dated 18 August 1965, in Stus, *Selected Poems*, 80–81. V. P. are the initials of Stus's wife, Valentyna Popeliuk.

4   The Ukrainian title of the poem is "Padolyst," the archaic Ukrainian name of November, meaning "falling leaves."

archivist at the State Historical Archive in Kyiv, he was soon also dismissed there and was unable to keep any job for long as a consequence of the administrative repressions against him. The news of Dziuba's recantation was a bitter surprise to Stus, and he found the psychological strength to face it only several years later. He wrote a harsh letter to Dziuba to express his disappointment, labelling Dziuba a "Lilliputian" and his recantation as intellectual suicide.

> I have long felt the need to come to an understanding with you, because the you I knew is dead, and that you whose birthday you announced loudly two years ago is incomprehensible to me.... You hope to be able to return to literature even though this return will be without [your] right to a civic voice and without a sense of your own ethical well-being.... Because having been repressed, you repressed yourself once again.[5]

Stus condemned Dziuba's betrayal, reminding him that his decision was "incomprehensible" if one considered the intellectual's duty toward his people, who were under the threat of "genocide." Something had changed ideologically: the shift between *shistdesiatnytstvo* and the new Ukrainian dissent, of which Stus would become the symbolic martyr, is touched upon in one of the letters he wrote in 1975. In this letter, usually published with the title "I Accuse," Stus holds the Soviet Union responsible for violating basic human rights.

> The case against me was subsequently based on my writings dealing with the persecutions of the 1920s and 1930s, with the genocide of the Ukrainian peasantry in 1933, and the destruction of Ukrainian intellectuals in the 1930s and following decades. My description of the internal-passport system that prevents peasants from moving freely within their own country as a new form of serfdom was deemed anti-Soviet by the court.... By judging all those statements as anti-Soviet, the KGB took on the role of direct culprits of past crimes and accomplices in the state's exploitation of the people. By concealing the well-known facts of unprecedented repression in the past, today's KGB maintains its kinship with the banditry of Yezhov and Beria and assumes responsibility for their crimes. I deem the KGB a parasitic, exploitative, and pernicious organization on whose

---

5   Vasyl' Stus, "Vidkrytyi lyst do Ivana Dziuby," in his *Tvory v shesty tomakh, dev'iaty knyhakh*, vol. 4 (Lviv, 1994), 441–42.

conscience lie the millions upon millions of souls shot, tortured, or starved to death.[6]

In "I Accuse" Stus blamed the KGB for the violations of the Ukrainian nation's rights during the political pogrom of 1972–73. Any reference to Soviet legality or Marxism-Leninism was notably absent, for Stus had given up invoking the Communist ideology to defend himself. Instead he challenged the Soviet state solely on the basis of universal human rights.

> They ascribed guilt to me, saying that in my writings a class approach is missing, and that as a writer I am not a member of the Party or the Union of Writers, that I do not support the principle of the Communist Party's spirit or the principles of socialist realism, that I stand on positions of abstract humanitarianism, and that in some of my works there is an existential mood (range of problems). In this way [my] crime is that a person holds certain non-communist ideals. This person is simply forbidden to exist. Therefore I identify the KGB as criminal for violating the most elementary human rights.[7]

Stus was not denying that he was not a Communist, but he claimed that his different beliefs were a human right. He had taken a step that Dziuba and Dziuba's followers had been unable to take—abandoning hope in a bright future for Communism.

What Remained of the Politics

Once he had been arrested, Chornovil was unable to prepare the sixth issue of *Ukraïns'kyi visnyk*. But three other dissidents decided to assume that role and disseminate the news about the wave of arrests in 1972—Yevhen Proniuk, Vasyl Lisovy (1937–2012), and Vasyl Ovsiienko.[8] The first two wrote articles about the arrests, while Ovsiienko was responsible for printing and disseminating them. To maintain continuity with the past issues of *Ukraïns'kyi visnyk*, in the sixth "Kyiv issue" that they prepared they included the "Tasks" of *Ukraïns'kyi visnyk* that Chornovil

---

6   Vasyl' Stus, *Ia obvynuvachuiu*, in ibidem, 495–96.
7   Ibidem, 496.
8   About Proniuk, see chapter two, n. 47. Lisovy (1937–2012), was a research associate at the Institute of Philosophy of the AN URSR and taught logic at Kyiv State University. He was active from the second half of the 1960s and was acquainted with many *shistdesiatnyky*.

had formulated. Proniuk and Lisovy were also arrested, in July and August 1972 respectively, but Ovsiienko continued disseminating the underground documents for almost a year until he was arrested in March 1973 and sentenced to hard labour in the Mordovian Gulag. Ovsiienko considered what the *shistdesiatnyky* had written not to be nationalist enough and even insincere to some extent.[9] While their writings were a revelation, he nonetheless preferred Valentyn Moroz's point of view to the Dziuba's diplomatic tone in *Internationalism or Russification?*

> I was absolutely convinced that the circle of Ivan Dziuba, Ivan Svitlychny, Yevhen Sverstiuk, and Viacheslav Chornovil had somewhat different ideas from those expressed in this work [*Internationalism or Russification?*], and were more critical toward the existing regime. But clearly that tactic had been chosen intentionally.[10]

This interpretation of how the *shistdesiatnyky* had treated the national question was a sign that they had not been able to communicate their world view to the younger generation. Faith in the Soviet Union and socialism, which had restrained the *shistdesiatnyky* from condemning the Soviet authorities outright, was no longer among the values of those who continued fighting in support of Ukrainian culture in the 1970s.

After the publication of the "Kyiv Issue" of *Ukraïns'kyi visnyk*, the main initiative in defending the Ukrainian nation took place on 9 November 1976 in Moscow at Aleksandr Ginzburg's apartment. There the Ukrainian writer and former Communist Mykola Rudenko (1920–2004)

---

9 Ovsiienko was born in a village in Zhytomyr oblast on 8 April 1949. During my interview with him on 29 May 2009, he said that he was from a peasant family, and that his parents always perceived the Soviet regime as alien. He has told me that the border between "us" and "them" was well defined in the rural society where he used to live. For example, for him the OUN's leader Stepan Bandera (1909–59), who was assassinated by a Soviet agent, was "one of us." Being younger than the *shistdesiatnyky*, Ovsiienko joined the Komsomol because he knew that it would guarantee an easier life (e.g., passing university entrance exams), but he never believed in Communism. When he started attending Kyiv State University in 1967, he was struck by the hostility with which Kyivans reacted to people from rural parts of the country who spoke in Ukrainian. The insults and invectives he heard, such as "Why don't you speak human?" (i.e., Russian), "*khokhol!*" (a Russian pejorative for a Ukrainian), and *derevnia!* ("village"" in Russian, i.e., "you yokel!") made him feel uncomfortable speaking Ukrainian.

10 Vasyl' Ovsiienko, "Moï universytety" (interview with Borys Zakharov) in his *Svitlo liudei*, vol. 1, *Memuary ta publitsystyka* (Kharkiv, 2007), 14.

announced the creation of the Ukrainian Helsinki Group (UHG) on the example of the Helsinki Group founded in Moscow in May of that year.[11] Inspired by the Helsinki Final Act on human rights, these watch groups monitored the Soviet government's compliance with this international treaty and called on the Soviet Union to respect civil rights, with the goal of drawing the global public's attention to Soviet human-rights violations. The document the UHG released to the press emphasized the importance of freedom of expression.

> The group is led in its activity not by political motives but only by the defence of human rights. We are aware that the perennial bureaucratization of state life, which is ever increasing, is able to persecute us for our legal actions. But we also know well that the bureaucratic interpretation of Human Rights cannot empty the international juridical documents signed by the government of the USSR of their contents. We accept these documents in their entire meaning—without bureaucratic misrepresentation or arbitrary excisions by state officials or institutions. We are deeply convinced that only this understanding of the Universal Declaration of Human Rights and the Helsinki Accords is able to foster a real détente in international relations.[12]

This strategy was a consequence of the evolution of the tactics of the *shistdesiatnyky*, with increasing importance being conferred on international public opinion about the internal struggle. As some of the *shistdesiatnyky* had foreshadowed, the UHG's members were convinced of the need to make the USSR abide by the international agreements it had sanctioned. A human-rights agenda had entered the culture of Soviet citizens through the revival of the self propagated by *shistdesiatnytstvo*, which restored the significance of the individual over the prominence in Stalin's time of the collective. The Universal Declaration of Human Rights and the Helsinki Accords were an organic part of 1970s dissidents' political culture thanks to the *shistdesiatnyky*: the importance attributed to the rights of the individual is an original and unique legacy of the

---

11 Vasyl' Ovsiienko, "Pravozakhysnyi rukh v Ukraïni (seredyna 1950-kh – 1980-i roky)," in Ievhen Zakharov, *Ukraïns'ka hromads'ka hrupa spryiannia vykonanniu Hel'sins'kykh uhod*, vol. 1, *Osobystosti* (Kharkiv, 2001), 26.

12 *Deklaratsiia Ukraïns'koï hromads'koï hrupy spryiannia vykonanniu Hel'sinks'kykh uhod*, in Zakharov, *Ukraïns'ka hromads'ka hrupa spryiannia vykonanniu Hel'sins'kykh uhod*, vol. 2, *Dokumenty i materialy, 9 lystopada 1976 – 2 lypnia 1977* (Kharkiv, 2001), 23.

shistdesiatnyky and did not derive from Ukrainian nationalism or Marxism-Leninism.

I have used the term "dissident" to refer to the activists of the Ukrainian national movement that followed the *shistdesiatnyky*. They had abandoned any faith in the Soviet Union and in Marxism, and they can reasonably be considered dissidents and not simply "nonconformist" intellectuals such as the *shistdesiatnyky*. The dissidents inherited the "law-abiding" strategy, but their political goals had changed. Throughout the 1970s and 1980s the question of national liberation would gain importance, and the goal of the UHG would become secession from the USSR through a referendum.[13] The movement born with the UHG did not have the artistic connotations of *shistdesiatnytstvo*. There were some artists in the UHG, but it was not their cultural engagement that made them members. The UHG's claims were political, and its members were interested in political change, not poetic expression. The political affiliations of the *shistdesiatnyky* and the UHG's members were radically different. The *shistdesiatnyky* would hardly consider Danylo Shumuk and Levko Lukianenko two of their own. But people with various world views shared the UHG's political claims.

Besides Viacheslav Chornovil, the key figures of *shistdesiatnytstvo* did not join the UHG. The UHG's members had various backgrounds but were united by their labour-camp experiences—by the "Mordovian university."[14] This should be the starting point of subsequent research on Ukrainian dissent of the 1970s and 1980s. I have tried to contribute to and illustrate possible developments through the analysis of Lukianenko's writings. Further research should begin with the study of life in the Soviet labour camps and of the complex relationships among the inmates. Intellectual prisoners were imprisoned in at least three camps in the Mordovian Gulag, and their dislocation and consequent opportunities for interaction influenced the subsequent dissent. The labour camp was also the starting point of a closer relationship with the Russian and other Soviet dissident groups, whose representatives were fellow inmates of the Ukrainians.

---

13 See Zakharov, *Ukraïns'ka hromads'ka hrupa spryiannia vykonanniu Hel'sins'kykh uhod*, vols. 2–4 (Kharkiv, 2001).

14 Mykhailo Horyn used this expression, but it was not typical. See Ovsiienko, *Moï universytety*.

In Sum: Who the *Shistdesiatnyky* Were

The first common experience of the *shistdesiatnyky* was of a radically different nature than that of later dissidents. As Yevhen Sverstiuk noted in *A Cathedral in Scaffolding*, *shistdesiatnytstvo* was a consequence of the reawakening of the Ukrainian countryside, whose youngest and most deserving children were moving to the city. Nearly all *shistdesiatnyky* had in common a childhood spent in a rural Ukrainian environment. Every time he has had the opportunity, Ivan Dziuba has stressed that he was born in the almost entirely Ukrainophone countryside of Donetsk (formerly Stalino) Oblast. (The city of Donetsk, itself, however, evolved into one of the principal hubs of Ukraine's ethnic Russian and Russian-speaking population.) It was in a rural environment that the *shistdesiatnyky* learned to love traditional Ukrainian culture. At the same time, however, they did not view Russian culture as alien. Some of them spoke Russian, many of the books their parents had were in Russian, and Russian was sometimes the language used in their schools. The *shistdesiatnyky* also studied and loved the Russian language, literature, and culture. Dziuba and Lina Kostenko are two of the brightest examples.

After finishing their elementary and secondary schooling in the countryside, the *shistdesiatnyky* moved to bigger cities to attend university. They were the beneficiaries of the economic dynamics of postwar Ukraine and its increasing urbanization. It was not only a single city or a single university that contributed to their educations: Kyiv, Lviv, Stalino, Kharkiv, and even Moscow shaped important members of the core of *shistdesiatnytstvo*, which should not be seen as a revival of Ukrainian culture in Galicia or Kyiv. Benjamin Tromly has proposed that the emergence of *shistdesiatnytstvo* was partly the consequence of the Ukrainian educational system, which had particular institutions where the students could be educated in the spirit of respect for Ukrainian culture.[15] While it is true that some *shistdesiatnyky*, such as Ivan Svitlychny, Mykhailyna Kotsiubynska, and Valentyn Moroz, studied Ukrainian philology or Ukrainian history at university, they were not a majority. Many studied journalism (e.g., Viacheslav Chornovil and Vasyl Symonenko), medicine (Yaroslav Hevrych and Mykola Plakhotniuk), theatre arts (Les Taniuk), Russian philology (Ivan Dziuba and Lina

---

15 Benjamin Tromly, "An Unlikely National Revival: Soviet Higher Learning and the Ukrainian 'Sixtiers,' 1953–65," *The Russian Review* 68, no. 4 (October 2008): 607–22.

Kostenko), or visual art (Alla Horska, Opanas Zalyvakha, Viktor Zaretsky).

For the *shistdesiatnyky*, studying Ukrainian literature seems to have been a consequence of their sense of national belonging, and a significant number became graduate students at the Institute of Literature of the AN URSR (Ivan Svitlychny, Mykhailyna Kotsiubynska, Zynoviia Franko, and Vasyl Stus). Other environments, such as the SPU and the editorial boards of the literary journals *Vitchyzna*, *Zhovten'*, and *Dnipro*, were also important in shaping them. Another common experience was the alienation the *shistdesiatnyky* felt in the cities where they studied and worked. Many a *shistdesiatnyk* had been reprimanded for speaking Ukrainian in public or had to experience the consequences of Russification in daily life—reflected, for example, in the lack of Ukrainian manuals and the impossibility of sending telegrams in Ukrainian. The degree of Russian chauvinism in the cities and the concomitant conceit of their inhabitants toward those who recently arrived from the countryside contributed to an opposite reaction—a rise in the level of Ukrainian national consciousness among the new city dwellers.

Many *shistdesiatnyky* were active in the Komsomol. If joining this organization was a compulsory step for any enterprising young person, the fact that the first organization imbued with *shistdesiatnytstvo*, the Club of Creative Youth/KTM, was under the Komsomol's aegis is more significant, especially if one considers that the *shistdesiatnyky* declared their belief in communism until the end of the 1960s and several of them were Party members until 1991. An important element in the KTM's members' cohesiveness was their mutual friendship, which was strengthened by the intellectual esteem the *shistdesiatnyky* had for each other's work. *Shistdesiatnytstvo* emerged as a cultural movement that was able to influence the entire cultural climate in Ukraine. It even attracted the attention of an entire congress of the SPU. *Shistdesiatnytstvo*'s values were revolutionary culturally (with the liquidation of socialist realism) and, more broadly, socially (honesty and truth instead of Soviet duplicity; the importance of the individual instead of the prominence of the collective; and trust in and love of personal ties instead of the regime's suspicion and terror).

Despite *shistdesiatnytstvo*'s radical themes, its adherents did not want to be in conflict with the regime, and they even tried mediation by way of the KTM. As the events of the evening in memory of Lesia Ukrainka on 31 July 1963 demonstrated, the KTM's members tried to reach an understanding with the political authorities, and they only decided to act outside the rules when they encountered an inflexible prohibition from the latter. This was due to two factors: first, although the KTM's initiatives had some civil content, they were mainly cultural and not political; and second, the members did not want to engage in a political struggle against the Soviet leadership, for they were convinced that it was possible to contribute to the future development of the Soviet Ukrainian republic. The *kompaniia* of the *shistdesiatnyky* tried to build a new *hromadskist* (civic consciousness) within the framework of Soviet legality. The members of the *shistdesiatnytstvo* movement did not perceive themselves as extraneous to Soviet society: they had identified Soviet culture's shortcomings but wanted to find a solution through recovering what they believed to be the "real Leninism," similarly to what was happening elsewhere in the Soviet Union and Eastern Europe. As intellectual workers who had experienced discrimination against Ukrainian culture, they understandably focussed their attention on this topic. At the beginning the collaboration with Soviet institutions seemed possible, as represented by the help that Oles Honchar offered as leader of the SPU.

After a short period of collaboration, the Soviet authorities understood the potential threat that the values of *shistdesiatnytstvo* presented and decided to contain and repress it. The arrests in 1965 were a declaration that the new Soviet political leadership, which was no less tolerant but more resolute, was not willing to accept significant deviations from Soviet orthodoxy. This is when the *shistdesiatnyky* began activities independently of the Soviet state. It was not a total "war," for the *shistdesiatnyky* did not denounce Soviet power entirely, but only those institutions and sectors that supported a return to Stalinism. They hoped that some in the Soviet leadership would support their claims, trusting Petro Shelest in particular to protect and help them.

The *shistdesiatnyky* began competing with official Soviet media in an effort to inform and influence public opinion. Dziuba's speech at the Ukraina movie theatre and Chornovil's *Woe from Wit* are examples of this kind of counter-information. The *shistdesiatnyky* proposed a different *hromadskist* to Ukrainian society—new values expressed in essays and treatises (e.g., Dziuba's *Internationalism or Russification?*) and at public meetings. After 1965 the *kompaniia* of the *shistdesiatnyky* had to deal with a less definite structure. Their movement was able to mobilize enough people to be seen as a menace by the Soviet state, but they were not organized. Not all of them took part in all of the initiatives. Lina Kostenko, for example, was very active in attending the trials against her friends, but she did not take part in public meetings or participate in the distribution of *samvydav*. Furthermore, the movement lacked an institutionalized leadership. People looked to Dziuba for his intellectual acumen, but he was unwilling to be a leader, while the more politically engaged figures, such as the Horyn brothers or Chornovil, were imprisoned long enough to limit their potential leadership roles. In the period between 1965 and 1968 *shistdesiatnytstvo* was in limbo—not quite a group of private citizens nor a public organization. However, as it continued to gain support within the population, this organizational problem was not always evident.

In 1968 the Prague Spring convinced the Soviet authorities of the dangerous nature of uncontrolled, of nonconformist movements in the spheres of culture and politics and, of course, nationalities policy. The unrest in Czechoslovakia provoked a second and broader wave of repression in Soviet Ukraine. During the first stage of this wave—that is, political defamation via accusations of bourgeois nationalism, fascism, and betrayal of the Soviet fatherland—*shistdesiatnytstvo* was not prepared to engage in a struggle against the state. I have discussed how the lack of a shared ideological platform and of a structured organization contributed to the movement's defeat.

The most dangerous threat that *shistdesiatnytstvo* represented was its accusation that the Soviet regime had misinterpreted and violated Marxism-Leninism, to which the regime responded by tenaciously attacking Ivan Dziuba's *Internationalism or Russification?* But the *shistdesiatnyky* did not denounce the Soviet Union as a fallacy and were reluctant to condemn the society that had engendered them. This reluctance gave birth to a broad spectrum of different behaviours. After the forced closure of the KTM in Kyiv, Les Taniuk continued working as a theatre director. But he had to leave Kyiv, and after a brief, less successful interlude in Kharkiv he became an influential theatre and television director in Moscow. Lina Kostenko kept on writing, penning some of the most significant works in Ukrainian verse, but she did not become a political dissident even though she was blacklisted and was not published from 1968 to 1976. Ivan Dziuba, who was accused of siding with Ukrainian nationalists who had collaborated with the Nazis, resolutely denied the accusations and sought a modus vivendi with the Soviet authorities from 1970 on. His recantation in 1973 was dictated by his desire to avoid imprisonment, but even after Ukraine became independent in 1991 he continued to claim that his motivation was searching for other ways to attain the same goals. These are just three examples, but they are also the stories of three key figures in the *shistdesiatnytstvo* movement, with whom I began this study. But explaining their conduct as betrayals of the values they previously espoused is too simplistic.

The *shistdesiatnyky* were brought up believing in the values of justice and equality communicated by Soviet propaganda, and they continued (and continue) to believe in those values reinterpreting them in an original way. In the years between their birth and the 1972 repressions, they watched many violations of those values, but at the same time they witnessed an unprecedented improvement in the conditions of everyday life—an improvement that, more often than one can imagine, touched upon their own lives. While I was interviewing him, Ivan Dziuba told me that he was grateful to the Soviet state for the medical treatments he received for his tuberculosis: though was the a son of two very poor workers, he was able to convalesce in the best sanatoriums, which in today's Ukraine are reserved for the rich. Questioning the entire enterprise of the Soviet Union, beginning with its Marxist-Leninist doctrine, was a very long, difficult, and painful process that the generation of the 1960s was able to undertake completely only after 1991.

Soviet identity was complex enough to allow various ways of dealing with the shortcomings of Soviet reality, especially regarding the question of national consciousness. An original approach to this question comes from Paul Robert Magocsi. Tired of the exclusion from historical research of occurrences and subjects that cannot be forced into a teleological narrative, he proposed a pair of analytical concepts—"multiple loyalties" and "mutually exclusive loyalties."[16] In Magocsi's interpretation, before the French Revolution and the spread of nineteenth-century nationalism, Ukrainian society was characterized by a peculiar cultural permeability that blended different linguistic, religious, social, and ethnic identities. Ukraine's inhabitants, individuals as well as groups, had various loyalties, which sometimes overlapped or contradicted one another. But none them dominated over the others.

Having embraced nationalism, nineteenth-century Ukrainian intellectuals acquired the idea that one, single national belonging was predominant and that it excluded or subordinated other loyalties. Consequently, Ukraine's later history can be read as a series of attempts

---

16   See Paul Robert Magocsi, *A History of Ukraine: The Land and Its Peoples,* second, revised and expanded ed. (Toronto, 2010), 374–88.

by intellectuals to spread this exclusive loyalty among the masses, but, because of the masses' "multicultural" nature, they encountered significant resistance that generated unexpected results. Sometimes, especially under Soviet rule, the intellectuals themselves manifested multiple loyalties in order to oppose Soviet standardization. Commenting on the increase in the number of Ukraine inhabitants who considered themselves Ukrainian in post-Stalinist Ukraine and on Ukrainian society in the 1970s, Magocsi writes that

> ... the vast majority of Soviet Ukraine's inhabitants, better off economically than ever before and spared from foreign invasion for more than a third of a century because of the protective shield of Soviet military might, seemed resigned to or even satisfied with functioning within a system that reflected the principle of a hierarchy of multiple loyalties. In effect, it seemed possible to be simultaneously an ethnic Ukrainian and a Soviet citizen. Of course, such complementary loyalties could realistically be maintained only on the understanding that while a Ukrainian identity and cultural framework was possible in many circumstances, higher forms of cultural and educational endeavor were to be carried out in the "universal Soviet" medium, Russian.
>
> Notwithstanding this analogy, there was at least one crucial difference between the nineteenth century and the last decades of Soviet rule. Whereas in tsarist times being a "Little Russian" Russian often led one to complete national assimilation, Soviet Ukrainianism was a form of political accommodation without assimilation. Despite the increasing dominance of Russian forms in Soviet Ukrainian political, social, and cultural life (including an increase in the number of Russian-language schools and publications and the encouragement of bilingualism in elementary schools), the Soviet system at the same time produced a highly educated and nationally conscious Ukrainian stratum of the population. Also, because of socio-demographic changes, it was cities and not rural villages, especially in eastern Ukraine, that became the carriers of the Ukrainian ethos.[17]

The dynamics Magocsi describes do not illustrate the story of the *shistdesiatnyky*. But considering the landscape that surrounded them and their non-awareness of the economic crisis that would lead the Soviet Union to dissolution, it is less difficult to understand how Dziuba's

---

17   Ibidem, 712–13.

method (as well Taniuk's and Kostenko's) of looking for other ways to continue his struggle by exploiting "Soviet Ukrainianism" could seem a realistic option. What I want to stress is that dissent was just one of the many possible outcomes of *shistdesiatnytstvo*, but not the only one. Some *shistdesiatnyky*—for example, Viacheslav Chornovil and Vasyl Stus— joined the dissident movement in the 1970s, but many others did not.

At the end of her study of Russia after the Second World War, Elena Zubkova affirms that the reason for the failure of the postwar attempts at reform lay in the inability of both the Communist Party and Soviet civil society to give birth to real reforms transcending a "return to Lenin."[18] And even more powerfully, summarizing the Khrushchev era, Cynthia Hooper writes that

> what the short-lived regime *did* do—both in initially disrupting established rules of openness and then in attempting to 'manage' that disruption—was to call the attention of ordinary Bolsheviks to Soviet government processes of censorship and secrecy, and to the importance of both to the Communist Party. The Khrushchev regime raised a dilemma it failed to resolve, one that Mikhail Gorbachev would once again face in his later efforts to implement reform: the question of whether truth, of whatever stripe, was preferable to an illusion, even when that illusion was socialism itself ...[19]

It is possible to agree with Zubkova's and Hooper's conclusions, which explain the reason why Ukraine's national democrats were so well disposed toward a compromise with the old Soviet *nomenklatura* after 1991. Nevertheless both of these reflections have to be supplemented with other considerations about the legacy of *shistdesiatnytstvo*. Though in most cases the *shistdesiatnyky* were unable to denounce the Marxist-Leninist doctrine, it was the implicit affirmation of the rights of the individual in *shistdesiatnytstvo* that started the process that led to the abandonment of Leninism. Thanks to the *shistdesiatnyky* the subsequent national dissident movement was able to rearrange its struggle on the basis of the peaceful defence of human rights instead of the armed struggle represented by the OUN and the UPA. This, in conjunction with *shistdesiatnytstvo*'s moderate

---

18 See her "Conclusion" in *Russia after the War*.
19 Cynthia Hooper, "What Can and Cannot Be Said: Between the Stalinist Past and New Soviet Future," in *The Relaunch of the Soviet Project, 1945–1964*, ed. Juliane Fürst, Polly Jones, and Susan Morrissey, special issue of *The Slavonic and East European Review* 86, no. 2 (April 2008): 327.

sense of national belonging, according to which it embraced Russian culture and disapproved only of Russian chauvinism, significantly contributed to the peaceful dissolution of the Soviet Union in 1991. The Ukrainian republic, with its complex ethnic landscape, could have been a bloody battlefield if a movement with a more rigid conception of national belonging and a lesser respect for human rights had been at the forefront of the independence drive in 1991 instead of the national democrats, who inherited and further developed *shistdesiatnytstvo*'s cultural and political legacy.

The second great merit of *shistdesiatnytstvo* is its artistic heritage. The art of the *shistdesiatnyky*, owing to their interest in and attraction to other cultures, generated writing on a high level, especially in poetry, and integrated Ukrainian culture with European and world culture. The *shistdesiatnyky* represented a rebirth for Ukraine, which had been suffering from the intellectual suppression and standardization by Stalinism since the late 1920s.[20] I believe that the postmodernist character of the Bu-Ba-Bu generation of Ukrainian writers of the late 1980s and the 1990s, with its unconventional notion of national belonging and its aspirations to address a world audience, was influenced by the culture of *shistdesiatnytstvo*. The *shistdesiatnyky* may have been reduced to silence for some time, but their ideas continued to be effective and influence the further evolution of Ukrainian society. This is the sense of the epigraph with which this cultural study begins.

---

20 Although I disagree with Oksana Pakhl'ovs'ka's other, mainly political, observations in her article "Ukraïns'ki shistdesiatnyky: Filosofiia buntu" in *Suchasnist'*, 2000, no. 4: 65–84, I agree with her on this point.

Bibliography

Archives

Haluzevyi Derzhavnyi Arkhiv Sluzhby Bezpeky Ukraïny (Branch State Archive of the Security Service of Ukraine), Kyiv. File no. 58114fp, "Ugolovnoe delo no. 24 po faktu rasprostraneniia v gor. Kieve antisovetskoi knigi A. Avtorkhanova 'Tekhnologiia vlasti' po priznakam st. 62 ch. 1 KK URSR."

———. File no. 68805fp, "Ugolovnoe delo no. 45 po obvineniiu Svitlychnogo Ivana Oleksiiovycha za st. 62 ch. 1 KK URSR."

———. File no. 69260fp, "Dziuba Ivan Mykhailovych za st. 62 ch. 1 KK URSR"

Tsentral'nyi derzhavnyi arkhiv hromads'kykh ob'iednan' Ukraïny (Central State Archive of Public Organizations of Ukraine), Kyiv. Fond no. 1, "Central Committee of the Communist Party of Ukraine, Central Department."

Tsentral'nyi derzhavnyi arkhiv Muzeiu literatury i mystevtstva Ukraïny (Central State Archive Museum of Literature and Art of Ukraine), Kyiv. Fond no. 22, "Malyshko, Andrii Samiilovych, ukraïns'kyi radians'kyi poet."

———. Fond no. 590, "Spilka pys'mennykiv Ukraïny" (Union of Writers of Ukraine).

———. Fond no. 1242, "Dziuba, Ivan Mykhailovych."

Bibliographies

Babych, Ievdokiia K., and Valentyna V. Patoka. *Represiï v Ukraïni (1917–1990 rr.): Naukovo-dopomizhnyi bibliohrafichnyi pokazhyk.* Kyiv: Smoloskyp, 2007.

Liber, George, and Anna Mostovych. *Nonconformity and Dissent in the Ukrainian SSR, 1955–1975: An Annotated Bibliography.* Cambridge, Mass.: Harvard Ukrainian Research Institute, 1978.

Periodicals

Dnipro, Kyiv.
Kommunist Ukrainy, Kyiv.
Literaturna Ukraïna [until 1962 *Literaturna hazeta*], Kyiv.
Perets', Kyiv.
Vitchyzna, Kyiv.
Zhovten', Lviv.

Books and Selected Articles

Alexeieva, Liudmila. *Soviet Dissent: Contemporary Movements for National, Religious, and Human Rights.* Middleton, Conn.: Wesleyan University Press, 1985.

———. *The Thaw Generation: Coming of Age in the Post-Stalin Era.* Boston: Brown, 1990.

Alpatov, Vladimir M. *Istoriia odnogo mifa: Marr i Marrizm.* Moscow: Nauka, 1991.

Anatoly A. [Kuznetsov, Anatolii]. *Babi Yar: A Document in the Form of a Novel.* Translated by David Floyd. New York: Farrar, Straus, and Giroux, 1970.

"The Art of Painting in Soviet Ukraine." *The Ukrainian Review* 6, no. 1 (Spring 1959): 73–75.

Avtorkhanov, Abdurakhman. *Stalin and the Soviet Communist Party: A Study in the Technology of Power.* New York: Praeger, 1959.

Balestrini, Nanni, and Primo Moroni, eds. *L'orda d'oro, 1968–1977: La grande ondata rivoluzionaria e creativa, politica ed esistenziale*, 3rd ed. Milan: Feltrinelli, 2005 [first ed.: Sugarco, 1988].

Baran, Volodymyr K. *Ukraïna 1950–1960-kh rr.: Evolutsiia totalitarnoï systemy.* Lviv: Instytut ukraïnoznavstva im. I. Kryp'iakevycha NAN Ukraïny, 1996.

—— and Vasyl' M. Danylenko. *Ukraïna v umovakh systemnoï kryzy (1946–1980-i rr.).* Kyiv: Al'ternatyvy, 1999.

Batenko, Taras. *Opozytsiina osobystist': Druha polovyna XX st. Politychnyi portret Bohdana Horynia.* Lviv: Kal'variia, 1997.

Bazhan, Oleh H. "Dysydents'kyi rukh na Dnipropetrovshchyni v 1960–80-kh rr." In *Istoriia Ukraïny: Malovidomi imena, podiï, fakty*, edited by Petro T. Tron'ko, 326–32. Kyiv: Ridnyi krai, 1999.

——. "Narostannia oporu politytsi rusyfikatsiï v Ukraïns'kii RSR u druhii polovyni 1950-kh–1960-kh rr." *Ukraïns'kyi istorychnyi zhurnal*, 2008, no. 5: 147–59.

Berdykhovs'ka, Bogumila, and Olia Hnatiuk. *Bunt pokolinnia: Rozmovy z ukraïns'kymy intelektualamy.* Kyiv: Dukh i litera, 2004.

Bilas, Lev. "How History Is Written in Soviet Ukraine." *The Ukrainian Review* 5, no. 4 (1958): 39–47.

Bilets'kyi, Myroslav. "Iak hotuvavsia 'Kyivs'kyi lyst.'" *Suchasnist'*, 1999, no. 1: 91–96.

Bilocerkowycz, Jaroslaw. *Soviet Ukrainian Dissent: A Study of Political Alienation.* Boulder and London: Westview Press, 1988.

Birch, Julian. "The Ukrainian Nationalist Movement in the U.S.S.R. since 1956." *The Ukrainian Review* 17, no. 4 (1970): 2–47.

Boiko, Leonid. "Vid'oms'ki poliuvannia na 'Vatchyni.'" *Vitchyzna*, 1999, no. 11–12: 111–25.

Braichevs'kyi, Mykhailo Iu. *Pryiednannia chy vozz'iednannia? Krytychni zauvahy z pryvodu odniieï kontseptsiï.* Toronto: Novi dni, 1972.

Browne, Michael, ed. *Ferment in the Ukraine: Documents by V. Chornovil, I. Kandyba, L. Lukyanenko, V. Moroz and Others.* Foreword by Max Hayward. Woodhaven, N.Y.: Crisis Press, 1973.

Carynnyk, Marco. "Vasyl Stus." *Journal of Ukrainian Graduate Studies* 1, no. 1 (1976): 62–67.

Chaplenko, Vasyl. "The Struggle against the Russification of the Ukrainian Language." *The Ukrainian Review* 14, no. 2 (1967): 2–16.

Chernov, Pavlo [Szporluk, Roman]. "Do natsional'nykh vidnosyn v URSR – misto, mova i presa skhidnikh oblastei." *Suchasnist'*, 1964, no. 6: 73–89.

——. "Mis'ki hazety v URSR." *Suchasnist'*, 1961, no. 5: 11–21.

——. "Presa URSR za mynule desiatyrichchia." *Suchasnist'*, 1962, no. 3: 73–84.
——. "Shcho chytaiut' u nas na Ukraïni?" *Suchasnist'*, 1963, no. 11: 57–68.
——. "Zamitky pro polityku peretryvannia i vik chesnosty." *Suchasnist'*, 1961, no. 11: 34–41.
Chornovil, Viacheslav/Vyacheslav. *The Chornovil Papers*. Introduction by Frederick C. Narghoorn. New York: McGraw-Hill, 1968.
——. *Ia nichoho u vas ne proshu: Lyst V. Chornovola do sekretaria TsK KPU P. Iu. Shelesta*. Toronto: Kraiova eksekutyva UNO, 1968.
——. *Lykho z rozumu: Portrety dvadtsiaty zlochyntsiv. Zbirnyk materiialiv.* Paris: Persha ukraïns'ka drukarnia u Frantsiï, 1968.
——. *Tvory v desiaty tomakh*. Vols. 1–6. Kyiv: Smoloskyp, 2002–2011.
——. Pavlo Skochok, and Liudmyla Sheremet'ieva. "Kolektyvovi zhurnala «Perets'»." *Suchasnist'*, 1967, no. 11: 53–61.
Clementi, Marco. *Storia del dissenso sovietico*. Rome: Odradek, 2007.
V. D. [Volodymyr Derzhavyn]. "School and Russification." *The Ukrainian Review* 6, no. 3 (Autumn 1959): 12–20.
Danko, Osyp. "Suchasnyi stan ukraïns'koï istorychnoï nauky ta suspil'no-politychnykh dystsyplyn." *Suchasnist'*, 1962, no. 12: 58–68.
Danyliuk, Iurii Z., and Oleh H. Bazhan. *Opozytsiia v Ukraïni (druha polovyna 50-kh – 80-kh rr. XX st.)*. Kyiv: Ridnyi krai, 2000.
Derzhavyn, V. [Volodymyr]. "The Soviet Language-Policy in Ukraine." *The Ukrainian Review* 6, no. 2 (Summer 1959): 29–41.
Do 70-richchia Viacheslava Chornovola (1937–2007). Special issue of *Moloda natsiia*, no. 50 (2009).
"Dokumenty chasu." *Suchasnist'*, 1972, no. 5: 84–107.
Dontsov, Dmytro. *Natsionalizm*. Vinnytsia: DP DKF, 2006.
Dovzhenko, Oleksandr. "The Art of Painting and Contemporaneity." *Literaturnaia gazeta*, 21 July 1954.
——. *The Enchanted Desna*. Kyiv: Dnipro, 1982
Drach, Ivan. "O, bud'te prokliati vy shche raz! Vidpovid' panovi Kravtsivu i ko." *Literaturna Ukraïna*, 22 July 1966.
——. *Orchard Lamps*. Edited, with an introduction, by Stanley Kunitz. New York: The Sheep Meadow Press, 1978.
Dunham, Vera. *In Stalin's Time: Middleclass Values in Soviet Fiction*. Cambridge: Cambridge University Press, 1976.
Dziuba, Ivan. *Internatsionalizm chy rusyfikatsiia?* Edited, with an afterword and bibliography, by Iurii [George] Liber. Foreword by Iurii Shapoval. Kyiv: Vydavnychyi dim "Kyievo-Mohylians'ka akademiia, 2005.
"Ivan Dziuba Replies." *The Ukrainian Review* 14, no. 2 (Summer 1967): 21–23.
——. *L'oppressione delle nazionalità in URSS*. Roma: Samonà e Savelli 1971.
——. "Poiasniuval'na zapyska." *Suchasnist'*, 1968, no. 8: 87–94.
——. *Spohady i rozdumy na finishnii priamii*. Introduction by M. H. Zhulyns'kyi. Kyiv: Krynytsia, 2008.

———. "U 25 rokovyny rostriliv u Babynomu Iaru." *Suchasnist'*, 1967, no. 11: 32–35.

———. "Vasyl Symonenko: A Speech Commemorating the 30th Birthday of the Poet, Delivered on January 10th, 1965, at the Republican Building of Literature in Kyïv." *The Ukrainian Review* 14, no. 1 (Spring 1967): 43–49.

———. "Zaiava Ivana Dziuby." *Suchasnist'*, 1970, no. 1: 79–80.

———. *Zvychaina liudyna chy mishchanyn? Literaturno-krytychni statti*. Kyiv: Radians'kyi pys'mennyk, 1959.

Dzyuba [Dziuba], Ivan. *Internationalism or Russification? A Study in the Soviet Nationality Problem*. New York: Monad Press, 1974.

Farmer, Kenneth C. *Ukrainian Nationalism in the Post-Stalin Era: Myth, Symbols and Ideology in Soviet Nationalities Policy*. The Hague, Boston, and London: Martinus Nijhoff, 1980.

Feldbrugge, Ferdinand J.M. *Samizdat and Political Dissent in the Soviet Union*. Leyden: A.W. Sijthoff, 1975.

Figes, Orlando. *The Whisperers: Private Life in Stalin's Russia*. London: Penguin, 2007.

Fireside, Harvey. "Valentyn Moroz: Individualist in Jeopardy." *Survey* 22, no. 1 (1976): 132–140

Fürst, Juliane. "Friends in Private, Friends in Public: The Phenomenon of the *Kompaniia* among Soviet Youth in the 1950s and 1960s." In *Borders of Socialism: Private Spheres of Soviet Russia*, edited by Lewis H. Siegelbaum, 229–49. New York and Houndmills: Palgrave Macmillan, 2006.

———. *Stalin's Last Generation: Soviet Post-War Youth and the Emergence of Mature Socialism*. Oxford: Oxford University Press, 2010.

———, Polly Jones, and Susan Morrissey, eds. *The Relaunch of the Soviet Project, 1945–1964*. Special issue of *The Slavonic and East European Review* 86, no. 2 (April 2008).

Graziosi, Andrea. *L'Urss dal trionfo al degrado: Storia dell'Unione Sovietica, 1945–1991*. Bologna: Il Mulino, 2008.

Heneha, R. Ia. [Roman Iaroslavovych]. "Uchast' lvivs'koho studenstva v rusi oporu v druhii polovyni 1940-kh – na pochatku 1950-kh rr." *Ukraïns'kyi istorychnyi zhurnal*, 2007, no. 3: 97–112.

Himka, Jean-Paul. "Leonid Plyushch: the Ukrainian Marxist Resurgent." *Journal of Ukrainian Studies* 5, no. 2 (1980): 61–79.

Hnatiuk, Ola/Olia. "Nativists vs Westernizers: Problems of Cultural Identity in Ukrainian Literature in the 1990s." *The Slavic and East European Journal* 50, no. 3 (2006): 434–51.

———. *Mizh literaturoiu i politikoiu: Eseï ta intermediï*. Kyiv: Dukh i litera, 2012.

Hodnett, Grey, and Peter J. Potichnyj. *The Ukraine and the Czechoslovak Crisis*. Occasional Paper No. 6 (1970), Department of Political Science, Research School of Social Sciences, Australian National University.

Hoffmann, David L. *Stalinist Values: The Cultural Norms of Soviet Modernity, 1917–1941*. Ithaca and London: Cornell University Press, 2003.

Honchar, Oles'. *The Cathedral: A Novel*. Washington and Toronto: St. Sophia Religious Association of Ukrainian Catholics, 1989.
——. "Slovo do molodykh." *Dnipro* 30, kn. 2 (1956): 120–22.
——. "Slovo na vechori 3 kvitnia 1968 roku." *Journal of Ukrainian Graduate Studies* 1, no. 1 (1976): 48–50.
——. *Shchodennyky*. Kyiv: Veselka, 2008.
——. *Tronka – Sobor*. Kyiv: Saktsent Plius, 2005.
Horbach, Oleksa. "Pisliavoienni movoznavchi publikatsiï v URSR." *Suchasnist'*, 1961, no. 12: 81–113.
Horbatch, Anna-Halia. "The Young Generation of Ukrainian Poets." *The Ukrainian Review* 12, no. 4 (1965): 23–34.
Hornsby, Robert. *Protest, Reform and Repression in Khrushchev's Soviet Union*. Cambridge: Cambridge University Press, 2013.
Hrupa tovaryshiv. "Vasyl Symonenko." *Literaturna Ukraïna*, 19 December 1963.
Iaremchuk, Vitalii. *Mynule Ukraïny v istorychnyi nautsi URSR pisliastalins'koï doby*. Ostroh: Vydavnytstvo Natsional'noho universytetu "Ostroz'ka akademiia," 2009.
Iurchuk Vasyl' I. *Kul'turne zhyttia v Ukraïni u povoienni roky: Svitlo i tini*. Kyiv: Asotsiatsiia «Ukraïno!», 1995.
Jones, Polly, ed. *The Dilemmas of De-Stalinization: Negotiating Cultural and Social Change in the Khrushchev Era*. London and New York: Routledge, 2006.
Kas'ianov, Heorhii. *Nezhodni: Ukraïns'ka intelihentsiia v rusi oporu 1960 – 80-kh rokiv*. Kyiv: Lybid', 1995.
——. *Ukraïna, 1991–2007: Narysy novitn'oï istoriï*. Kyiv: Nash chas, 2008.
Khodorovich, Tatiana S., ed. *Istoriia bolezni Leonida Pliushcha*. Amsterdam: Fond imeni Gertsena, 1974.
Khom'iak, Rostyslav L. "Sichnevi areshty ta reaktsiia svitu." *Suchasnist'*, 1972, no. 3: 113–22.
Khrushchov, Mykyta [Khrushchev, Nikita]. "Za tisnyi zv'iazok literatury i mystetstva z zhyttiam narodu." *Zhovten'* 7, no. 9 (1957): i–xx.
Knight, Amy. *Beria: Stalin's First Lieutenant*. Princeton: Princeton University Press, 1993.
Kolasky, John. *Two Years in Soviet Ukraine*. Toronto: Peter Martin Associates, 1970.
Komaromi, Ann. "The Material Existence of Soviet Samizdat." *Slavic Review* 63, no. 3 (Autumn 2004): 597–618.
Kurnosov, Iurii O. *Inakomyslennia v Ukraïni (60-ti – persha polovyna 80-kh rr. XX st.)*. Kyiv: Instytut istoriï Ukraïny NAN Ukraïny, 1994.
Korohods'kyi, Roman. *Brama svitla: Shistdesiatnyky*. Lviv: Vydavnytstvo Ukraïns'koho katolyts'koho universytetu, 2009.
Koshelivets', Ivan. *Panorama nainovishoï literatury v URSR: Poeziia, proza, krytyka*. New York: Proloh, 1963.
——. "Pro «Sobor» Olesia Honchara." *Suchasnist'*, 1968, nos. 8: 62–74 and 9: 44–53.
Kostenko, Lina. "Alternatyva barykad." *Dnipro*,1964, no. 12: 60–61.

———."Ia vyrostala u sadakh." *Dnipro,* 1956, no. 10: 36.
———. "If You Cannot Paint the Wind," *The Ukrainian Review,* 21 (1975), no. 3: 84.
———. "Kobzarevi." *Zhovten',* 1961, no. 3: 3–5.
———. "Kryla." *Vitchyzna,* 1961, no. 2: 5.
———. "Lidiia Koidula na chuzhyni." *Dnipro,* 1957, no. 6: 39–40.
———. "Na sviti mozhna zhyt' bez etaloniv." *Dnipro,* 1958, no. 2: 62.
———. "Narodzhennyi pid znakom Stril'tsia." *Kinoteatr,* 2002, no. 2: 4–7.
———. *Selected Poems: Wanderings of the Heart.* Translated, with a foreword, by Michael Naydan. New York and London: Garland, 1990.
———. "To Kobzar," *Nashe zhyttia,* 1970, no. 3: 26.
———. "Vse bil'she na zemli poetiv." *Vitchyzna,* 1962, no. 7: 123.
———. *Vybrane.* Kyiv: Dnipro,1989.
——— and Arkadii Dobrovol's'kyi. "Perevirte svoï hodynnyky." *Dnipro,* 1963, no. 2 (1963): 5–43.
Kotsiubyns'ka, Mykhailyna. "Ivan Svitlychnyi shistdesiatnyk." In Ivan Svitlychnyi, *U mene ie til'ky slovo,* 5–27. Kharkiv: Folio, 1994.
———. "Kriz' velyku pryzmu." In Ievhen Sverstiuk, *Na sviati nadii: Vybrane,* 6–9. Kyiv: Nasha vira, 1999.
Koval', Vitalii. "«Sobor» i navkolo n'oho," *Dnipro,* 1988, no. 4: 6–50.
Kozlov, Denis. *The Readers of* Novyi Mir*: Coming to Terms with the Stalinist Past.* Cambridge, Mass.: Harvard University Press, 2013
Kravtsiv, Bohdan. "'Velyka vedmedytsia' i 'honchi psy.'" *Suchasnist',* 1962, no. 2: 24–49.
Krawchenko, Bohdan. *Social Change and National Consciousness in Twentieth-Century Ukraine.* Londone: Macmillan, 1985.
Kul'chyts'kyi, Stanislav V., ed. *M. S. Khrushchov i Ukraïna: Materialy naukovoho seminaru 14 kvitnia 1994 r., prysviachenoho 100-richchiu vid dnia narodzhennia M. S. Khrushchova.* Kyiv: Instytut istoriï NAN Ukraïny, 1995.
———, ed. *Pochatok destalinizatsiï v Ukraïni (do 40-richchia zakrytoï dopovidi M. Khrushchova na XX z'ïzdi KPRS).* Kyiv: Instytut istoriï NAN Ukraïny, 1997.
Kvitnevyi, Volodymyr, ed. *U vyri shistdesiatnyts'koho rukhu: Pohliad z vidstani chasu,* Lviv: Kameniar, 2003.
Lavrinenko, Iurii. *Rozstriliane vidrodzhennia: Antolohiia, 1917–1933. Poeziia, proza, drama, eseï.* Paris: Kultura, 1959, and Kyiv: Smoloskyp, 2002.
Lewytzkyj, Boris. *Politics and Society in Soviet Ukraine, 1953–1980.* Edmonton: Canadian Institute of Ukrainian Studies, 1984.
Liber, George O. *Alexander Dovzhenko: A Life in Soviet Film.* LondonIII British Film Institute, 2002.
Liehm, Antonín J., ed. *Serghiej Paradjanov: Testimonianze e documenti su l'opera e la vita.* Venice: La Biennale di Venezia/Marsilio, 1977.
Loewenstein, Karl. "Obshchestvennost' as Key to Understanding Soviet Writers of the 1950s: Moskovskii *Literator,* October 1956–March 1957." *Journal of Contemporary History* 44, no. 3 (July 2009): 473–492.

Luckyj, George S. N. "Polarity in Ukrainian Dissent." *Canadian Slavonic Papers* 14, no. 2 (June 1972): 269–79.
——. "The Ukrainian Literary Scene Today." *Slavic Review* 31, no. 4 (December 1972): 863–869.
——. *Ukrainian Literature in the Twentieth Century: A Reader's Guide*. Toronto: University of Toronto Press, 1992.
Luk'ianenko, Levko. *Ne dam zahynut' Ukraïni!* Kyiv: Vydavnycho-kul'turolohichnyi tsentr «Sofiia», 1994.
——. *Spovid' u kameri smertnyka*. Kyiv: Nora-druk, 2005.
——. *Z chasiv nevoli: Sosnovka-7*. Kyiv: Mizhrehional'na akademiia upravlinnia personalom, 2005.
——. *Z chasiv nevoli: Knyha druha*. Kyiv: Mizhrehional'na akademiia upravlinnia personalom, 2007.
Lupii, Oles'. "Sobory dush liuds'kykh." *Literaturna Ukraïna*, 29 March 1968.
"Lyst do Olesia Honchara i sekretariv SPU." *Suchasnist'*, 1968, no. 12: 50–60.
"Lystivka z Ukraïny pro areshty diiachiv ukraïns'koï kul'tury." *Suchasnist'*, 1972, no. 9: 108–109.
Mace, James E. *Communism and the Dilemmas of National Liberation: National Communism in Soviet Ukraine, 1918–1933*. Cambridge, Mass.: Harvard University Press, 1983.
Magocsi, Paul Robert. *A History of Ukraine: The Land and Its Peoples*. Second, revised and expanded edition. Toronto: University of Toronto Press, 2010.
Malynovs'ka, Marharyta. "Zhyttia v romani." *Literaturna Ukraïna*, 19 January, 1968.
Mal'cev, Jurij V. *L'altra letteratura (1957–1975): La letteratura del samizdat da Pasternak a Solzenicyn*. Milan: La casa di Matriona, 1976.
Markus', Vasyl. "Ukraïns'ka kul'tura v prokrustovomu lozhi." *Suchasnist'*, 1961, no. 2: 8–21.
Marochko, Vasyl. *Zacharovanyi Desnoiu: Istorychnyi portret Oleksandra Dovzhenka*. Kyiv: Vydavnychyi dim «Kyievo-Mohylians'ka akademiia», 2006.
Marples, David R. *Heroes and Villains: Creating National History in Contemporary Ukraine*. Budapest and New York: CEU Press, 2007.
Mizhnarodnyi biohrafichnyi slovnyk dysydentiv kraïn Tsental'noï ta Skhidnoï Ievropy i kolyshn'oho SRSR, vol. 1, *Ukraïna*. Kharkiv: Kharkivs'ka pravozakhysna hrupa-Prava liudyny, 2006.
Molod' Dnipropetrovs'ka v borot'bi proty rusyfikatsiï. Munich: Suchasnist', 1971.
Moroz, Raïsa. *Proty vitru: Spohady druzhyny ukraïns'koho politv'iaznia.*, Lviv: Svichado, 2005.
Moroz, Valentyn. *Boomerang: The Works of Valentyn Moroz*. Edited by Yaroslav Bihun. Introduction by Paul L. Gersper. Baltimore, Paris, and Toronto: Smoloskyp, 1974.
Nahaylo, Bohdan P. "Dziuba's "Internationalism or Russification?" Revisited: a Reappraisal of Dziuba's Treatement of Leninist Nationalities Policy." *Journal of Ukrainian Studies* 2, no. 2 (Fall 1977): 31–53.

Naspravdi bulo tak: Interv'iu Iuriia Zaitseva z Ivanom Dziuboiu. Lviv: Instytut ukraïnoznavstva im. I. Kryp'iakevycha NAN Ukraïny, 2001.

Nebesio, Bohdan Y. "Questionable Foundations for a National Cinema: Ukrainian Poetic Cinema of the 1960s." *Canadian Slavonic Papers* 42, no. 1-2 (March-June 2000): 35-46.

Novichenko, Leonid. "Bol'shaia otvetstvennost' khudozhnika pered narodom." *Kommunist Ukrainy*, 1963, no. 4: 65-70.

Obertas, Oles'. *Ukraïns'kyi samvydav: literaturna krytyka ta publitsystyka (1960-i – pochatok 1970-kh rokiv)*. Kyiv: Smoloskyp, 2010.

Ocheretianko, Viktor I. "Petro Iukhymovych Shelest i ukraïns'ka kul'tura." In *Istoriia Ukraïny: Malovidomi imena, podiï, fakty*., issue 28, ed. Petro Tron'ko, 237-47. Kyiv, Khmelnytskyi, and Kamianets-Podilskyi: Abetka nova, 2004.

Ohnieva, Liudmyla, ed. *Alla Hors'ka: Dusha ukraïns'koho shistdesiatnytstva*. Kyiv: Smoloskyp, 2015.

Osadchuk, Bohdan. "Skandal u Kyievi, abo deshcho pro suchasnyi radians'kyi antysemityzm." *Suchasnist'*, 1964, no. 6: 115-17.

Osadchy, Mykhailo. *Cataract*. Translated, edited, and annotated byMarco Carynnyk. New York and London: Harcourt Brace Jovanovich, 1976.

Osadchyi, Vasyl'. "Pro Mistera Stets'ka i velykomuchenyts'ke zhabenia." *Perets* 40, no. 17 (1966): 5.

Ovsiienko, Vasyl'. *Svitlo liudei*,vol. 1, *Memuary ta publitsystyka*. Kharkiv: Prava liudyny, 2007.

—— and Vakhtang Kipiani, eds. "Interv'iu z Nadiieiu Svitlychnoiu." *Moloda natsiia*, 2006, no. 2: 22-57.

Ovsiienko, Vasyl. *Svitlo liudei*, kn. 1, *Memuary ta publitsystyka*. Kharkiv: Prava liudyny, 2007.

Pakhl'ovs'ka, Oksana. "Ukraïns'ki shistdesiatnyky: Filosofiia buntu." *Suchasnist'*, 2000, no. 4: 65-84.

Pasolini, Pier Paolo. *Lutheran Letters*. Translated by Stuart Hood. Manchester and Dublin: Carcanet New Press-Raven Arts Press, 1983.

Pavlychko, Dmytro. *Hranoslov*. Kyiv: Radians'kyi pys'mennyk, 1968.

Pavlyshyn, Marko. "Literary Canons and National Identities in Contemporary Ukraine." *Canadian-American Slavic Studies* 40, no. 1 (2006): 5-19.

Perepadia, Anatolii. "Everest pidlosti." *Radians'ka Ukraïna*, 15 April 1965.

Piretto, Gian Piero. *Il radioso avvenire: Mitologie culturali sovietiche*. Turin: Einaudi, 2001.

Plyushch, Leonid. *History's Carnival: A Dissident's Autobiography*. With a contribution by Tatyana Plyushch. Edited and translated by Marco Carynnyk. New York and London: Harcourt Brace Jovanovich, 1979.

Poklad, Natalka. ed. *Master, abo Terny i lavry Ivana Honchara*. Kyiv: MAUP, 2007.

Pospielovsky, D. [Dimitry]. "From *Gosizdat* to *Samizdat* and *Tamizdat*." *Canadian Slavonic Papers* 20, no. 1 (March 1978): 44-62.

Psychiatric Abuse of Political Prisoners in the Soviet Union: Testimony by Leonid Plyushch, Washington, D.C.: U.S. Government Printing Office, 1976.

Redlich, Shimon. *War, Holocaust and Stalinism: A Documented Study of the Jewish Anti-Fascist Committee in the USSR*. Luxembourg: Harwood Academic Publishers, 1995.

Revolutionary Voices: Ukrainian Political Prisoners Condemn Russian Colonialism. Munich: Press Bureau of the Anti-Bolshevik Bloc of Nations, 1969.

Risch, William Jay. *The Ukrainian West: Culture and the Fate of Empire in Soviet Lviv*. Cambridge, Mass.: Harvard University Press, 2011.

Rubenstein, Joshua, and Vladimir P. Naumov, eds. *Stalin's Secret Pogrom: The Postwar Inquisition of the Jewish Anti-Fascist Committee*. New Haven: Yale University Press, 2001.

Rubl'ov, Oleksandr S. "'Ukraïns'kyi istorychnyi zhurnal': Istoriia ofitsiina i zalashtunkova (1957–1988 rr.)." *Ukraïns'kyi istorychnyi zhurnal*, 2007, no. 6: 18–55.

Rusnachenko, Anatolii. *Rozdumom i sertsem: Ukraïns'ka suspil'no-polityčhna dumka 1940–1980kh rokiv*. Kyiv: Vydavnychyi dim "KM Academia," 1999.

Salomoni, Antonella. *L'Unione Sovietica e la Shoah: Genocidio, resistenza, rimozione*. Bologna: Il Mulino, 2006.

Savka, Mar'iana. "'Ia vybrala doliu sobi sama': Zhyttievymy shliakhamy Liny Kostenko." *Use dlia shkoly*, 2001, issue 6: 5–13.

Serbyn, Roman. "Moia persha zustrich z Ivanom Dziuboiu." *Suchasnist'*, 2001, no. 7–8: 124–25.

Shankovsky, Igor Peter. "Vasyl Symonenko and His Background." *The Ukrainian Review* 14 (1967), nos. 1: 20–37, 2: 33–43, and 4: 44–55.

Shapoval, Iurii. "Internatsionalizm chy rusyfikatsiia? (Do istoriï zapytannia)." *Naukovi zapysky*, Instytut politychnykh i etnonatsional'nykh doslidzhen' im. I. F. Kurasa, Natsional'na akademiia nauk Ukraïny, issue 33 (2003): 33–50.

——. "Internatsionalizm iak rusyfikatsiia, abo shcho i iak obstoiuvav Ivan Dziuba 40 rokiv tomu." In Ivan Dziuba, *Internatsionalizm chy rusyfikatsiia?* Edited, with an afterword and a bibliography, by Iurii [George] Liber. Kyiv: Vydavnychyi dim "Kyievo-Mohylians'ka akademiia," 2005. 15–27.

——. *Nevyhadani istoriï*. Kyiv: Svitohliad, 2004.

Shelest, Petro E. *Istoricheskoe prizvanie molodezhi*. Moscow: Molodaia жvardiia, 1968.

——. *Da ne sudimy budete: Dnevnikovye zapisi, vospominaniia chlena Politbiuro TsK KPSS*. Moscow: Kvintessentsiia, 1994.

——. *"Spravzhnii sud istoriï shche poperedu ...": Spohady, shchodennyky, dokumenty, materialy*. Ed. Iurii Shapoval. Kyiv: Heneza, 2003.

Shevchenko, Lesia A. "Kul'turno-ideolohichni protsesy v Ukraïni pislia XX z'ïzdu KPRS" In *Pochatok destalinizatsiï v Ukraïni (do 40-richchia zakrytoï dopovidi M. Khrushchova na XX z'ïzdi KPRS)*. Ed. Stanislav V. Kul'chyts'kyi, 98. Kyiv: n.p., 1997.

Shevelov, Iurii. *The Ukrainian Language in the First Half of the Twentieth Century (1900–1941): Its State and Status*. Cambridge, Mass.: Harvard University Press, 1989.

Shlapentokh, Viktor. *Soviet Intellectuals and Political Power: The Post-Stalin Era*, London and New York: I. B. Tauris, 1990.
Shumuk, Danylo. *Za skhidnim obriiem: Spomyny*. Peredruk samvydavnoho tvoru z Ukraïny. Paris: Smoloskyp, 1974.
Shyroke more Ukraïny: Dokumenty samvydavu z Ukraïny. Paris and Baltimore: Persha ukraïns'ka drukarnia v Frantsiï and Smoloskyp, 1972.
Slavutych, Iar. "Naklady seriinykh vydan' na Ukraïni." *Suchasnist'*, 1964, no. 5: 68–77.
Slovo molodykh: Al'manakh. Kyiv: Radians'kyi pys'mennyk, 1955.
Sobranie dokumentov samizdata: Arkhiv samizdata. Ukrainskii samizdat. Munich: Issledovatel'skii otdel Radiostantsii "Svoboda" v Miukhene, 1973.
Solovei, Eleonora, ed. *"U merekhtinni naidorozhchykh lyts'": Zhaduiuchy Mykhailynu Kotsiubyns'ku*. Kyiv: Dukh i litera, 2012.
Solzhenitsyn, Aleksandr I. *The Gulag Archipelago, 1918–1956: An Experiment in Literary Investigation*. Boulder: Westview Press, 1991.
Stakhiv, Volodymyr P. "Kryza «ideolohichnoï nadbudovy», shcho ïï podolaty ne mozhna." *Suchasnist'*, 1963, serpen': 67–76.
Stenchuk, Bohdan. *Shcho i iak obstoiue I. Dziuba (Shche raz pro knyhu "Internatsionalizm chy rusyfikatsiia?")*. Kyiv: Tovarystvo kul'turnykh zv'iazkiv z ukraïntsiamy za kordonom, 1969.
Strauss, Wolfgang. "The Symonenko Case." *The Ukrainian Review* 12, no. 4 (1965): 35–37.
Struk, Danylo Husar. "The Summing-up of Silence: The Poetry of Ihor Kalynets'." *Slavic Review* 38, no. 1 (1979): 17–29.
Stus, Vasyl. *Selected Poems*. Translated and edited by Jaropolk Lassowsky. Munich and New York: The Ukrainian Free University and the Larysa and Ulana Celewych-Steciuk Memorial Foundation, 1987.
——. *Tvory v 4 t. 9 kn*. Lviv: Prosvita, 1994–1999.
——. *Zibrannia tvoriv u dvanadtsiaty tomakh*. Vols. 1 and 3. Kyiv: Fakt, 2007–2008.
Sverstiuk, Ievhen. *Clandestine Essays*. Translated and edited by George S.N. Luckyj. Littleton, Col.: Ukrainian Academic Press, 1976.
——. *Sobor u ryshtovanni*. Paris and Baltimore: Smoloskyp, 1970.
——. "'Vony ne znaly, khto taka Nadiia Svitlychna ...'" *Moloda natsiia*, 2006, no. 2: 12–14.
[Sverstiuk, Ievhen]. "Z pryvody protsesu nad Pohruzhal's'kym." *Suchasnist'*,1965, liutyi: 78–84.
Svitlychnyi, Ivan. "Harmoniia i alhebra." *Dnipro* 39, no. 3 (1965): 142–150.
——. "Krytsia ne irzhaviie." *Zhovten'*, 1963, no. 8: 129–35.
——. "Steel does not Rust (Excerpts)." *The Ukrainian Review* 18, no. 2 (Summer 1971): 39–44.
Symonenko, Vasyl. *Bereh chekan'*. Munich: Suchasnist', 1965, 2d ed. 1973.
——. *Hranitni obelisky / Granite Obelisks*. Trans., with an intro., by Andriy M. Freishyn-Chirovsky. Jersey City: Svoboda, 1975.
——. *Spadshchyna*. Kyiv: Personal, 2008.

Shporliuk [Szporluk], Roman. *U poshukakh maibutn'oho chasu*. Kyiv: Harni-T, 2010.
Szporluk, Roman. "Valentyn Moroz: His Political Ideas in Historical Perspective." *Canadian Slavonic Papers* 19, no. 1 (1976): 80–90.
Taniuk, Les'. *Parastas*. Kyiv: Sfera, 1998.
———. *Slovo, teatr, zhyttia*. Vol. 3. *Zhyttia*. Kyiv: Al'terpres, 2003.
———. *Tvory*. Vol. 4. *Shchodennyky 1959–1960 rr*. Kyiv: Al'terpres, 2004.
Tarnashyns'ka, Liudmyla. *Ukraïns'ke shistdesiatnytstvo: Profili na tli pokolinnia (Istoryko-literaturnyi ta poetykal'nyi aspekty)*. Kyiv: Smoloskyp, 2010.
Tarnawsky, Ostap. "Dissident Poets in Ukraine." *Journal of Ukrainian Studies* 6, no. 2 (1981): 17–27.
Taubman, William. *Khrushchev: The Man and His Era*. New York and London: W.W. Norton, 2003.
"The Witches' Sabbath of the Chauvinists: Open Letter from Young Creative Intellectuals of Dnipropetrovsk." *The Ukrainian Review* 16, no. 3 (Autumn 1969): 46–52.
Tillett, Lowell. "Ukrainian Nationalism and the Fall of Shelest." *Slavic Review* 34, no. 4 (December 1975): 752–68.
Tromly, Benjamin. "An Unlikely National Revival: Soviet Higher Learning and the Ukrainian 'Sixtiers," 1953–65." *The Russian Review* 68, no. 4 (October 2009): 607–22.
———. *Making the Soviet Intelligentsia: Universities and Intellectual Life under Stalin and Khrushchev*. Cambridge: Cambridge University Press, 2015.
———. "Soviet Patriotism and its Discontents among Higher Education Students in Khrushchev-Era Russia and Ukraine." *Nationalities Papers* 37, no. 3 (May 2009): 299–326.
Tron'ko, Petro T., Oleh H. Bazhan, and Danylyuk, Iurii Z., eds. *Ternystym shliakhom do khramu: Oles' Honchar v suspil'no-politychnomu zhytti Ukraïny, 60–80-i rr. XX st*. Kyiv: Ridnyi ikrai, 1999.
Tsalyk, Stanislav, and Pylyp Selihei. *Taiemnytsi pys'mennyts'kykh shukhliad: Detektyvna istoriia ukraïns'koï literatury*. Kyiv: Nash chas, 2011.
Tsukanov, Fedir. "The Mask and the Face of Slanderers." *Digest of the Soviet Ukrainian Press*, October 1970, 3–5.
The Ukrainian Herald, Issue 6: Dissent in Ukraine. An Underground Journal from Soviet Ukraine. Intrduction by Yaroslav Bilinsky. Translated and edited by Lesya Jones and Bohdan Yasen. Baltimore, Paris, and Toronto: Smoloskyp, 1977.
The Ukrainian Herald, Issue 7–8: Ethnocide of Ukrainians in the U.S.S.R., Spring 1974. An Underground Journal from Soviet Ukraine. Compiled by Maksym Sahaydak. Introduction by Robert Conquest. Translated by Olena Saciuk and Bohdan Yasen. Baltimore, Paris, and Toronto: Smoloskyp, 1976.
Ukraïns'ka inteligentsiia pid sudom KGB: Materiialy z protsesiv V. Chornovola, M. Masiutka, M. Ozernoho ta in. Munich: Suchasnist', 1970.
Ukraïns'ki iurysty pid sudom KGB. Munich: Suchasnist', 1968.
Ukraïns'kyi visnyk, vypusk I–II, sichen' 1970–traven' 1970. Paris and Baltimore: Persha ukraïns'ka drukarnia u Frantsiï and Smoloskyp, 1971.

Ukraïns'kyi visnyk, vypusk III, zhovten' 1970. Winnipeg and Baltimore: Novyi shliakh and Smoloskyp, 1971.
Ukraïns'kyi visnyk, vypusk IV, sichen' 1971. Winnipeg and Baltimore: Novyi Shliakh and Smoloskyp, 1971.
U pivstolittia radians'koï vlady. Parizh: Persha ukraïns'ka drukarnia u Frantsiï, 1968.
V. D. [Volodymyr Derzhavyn]. "School and Russification." *The Ukrainian Review* 6, no. 3 (Autumn 1959): 12–20.
V. P. S. [Volodymyr P. Stakhiv]. "Dekada pol's'koï knyhy na Ukraïni." *Suchasnist'*, 1963, no. 1: 124–26.
———. "Rusyfikatsiia nauky, literatury, pobutu." *Suchasnist'*, 1965, no. 6: 119–22.
Vashchenko, H [Hryhorii]. "Soviet Educational Policy." *The Ukrainian Review* 3, no. 4 (December 1956): 55–60.
Wilson, Andrew. *Ukrainian Nationalism in the 1990s: A Minority Faith.* Cambridge: Cambridge University Press, 1997.
———. *The Ukrainians: Unexpected Nation.* New Haven: Yale University Press, 2000, 2002.
———. *Virtual Politics: Faking Democracy in the Post-Soviet World.* New Haven: Yale University Press, 2005.
Wojnowski, Zbigniew. "De-Stalinization and Soviet Patriotism: Ukrainian Reactions to East European Unrest in 1956." *Kritika* 13, no. 4 (2012): 799–829.
Yekelchyk, Serhy. *Stalin's Empire of Memory: Russian-Ukrainian Relations in the Soviet Historical Imagination.* Toronto: University of Toronto Press, 2004.
Zabuzhko, Oksana. "Reinventing the Poet in Modern Ukrainian Culture." *The Slavic and East European Journal* 39, no. 2 (Summer 1995):. 270–75.
Zakharov, Ievhen. *Ukraïns'ka hromads'ka hrupa spryiannia vykonanniu Hel'sins'kykh uhod.* Vols. 1–4. Kharkiv: Folio, 2001.
Zaplotyns'ka, O. [Olena]. "Ukraïns'ke shistdesiatnytstvo: Vyznachennia definitsiï ta istoriohrafiia problemy." In *Ukraïns'kyi istorichnyi zbirnyk,* issue 5 (2003), 448–58.
Zarets'kyi, Oleksii, and Mykola Marychevs'kyi, eds. *Alla Hors'ka: Chervona tin' kalyny.* Kyiv: Spalakh, 1996.
Za shcho i iak usunuly Shelesta? Dokumenty. Munich: Suchasnist', 1973.
"Znyshchennia vitrazhu T. Shevchenka v Kyivs'komu universyteti." *Suchasnist'*, 1965, no. 6: 104–107.
Zhylenko, Iryna. *Homo feriens: Spohady.* Kyiv: Smoloskyp, 2011.
Zinkevych, Osyp. *Svitlychny and Dziuba: Ukrainian Writers under Fire.* Baltimore and Toronto: Smoloskyp, 1966.
———. *Z generatsiï novatoriv: Svitlychnyi i Dziuba. U dzherel modernoï ukraïns'koï krytyky.* Baltimore and Toronto: Smoloskyp, 1967.
———, et al, eds. *Rukh oporu v Ukraïni, 1960–1990: Entsyklopedychnyi dovidnyk.* Kyiv: Smoloskyp, 2010, 2012.
Zubkova, Elena. *Russia after the War: Hopes, Illusions and Disappointments, 1945–1957.* London and Armonk: M. E. Sharpe, 1998.
Zubok, Vladislav. *Zhivago's Children: The Last Russian Intelligentsia.* Cambridge, Mass. And London: The Belknap Press of Harvard University Press, 2009.

Index

Adelheim, Yevhen, 25n88
Agaev, Akhed, 193
Aleksei Mikhailovich (tsar of Russia), 1n3
Alexander II (emperor of Russia), 198n261
Alexeyeva, Liudmila, xviii, 188
Alpatov, Vladimir, 94n5
Amalrik, Andrei, 261
Anatoli, A. See Kuznetsov, Anatolii
Andreyeva, Zoia, 275
Androshchuk, Oleksandr, ix
Anti-Bolshevik Bloc of Nations (ABN), 186n235
Antonenko-Davydovych, Borys, 27, 55, 98, 100, 181, 183, 189, 250, 260, 282
Antonov, Oleg, 253, 292
Arkhypenko, Oleksandr (Archipenko, Alexander), 254
Auschwitz, 167
Australia, xx
Austria, 74–75
Avtorkhanov,

Abdurakhman, 282–83

Babych, Ievdokiia, xxi
Babyn Yar (landmark), 182–84, 190
Badzo, Yurii, 120, 129, 185
Baidebura, Pavlo, 54, 192
Balestrini, Nanni, 234n48
Bandera, Stepan, 106, 214, 317n9
Barale, Lorena, ix
Baran, Volodymyr, 5n18, 15n55, 17, 19n69
Barbieri, Sara, ix
Bash, Yakiv, 26
Batenko, Taras, 107n42, 164n183
Baudelaire, Charles, 155
Bazhan, Mykola, 19–20, 24–27, 64n181, 64n183, 203–4
Bazhan, Oleh, 6n30, 18n63, 191n247, 200n266, 211n307
Berdychowska, Bogumiła (Berdykhovska, Bogumila), 52n150, 105n37, 180n220, 207n297
Berezovka, 73

Beria, Lavrentii, 1, 39, 315
Bihun, Yaroslav, 165
Biivtsi, 41
Bilas, Lev, 173
Bilenko, Anatole, 8n32
Biletsky, Mykhailo, 220–21, 262
Biletsky, Oleksandr, 15,
Bilinsky, Yaroslav, 237n52
Bilocerkowycz, Jaroslaw, xiiin4
Birch, Julian, xiiin4
Bishkek. See Frunze
Blakytny, Vasyl, 5–6
Blashkiv, Oksana, ix
Bloch, Marc, xvin10
Blok, Aleksandr, 33
Bochkovskaya, Nina, 300
Boichenko, Vasyl, 113
Boichuk, Mykhailo, 253–54
Boiko, Leonid, 202n279
Bondarchuk, Viktor, 220, 261, 283
Borovnytsky, Yosip, 79–80, 89
Borysivka, 262
Borzna, 270
Braichenko, Fedir, 129–30
Braichevsky, Mykhailo, 69, 170,

Index 341

173–78, 253, 306
Bratun, Rostyslav,
    104, 105n35, 107–
    8, 110, 135
Brecht, Bertold, 104
Brezhnev, Leonid,
    111, 198, 200,
    202n279, 213, 218,
    221, 228, 286,
    302–3, 306, 308
Brontë, Charlotte,
    152
Browne, Michael,
    79n219, 85n231,
    88n238, 153n158,
    160n171,
    162n174,
    179n219, 219n7,
    221n219, 223n14,
    269n129
Buchenwald, 300n199
Budzynsky, Herman
    (Hryhorii), 259
Buhaievska, Nadia,
    76
Bukovyna, 171
Bulgaria, 133
Bunin, Ivan, 71
Bykivnia, 104, 253

Canada, xx, 255n101
Carynnyk, Marco,
    144n135,
    269n130, 313n2
Caucasus
    Mountains, 267
Chaplenko, Vasyl,
    18n64, 20n71
Chechnia, 283
Chendei, Ivan, 192
Cherkasy, 41, 48, 66,
    68, 101, 109, 116,
    214

Chernihiv, 73, 78,
    180, 198n261, 270
Chernov, Pavlo. See
    Szporluk, Roman
Chernyshevsky,
    Nikolai, 307
Chervonenko,
    Stepan, 10
Chmykhalo,
    Yevheniia, 102–3
Chornovil,
    Viacheslav, xii,
    xxii, 66–67, 107,
    113n61, 125n94,
    130, 141, 144,
    145n138, 147–51,
    152n153, 153–56,
    168, 187, 189,
    203–5, 215, 217–
    20, 222–23, 229,
    235–38, 249–50,
    255–59, 262–67,
    277, 282, 291,
    310–11, 314, 316–
    17, 319–20, 322–
    23, 326
Chumak, Vasyl, 5,
    6n19, 100
Clementi, Marco,
    263n118, 295n185
Club of the Creative
    Youth (KTM),
    61–69, 91, 101–6,
    109, 114, 118, 120,
    173, 180–81, 188–
    89, 239, 251–52,
    255, 309, 321–23
Conquest, Robert,
    291n175
Cracow, 95, 113
Cuba, 212
Czechoslovakia, xx,
    56, 125, 169–70,

205–6, 213, 216,
218–21, 228–29,
254n98, 289n172,
303, 309, 323

Dadenkov, Yurii, 152
Daloja, Chiara, ix
Daniel, Yulii, 165
Danko, Osyp, 173
Danylenko, Viktor,
    5n17, 15n55,
    19n69
Danyliuk, Yurii,
    191n247,
    199n266, 211n307
Dashkevych,
    Yaroslav, 257n107
Derzhavyn,
    Volodymyr, 19n68
Diachenko,
    Oleksandr, 119
Đilas, Milovan, 173
Dmyterko, Liubomyr,
    5, 6n19, 22, 229–
    31, 290
Dniprodzerzhynsk
    (now Kamianske),
    200
Dnipropetrovsk
    (now Dnipro),
    111, 193, 200, 202,
    206, 211n307,
    223–27, 229, 255,
    259, 295, 299
Dobosh, Yaroslav,
    282
Dobroliubov
    (Dobrolyubov),
    Nikolai, 224, 307
Dobrovolsky,
    Aleksei, 221
Dobrovolsky,
    Arkadii, 126–27

Dobryk, 200
Dokuchaievsk (Olenivski Kariery), 54n157
Dold-Mykhailyk, Yurii, 26
Donbas, 93, 192
Donchyk, Vitalii, 199
Donetsk (Stalino), 10, 21, 51, 54, 124, 143, 230, 313n2, 320
Dontsov, Dmytro, 62, 243, 248, 286–87
Dostoevsky, Fyodor, 208
Dovbush, Oleksa, 244, 247
Dovzhenko, Oleksandr, 2, 8–9, 20, 27–28, 32, 58, 60, 67, 98, 125
Drach, Ivan, xin*, xii, 31n110, 56, 95–98, 100–101, 104, 110–11, 120, 124, 144, 178–79, 204, 211, 241–42, 273
Drahomanov, Mykhailo, 15, 55, 70, 136
Drobot, Stanislav, 119
Drohobych, 7
Drozd, Volodymyr, 98, 281
Dubček, Alexander, 215, 220, 294
Dubno, 225
Dudintsev, Vladimir, 8–10, 16, 24, 27, 61, 64, 194, 272
Dunaivtsi, 171

Dunham, Vera, 40n127
Dziuba, Ivan, ix, xix, xxii, 21, 25, 31, 52–61, 65, 69, 92n*, 95–97, 100–101, 103–4, 107, 110–12, 117–18, 120, 123–24, 129–42, 155, 164, 178–80, 183–89, 204–7, 211, 213, 215, 218, 220, 222, 229–36, 238, 240–44, 249–50, 254–56, 259, 261–67, 273–74, 277–78, 282, 287–95, 309–11, 314–17, 320, 322–25
Dziuba, Marta, 107
Dzyra, Yaroslav, 173

Echmiadzin, 247
Ehrenburg, Ilya, 183, 193, 272
Eisenhower, Dwight, 55
Engels, Friedrich, 82, 84, 132, 174, 235
Epik, Hryhorii, 20n72

Farmer, Kenneth, xiiin4
Fed, Nikolai, 203n283
Feldbrugge, Ferdinand, 29n103
Feltrinelli, Giangiacomo, 234
Figes, Orlando, 123n87
Filippo, Eduardo de, 63

Fireside, Harvey, 248
Floyd, David, 183n228
France, xx, 28n100, 66, 71, 218, 269, 301
Franco, Francisco, 211
Franko, Ivan, 7, 15, 24, 102, 107, 136, 239
Franko, Taras, 18
Franko, Zynoviia, 239, 249, 266–67
Freishyn-Chirovsky, Andriy, 45n135
Frunze (now Bishkek), 270
Fürst, Juliane, xvin8, xviii, 55n159, 326n19
Fylypovych, Pavlo, 20n72

Galanskov, Yurii, 220
Galicia, 106, 135, 148, 171n199, 172, 186n235, 259, 274, 320
Gaulle, Charles de, 66
Geevsky, V., 7
Georgia, 218
Germany, xvi, xx, 74, 93, 158, 154n98
Gersper, Paul, 165
Ginzburg, Aleksandr, 165, 220, 317
Goldberg, Paul, xviiin13
Gorbachev, Mikhail, 326
Gorky, Maxim, 57–58
Gramsci, Antonio, 133

Graziosi, Andrea, ix, 1n2, 219n6
Great Britain, xx, 183n228
Grigorenko, Petr (Hryhorenko, Petro), 262, 275
Grybov, Vitalii, x
Guerra, Davide, ix
Gumilev, Nikolai, 46n77

Halpern, Daniel, xin*
Havel, Václav, 294
Hel, Ivan, 108, 119, 255–56, 282, 291
Heneha, Roman, 13n49
Herzen, Alexander, 132, 307
Hevrych, Yaroslav, 189, 320
Himka, John-Paul, xiii, 272, 276
Hlavak, Tamara, 102
Hnatiuk, Ola, xin1, 23n85, 52n150, 105n37, 180n220, 207n297
Hodnett, Grey, 205n291, 220n8
Hoffmann, David, 30n107, 196n257
Holoborodko, Vasyl, 121
Holobutsky, Volodymyr, 171
Holovko, Andrii, 201
Honchar, Ivan, 280, 281n155
Honchar, Oles, 5, 6n19, 7, 19–20, 23–27, 90, 99, 112, 160, 191, 193–96, 198–208, 210–15, 217, 222–24, 229, 249–50, 304, 308, 322
Hooper, Cynthia, 326
Horbach, Oleksa (Horbatsch, Olexa), 18n66, 93–94
Horbatch, Anna-Halia, 31n110
Hornsby, Robert, 8n28, 78n216
Horska, Alla, 29, 67–68, 95n10, 104–5, 112–13, 120, 123, 181, 239, 251–56, 314, 321
Horsky, Oleksandr, 252
Horyn, Bohdan, 105–8, 115, 119, 124, 164, 179, 323
Horyn, Mykhailo, xii, 105–9, 115, 119, 124, 144–47, 156–57, 159–60, 164–65, 179, 229, 268, 319n14, 323
Hrabovsky, Pavlo, 15, 203
Hrek, Stefaniia, 106
Hrinchenko, Borys, 15, 55
Hrushetsky, Ivan, 211–12
Hrushevsky, Mykhailo, 70–71, 78, 136, 173
Hryhorenko, Petro. See Petr Grigorenko
Hryhoriiv, Nykyfor (Matvii), 170
Hrynko, Hryhorii, 132, 133n113
Hubanov (journalism student), 36–37
Hubenko, Pavlo, 144
Hungary, 10–11, 13–14
Hurzhii, Ivan, 171
Huslysty, Kostiantyn, 171
Hutsalo, Yevhen, 98, 204

Iaremchuk, Vitalii. See Yaremchuk, Vitalii
Ilnytsky, Mykhailo, 108n44, 109n48
Illienko, Yurii, 128
Irchan, Myroslav, 5, 6n19, 20n72
Ivano-Frankivsk (Stanislav), 5, 119, 124, 142–43
Ivanysenko, Viktor, 203n281
Ivashchenko, Dmytro, 125, 142

Jannsen, Lydia. See Koidula, Lydia
Jones, Lesya, 237n52
Jones, Polly, xvin8, 196n254, 326n19
Julfa, 74

Kabardino-Balkaria, 267
Kaganovich, Lazar, 6, 17

Kalynets, Ihor, 106, 121, 267n27, 291
Kalynets, Iryna. See Stasiv, Iryna
Kamenetskaya, Ella, 300
Kamianets-Podilskyi, 174, 230n36
Kamianske. See Dniprodzerzhynsk
Kandyba, Ivan, 72, 79–80, 85–86, 88–89, 160, 268
Kandyba, Oleksander. See Oles, Oleksander
Kaniv, 108–9, 279
Karavansky, Sviatoslav, 142n131, 151–53, 204–5, 222, 259, 262, 266
Karelia, 20n72, 151n150
Karpenko, Oleksandr, 172
Kashei, Iryna, ix
Kasianov, Heorhii, xii, xiv–xv, 89, 90n241, 102n31, 115n68, 188n240, 217n1, 229, 243n69, 249n82
Katyn, 153
Kendzor, Yaroslav, 257
Kennedy, John F., 110
Kharkiv, 12, 70, 95, 120, 123, 302, 320, 323
Khmelnytsky, Bohdan (Ukrainian hetman), 1n3, 171, 177, 208
Khodoriv, 107
Khodorovich, Tatiana, 299n196
Kholodny, Mykola, 144
Kholoniv, 124
Khomiak, Rostyslav, 282n162
Khrushchev, Nikita, xi, xvi–xvii, xixn17, 2–3, 6, 8n28, 10, 12, 15–17, 19–20, 24, 26–27, 29, 55, 57, 60–61, 66, 76–78, 90, 106, 110–11, 132–33, 145–46, 170, 193, 271, 273, 286, 303, 308, 326
Khrypivtsi, 73
Khvylovy, Mykola, 30, 54, 59n167, 171, 233, 254
Khyzhniak, Anton, 18
Kibalchich, Nikolai, 197, 198n261
Kipysh, Ivan, 79–80, 89
Kirghiz SSR, 270
Kirov, Sergei, 150
Kirovohrad. See Kropyvnytskyi
Klochchia, Andrii, 54, 97
Knight, Amy, 1n2
Kobylytsia, Lukian, 171
Koch, Ilse, 300
Koch, Karl, 300n199
Koidula (Jannsen), Lydia, 34–35
Kolasky, John, 113n60
Koloda, Panko, 186
Komaromi, Ann, xxn19
Komi ASSR, 291
Kompan, Olena, 60n167, 173
Komsomol, 6, 12–14, 20, 41–43, 47, 53–55, 58, 61, 65–67, 69, 75, 90–91, 100, 102, 106–7, 123–24, 127, 137, 143, 148, 151, 158, 180, 199, 221–22, 224, 226, 228, 230, 240, 252, 271, 281, 304, 317n9, 321
Kononenko, Musii, 70–71
Korenevych, Leonid, 12
Korniichuk, Oleksandr, 5
Korniienko, Nelli, 68
Kornusov, Iurii, xiiin3, 189n242
Korohodsky, Roman, xxn18
Korop, 198n261
Korotych, Vitalii, 31, 95, 111, 191–92, 204
Korzh, Viktor, 192
Koshelivets, Ivan, xxi, 195n257, 218
Kosiv, 244
Kosiv, Mykhailo, 105–6, 109, 112n58, 257

Kosmach, 244–50
Kostenko, Lina, ix,
    xii, xviii, xxii,
    1n*, 21, 26, 31–42,
    57, 61, 69, 96, 100,
    112, 124, 126–27,
    144, 155, 182, 191,
    205, 211, 217, 222,
    244, 274, 276,
    320–23, 326
Kostomarov,
    Mykola, 15
Kosygin, Aleksei,
    221
Kotsiuba, Oleh, ix
Kotsiubera, Vasyl, 74
Kotsiubynska,
    Mykhailyna, 69,
    120, 123, 129, 155,
    179–81, 205-206,
    207n296, 222, 267,
    283, 320–21
Kotsiubynsky,
    Mykhailo, 15, 59,
    128, 180–81
Koval, Vitalii,
    191n247
Kovalchuk, Yakiv,
    20n72
Kovalenko, Leonid,
    4, 56
Kozachenko, Vasyl,
    56
Kozak, Bohdan, 106
Kozlov, Denis, 8n29
Krasnopevtsev, Lev,
    77, 78n216
Kravtsiv, Bohdan,
    xxi, 31n110, 179
Krawchenko,
    Bohdan, xiiin4
Kropyvnytskyi
    (Kirovohrad),

107, 313n2
Krushelnytska,
    Larysa, 106
Krushelnytsky,
    Antin, 20n72
Krushelnytsky,
    Marian, 63, 65–66,
    68
Krutikova, Nina, 4–5
Kryvyi Rih, 202n280
KTM. See Club of the
    Creative Youth
Kudin, Viacheslav,
    27
Kulchytsky,
    Stanislav, 15n56
Kulchynsky,
    Mykola, 225–28
Kulish, Mykola, 5,
    20, 64, 67–68,
    104–5, 273
Kulish, Panteleimon,
    15, 98
Kulmagambetov,
    Makhmed, 165
Kunitz, Stanley, xin*,
    101n25
Kurbas, Les, 20, 25,
    64, 67–68, 102,
    150
Kursk, 189n241
Kuzmenko,
    Oleksandr, 226
Kuznetsov, Anatolii
    (Anatoli, A.), 183
Kvitka-
    Osnovianenko,
    Hryhorii, 59, 63
Kvitnevy,
    Volodymyr,
    105n35–36, 106,
    108,
Kyiv, ix, xix, xxi–

xxii, 3, 4, 6, 10–15,
    18, 20, 22, 25n88,
    31–35, 41–42, 55–
    56, 60–63, 66–68,
    69n197, 70n200,
    74, 76, 95, 100–2,
    104–5, 107–9,
    111–14, 117, 119–
    21, 123, 125, 129,
    142–43, 146, 156,
    159, 168, 174, 178,
    180-183, 188–90,
    204, 207n297, 214,
    220, 227, 229,
    230n36, 231, 239,
    244, 251–53, 256–
    57, 259, 261–62,
    265, 271, 273,
    278–80, 282–83,
    289, 292–93,
    297n189, 302, 306,
    309, 313n2, 317,
    320, 323
Kyrychenko, Oleksii,
    3, 5, 6n19–22,
    7n23, 8, 12–13, 17

Lafargue, Paul, 133
Lashkova, Vera,
    220–21
Lassowsky,
    Jaropolk, 313n2
Lavrinenko, Yurii, 29
Lazarenko, Yevhen,
    104, 105n35, 107
Lebedenko, F.,
    203n281
Lebid, Mykola, 106
Lenin, Vladimir,
    xvi–xix, 7, 13–14,
    57, 60, 62–63, 71,
    82, 84, 95, 108,
    132–33, 138–41,

144, 146, 154–55, 169, 175, 184, 191, 208–9, 212–13, 224, 227, 235–37, 243, 262, 273, 284–87, 293–94, 298, 303, 326
Leningrad (now Saint-Petersburg), xvii, 94, 151, 252, 266
Levterova, Raisa. See Moroz, Raisa
Levytska, Iryna, 252
Lewytzkyj, Borys, 1, 111n55, 112n57, 170n198
Liber, George, xx, xxin20, 8n32
Libovych, Oleksandr, 79–80, 89
Liehm, Antonin, 128n101
Lisovy, Vasyl, 316–17
Lobko, Vasyl, 119
Loewenstein, Karl, xviii
Lohvyn, Hryhorii, 104, 253
Los, Evdokiia, 244
Lubni, 70n201
Luckyj, George, 8n31, 210n299, 248n81, 261, 262n116
Luhansk (Voroshylovhrad), 120, 123, 127
Luhova, Olena, 172
Lukianenko, Levko, xii, xx, 72–86, 88–89, 146, 156–64, 218, 266, 268, 276,

319
Lupii, Oles, 198, 199n263
Lupynis, Anatolii, 279–80, 295
Lutsk, 61, 20
Lutskiv, Vasyl, 72, 79, 88–89,160
Lviv, xxi, 4, 13, 20, 22, 67, 72, 78–80, 89, 94, 104–9, 119, 121, 124, 129, 143–44, 156, 160, 172, 178, 189, 208n297, 225, 229, 230n36, 255, 257n107, 267n27, 320
Lykholat, Andrii, 2

Mace, James, 30n106, 171n199
Magocsi, Paul Robert, 324–25
Majdanek, 300n199
Makhno, Nestor, 170
Makukh, Vasyl, 229
Malcev, Jurij, 29n103
Malynovska, Marharyta, 198
Malyshko, Andrii, 5–8, 19
Mao Tse-tung, 219
Marian (journalism student), 12–13
Marianivka, 124
Markus, Vasyl, 17n57, 20
Marochko, Vasyl, 8n32
Marples, David R., xiiin3
Marr, Nikolai, 94n5
Marx, Karl, 7, 84,

132–33, 208–9, 224, 235
Marychevsky, Mykola, 104n33, 252n92, 255n97
Maryniak, Ksenia, ix
Masaryk, Tomáš, 246
Masiutko, Mykhailo, 119, 156–57, 159 164
Masokha, Petro, 67
Mayakovsky, Vladimir, 53–55, 212
Mazepa, Ivan (Ukrainian hetman), 70
Mazurkevych, Oleksandr, 203
Melnikov, Leonid, 1
Menkush, Halyna, 109
Mikoyan, Anastas, 170
Mödling, 74
Moldavia, 218
Monaco, 192
Mordovia, 80, 89, 120, 125, 153, 156, 162, 165, 168, 189, 238, 248, 259n111, 279, 291, 317, 319
Moroni, Primo, 234n48
Moroz, Anatolii, 24
Moroz (Levterova), Raisa, 124, 128, 142, 238–39,
Moroz, Valentyn, 120, 124–25, 128, 142, 156–57, 159, 164–70, 184, 229, 238–51, 255, 261,

263–64, 266, 281–
  82, 286–87, 309–
  11, 317, 320
Morrissey, Susan,
  xviii8, 326n19
Moscow, xi, xvii, xx,
  2, 8, 14, 18, 33–34,
  55, 61n171, 72,
  75–78, 90, 94, 96,
  98, 103, 111, 115,
  135, 139, 156, 165,
  171, 177, 182, 203,
  206, 218, 220–21,
  248, 254, 257,
  261–63, 267, 272,
  274, 283, 301, 303,
  306, 310, 317–18,
  320, 323
Mostovych, Anna,
  xxi
Movchan, Pavlo, xii
Munich, xxi, 93, 116,
  131n110, 217,
  283n164
Muratov, Ihor, 95
Mušinka, Mikuláš
  (Mushynka,
  Mykola), 289
Mykhailenko, V., 14
Mykolaichuk, Ivan,
  128
Mykolaivka, 52
Mysnyk, Prokip,
  25n88

Nagy, Imre, 11
Nahaylo, Bohdan,
  xiii, 293
Nalchik, 267
Narodnaia Volia
  (People's Will),
  198n261
Naryn, 270

Naumov, Vladimir,
  182n225
Nazarenko, Ivan, 185
Nebesio, Bohdan,
  126
Nehoda, Mykola,
  118
Nehrebetsky,
  Oleksandr, 119
Nehru, Jawaharlal,
  243
Nekrasov, Viktor,
  111, 183, 205, 222
New York, 179,
  254n98
Nicholas II (emperor
  of Russia), 237
Nikitin (student), 6
Novomoskovsk, 225
Novychenko, Leonid,
  96, 110–11, 118,
  193, 203, 213

Obertas, Oles, ix,
  116n70, 249n82,
  278
Oblast Yednannia
  (Realm of
  Unification), 163
Ocheretianko,
  Viktor, 304n207
Odesa, 142, 151–52,
  266–67, 270–71
Ohnieva, Liudmyla,
  252n91
Olenivski Kariery.
  See Dokuchaievsk
Oles (Kandyba),
  Oleksander, 5,
  6n19, 20
Olesnevych,
  Liubomyr, 22
Olitskaya, Ekaterina,

275
Organization of
  Ukrainian
  Nationalists
  (OUN), xv, 74,
  106, 109n47, 152,
  156, 162–64, 186,
  205, 207n297,
  214–15, 222, 226,
  230, 267n127,
  317n9, 326
Osadchuk, Bohdan,
  183n227
Osadchy, Mykhailo,
  119, 123, 144, 148,
  282, 291
Osadchy, Vasyl,
  185–87
Osmachka, Todos,
  67
Ostryk, Mykhailo,
  213
Ovcharenko, Fedir,
  12, 204, 207n296,
  223
Ovsiienko, Vasyl, ix,
  xxii, 100n23,
  120n78, 316–17,
  318n11, 319n14
Ozerny, Mykhailo,
  142–43

Pachlowski, Jerzy,
  34, 127n98
Pakhlovska Oksana
  (Pachlovska,
  Oxana), 327n20
Palach, Jan, 229
Paniv, Andrii, 20n72
Pankratova, Anna,
  170
Paradzhanov, Serhii
  (Sergei), 125–26,

128–29, 135, 143,
178, 244, 247, 249
Paris, 66, 98, 217–18,
254n98
Pashko, Atena, 257
Pasolini, Pier Paolo,
190n246
Pasternak, Boris, 25,
33
Pastushenko,
Tetiana, ix
Patoka, Valentyna,
xxi
Patyk, Volodymyr,
107
Pavlychko, Dmytro,
xxii, 99–100, 104,
107, 117, 199,
203–4, 211–13,
223, 234, 242, 290
Pavlyshyn, Marko,
xin1
People's Will. See
Narodnaia Volia
Pereiaslav, 1, 174,
176–77, 306
Perepadia, Anatol,
118, 119n75
Perm, 291, 313
Pervomaisky,
Leonid, 22, 26
Petliura, Symon, 163,
262
Pianov, Volodymyr,
56
Pichoia, Rudolf, 218
Pidhirny, Mykola
(Podgorny,
Nikolai), 72, 111,
206, 221, 302
Pidmohylny,
Valeriian, 20n72
Piretto, Gian Piero,

182n226
Plachynda, Serhii,
28, 56, 57n162
Plakhotniuk,
Mykola, ix, xxii,
68, 188–89, 227–
28, 238, 239n56,
257, 276, 282, 291,
295, 320
Plekhanov, Georgii,
78
Pliushch, Leonid,
xxii, 261, 263,
269–77, 282, 295–
301, 310
Pliushch, Tania. See
Zhitnikova, Tania
Plokhii, Serhii, ix
Pochaiv, 207n297
Podillia, 171
Podolynsky, Serhii,
15
Pohruzhalsky,
Viktor, 113–14
Poklad, Natalka,
281n155
Poland, xx, 10–13,
16, 22, 87, 94, 113,
125, 177, 207n297,
218, 227
Polishchuk,
Valeriian, 20n72
Polovynkyne, 120
Poltava, 41, 63,
70n201, 207n297
Poltoratsky, Oleksii,
25–26, 56, 193,
204–5, 222
Popeliuk, Valentyna,
314n3
Pospielovsky,
Dimitri, 29n103
Potebnia (Potebnya),

Oleksander, 137,
138n122
Potichnyj, Peter,
205n291, 220n8
Prague, 170, 205,
216–20, 228–29,
308, 323
Prešov, 95n10, 187,
219, 289n172
Prolisok Youth Club,
104, 106–9, 119,
144, 225
Proniuk, Yevhen,
109n47, 316–17
Pyvovarov
(historian), 70–71

Rakhmannyi,
Roman, 175
Rakhnivka, 314n2
Rakovsky, Christian,
133
Raskolnikov, Fedor,
272
Realm of Unification.
See Oblast
Yednannia
Recoursé, Nathaël, ix
Redlich, Shimon,
182n225
Revolutionary
Ukrainian Party
(RUP), 102
Risch, William,
195n35
Rokossovsky,
Konstantin, 11
Ronsard, Pierre de,
155
Ruban, Vasyl, 265
Rubenstein, Joshua,
182n225
Rublov, Oleksandr,

172n202,
174n205,
Rudenko, Mykola,
317
Rudenko, Roman,
160
Rudnytsky,
Mykhailo, 107
Rudnytzky, Leonid,
194n255
Rylsky, Maksym, 11,
15–16, 19–20,
21n74, 23, 29, 63,
65, 98, 104, 179–80
Rzhyshchiv, 31

Saciuk, Olena,
291n175
Sahaydak, Maksym,
291n175
Saint-Exupery,
Antoine de, 272
Saint-Petersburg. See
Leningrad
Salomoni, Antonella,
182n225
Savka, Mariana,
35n118
Schattenberg,
Susanne, 193,
194n254
Selianska, Vira
(Selansky, Wira).
See Vovk, Vira
Semykina,
Liudmyla, 113
Senchenko, Ivan, 59
Senkus, Roman, ix
Serbyn, Roman, 293
Serhiienko,
Oleksandr, 255
Sevastopol, 275n138
Sevruk, Halyna, 121

Shamota, Mykola,
181, 202, 203n281,
241, 289, 306, 308
Shankovsky, Igor,
42n132
Shapoval, Yurii, 294,
301–2, 306
Shaw, George
Bernard, 63
Shcherbytsky,
Volodymyr, 111,
131, 220, 223,
306–7
Shelest, Petro, 110–
12, 131, 149, 151,
169–70, 185, 189,
191, 200-206, 212–
13, 215, 220, 228–
29, 281, 301–8, 322
Sheremetieva,
Liudmyla, 257
Shevchenko, Fedir,
171–73
Shevchenko, Lesia,
15n56
Shevchenko, Taras,
15, 36–37, 40, 46,
59, 80, 95n10, 96,
101–2, 108–9,
112–13, 115, 117,
121, 124, 164, 181,
184, 188–90, 197,
208, 214, 224, 227,
241, 253, 279, 307,
Shevchuk, Tatiana,
37n122
Shevelov, George,
260n114
Shlapentokh,
Vladimir, 30n108
Shostakovich,
Dmitrii, 182
Shpol, Yuliian. See

Yalovy,
Mykhailo
Shumsky, Oleksander,
171, 233
Shumuk, Danylo,
255, 282, 319
Shumylo, Mykyta, 7
Shvets, Ivan, 113
Shvets, Vasyl, 7
Shylo, Ivan, 226–27
Shypenko, Borys,
13–14
Siberia, 27n97, 73,
144n135, 152, 196,
259n111
Simferopol, 165
Siniavsky, Andrei,
165
Skaba, Andrii, 70–72,
111, 113, 149,
204n286, 289
Skrypnyk, Mykola,
30, 95, 132,
133n113, 171
Slavutych, Yar, 93n1
Slisarenko, Oleksa,
20n72
Slovakia, 95, 134,
187, 289
Smolych, Yurii,
24n87
Sokulsky, Ivan,
202n279, 225–28,
281, 309
Soldani, Maria Elisa, ix
Solovei, Eleonora,
180n220
Solovets Islands, 151
Solzhenitsyn,
Aleksandr, 247,
272, 296n187
Soroka, Mykhailo,
164

Sosiura, Volodymyr,
    4–5, 29, 180
Stakhiv, Volodymyr,
    94n6, 94n9, 111n56
Stalin, Joseph, xvi–
    xvii, 1, 3–4, 6–7,
    10, 16–18, 23, 26–
    27, 34, 48, 53, 55,
    57, 61–62, 64, 80,
    90, 96–99, 101,
    107, 127, 132–35,
    146–47, 150, 166–
    68, 171, 184, 195,
    208, 219, 229–30,
    233, 243, 246, 271–
    72, 286–87, 303
Stalino. See Donetsk
Stanislav. See Ivano
    Frankivsk
Stasiv (Kalynets),
    Iryna, 106, 267,
    277, 282, 291
Stech, Marko R., ix
Stelmakh, Mykhailo,
    27, 72, 96, 104,
    109, 113, 180
Stenchuk, Bohdan,
    231–33, 237–38,
    256
Stetsko, Slava,
    183n230
Stetsko, Yaroslav,
    186n235
Strauss, Wolfgang,
    116n69
Strokata, Nina, 142,
    262, 266–68
Struk, Danylo
    Husar, 277n143
Stus, Vasyl, 54, 121,
    130, 178, 230–31,
    256, 263, 267, 282,
    291, 313–16, 321,
    326
Sukarno, 243
Sumy, 144
Sun Yat-sen, 243
Suprunenko,
    Mykola, 170,
    171n199, 172
Surovtseva, Nadia,
    275
Sverstiuk, Yevhen,
    xii, 29, 56, 114–17,
    123, 179-180, 205,
    207–11, 214–15,
    217, 222, 241, 249,
    251, 255, 264, 275,
    282, 291, 310, 314,
    317, 320
Svitlychna, Nadia,
    123–24, 143, 155,
    217n*, 251, 282,
    283n165, 291
Svitlychny, Ivan, 25,
    56, 68, 69n199,
    105, 108–9, 118–
    23, 142, 146, 155,
    159, 161, 178, 181,
    207n297, 220, 239,
    241, 249, 262-267,
    275, 282–83, 287,
    289, 310, 314, 317,
    320–21
Symonenko, Petro
    (Petr), 200n266
Symonenko, Vasyl,
    v, 28, 31, 41–52,
    57, 61, 68–69, 101,
    109–10, 112, 116–
    20, 123–24,
    168n193, 182, 191,
    214, 240–41, 244,
    253, 256, 259,
    313n*, 320
Synytsia, Hryhorii,
    13n48, 253
Szporluk, Roman
    (Chernov, Pavlo),
    ix, xiii, xxi, 1n*,
    16, 19n67, 93,
    225n21, 247

Tambov, 153
Taniuk, Les, ix, xxii,
    61–68, 91, 104–5,
    123, 252–53, 276,
    320, 323, 326
Tarasenko, Vasyl, 22
Tarnashynska,
    Liudmyla, 31n109
Tarnawsky, Ostap,
    31n110
Tatev, 247
Taubman, William,
    xvin8
Telizhyntsi, 100
Telniuk, Stanislav, 68
Tillett, Lowell, 306–7
Tiutiunnyk, Hryhir,
    199–200
Tiutiunnyk, Hryhorii,
    95
Tkach, Yuri, 194n255
Togliatti, Palmiro,
    68, 173
Tolkunov, Lev, 206
Tolstoy, Leo, 208, 272
Toronto, 18
Tromly, Benjamin,
    xviii, xixn17, 320
Tronko, Petro,
    200n266, 211n307,
    304n207
Tsekhmistrenko,
    Yurii, 220
Tsukanov, Fedir,
    226–28

Tsvetaeva, Marina, 22n77, 33
Tsvirkunov, Vasyl, 127
Tula, 183
Tvardovsky, Aleksandr, 161
Twain, Mark, 41
Tychyna, Pavlo, 20, 21n74, 29, 36, 56, 179–80, 273
Tymchuk, Leonid, 267

Ukrainian Helsinki Group, 108, 313, 318
Ukrainian Insurgent Army (UPA), xv, 72, 74, 106, 156, 158, 162–63, 211, 215, 229, 274, 326
Ukrainian Workers' and Peasants' Union (URSS), 72–73, 80–85, 87–89, 160, 164
Ukrainka, Lesia, 15, 59, 102, 108, 121–22, 184, 241, 273, 321
Union for the Liberation of Ukraine (SVU), 174
Union of Cinema Workers, 15
Union of Writers of Ukraine (SPU), xxi–xxii, 5, 7–8, 19–20, 22–27, 61, 68, 71, 90, 95, 99–100, 103, 117–18, 191, 203–4, 205n291, 206n291, 212–14, 223, 234, 236, 241, 249, 259, 261, 288, 290–91, 321–22
United Nations, 15, 22n80, 263, 268
United States of America (USA), xx, 111, 119, 179, 246, 283n164
Uruguay, 192

Vakulík, Ludvík, 215
Vaplite, 24n87, 59n167, 64, 150n150
Vashchenko, Hryhorii, 17n62
Vasylkiv, 251
Vatchenko, Oleksii, 200, 202, 204, 211n307, 212, 223
Velyka Novosilka (Velyki Yanisol), 124
Viblaia, Larisa, 226–27
Vilde, Iryna, 107
Vinhranovsky, Ivan, 31n110, 95, 104, 110–11
Vinnytsia, 100, 156, 179, 143n69, 313n2
Virun, Stepan, 72, 79–80, 85, 89, 160
Vladimir (city), 262, 279
Vodolazhchenko, Oleksandr, 225n21
Volhynia, 171n199, 207n297
Voloshchak (Lviv student), 113
Voronko, Platon, 95
Vorony, Marko, 20n72
Voroshylovhrad. See Luhansk
Vovk (Selianska), Vira (Selansky, Wira), 289
Vynnychenko, Volodymyr, 28, 54, 99, 136
Vysheslavsky, Leonid, 5
Vyshnia, Ostap, 59, 144, 150

Wasilewska, Wanda, 8
Whitney, Thomas, 296n187
Wilson, Andrew, xiin2, xiiin3
Wojnowski, Zbigniew, 13n51
Wood, Hannah, ix

Yacheikin, Yurii, 41–42
Yakir, Petr, 220, 262–63, 267, 274–75
Yakir, Sara, 275
Yalovy, Mykhailo (Shpol, Yuliian), 20n72, 150
Yalta, 252
Yaremchuk, Vitalii, 2n6, 171, 172n201, 173n204, 174n206
Yasen, Bohdan, 237n52, 291n175

Yashchenko, Leopold, 278–80
Yatskiv, Mykhailo, 107
Yavorivsky, Volodymyr, xii
Yavornytsky, Dmytro, 195n256
Yekelchyk, Serhy, 2n4, 171n200
Yerevan, 220
Yevtushenko, Yevgeny, 182, 273
Yezhov, Nikolai, 101, 150–51, 283n164, 315
Yugoslavia, 12, 219
Yurchuk, M., 203n281

Zabuzhko, Oksana, xin1
Zahrebelny, Pavlo, 95, 203–4, 213
Zaitsev, Yurii, xiiin3, 105n35
Zakharov, Bohdan, 120n78
Zakharov, Borys, 317n10
Zakharov, Yevhen, 100n23, 318n11, 319n13
Zalyvakha, Opanas, 120, 179, 253–54, 321
Zaplotynska, Olena, ix, xiii–xiv
Zaporizhzhia, 69n197, 127, 262, 304
Zaretsky, Ivan, 251–52
Zaretsky, Oleksii, 104n33, 254n97
Zaretsky, Viktor, 104, 112, 251–52, 255, 321
Zasenko, Petro, 4
Zaslavska, Iryna, 220
Zavhorodnii, Oleksandr, 225n21
Zbanatsky, Yurii, 5, 6n19, 8–9, 23, 99, 204, 212, 289
Zerov, Mykola, 20n72
Zhdanov, Andrei, 1–2
Zhitnikova (Pliushch), Tania, 271, 275, 205
Zhukyn, 61
Zhulynsky, Mykola, xii
Zhurakhovych, Semen, 27
Zhylenko, Iryna, xxn18
Zhytomyr, 143, 317n9
Zinkevych, Osyp, 217
Zubchenko, Halyna, 253n94
Zubkova, Elena, xvi, 326
Zubok, Vladislav, xvi, xviin11, xviii, 76n214, 110n51, 147n142, 221n10, 257n106
Zuiev, 12–13
Zvarychevska, Myroslava, 108, 144